THE POLITICS OF DISCLOSURE, 1674–1725:
SECRET HISTORY NARRATIVES

POLITICAL AND POPULAR CULTURE IN THE EARLY
MODERN PERIOD

Series Editors: *Alastair Bellany*
　　　　　　　　　Krista Kesselring
　　　　　　　　　Jason Peacey
　　　　　　　　　Ted Vallance

Credibility in Elizabethan and Early Stuart Military News
David Randall

FORTHCOMING TITLES

'Commotion Time': The English Risings of 1549
Amanda Jones

THE POLITICS OF DISCLOSURE, 1674–1725: SECRET HISTORY NARRATIVES

BY

Rebecca Bullard

LONDON
PICKERING & CHATTO
2009

Published by Pickering & Chatto (Publishers) Limited
21 Bloomsbury Way, London WC1A 2TH

2252 Ridge Road, Brookfield, Vermont 05036-9704, USA

www.pickeringchatto.com

All rights reserved.
No part of this publication may be reproduced,
stored in a retrieval system, or transmitted in any form or by any means,
electronic, mechanical, photocopying, recording, or otherwise
without prior permission of the publisher.

© Pickering & Chatto (Publishers) Ltd 2009
© Rebecca Bullard 2009

BRITISH LIBRARY CATALOGUING IN PUBLICATION DATA
Bullard, Rebecca, 1979–
The politics of disclosure, 1674–1725 : secret history narratives. – (Political and popular culture in the early modern period)
1. Political culture – Great Britain – History – 17th century 2. Political culture – Great Britain – History – 18th century 3. Politics and literature – Great Britain – History – 17th century 4. Politics and literature – Great Britain – History – 18th century 5. Historiography – Great Britain – History – 17th century 6. Historiography – Great Britain – History – 18th century 7. Great Britain – History – Stuarts, 1603–1714 – Historiography 8. Great Britain – History – 18th century – Historiography 9. Great Britain – Politics and government – 1603–1714
I. Title
306.2'0941'09032
ISBN: 9781851969692
e: 9781851965915

This publication is printed on acid-free paper that conforms to the American National Standard for the Permanence of Paper for Printed Library Materials.

Typeset by Pickering & Chatto (Publishers) Limited
Printed in the UK by the MPG Books Group

CONTENTS

Acknowledgements	vii
Conventions	viii
Introduction	1
Section 1 Whig Secret History: the Core Traditions	27
1 Procopius of Caesarea and *The Secret History of the Court of the Emperor Justinian*	29
2 Secret History and Whig Historiography, 1688–1702	45
3 Secret History, the 'Revolution' of 1714 and the Case of John Dunton	63
Section 2 Secret History in the Eighteenth Century: Variations and Adaptations	81
4 Delarivier Manley and Tory Uses of Secret History	85
5 Secrecy and Secret History in the *Spectator* (1711–14)	111
6 Daniel Defoe: Harleyite Secret History and the Early Novel	133
7 Eliza Haywood: Secret History, Curiosity and Disappointment	161
Conclusion	183
Notes	189
Works Cited	229
Index	245

In memory of my grandmothers,
Lena Price (1907–2007)
and
Thelma Rees (1920–1998)

ACKNOWLEDGEMENTS

I have received a great deal of help, advice and encouragement while this book has been in preparation. Ros Ballaster was an exemplary doctoral supervisor and continues to be a wonderful mentor. She, along with Eve Tavor Bannet, Alan Downie, Brean Hammond, Kate Loveman, Kathryn King and Abigail Williams, gave up valuable time to read and improve earlier drafts. Crofton Black translated passages of Latin for me; Chris Miller and Richard Parish generously corrected my translations of passages in French. The Arts and Humanities Research Council, the English Faculty at Oxford University, Lincoln College, Oxford and University College, Oxford provided funding during the early stages of this research project. A Junior Research Fellowship at Merton College, Oxford allowed me to complete my book in good company and beautiful surroundings.

I am deeply grateful to my family for their ongoing support. My parents, Frank and Anne Rees, have always given unstintingly of their time and their love. Paddy Bullard is my best reader and best imaginable husbandman. Clement Bullard made his appearance during the production of this book, enriching all of our lives immeasurably.

CONVENTIONS

Texts published before the twentieth century were published in London, unless otherwise specified.

The first letter of each quotation is silently capitalized or lowered according to context. When quoting from prefaces and dedications, italics are often silently reversed.

The Acts of Union (1707) turned Scotland and England into the Kingdom of Great Britain. When discussing texts published before 1707, I generally refer to England; in discussions of texts published after this date or when I make comments that apply to the entire period, I refer to Britain.

Robert Harley became Earl of Oxford and Mortimer in 1711. For the sake of clarity, I refer to him as Robert Harley throughout.

INTRODUCTION

During the late seventeenth and early eighteenth centuries, Britain experienced an extraordinary and unprecedented vogue for texts calling themselves 'secret histories'. Secret history undermines received or official accounts of the recent political past by exposing the seamy side of public life. As an early commentator on the form puts it, the orthodox historian 'considers almost ever Men in Publick', whereas the secret historian 'only examines 'em in private':

> Th'one thinks he has perform'd his duty, when he draws them such as they were in the Army, or in the tumult of Cities, and th'other endeavours by all means to get open their Closet-door; th'one sees them in Ceremony, and th'other in Conversation; th'one fixes principally upon their Actions, and th'other wou'd be a Witness of their inward Life, and assist at the most private hours of their Leisure: In a word, the one has barely Command and Authority for Object, and the other makes his Main of what occurs in Secret and Solitude.[1]

Inside the closets and cabinets of those in power, secret historians discover sexual intrigue and political chicanery. They reveal that monarchs and ministers routinely attempt to dupe their people in an effort to extend their own power. Secret history presents itself as a defender of British political liberties at the vanguard of the battle against French-style absolute rule. But secret history is also self-conscious about its status as a literary form. A revisionist mode of historiography, it re-plots received accounts of recent political history along partisan lines. It encourages its readers to consider the relationship between historical narratives and political power and the function of secrecy and revelation in each.

The discoveries that secret historians make in the cabinets and closets of the powerful vary according to period. The first English text to bear the title 'secret history' is *The Secret History of the Court of the Emperor Justinian* (1674), an anonymous translation of the *Anekdota* or 'unpublished things' by the sixth-century Byzantine historian, Procopius of Caesarea. This secret history's revelations about the debauched and tyrannical behaviour of the Emperor Justinian were interpreted by many contemporaries as reflections upon Charles II. Later secret historians were more direct in their attacks on the Stuart monarchs. In the wake of the Revolution of 1688–9, at the height of secret history's popularity in

England, almost all secret histories reveal the political and sexual secrets of the Stuart kings, Charles II and James II, and the French monarch, Louis XIV. Texts such as *The Secret History of the Reigns of K. Charles II and K. James II* (1690), *The Secret History of the Duchess of Portsmouth* (1690), *The Cabinet Open'd: or, the Secret History of the Amours of Madam de Maintenon with the French King* (1690) and *The Royal Mistresses of France, or, The Secret History of the Amours of All the French Kings* (1695) focus on the power of royal mistresses at both the Stuart and Bourbon Courts. They give their readers a titillating glimpse of kings and courtesans in a state of undress, but they also reinforce important political ideas: in particular, that France gained insidious control over Charles II through his mistress, Louise de Kéroualle, Duchess of Portsmouth; more generally, that absolute or would-be absolute monarchs are, in fact, ruled by the women at their Courts. Arbitrary government, secret historians claim, is little more than petticoat government.

Other closet discoveries are more overtly and straightforwardly political. Secret leagues between England and France – to the detriment of the Protestant religion and political liberty – occupy much space in *The Secret History of White-hall* (1697) and *The True Secret History of the Reigns of All the Kings and Queens of England* (1702). Among these conspiratorial leagues to enslave the English people, the secret treaty of Dover consistently generates the highest level of interest among secret historians. Signed by Charles II and Louis XIV in 1670, it annihilated the defensive Triple League between the Protestant nations, England, the United Provinces and Sweden. Within two years, England was at war against the United Provinces on the side of Roman Catholic France. The fact that the Duchess of Orléans, Charles II's sister, died soon after the treaty was signed led to allegations that she had been poisoned by the French having played her part in the negotiations.[2] Scandal, sensation and polemic are the stuff of post-Revolution secret history, which thrills and shocks its readership into believing that their political liberties had only very recently been in the greatest peril.

During the eighteenth century, the detail of secret historians' closet discoveries changes, but secret history's intrusive character and iconoclastic purpose endure. With the Stuart Court in exile at St Germain-en-Laye, Jacobite conspirators, assisted by French finances, represented a new threat to British political liberties. Secret histories of this period focus not so much on the Jacobite plotters themselves as on the intrigues of Queen Anne's Tory ministers. The Whig opponents of Robert Harley, Earl of Oxford, and Henry St John, Viscount Bolingbroke, argued that these ministers were secret supporters of the Pretender attempting to undermine limited monarchy in Britain. During the early eighteenth century, then, secret historians shift their attention from monarchs to ministers and they narrow their focus so that sexual intrigue becomes less important to their arguments than political scheming. But they continue to oppose the threat of arbitrary government, even when the nature of that threat alters.

The first three decades of the eighteenth century witness not only changes in the typical content of secret history, but also the appropriation and adaptation of this form's generic conventions by writers working in genres other than secret history itself. Between 1709 and 1725, texts as diverse as Delarivier Manley's scandalous *roman à clef*, *The New Atalantis* (1709), the polite periodical, *The Spectator* (1711–14), and Daniel Defoe's dark, late novel, *Roxana* (1724) – to name just a few – manipulate in a variety of different ways secret history's central claim to disclose previously undiscovered intelligence. Eighteenth-century authors create a range of rhetorical effects out of raw material provided by secret history's revelatory narratives. In each case, however, the act of adaptation can be read as a political statement. Sometimes these writers affirm the connection between secret history and the Whig opposition to excessive royal prerogative but more often they modify, question or even challenge it. During the early eighteenth century, allusions to secret history are used to shore up support for the Tory party, condemn Robert Harley's intelligence-based style of political management, celebrate the triumph of Whiggism after the accession of George I to the throne, decry the ministerial Whigs' abandonment of Revolution principles, and attack the prime minister, Robert Walpole. The sheer range of political uses to which secret history's literary conventions are put reveals the flexibility and enduring appeal of this polemical form of historiography over the course of a turbulent half-century in British politics.

Secret History's Cultural Contexts

The fifty years on which this study focuses are an age of plots and plotting.[3] The later seventeenth century witnessed a cluster of high profile conspiracies, including the Popish Plot of 1679 (an alleged Jesuit conspiracy to assassinate Charles II and install his Roman Catholic brother, James Duke of York, to the throne), the Rye-House Plot of 1683 (a plot to murder both Charles II and his brother, James, by Exclusionists, or proto-Whigs, seeking to prevent the accession of a Roman Catholic monarch to the English throne), and the Assassination Plot of 1696 (in which Jacobite agents were convicted of conspiring to murder William III). Rebellions against the monarch, from the Monmouth uprising in 1685 to attempted Jacobite invasions in 1692, 1708 and 1715, add to the sense that conspiracy was never far from the surface of British politics during this period.

Early modern writers represented the Stuart monarchs not only as potential victims of conspiracy, however, but also as its perpetrators. Opposition polemicists accused Charles II, James II and their supporters of conspiring to undermine the political and religious freedoms of the British people. In his *Account of the*

Growth of Popery and Arbitrary Government (1677), Andrew Marvell repeatedly describes the parliamentary Court party as 'conspirators' against the nation, in league with the French king. The Revolution of 1688–9 was justified not only on the grounds that James II had fled to France and therefore vacated or abdicated his throne, but also that he had conspired to impose Roman Catholicism and arbitrary government upon his subjects and had thus forfeited their loyalty. James, his consort Mary of Modena and their counsellors were popularly believed to have conspired together to procure a suppositious heir to the throne: the infant Prince of Wales, later the Pretender, was allegedly smuggled into the birthing chamber in a warming pan.[4] Even Queen Anne was (albeit falsely) suspected in many quarters of conspiring to make the Pretender her successor, rather than the Protestant Hanoverians.[5] Secret history encourages its readers to believe that their rulers are in league against them and encourages suspicion of Courts in general, arguing that monarchs and ministers operate within a secret sphere of clandestine political activity. If late-Stuart Britain did, indeed, witness the emergence of a 'public sphere', then secret history undermines the idea that its foundations were the rational and free exchange of information and opinion. Secret history suggests that the contemporary reading public was both prurient and fearful about what it did not know. Each revelation of previously concealed intelligence increased awareness of the limits of public knowledge.[6]

The political culture of plots and plotting out of which secret history emerges raises difficult epistemic and generic questions about the relationship between fact and fiction and – even more significantly for secret history – about the ways in which historical events are turned into historical narratives. Where the discovery of secret conspiracy is concerned, it is easy to claim that plots have been invented, especially where there are obvious motives for covering up or fabricating evidence. Sceptical contemporaries speculated that Charles II or his supporters or even Whig activists invented the Rye-House Plot in order to damage their political opponents.[7] Reports of Jacobite conspiracies could, likewise, be dismissed as *ignes fatui* designed by the government to quell a factious public into political submission. The deregulation of the press that occured as a result of a temporary lapse of the Licensing Act in 1679 and a permanent lapse of this Act from 1695 allowed the proliferation of printed accounts of the recent past. In this milieu it was difficult to tell what to believe, since behind every account of contemporary political history lay the potential for numerous, competing versions of past.

Connections between the epistemic problems raised by late Stuart political culture and contemporary literary interest in the concepts of fact and fiction have been explored in much recent scholarship, most notably by Mark Knights and Kate Loveman.[8] The relationship between political and literary questions about how to determine what to believe and similar enquiries in variety of spheres – among them the law, natural philosophy, religion and accounts of travels in far-flung places – has also received substantial critical attention over recent decades.[9] It has less often been observed, however, that such questions about belief necessarily lead on to questions about the business of plotting the past.[10] Asserting the credibility of a previously undiscovered piece of intelligence inevitably involves making an adjustment to received historical narratives. Indeed, even if readers refuse to believe that a particular piece of information is true, the rhetorical act of revelation encourages them to consider the ways in which narratives of the past are constructed out of a selected and therefore contingent set of events. The act of disclosure demonstrates that secrets are narratives, created by rearranging sequences of events in such a way as to obscure the truth. It is the connections between secrecy, revelation, narrative and political power, more than questions about fact and fiction *per se*, that preoccupy early modern secret historians.

Secret history, with its claims to discover previously concealed intelligence, invites from its readers the same kind of scepticism as contemporary political plots. But secret histories differ from most other contemporary accounts of conspiracy and political intrigue because of the highly self-conscious approach that they adopt towards the discourse of disclosure. Secret history not only claims to reveal secrets but also scrutinizes the ethical, epistemic, historiographical and political implications of its own revelatory gestures. Instead of seeking to convince its readers that the claims it makes are unquestionably true, secret histories often acknowledge and even make political capital out of the precarious position that they occupy on the borders of history and fiction. They draw attention to the impact of the disclosure of secrets upon received or familiar narratives of the past. They suggest that all historical narrative, including secret history itself, might be revised or reinterpreted should further information come to light, and that any version of events might be built on fictional rather than factual foundations. Its self-reflexive character makes secret history one of the early modern period's most complex forms of polemical writing.

In order to understand secret history fully, it is vital that we try to situate its distinctive polemical strategies within the partisan milieu that it seeks to influence. This study seeks to provide the first integrated account of early modern secret history, in which both its literary and its partisan characteristics are considered, in detail, together. And it is also the first account of secret history's influence upon a particular set of early eighteenth-century texts, each of which engages with both the literary and political conventions of this polemical form of historiography. The following chapters provide a secret history of secret history by revealing the complexity of this form and the central position that it occupies within early modern literary and political culture. But as it discloses secret history's own secrets, this study also illuminates hidden aspects of the culture of which secret history forms part. For instance, by demonstrating that many of secret history's polemical strategies are counter-intuitive rather than logical and straightforward, it suggests the existence of a politicized reading public capable not only of sophisticated analyses of individual texts but also comparing the rhetorical devices used by a variety of different authors within and across genres. It also shows that early modern party politics – the personalities involved as well as the ideas discussed – precipitated tremendous literary innovation during this period by encouraging a highly self-conscious approach towards questions of genre and narrative form. As the next section demonstrates, secret history's formal characteristics are tailored to its primary political function: opposing arbitrary government. The subseqent two sections explore the more complex and self-conscious rhetorical facets of this polemical form of historiography.

Secret History and the Opposition to Arbitrary Government

Secret history is a form of historiography designed to oppose arbitrary government. It responds to the importance of secrecy in the theory and practice of absolute rule.[11] One recent historian of European absolutism during the early modern period suggests that, 'under absolutism, the concept of secrecy had become morally neutral, far removed from its earlier association with deceit'.[12] Secrecy-based concepts such as political 'prudence', simulation (pretending to be what one is not), dissimulation (pretending not to be what one really is) and *arcana imperii*, or secrets of state, were central to early modern absolutism. These concepts underpinned *raison d'état* or 'reason of state': the adoption of extra-legal or apparently immoral methods of rule, ostensibly for the good of the country.[13] Some early modern writers castigated reason of state as Machiavellian; in other quarters, however, it was applauded as the best means to establish a strong, stable political system.[14] As well as being crucial to reason of state, secrecy was also an intrinsic element of the theological rationale for absolute rule. Absolute monarchs were deemed accountable to God alone and analogous to God as all-powerful rulers. Their motives and secret purposes were inscrutable.[15] In Britain, the association of absolutism with Roman Catholicism (evident in the collocation 'popery and arbitrary government') further added to the perception that mystery sustains arbitrary rule. In absolutist, Roman Catholic states such as France, secrecy appeared to uphold a system of civil and ecclesiastical government in which monarch and priests conspired to control and suppress the people by keeping them in ignorance.[16]

Against the clandestine world of the backstairs and closet, secret history pits the populist medium of print.[17] While secrets are created in private, passed on through whispers or manuscripts that can be destroyed at a moment's notice, secret historians expose secrets in a printed and therefore highly public form. The medium in which their texts appear is thus central to their iconoclastic political aims.[18] But if secret history's general claim to reveal secrets in print is in itself an assault on arbitrary government, then the particular nature of the secrets exposed by secret historians adds weight to the attack. Secret history offer its readers tales of sexual as well as political intrigue gathered from the closets and bedchambers of those who occupy positions of power. The capacity of secret history to titillate was not only commercially advantageous, but also politically significant. Secret history focuses attention on the body of the monarch, thereby compromising regal dignity and undermining the reverential distance between monarch and people.[19] It also presents the foundations of arbitrary rule as unsteady by locating them in the personal whims and appetites of an absolute ruler. When they depict bedchamber intrigues as the root cause of recent political events, secret historians are not necessarily arguing that the king's sexual appetite is the sole reason behind all political history (although, as we shall see, they do sometimes suggest that this is the case). Rather, salacious secret history reveals what happens when men, rather than laws, govern.[20]

The relationship between secret history and pre-existing versions of recent political history reinforces secret history's oppositional political aims. Secret history is never a standalone account of past events; it always supplements and revises earlier historical narratives. Procopius's *Anekdota* was written to undermine his *History of the Wars*, a laudatory account of the battles between the Roman army and the Persians, Goths and Vandals. David Jones's *Secret History of White-hall* claims to be a '*Supplemental Part*, as well for the detecting of past Falsities, as for the perfecting of past Discoveries' in Sir William Temple's *Memoirs* (1691) and Roger Coke's *Detection of the Court and State of England during the Four Last Reigns* (1694).[21] In his *True Secret History*, John Somers prefaces his secret history of each reign with an account of that reign's 'General History', thus highlighting the difference between the two.[22] Yet even when secret historians do not specify particular versions of events that their narratives challenge, secret history is still a revisionist form of historiography. By claiming to bring secrets to light, secret history sets out to undermine prevailing orthodoxies about the character of the reigns that it describes. Secret history's revisionist tendencies also demonstrate the political role of historians, who create or destroy the narratives that surround absolute rulers. This self-reflexive function of secret history had particular resonance for English historians and readers during the later seventeenth century: secret history represents a concerted effort to highlight the iconoclastic potential of historical narrative at a time when Courts across Europe were introducing the post of royal historiographer to promote official versions of the past.[23] Secret history's reflections upon its own status as a genre of iconoclastic historiography represent one of its most powerful polemical strategies.

So far, there appears to be a fairly straightforward political rationale behind secret history's principal rhetorical strategies. In order to attack the aura of secrecy that surrounds absolute rulers, secret history exposes their secrets; in order to highlight the unstable foundations of personal rule and to deprive monarchs of regal dignity, secret history reveals them in a state of undress; and in order to assert the role of the historian in sustaining or undermining arbitrary power, secret history supplements and challenges pre-existing accounts of the recent political past. But such a logical relationship between the political aims and stylistic characteristics of secret history only takes us some of the way towards appreciating the rhetorical strategies of this sophisticated form of historiography. If we look closely at secret histories written during the late seventeenth and early eighteenth centuries, we often find in them a self-conscious approach towards the central motif of revelation that is more hermeneutically demanding than recent scholarly accounts of this genre have acknowledged.

Given its generic title, secret history might logically be expected to reveal secrets and to make strong claims to historicity. Many of its early critics, however, protest that it fails to meet these expectations. One early, Latin commentary on secret history suggests that it should be classed as common satire rather than the prestigious genre of history, and that the information it contains is more accurately described as gossip than as secrets.[24] A later writer likewise observes that the 'Objection ... generally made to all *Anecdotes*' is that their intelligence is 'either False or Common'.[25] According to objectors against secret histories, these texts pretend to give their readers intelligence that is both historically accurate and previously undiscovered while peddling invented stories or common gossip. But do secret historians really claim to tell secrets? And do they genuinely regard their texts as history? The next two sections (respectively) address these questions. The answers that emerge reveal the rhetorical complexities of secret history, and the often counter-intuitive ways in which practitioners of this genre pursue their polemical ends.

A Rhetorical Approach towards the Motif of Revelation; or, Does Secret History Really Tell Secrets?

In order to understand secret history's more complex rhetorical strategies, it helps to begin by asking a simple question: in what sense does secret history tell secrets? The period under consideration does witness the publication of texts which reveal genuine secrets: that is, information never before published and probably unknown to the majority of its readers. Into this category we might place Marvell's *Account of the Growth of Popery*, which reveals the ongoing 'conspiracy' between the Court faction and France to introduce French-style arbitrary government into England through secret leagues.[26] Marvell provides

Introduction 9

his readers with verbatim reports of speeches from inside the *sanctum sanctorum*, the House of Commons – a practice that was illegal in and of itself – as well as incriminating documentary evidence of the Court faction's underhand activities.[27] In the early eighteenth century, Jonathan Swift's *The Conduct of the Allies* (1711) also tells its readers secrets. Swift asserts that 'the true Spring or Motive' of the War of Spanish Succession, which had raged since 1702, 'was the aggrandizing a particular Family' – that is, the Duke and Duchess of Marlborough and the Earl of Godolphin who stood to benefit politically and financially from the war's prolongation.[28] Swift's close contact with the Tory Lord Treasurer, Robert Harley, gave him access to privileged information which he exposed, at Harley's behest, in this propagandist pamphlet.[29] Throughout the period under consideration, writers of polemic clearly understood the importance of putting previously undiscovered intelligence into print as a means of manipulating public opinion.

Many self-professed secret historians likewise claim that their texts provide their readers with genuine, previously undiscovered intelligence. In the preface to *The Secret History of White-hall*, David Jones asserts that his text is intended 'to obviate a vulgar Error and Objection that I foresee would be made upon this Subject, *That all that could be Writ has been written already, concerning the late Reigns*'. Jones challenges 'the *Objector*' to state

> where it is he meets with an exact Account of the *Private League* between King *Charles II.* and the *French* King; The Duke of *York's* secret Correspondence with that Court; *Coleman's* intervention with both for his own Advantage; The Interest the *French* made both in *England* and *Holland* among the several *Sects* and *Parties* of Men, to prevent the late Queen's being married to his present Majesty: The Methods concerted to trapan her into *France* with her Father's concurrence, and how prevented; Father *St Germain's* attempting King *Charles* the Second in his Religion, with the King's Answer, *&c*. His unseasonable boasting of it, the Occasion of his flight into *France*, and the Censure he underwent from those of his Order for it; *Coleman's* Wife's Petition to the *French* King, the Answer, and her destroying her self; Monsieur *Le Tellier's* Speech about the *Invasion* of *England*; The Duke of *York* his perversion to the Church of *Rome*; King *James's Private League* with *France*, when Regnant; the Essay made by *Don Ronquillo*, the *Spanish* Ambasssador, to draw him into the *Austrian* Interest, with his Answer, and Refusal in favour of *France*; How Father *Petre* came to be made a Privy Councellor; wherefore Mr *Skelton* was imprisoned in the *Tower &c*. ... to name no more, though the rest are of equal Curiosity.[30]

This sensationalist preface *cum* table of contents is designed to advertise the novelty of Jones's revelations, but its brash tone perhaps raises more suspicions about the freshness and reliability of the intelligence contained in this text than it quells. Indeed, despite Jones's rhetoric of revelation, much of the information that he claims is new had long circulated in the public domain in printed form. Andrew Marvell had alerted his readers to 'the *Private League* between King *Charles* the Second, and the *French* King' – commonly known as the secret treaty of Dover – twenty years earlier in his *Account of the Growth of Popery*.[31] The secret treaty is the main topic of works such as *An Account of the Reasons Which Induced Charles II. King of England to Declare War Against the States-General of the United Povinces [sic] in 1672. And of the private league which he entred into at the same time with the French king to carry it on* (1689), which in turn was based on Primi Fassola di San Maiolo's suppressed account of the Third Dutch War, *Historia della guerra d'Olanda* (1682). The conspiracies between the Duke of York and the French Court to which Jones alludes had also been publicized in *An Account of the Private League betwixt the Late King James II and the French King. In a Letter from a Gentleman in London, to a Gentleman in the Country* (1689).

Many texts that proudly display the phrase 'secret history' on their title pages deal in similarly recycled material. *The Secret History of the Chevalier de St George* (1714), for instance, rehearses exactly the same stories about the birth of the Pretender that had circulated ever since the warming-pan scandal first broke in 1689, although its author claims to 'enumerate what others have carelessly or artfully pass'd by'.[32] And as late as 1718, John Dunton asserts in *The Hanover-Spy; or, Secret History of St. James's* that Charles II and James II's Roman Catholicism was 'a great Secret hitherto', which 'I positively affirm to be Matter of Fact' – a claim little short of laughable in the context of political events during the previous thirty years.[33] How are we to interpret the motif of revelation in texts like these, which clearly contain little that might be described, in any ordinary sense of the term, as secret?

In the almost total absence of archival evidence, it is impossible to know how readers responded to the claims made by secret histories to reveal secret intelligence, let alone to evaluate variations in the reception of these texts in metropolitan centres and the provinces, by readers with knowledge of the Court and those outside such privileged circles, or among readers of different political persuasions.[34] Even without firm evidence, however, it is safe to assume that readers of secret histories received these texts in a wide variety of different ways. At least some are likely to have approached the information contained in secret histories as genuine secrets – that is, as information brought to light for the first time. With the benefit of hindsight it is evident that much of the content of secret histories was already available to readers in printed form, and it is easy to suspect that still more was common political gossip in and around the Court and City of London. It is nonetheless reasonable to believe that there were many individual readers who really had never encountered the claims made by particular secret histories. The secret historian John Oldmixon seems particularly conscious of such a potential readership in his *Secret History of Europe* (1712–15) – a text which is comprised not of 'such Anecdotes, as are no where else to be met with', but rather of information scattered through so many disparate texts that it 'probably would never have fallen into the Hands of one Man' had Oldmixon not gathered it together.[35] On the other hand, there were readers who remained resolutely sceptical about any information conveyed in the form of a secret history because of the genre's reputation for invented, malicious scandal: as we will see shortly, secret history met with many critics keen to portray its claims to reveal secret intelligence as nothing more than unreliable partisan propaganda and/or profiteering. Most readers probably fell somewhere between these two extremes, evaluating the revelations made by individual texts on their own merits.

If we are to consider the full range of potential responses towards secret history, however, we need to adopt a rhetorical rather than a positivist approach towards the motif of revelation. Instead of attempting to deduce whether secret histories really revealed secrets or to conjecture about how actual readers responded to secret history, this study analyses the authorial strategies that are founded upon the claim to disclose secrets. Such an approach illuminates the possibility that many secret historians did not intend their claims to disclose secret intelligence to be taken as literally true but, rather, that they regarded such gestures as a rhetorical device. For many writers in this genre, the claim to reveal secrets is a statement in support of the Whig opposition to arbitrary government. Whig writers use secret history's central motif of revelation to present their political party as the party of openness rather than concealment, of candour rather than conspiracy, regardless of the quality of the intelligence contained in the secret histories themselves.

Interpreting the motif of revelation as rhetorical has significant implications for the way in which I approach early modern secret history. It means that I am not concerned to discover the real secrets of late Stuart politics, but rather to analyse the ways in which secret historians handled the discourse of disclosure. In this context, the actual details of the secrets that are revealed in any given text are important only insofar as they illuminate the rhetorical act of revelation. So, for instance, the fact that John Dunton claims to expose Charles II's and James II's Roman Catholicism is significant because it connects Dunton's text with an established tradition of Whig secret history and because, as a revelation made in 1718, its putative status as secret intelligence is so entirely implausible. Chapter 3 demonstrates that, although Dunton's text does not in a positive sense reveal secrets in the way that it claims to, its engagement with the discourse of disclosure is, nonetheless, politically motivated. Dunton's approach towards the motif of revelation is far from unusual in the late seventeenth and early eighteenth centuries. We will see that, instead of expressing embarrassment or concern at the lack of secrets in their texts, many writers who engage with the conventions of secret history ostentatiously draw attention to the mismatch between their texts' claims to expose secrets and their contents. Although, at first, Dunton's claim that the Stuart kings' sympathy for the Roman Catholic Church is 'a great Secret hitherto' appears risible, further analysis reveals that a wide disparity between the claim to reveal secret intelligence and the kind of information contained in a given text is a vital part of the polemical strategy of many secret historians.

A rhetorical approach towards the motif of revelation also draws attention to secret historians' ambivalent attitude towards the printed text as a revelatory mechanism. Secret historians contrast the publicity of print with the secrecy of underhand, political machinations but the act of doing so creates a paradox: the printed secret. In the preface to his translation of Antoine Varillas's *Anekdota Heterouiaka; Or, The Secret History of the House of Medicis* (1686), Ferrand Spence testily pre-empts any critics who might take issue with his use of the phrase 'secret history' on the grounds that the information in his text had already appeared in print:

> Some will, perhaps, carp at me, for calling my Traduction a Secret History, whereas the Original had already made the matter Publick; but against this, and other Cavils and Objections, I shall not stand to make a Defence, having, for what I have done, the Authority of all *Procopius* his Translators.[36]

Spence falls back on the same kinds of argument as the French neoclassical critic whose work he translates. He claims that the authority of precedents, particularly those closely related to an ancient text, negates the significance of any contradictions in secret history's claim to reveal secrets. Yet, when compared with later secret historians, Spence's defensive arguments represent something of a failure of imagination. When they describe information published in printed form as 'secret', secret historians create an inconsistency that becomes, for many of them, fertile rhetorical ground.

The fact that so many secret histories fail to provide their readers with genuine secret intelligence in spite of their claims to reveal secrets must have a bearing upon the ways in which we approach these texts. Instead of regarding secret history as a form that actually reveals secrets, we need to think of it as a form that *claims* to reveal secrets and often fails, quite deliberately, to live up to the expectations that it generates. As we shall see, secret historians manipulate the disparity between claim and content in a variety of ways, according to their particular rhetorical and partisan purposes. The coexistence of straightforward and counter-intuitive rhetorical strategies is, however, a feature of almost all secret histories published during the late seventeenth and early eighteenth centuries. This peculiar characteristic of secret history is very much in evidence in its distinctive, self-conscious approach towards questions of genre and narrative form.

A Generic Approach towards the Motif of Revelation; or, is Secret History Really Historical?

Throughout the period of secret history's prominence, ill-disposed commentators repeatedly attack this form's pretensions to historicity. Many of them do so on the grounds that secret history is more fiction than fact. *The Blatant Beast Muzzl'd* (1691) – an extended critique of secret history by writer who identifies himself only as N. N. – declares that *The Secret History of the Reigns of K. Charles II and K. James II* (1690) is 'Fantastick Stuff' which is 'so full of Forgery, that it disgraces *History* by being nam'd such, having scarce as much Truth in it as is generally Found in Romances'.[37] The French historiographer Nicolas Lenglet Dufresnoy likewise condemns the 'loose Imaginations' of secret historians, which blur the boundary between fact and fiction. 'Because in them are found some Truth', he asserts, 'therefore it is believed that there is nothing false', when in fact 'we shou'd regard the whole as false, upon Account of the Difficulty we have to trace out the Truth so enwrapped with Falsehood'.[38] Jonathan Swift has Gulliver discover and denounce 'the Roguery and Ignorance of those who pretend to write *Anecdotes*, or secret History; who send so many Kings to their Graves with a cup of Poison; will repeat the Discourse between a Prince and a chief Minister, where no Witness was by; unlock the Thoughts and Cabinets of Embassadors and Secretaries of State; and have the perpetual Misfortune to be mistaken'.[39] Gulliver implies that the ignorant rogues who write secret history invent the stuff that fills their narratives.

Gulliver's observations show that the motif of revelation, which is secret history's most distinctive characteristic, renders this genre particularly vulnerable to criticism, since intelligence about things that took place 'where no Witness was by' is nearly impossible to verify. Some secret histories advertise the fact that the information they contain was 'undiscoverable by any other Hand' – a claim that asserts the uniqueness and, hence, the high value of their contents.[40] But such claims also preclude the possibility of introducing the corroborative accounts of other witnesses. Secret history's main selling point – its claim to provide undiscovered secret intelligence – thus becomes a historiographical weakness.[41]

Critics of secret history regularly capitalize on this particular vulnerability. Nicolas Lenglet Dufresnoy asserts, with a degree of irony, that 'indeed difficult it is to know that which passes only between two where it is their Interest to conceal it'.[42] With rather more rancour, the author of *The Blatant Beast Muzzl'd* demands:

> In the Name of Wonder, how comes this inconsiderable Wretch [the author of *The Secret History of the Reigns of K. Charles II and K. James II*] to be better acquainted with the *Secrets* of State, than all the Heard [*sic*] of Mankind besides[?]... Was he ever Secretary to any of those several Princes or Popes, that he should be so well Vers't in

> their *most private* Transactions, and pronounce upon them with such a Confidence? Yet, he must be more than that; he must be of their *Cabinet-Council* too. Nor, will even such an intimate Familiarity with their *Persons* and *Outward* Transactions, justify the abominable Suggestions that are delivered as so many Certain & Evident Truths in this Libel of his. He assumes to himself yet a far greater Priviledge, than the knowing all the *Arcana Imperii*. This is too *superficial* an Object for his reaching Brain. He Fancies himself a little God Almighty, and dives into their very *Thoughts*; and (which is a Prerogative peculiar to the Divinity) searches their very Hearts and most retruse Intentions; and when he has done, he turns their Consciences inside-outwards.[43]

Secret history's pretensions to report on secret meetings, intimate conversations, and even private thoughts, beggar belief; they turn the eyewitness narrator of true history into an omniscient narrator more characteristic of romance. Secret history's central motif of revelation makes it impossible to determine whether or not its claims should be regarded as fact or fiction.

Several secret historians attempt to defend their chosen form against accusations of invention. In the preface to his *True Secret History*, John Somers contends with what he takes to be 'the main Objection against *Secret Histories* (that they are seldom True)'.[44] Somers cites his personal credentials to affirm the veracity of the information contained in his text. As a peer of the realm and former minister of state, he presents himself as a trustworthy eyewitness of many of the events he describes. He also notes that he has access to intelligence from 'the Rever[e]nd Mr. W. – Who was a Spy in the French Court, and by that means, took Minutes of the most Secret Transactions between *England* and *France* for many Years'.[45] Somers's personal wealth allows him to acquire 'all those scarce and Valuable Pieces of *Secret History* which were to be purchas'd', while his elevated social status grants him access to both 'Publick and Private Libraries' to see 'Authentick Authors and Manuscripts of Undoubted Credit'.[46] Somers thus advertises the fact that his secret history fulfils high standards of historical proof: his is an eyewitness narrative written by a participant in the events described; for earlier reigns and events that took place outside the Somers's immediate sphere of activity, the best documentary evidence – including unpublished, private material contained in manuscripts – is used to provide as full and factual an account as possible.

Other secret historians who lack Somers's social and political privileges use different criteria to assert the veracity of their accounts. David Jones affirms that the secrets revealed in his text can be corroborated 'not only by the Connection they have with many material passages in Sir *William Temple's Memoirs*, Mr. *Coke's Detection of the Court and State of England during the Four last Reigns*, &c. but by so natural an unfolding of what is obscurely, or but transiently hinted at by those learned Authors, who could not see beyond their Light'.[47] Jones thus highlights the revisionist character of secret history even as he attempts to substantiate his own revelations. The anonymous author of *The Secret History of the Reigns of K. Charles II and K. James II* employs yet another tactic, insisting that, 'as for the Truth of what is here contain'd, I will not Apologize for it; for as to the more secret Transactions, the Consequences and Events are my Testimonies; and for what was more publickly carried, there are the loud and general Complaints of the Kingdom to confirm it'.[48] While Somers's position as a Tacitean statesman-historian serves to underwrite the reliability of his account, and Jones encourages his readers to compare his account against other historical narratives, *The Secret History of the Reigns of K. Charles II and K. James II* appeals to the common experience of the people, his readers, reinforcing the iconoclastic political aims of this work.

The dubious reliability of the evidence put forward by secret history is not, however, the only ground upon which its critics attack its pretensions to historicity. Some opponents of secret history also assert that, whether it is true or false, the scandalous nature of secret history's contents violates generic decorum. In his commentary on a Latin translation of Procopius's *Anekdota*, an English jurist named Thomas Ryves rails against the title *Arcana Historia* ('secret history') because it makes too audacious a claim for Procopius's work. Ryves argues that the *Anekdota* is not a history – a prestigious generic label – but a 'satire of vices'.[49]

Even those writers who allow the *Anekdota* to be history criticize its historiographical method. In his *Instructions for History*, translated into English in 1680, René Rapin attacks Procopius's *Anekdota* on the grounds that it 'forget[s] to circumstance what is important, and is very careful in circumstancing what is not so'.[50] In particular, Rapin condemns secret history's efforts to explain historical change by reference to human passions and appetites. He mocks the idea 'that *Pericles* occasioned the *Peloponnesian* War, upon the score of his Amours to the Curtezan *Aspasia*. That *Xerxes* carried into *Greece* that dreadful Army, of which Historians give us an account, onely out of a design to eat Figs there. That *Anthony* lost the Empire, onely to avoid losing *Cleopatra*. That *Francis* the First of *France* had no motive to bring an Army into *Italy*, but the fair Eyes of a *Milanese* Lady named *Claricia*'.[51] Rapin denigrates this kind of historical method not only because its focus on love and sexual desire undermines the dignity of history, but also because it represents a highly reductive approach towards complex questions of historical causation. Indeed, Rapin's analysis seems designed to highlight the proximity of secret history and French *histoire galante*, which also prioritizes love as a causal force behind historical events.[52]

In making this implicit comparison, Rapin is, in fact, highlighting a generic relationship that is acknowledged in many secret histories. Changes in title between English and French editions of particular texts point towards correspondences between secret history and *histoire galante*: *The Royal Mistresses of France; or, the Secret History of the Amours of all the French Kings* (1695) is a translation of Claude Vanel's *Galanteries des Rois de France* (1694), while *The Court of St. Germains; or, The Secret History of James II* (1695) is translated from *La Cour de St. Germain, ou, les intrigues galantes du roy et de la reine d'Angleterre, depuis leur séjour en France* (1695). Secret histories that advertise their affiliation with *histoire galante* often do exhibit a simplistic sense of historical causation. The preface to the French translation of *The Secret History of the Duchess of Portsmouth* (1690), for instance, declares that 'if [Charles II] acted in a way that so little conformed to his judgement, to his powerful intelligence, to politics, to the interests not only of many nations in general, but also to his own realm, then it was a woman, it was the Duchess of Portsmouth, who drove him to it by means of the love that she had inspired in him, by her machinations, and by her power over his mind'.[53] Secret history's association with *histoire galante* draws together both of the principal criticisms against it: that it contains a promiscuous blend of fictional and factual material, and that it violates literary decorum by introducing frivolous, trivial subjects such as love and sexual desire into a serious genre designed to educate its readers through an analysis of the past.

While some secret historians – particularly those who translate works into or out of French – advertise secret history's proximity to *histoire galante*, others attempt to distance these two literary traditions by highlighting the characteristics that secret history shares with neoclassical historiography. In the first extended analysis of Procopian secret history, the French critic Antoine Varillas declares the importance of setting down rules for 'the Art of writing secret History', which he claims 'is still unknown, almost in its whole Extent' because 'no Philosopher, hitherto, has taken the pains to draw up the Method of it, nor Critick dar'd to shew its Defects'.[54] To this end, Varillas informs his reader that he will 'impose Laws on my self, according to which, I pretend to be try'd by an equitable Reader, on Condition I neither borrow them from my Reason nor Caprice, but only from the Examples of *Procopius*, whom I will ever have in ken, seeing I cannot find any other Guide'.[55] Varillas vows to follow Procopius just as other neoclassical historians imitate their ancient exemplars. In doing so, he implicitly elevates his model to the status enjoyed by other classical histories. To justify such an elevation, he insists that the secret historian 'cannot dispence himself from any of the Rules that *Aristotle, Cicero, Plutarch* and other the Masters of th'Art have so judiciously prescrib'd for Publick History'.[56] According to Varillas, Procopius '[performs] the Duty of a perfect Historian'.[57] By claiming that the *Anekdota* is 'perfect history', Varillas highlights the fact that it provides an account of the causes behind historical events as well as of the events themselves, according to the example of Procopius's own historiographical model, Thucydides.[58]

In fact, some of secret history's most forthright critics reveal the proximity of secret history to more orthodox forms of early modern perfect history. In his celebration of the best modern historical writing, René Rapin acknowledges that

> nothing is more divertive in a Narration, than the decyphering of what is secret and of importance, in the designs and intentions of those whose Actions it divulges: and as History has not any thing curious comparably [*sic*] to that, so are there not any Historians of any fame, who have not endeavoured to signalize themselves upon that score. For nothing does more excite the Curiosity of men, than when they have discover'd to them what is most conceal'd in the Heart of man, that is to say, the secret Springs and Resorts, which make him act in the Enterprizes, which are ordinary to him.[59]

Like the perfect historians whom Rapin praises, the secret historians whom he condemns aim to 'excite the Curiosity of men' by revealing 'the secret Springs and Resorts' behind public events; indeed, the 'secret springs' metaphor is a trope that secret historians frequently deploy in their own narratives.[60] In particular, Tacitus – whom Rapin cites as an example of an historian for whom motives are particularly important – is often criticized in early modern analyses of history writing in terms that seem pertinent to secret history.[61] In his short essay, 'Observations upon Salust and Tacitus', Charles de Saint-Evremond suggests that Tacitus 'turns every thing into Policy' and 'gives too far fetch Causes of some Actions, which are altogether Simple, Ordinary, and Natural'.[62] Rapin, too, accuses Tacitus of reading too much into every event, concluding that in the *Annals* and the *Histories*, 'the Political Reflection is the motive and general decypherer and disentangler of all things'.[63] As we will see, critics of secret history likewise accused its practitioners of seeing plots everywhere and over-interpreting historical events accordingly. If Tacitus wrote causal historical narratives that identify the reasons for the visible events of history as the secret motives and conspiracies of key figures, what is there to distinguish between orthodox and secret history?

In spite of the points of similarity between them, there are also several factors that set secret history apart from more orthodox forms of perfect history.[64] The first concerns the historian's qualification to narrate events. Tacitus and many of his latter-day imitators, such as Edward Hyde, Earl of Clarendon, assert the importance of their participation in the events that they describe to their authority as historians.[65] Unlike these orthodox narratives written by statesmen-historians, however, many secret historians reveal that their sources are ethically dubious – if they cite their sources at all. John Somers's emphasis on his personal acquaintance with affairs of state is unusual. Rather than writing about their firsthand experiences, secret historians often claim to have their intelligence through intercepted letters, whispered news and gossip, the intelligence of spies and the grumbling of cast-off mistresses. They thus give their readers the impression that the information contained in their texts is passed on expressly against the will of the powerful figures whom it concerns. The overtly iconoclastic purpose of secret history also distinguishes it from Tacitean history, which could be interpreted either as supportive of absolute rule because it gives instructions in reason of state, or as a revelatory form of historiography along the lines of secret history.[66] Secret historians' prurient interest in bedchamber intrigues puts their chosen form still further outside the historical pale. Rapin asserts that true history deals in 'what is secret *and of importance*'[67] – a category that does not include amatory affairs. Although Thomas Ryves meant to condemn secret history by describing it as a 'satire of vices', his analysis is close to the truth: secret history provides an alternative vision of the recent political past, which deliberately chafes against official accounts and orthodox historiographical methods.[68] Nonetheless, secret history's self-conscious interest in the business of plotting and re-plotting the past suggests that it has more to do with historiography than most other contemporary forms of satire. Indeed, it is important to secret history's polemical purpose that it both resembles and also subverts contemporary perfect history.

Some defenders of secret history actually seek to suggest that this form represents a new kind of perfect history which is more accurate in its representation of the past than Tacitean or other neoclassical perfect history. In his commentary on Procopius, Antoine Varillas suggests that it is precisely by peering into the hidden recesses of bedchambers and closets that Procopius carries out 'the Duty of a perfect Historian',[69] because it is only by doing so that the real causes of public events can be known. Indeed, Varillas insists that the interest that secret historians take in sexual intrigue not only allows them to provide a fuller account of the causes behind historical events than can other kinds of perfect historian, but that it also compels them to stick closer to historical facts than their more conventional counterparts. Varillas asserts that, 'what Liberty soever, not to say Libertinage, that's attributed to *Ἀνέκδοτα*, there is no kind of Writing more constrain'd, nor more reserv'd, since it has not a quarter of the Extent which the most scrupulous Historians propose to themselves', and that 'there's no kind of Slavery greater, for an Anecdoto-grapher, than to be ty'd to tell the truth in all its Circumstances, ev'n when he handles the nicest matters'.[70] Varillas implies that secret historians deal in sexual scandal – or, 'the nicest matters', as he modestly puts it – because it really is the driving force behind historical events, and not because they are prurient. Moreover, he affirms that the suspicion inevitably aroused by secret history's morally dubious content obliges practitioners of this form to adopt a particularly scrupulous approach towards questions of historical accuracy. Although he acknowledges it to be a 'Paradox',[71] Varillas suggests that the characteristics of secret history which this form shares with *histoire galante* are, in fact, those that make it a reliable, accurate form of historiography.

That secret historians should wish to affirm the accuracy and propriety of their own narratives is, of course, a logical response to the accusations of invention and indecorum that were made against them. But, as we have seen, secret history does not always fulfil the expectations that might be generated by a strictly logical approach to its central motif of revelation. Indeed, some secret historians respond to the accusations made against them in ways that appear decidedly counter-intuitive. Several of them, for instance, draw their readers' attention to ethical difficulties that are created by their claim to reveal secret intelligence. Antoine Varillas's observation that the secret historian 'endeavours by all means to get open [the] Closet-door'[72] of those in power creates an immediate impression of prurience and underhand dealing, which does little to inspire confidence in the honesty of such a writer. Other secret historians acknowledge the moral difficulties involved in publishing secret intelligence. The act of acquiring information in private and disclosing it in public inevitably involves a degree of bad faith, even if it is carried out in support of a laudable political cause. The revelation of secrets always involves a betrayal of trust, and the deeper the secret penetrated, the more profound the treachery involved.[73] By acknowledging the dubious ethical provenance of the intelligence that fills their texts, secret historians destabilize their own narrative authority – often, it seems, quite deliberately so. The sense of frisson that secret history generates for its readers derives not only from its promise to give a glimpse into cabinets of power, but also from its refusal to confirm whether or not the information it presents is, in fact, a true account of the past.

When they draw attention to the ethical challenges raised by the motif of revelation, secret historians call into question both the reliability of their historical narratives and the idea that those narratives provide a definitive account of the past. In the preface to his *True Secret History,* John Somers promises to reveal 'the Secret Springs and real Causes from whence so many strange and various Effects have proceeded; which oftentimes has [*sic*] been very different from what has been pretended'.[74] Somers implies that, while public history gives a partial account, secret history presents a full picture, showing what really happened in the past – an argument that we have also seen rehearsed in Varillas's analysis of Procopian secret history. Other secret historians, including David Jones in *The Secret History of White-Hall* and Daniel Defoe in his *Secret History of the White-Staff* (1714–15), vary Somers's mechanistic metaphor to suggest that secret history exposes not only 'secret Springs' but also 'wheels within wheels'.[75] Both metaphors imply that the visible events of history are like the hands on a watch, which are turned by hidden mechanisms. They suggest that public events can be caused in any number of ways by various configurations of motives and causes which, for the most part, can only be deduced from surface appearances.

But the idea that historical causation is a set of interlocking wheels within wheels also raises a prospect that unsettles Somers and Varillas's approach towards secret history. Instead of providing a definitive account of the past, secret history opens up the way for future narratives inspired by the discovery of still deeper, darker secrets – or yet smaller wheels within wheels.[76] If secret history supplements and undermines public versions of history, then the methods by which it does so also elicit (either knowingly or unwittingly) further accounts of what really happened. *The Blatant Beast Muzzl'd* asserts, sardonically, that 'our Godly Times, luxuriantly fruitful of such immodest Productions, do frequently teem with' secret histories.[77] His sexualized language reflects what he regards as secret history's prurient obsession with the sexual exploits of the powerful. But it also draws attention to the fact that the motif of revelation is fecund, having the potential to generate endless, competing accounts of the past. Indeed, in spite of his criticism of secret history, the author of *The Blatant Beast Muzzl'd* indulges in some scandalous revelations himself, asserting that Charles II's illegal act of closing down the exchequer was secretly 'done by the advice of the Earl of *Shaftesbury* to render that King odious'.[78] Even opponents of secret history, it seems, cannot resist exploiting its central motif of revelation. Yet as the number of narratives grows around any particular set of historical events, so the possibility of telling which are factual, and which fictional, diminishes. By taking the discourse of disclosure to its logical extreme, some secret historians suggest that all historical narrative, including secret history, is vulnerable to revision, reinterpretation, and fictional interpolation. These writers harness the iconoclastic force of secret history and direct it against secret history itself.

The Scope of This Study

Any study based on a particular genre of writing assumes that certain texts fall within its remit and that others are excluded. But this assumption raises difficult questions about how to define the characteristics that constitute the genre under consideration. In the case of secret history, early modern writers lend some assistance in this process. Several self-styled secret historians pen extensive and theoretically acute prefaces designed to explain secret history as a genre and justify their own engagement with its conventions. Antoine Varillas's *Anekdota Heterouiaka*, David Jones's *Secret History of White-hall* and John Somers's *True Secret History* all begin with detailed comments on the formal characteristics and/or the political functions of secret history. Critics of secret history also seek to define this form so that they might attack it with greater vigour. *The Blatant Beast Muzzl'd* is a book-length attack on *The Secret History of the Reigns of K. Charles II and K. James II* which, by analysing the polemical and rhetorical strategies used in one particular text, illuminates the entire genre to which it belongs. More scattered, usually hostile, but critically astute comments on the form are found in the works of French critics such as René Rapin and Nicolas Lenglet Dufresnoy, and English historiographers such as Thomas Hearne and Roger North. Deductions based on the characteristics of those texts that call themselves secret histories provide yet another means of understanding what contemporaries understood by the term. There are, of course, difficulties inherent in this deductive method. One later eighteenth-century writer jested that the 'secret history' label was nothing more than a marketing scam designed to allure potential readers into buying a text, be its contents ever so innocuous.[79] Nonetheless, the decision to label a text a secret history suggests that booksellers and authors perceived some common characteristics among such texts – a suggestion usually borne out by their contents.

According to these sources, secret history has a number of distinctive conventions. It invariably claims to reveal secrets about those in positions of power. Its revelations are almost always of a scandalous nature, whether they concern the bedchamber or political intrigues of monarchs or ministers. Secret history is designed to shock and outrage its readers. Most contemporaries therefore associate secret history with Whig politics – whether this entails justified resistance to arbitrary government (according to secret history's supporters) or an attempt to undermine the entire institution of the monarchy (according to its opponents). Secret historians' desire to establish a core tradition of Whig secret history is evident in their use of common metaphors, like those of secret springs and wheels within wheels, and allusion to one another's works: as we will see, John Dunton and John Somers quote key passages from *The Secret History of White-hall* and *The Secret History of the Reigns of K. Charles II and K. James II* in an attempt to reinforce the Whig heritage of this literary tradition.

Of equal importance to the act of revelation in defining secret history is the extent to which practitioners of and commentators on this form analyse its claim to expose secrets of state. Secret history's self-referential tendency is perhaps this genre's most distinctive characteristic. Often, it means that secret history's rhetorical and polemical strategies are counter-intuitive: some secret historians renounce the idea that their revelatory claims have historical authority; others reveal an awareness that their texts do not contain real secrets. Secret historians' scrutiny of the implications of their own claim to disclose intelligence is, however, an essential aspect of this form and one that clearly appealed to many of the writers who adapted its conventions. In its origins, then, secret history is a Whig form that not only claims to disclose secrets of state but that also examines the epistemic, historiographical and political consequences of its own revelatory tendencies. During the early eighteenth century, writers from across the political spectrum – Tories and Jacobites, Court Whigs and Old Whigs – exploit both secret history's early association with the Whig opposition to arbitrary government and its self-reflexive literary characteristics as they rework its conventions to serve a variety of political causes.[80]

The structure of this study reflects my belief that secret history is, at its heart, a self-conscious form with Whig origins, which was nonetheless appropriated by eighteenth-century writers of different political opinions. The first section analyses what I take to be secret history's 'core tradition'. Each of the three chapters of this section provides a snapshot of secret history at a different stage in its historical development: during the 1670s, when the first self-styled secret history was published in England; during the reign of William III, when secret history became a distinctively English but also a surprisingly sceptical form of historiography; and in the wake of the Hanoverian accession of 1714, when the decline of secret history seemed to some practitioners of this form to reflect the fate of Revolution principles under the Whig ministries of George I's reign. The second section explores eighteenth-century adaptations of and variations on the core tradition of secret history. In four chapters, each of which focuses on a different author or text, it analyses the ways in which eighteenth-century writers manipulate and rework both the literary conventions and the political connotations of secret history. It shows the variety of political ends to which Delarivier Manley, the contributors to *The Spectator*, Daniel Defoe, and Eliza Haywood put secret history's conventions. The structure of my study is designed to support its central argument: that the complexity and sophistication of secret history's formal, literary characteristics render it peculiarly apt to engage with the political vicissitudes of the first age of party politics.

This study focuses on a fairly small range of texts in a substantial amount of detail. In each of the chapters – particularly the chapters of Section 2, which address variations and adaptations of secret history's conventions in the eighteenth century – close reading of the texts in question underpins a historicized analysis of the ways in which these texts engage in contemporary party political debate. One effect of my decision to focus on depth of analysis rather than breadth of coverage is that I have not addressed some texts which, while they share some of the rhetorical characteristics of the Whig tradition of secret history, nonetheless engage with it either at a relatively superficial level, or in a somewhat incidental way, or not at all. Aphra Behn's *Love-Letters Between a Nobleman and His Sister* (1685, 1685, 1687), collections of poems on affairs of state such as *Poems on Affairs of State from the Time of Oliver Cromwell to the Abdication of K. James the Second* (1697), the Earl of Clarendon's *History of the Great Rebellion* (1702), Jonathan Swift's *Travels into Several Remote Regions of the World* (1726) – better known as *Gulliver's Travels* – and Gilbert Burnet's *History of His Own Times* (1724, 1734), engage in a variety of ways with ideas about secrecy.[81] None of them, however, reveal the combination of self-consciousness towards the rhetorical act of disclosure and the deployment of this self-consciousness to a partisan end that characterize the Whig tradition of secret history and are central to the texts considered in Section 2 of this study.

My contextualized study of secret history's rhetorical characteristics represents a new departure in scholarship on this genre. Although secret history has enjoyed a considerable amount of critical attention in recent years, it has almost always been incorporated into broader narratives of early modern and eighteenth-century cultural, literary and political history. Among literary scholars, secret history has often been used to illuminate developments in other literary genres during the early modern period. Melinda Alliker Rabb, for instance, has recently suggested that secret history is crucial to understanding eighteenth-century satire.[82] Many more literary historians have incorporated secret history into accounts of the rise of the novel. According to Robert Mayer, secret history displays the kind of experimental attitude towards 'matters of fact' which was crucial to the novel's emergence.[83] Michael McKeon draws attention to the fact that, like the early novel, secret history claims to give its readers access to private spaces and to the private lives of public individuals, while William B. Warner argues that the erotic elements of secret history are assimilated and 'elevated' by the eighteenth century novel.[84] Secret history appears to be one of the many voices – belonging to both high and low cultural forms – that, according to Mikhail Bakhtin's highly influential analysis, make up this 'heteroglossic' genre.[85]

Recent scholarly interest in ephemeral forms of writing such as secret history has vastly increased our understanding of the culture out of which major genres such as the novel emerged.[86] But one effect of this movement has been the creation of teleological narratives of early eighteenth-century literary history in which distinctive genres such as secret history are subsumed into the history of the novel.[87] My study goes some way towards redressing this balance. It reveals facets of secret history that are invariably flattened out or passed over in accounts of the early novel. For instance, instead of attempting to establish grounds that would allow its readers to believe, with a degree of confidence, in its revelations, many secret historians draw attention to the idea that, where secrets are concerned, it is impossible to distinguish between fact and fiction. And because of its sceptical approach towards epistemic or generic questions of fact and fiction, secret history is much more self-conscious than any early novel (with the exception of Defoe's *Moll Flanders* and *Roxana*, discussed in Chapter 6) about narrative form and different ways of plotting the past.[88] Moreover, secret history – unlike the early novel – deploys its self-conscious approach towards genre and narrative form to an explicitly party-political end. Although this close engagement with party politics inevitably limits the readability of secret history for modern, general readers, it contributes enormously to our scholarly understanding of the complex ways in which early modern polemicists deploy essentially literary devices in the services of highly partisan causes. As it reveals the narratological and political consequences of secret history's distinctive approach towards questions of fact and fiction, this study demonstrates that at least one of the minor genres out of which the novel emerges stands up to detailed scholarly analysis in its own right.

As well as being a subject of interest in recent literary history, secret history has also been considered as an index of broader changes in early modern political thought. Michael McKeon presents this genre as the epitome of a more general 'devolution of absolutism' that occurs between the sixteenth and eighteenth centuries. According to McKeon's analysis, secret history spreads knowledge and therefore power as its revelation of state secrets renders 'explicit' mysteries of state that, while only 'tacit', had underpinned absolute rule.[89] The idea that secret history articulates secrets of state in order to challenge royal prerogative is also put forward by Annabel Patterson. Patterson asserts that secret history is the preserve of 'the leftward or liberal side of the ideological spectrum', since its aim is 'to outsmart the government in its control of information'.[90] In my own study, I build on both of these earlier political analyses of secret history, but am more concerned than either Patterson or McKeon to connect secret history's conventions to the specific party political contexts of late seventeenth and early eighteenth century Britain. Secret history is an iconoclastic form of historiography that was used by Whig polemicists to ward off a perceived threat of arbitrary government, but its literary conventions were appropriated and reworked by writers from across the eighteenth-century political spectrum in spite of or, more accurately, because of its early association with Whiggism. I suggest that the only way in which we can gauge the shades of political opinion expressed by the large number of writers who exploit the conventions of secret history is by attending closely to the stylistic, rhetorical and literary devices that they deploy. By adopting a more literary critical approach towards secret history than either McKeon or Patterson, I demonstrate the flexibility of this genre and the central role that it plays in the literary and political culture fostered by late seventeenth- and early eighteenth-century party conflict.

As a site of party-political contest, secret history provides a new way of thinking about the relationship between political and literary culture during the early eighteenth century. Much previous scholarship in this area has focused on the importance of attending to the vocabulary of political argument during the early modern period as a way of accessing contemporary ideas and attitudes as well as modes of debate.[91] This linguistic approach has illuminated the political culture of the first age of party, when polemicists jostled over key terms as they promoted their own political beliefs and denigrated those of their opponents. Words such as 'loyalty', 'liberty', 'slavery', 'faction' and 'moderation' – to name but a few – were claimed and contested by partisans from all sides.[92] Mark Knights has recently argued that late-Stuart politics created a culture in which partisan struggles over slogans, words and phrases undermined any basis for common understanding and precipitated enormous anxiety over the perpetual possibility of misrepresentation and misunderstanding.[93] Secret history, however, suggests that such partisan contests were not limited to individual words or even key phrases. It reveals that generic conventions also become sites of struggle in the febrile political atmosphere of early eighteenth-century Britain. Secret history's scandalous revelatory gestures and revisionist historiographical impulses originate as a form of Whig polemic, but they are reworked by writers of various political opinions in order to attack Whig partisans and promote other social and political causes.

Tracing the appropriation of conventions by competing interest groups is in many ways more problematic than charting the ways in which individual words and their cognates are used and abused, if only because they are more difficult to define. Secret history's central motif of revelation can sometimes be identified by an explicit promise to give readers information 'never before publish'd' or 'hitherto undiscoverable', but often it is evident in less direct ways – the use of spy narrators or private, courtly settings and allusions to earlier secret histories among them. Analysing the ways in which conventions are passed between authors and modified through time requires a literary critical approach towards secret history. It demands close attention to both the language and the tone that particular texts adopt when they claim to disclose secrets, and to the formal and structural characteristics of the texts in which such revelatory gestures are made. It suggests that early modern and eighteenth-century authors – even of popular and partisan texts – regarded close reading and the detailed interpretation of texts as activities of which their readership would be thoroughly capable.[94] But it also entails substantial risks of misreading and over-reading, as it places heavy hermeneutic demands upon its readers, both contemporary and modern. I hope that in this study I have avoided most of these potential pitfalls and done justice to the rhetorical complexities of a supremely sophisticated form of polemical writing.

SECTION 1
WHIG SECRET HISTORY: THE CORE TRADITION

Section 1 is divided into three chapters that chart Whig secret history over the course of half a century. Each of the chapters addresses a different stage in this genre's development.

Chapter 1 focuses on Procopius's *Anekdota*. It describes the kind of model that Procopius's text provides for later writers in this tradition through an analysis of the internal, rhetorical features of the *Anekdota* and of the reception of this text in early modern Europe. This chapter reveals that early modern secret historians inherit from Procopius a complex literary and historiographical paradigm. Instead of simply revealing the secrets of those in power, the *Anekdota* also encourages its readers to reflect on and theorize the ethical and epistemic as well as the political consequences of its revelatory rhetoric.

Chapter 2 explores the boom in Whig secret history that happened during the 1690s. It demonstrates that, during this period, secret history developed into a peculiarly English form of historiography. It also analyses this form's engagement with what is now known as 'whig' historiography. This chapter shows that some secret historians, including John Somers and the anonymous author of the highly popular *Secret History of the Reigns of K. Charles II and K. James II*, present secret history as a token of newfound political liberties – a sign of the historical watershed that was created by the Revolution of 1688–9. Other secret historians, however, approach their chosen form in a less positive fashion. Instead of affirming the security of the Revolution settlement, writers like David Jones manipulate the conventions of secret history to suggest that the forces of arbitrary government pose an ongoing threat to English liberty and that the general populace remains powerless to act against such forces. Although several contemporary commentators accuse such secret historians of sedition, Chapter 2 argues that this highly sceptical form of historiography is designed to challenge not the government of William III, but rather the kind of political complacency that posed an indirect threat to English political liberty during the 1690s.

The third and final chapter in this section turns to consider the response of secret historians to the Hanoverian accession in 1714. It focuses on the work of the bookseller and Whig polemicist, John Dunton. Like many of his contemporaries, Dunton uses secret history to draw parallels between the two Protestant 'revolutions', in which the advent of a virtuous, Protestant (albeit foreign) monarch brought to an end a four-year, internal threat of popery and arbitrary government: the reign of James II in the 1680s, and the Tory ministry of the Lord Treasurer, Robert Harley, during the last four years of the reign of Queen Anne. By 1718, however, it was clear that Dunton's secret histories would bring him neither the political nor the commercial success that he had anticipated. In streightened circumstances, Dunton begins to suggest that his failure is itself an index of contemporary political corruption. By reasserting the connection between secret history and Revolution principles, Dunton not only attacks the current Whig ministry but also reveals secret history's capacity to function polemically even when it appears to be a form in decline.

The three chapters of section 1 reveal that, over the course of the period under consideration, Whig secret historians continue to deploy very similar rhetorical devices: all claim to reveal secret intelligence; all associate their claims with the opposition to arbitrary government; many use a set of common metaphors (for instance, secret springs) or even quote particular phrases found in earlier secret histories to assert their membership of a common tradition. But this section also demonstrates that the potential effects of these devices upon their readers vary considerably according to historical circumstances. In order to understand the significance of secret history's key rhetorical conventions, therefore, we need to attempt to reconstruct the possible range of meanings that they possessed within their original political context, and to assess the ways in which their redeployment over the course of time reflects both change and continuity within the secret history tradition.

1 PROCOPIUS OF CAESAREA AND THE SECRET HISTORY OF THE COURT OF THE EMPEROR JUSTINIAN (1674)

The first printed, English text to call itself a secret history is a slim octavo volume entitled *The Secret History of the Court of the Emperor Justinian* (1674) – an anonymous translation of the *Anekdota* (or 'unpublished things') by the sixth-century Byzantine historian Procopius of Caesarea.[1] Procopius's shocking descriptions of the political tyranny and sexual debauchery of the Empire's leading figures – Justinian, his Empress Theodora, and General Belisarius – ensured that the *Anekdota* had achieved a significant degree of notoriety by the time it appeared in English. It was already known to European intellectual circles as a result of several earlier published editions. The first of these was a Greek text with parallel Latin translation which appeared in 1623 under the title *Arcana Historia*. It was followed in 1669 by the first vernacular translation: a French edition with the title *Ἀνέκδοτα; ou Histoire secrète de Justinien*. The first English translation, published five years later, was based on both the Latin and French translations which preceded it.[2]

The Secret History of the Court of the Emperor Justinian seems at first glance to be an opposition polemic. Published in the wake of the Third Dutch War and in the midst of increasing fears that Charles II was becoming little more than a puppet of France, the English version of the *Anekdota* apparently challenges the absolutist ambitions of the Stuarts. In the opening pages of his narrative, Procopius declares that 'nothing excited me so strongly to this work, as that such persons who are desirous to govern in an Arbitrary way, might discover, by the misfortune of those whom I mention, the destiny that attends them, and the just recompence they are to expect of their crimes'.[3] His ambition held great appeal for opponents of the Court during the mid 1670s. The fact that *The Secret History of the Emperor Justinian* is the first English text to describe itself as a secret history, coupled with this overtly oppositional manifesto, means that it is often cited as the foundation of the close relationship between secret history and the

Whig political cause during the late seventeenth and early eighteenth centuries.[4]

In this chapter, however, I want to complicate the received analysis of the politics of *The Secret History of the Court of the Emperor Justininian*. Although secret history does undoubtedly become associated with the Whig cause – and particularly with Whiggism's more radical elements – over the course of the later seventeenth century, the idea that *The Secret History of the Court of the Emperor Justinian* is a Whig polemic is not incontrovertible. As we will see, the first translations of the *Anekdota* into Latin and French originate not in radical, anti-establishment political circles, but rather among a highly respectable educational elite. The notion that Procopius provides a literary model for anti-absolutist polemicists in Restoration England is further challenged by the internal, rhetorical characteristics of the *Anekdota*. Towards the beginning of his narrative, Procopius claims that he will reveal secrets relating to the reign of the tyrannical Emperor Justinian. It soon becomes apparent, however, that the information contained in his text is often common gossip or open secrets rather than 'genuine' *arcana imperii*. Moreover, the fact that the text of the *Anekdota* remained unpublished not only during Procopius's lifetime, but for almost a thousand years afterwards, qualifies the idea that this is a bold, revelatory text designed to challenge absolute rule.

Both in its internal, rhetorical strategies and its publication history, then, the *Anekdota* provides an ambivalent model to seventeenth-century secret historians in England. Instead of simply assuming that *The Secret History of the Court of the Emperor Justinian* was the founding text of the Whig secret history tradition, it is crucial that we analyse in detail the complex model that the *Anekdota* presents to seventeenth-century English polemicists.

The Reception of the *Anekdota* in Early Modern Europe

Procopius clearly regarded the *Anekdota* as a dangerous and seditious work. He informs his readers that, although he was determined to commit to writing the atrocities carried out by Justinian and Theodora during their reigns, publication of this information was impossible, since 'I could not long have concealed, or secured my self against some exemplary punishment if my Book should have been published: and I judged it very dangerous to commit such a secret to any Friend whatsoever'.[5] In fact, Procopius suppressed the *Anekdota* so effectively that it remained unpublished for over a millennium. In 1623, the manuscript was discovered in the Vatican Library by a German scholar, Nicolaus Alemannus, who published a Latin translation alongside the original Greek text under the title *Arcana Historia* (Lyon, 1623). Some contemporaries clearly believed that Alemannus's translation was as unpalatable and potentially seditious as Procopius's original. Three years after the appearance of the *Arcana Historia*, the first published response to this text complained that Alemannus's translation 'did not seem to pertain to the infamy of this emperor [Justinian] more than to the injury of all kings and leaders'.[6] Such an accusation suggests that, even in translation and a thousand years after it was first published, Procopius's *Anekdota* remained a politically dangerous text.

Not all early modern commentators agreed that translations of Procopius's *Anekdota* were necessarily seditious. Nearly fifty years after the publication of Alemannus' *Arcana Historia*, Leonor de Mauger produced the first vernacular translation of the *Anekdota* – a French text bearing the title Ἀνεκδοτα; ou Histoire secrète de Justinien (Paris, 1669). For the most part, the Latin and French translations of the *Anekdota* follow Procopius's original faithfully but they differ from the original text in two significant and interrelated respects. First, the Latin translation of the *Anekdota* is heavily censored.[7] It cuts from its opening pages a description of the debauched life led by Antonina, wife of General Belisarius, prior to her marriage and, more significantly, a lengthy passage which depicts, in graphic detail, the bizarre sexual acts committed by Theodora in the public theatre before her marriage to Justinian. The French translation of 1669, which is probably based on Alemannus's earlier Latin translation, retains these excisions. The second difference between Procopius's *Anekdota* and its seventeenth-century translations is the legal status of these texts. As we have seen, Procopius considered his attack on Justinian far too dangerous to publish immediately after it was written, and it remained an illegitimate and, ultimately, forgotten manuscript. In sharp contrast, both the Latin and French translations are beautifully produced folios which advertise on their title pages the fact that they are printed with royal permission. Indeed, the French translation is the final volume of a handsome set of the complete works of Procopius. Its publication in this format suggests that the *Anekdota* was regarded as equal in status to Procopius's other works: his prestigious *History of the Wars* and his architectural history, *On Buildings*. By 1685, as we have seen, the neoclassical critic Antoine Varillas felt it appropriate to write a treatise on 'the Art of writing secret History' as the preface to his own secret history, *Anekdota Heterouiaka*.[8] It seems that by the late seventeenth-century – on the European continent, at least – Procopius's *Anekdota* had been transformed from a seditious, unpublished manuscript into a published text that could either be regarded as a harmless antiquarian curiosity or even as a prestigious form of neoclassical history worthy of high-quality reproduction and imitation.

Even those commentators who responded enthusiastically to the new availability of Procopius's narrative in Latin and French translations, however, express some embarrassment at the contents of this work. Varillas emphasizes his adherence to his ancient exemplar, declaring that his historiographical method is derived neither 'from my Reason nor Caprice, but only from the Examples of *Procopius*, whom I will ever have in ken, seeing I cannot find any other Guide'.[9] There is, however, a note of reluctance in Varillas's self defence: any other guide, he seems to imply, might have been preferable to the prurient Procopius. Indeed, he goes on to suggest that the modern translations of Procopius have significant advantages over the ancient original. He commends the 'Modesty' of Nicolaus Alemannus, 'who, causing his Ἀνέκδοτα to be Printed, has retrench'd such Passages, wherein the Infamies of the Empress *Theodora* ... were too lively represented'.[10] Varillas asserts, decisively: 'I wish this Vacuum may never be fill'd, and that those who are able to do it, may have neither the Will nor the Leisure'.[11] In spite of his overtly neoclassical method, Varillas expresses relief that Alemannus, a modern intermediary, has tempered the worst excesses of his ancient original.

In his *Jugement sur les Anciens et Principaux Historiens Grecs & Latins* (1646), François de la Mothe le Vayer registers some of the same anxieties as Varillas. He suggests that modesty caused Alemannus to cut the most sexually explicit passages from his translation of Procopius.[12] Indeed, la Mothe le Vayer claims that Procopius – who was celebrated for his *History of the Wars* and *On Buildings* before the publication of the *Anekdota* – may not have written the seditious and satirical *Anekdota* at all.[13] He goes on to assert, however, that if Procopius really was the author of the *Anekdota*, then he was clearly embarrassed by his own narrative: 'the title *Anecdotes*', la Mothe le Vayer states, 'shows that this is a secret work and that its author did not want [his name] to be revealed'.[14] La Mothe le Vayer thus exploits a convenient ambivalence in the adjective 'secret' in the phrase 'secret history', which had first become attached to the *Anekdota* with the Latin translation. He suggests that, instead of referring to the contents of Procopius's narrative – that is, to the fact that it reveals previously unpublished *arcana imperii* – the adjective 'secret' should be applied to the text of the *Anekdota* itself.[15] The fact that Procopius's work had remained hidden in manuscript for over a millennium after its composition helped to facilitate such an interpretation.

La Mothe le Vayer's apparent disgust at the contents of the *Anekdota* is, however, somewhat disingenuous. Even as he praises the textual excisions made by Alemannus in the service of modesty, the tone of his writing betrays more complex motives behind his apparently straightforward moral stance. In his discussion of Alemannus's cleaned-up translation of the *Anekdota*, for instance, he observes:

> I have been sent from Rome that which shame has caused to be cut from page forty-one and forty-two of the printed *Anecdotes*, where Procopius has that woman [Empress Theodora] perform such strange, lewd acts, especially when, in full view of the theatre, some geese went to search for grains of wheat where they should least

have been, that I believe no one envies the complete original in the Vatican Library on that account, nor that anyone has ever heard tell of the like abominations.[16]

La Mothe le Vayer alludes here to a section of the *Anekdota* that describes in graphic detail some of Theodora's sexually explicit public performances, which was cut from the Latin and French translations. His ostensible purpose in mentioning it is to praise Alemannus for retrenching the more pornographic elements of Procopius's narrative. La Mothe le Vayer's own prose here is, however, titillating. His elliptical comments encourage his readers to imagine the scene described by Procopius. His references to the pages from which the cuts have been made send the reader to check the context of this lurid scene (readers who wished to pursue this path were assisted by the fact that, in both the Latin and French translations, asterisks indicate the point at which material has been excised). The teasing quality of la Mothe le Vayer's prose becomes particularly evident when compared with the first English translation of this passage by the ecclesiastical historian John Jortin, which removes any reference either to the geese or to the page of the original from which the cuts were made, recording only that 'Procopius represents this woman as guilty of such strange acts of lust and immodesty, even upon the theatre, that no one ever heard of the like abominations, or ought to envy the Vatican Library for having a complete copy of the Original'.[17] Jortin explains his own circumspection by referring to the context of his translation: 'I know that Latin and Greek obscenities never passed for contraband goods amongst Critics and Philologers, and that castrated editions are generally disapproved by the Learned. But, without entering into a discussion of that nice subject, I shall only say, that I will not insert such sort of ribaldry in these Remarks on Ecclesiastical History'.[18] La Mothe le Vayer may claim that no one should envy those who have read the original of Procopius's narrative and that the pornographic elements of this text are shameful, but he does so in such a way as to arouse the reader's curiosity and to assert his own privileged membership of a group which has access to the full text of the *Anekdota*.

La Mothe le Vayer's ambivalent response towards Procopius is far from unusual in the early modern period. The idea that the *Anekdota* is a secret text capable of segregating an educated elite from the rest of the reading public clearly held great appeal for many seventeenth and eighteenth-century commentators on Procopius. In the mid-eighteenth century Edward Gibbon's account of the *Anekdota*, like that of la Mothe le Vayer, combines censure of the 'satirical historian' with a strong sense of satisfaction at having access to the entire text of Procopius's narrative. Gibbon inserts a footnote – written, notably, in Greek – in which he recounts the story about Theodora's goose trick to which la Mothe le Vayer had also alluded, observing that 'a learned prelate, now deceased, was fond of quoting this passage in conversation'.[19] By the time Gibbon was writing, the excised portions of the Greek original had, in fact, appeared in print, in a parallel Greek and Latin text published as part of a French miscellany in 1715.[20] Yet these passages remain, in Gibbon's words, 'veiled in the obscurity of a learned language'.[21] In 1626, Thomas Ryves had opined that Justinian's misdeeds should have remained in a 'veil of silence' instead of being put into print, but Gibbon's use of the same metaphor here suggests a rather different attitude towards Procopius's text.[22] The 'veil' which only those with a classical education can penetrate appears to titillate as much as Procopius's words themselves. Here, the *Anekdota* is portrayed as a secret text, rather than a text that reveals secrets.

In opposition to this conservative approach towards the *Anekdota*, some early modern writers wished to make Procopius's work more widely available to the reading public through published, vernacular translations. We can see evidence of a growing desire to make the *Anekdota* more widely available in the first printed reference in English to this text, which is found in the preface to *The History of the Warres* (1653), a translation of Procopius's more respectable, orthodox history of Justinian's reign by Sir Henry Holcroft. An anonymous preface – probably by Holcroft's assistant Edmund Chilmead – reflects on the *Anekdota* in a fascinating parenthetical aside:[23]

> (...Sir *Henry* hath (as I am informed by those that should know) translated the Ανεχδοτα; or Secret History (a book which none of the Ancients met with, but *Suidas* only, as appears by *Evagrius, Agathias, Epiphanesis, Simon Metaphrastes* in vita *S. Sabae, Porphyrius,* and *Photius* in his *Bibliothecâ*; as neither many other Learned men who wrote since *Suidas,* as *Zonaras, Cedrenus, Anonymus* in his *Chronicon Vatican* & others, amongst whom was *Cardinal Baronius,* who could never attain the sight of it, though he much desired it) ... & to my own knowledge, *Agathias* his History, who takes up the story, where *Procopius* leaves off: All which may see the light, kind Reader, if thy acceptation of this [i.e. *The History of the Warres*] encourage their Impression.)[24]

The parentheses within parentheses in this passage represent, both typographically and syntactically, the inaccessibility of Procopius's secret text: a point reinforced by the catalogue of disappointed figures who died without setting eyes upon the grail-like *Anekdota*. But Chilmead's comments suggest that a new force – popular demand – has the potential to unveil the *Anekdota*. Chilmead does not portray his desire to publish the *Anekdota* in an English translation as a populist political move. Nonetheless, the idea that the public could use market pressure to force this 'secret' narrative into print represents an approach towards the secret history that differs starkly from the much more conservative attitude that we find in la Mothe le Vayer and Gibbon. It raises the possibility that the reason why Procopius's *Anekdota* provides an inspiring model for later secret historians is not only that it reveals the secrets of those in power, but also because the publication of a vernacular version of this text flies in the face of repeated attempts during the early modern period to keep it concealed.

It is in the context of these earlier approaches towards the *Anekdota* that we need to consider the first published English translation of this work, *The Secret History of the Court of the Emperor Justinian*. The *Secret History* is almost certainly not Sir Henry Holcroft's translation, to which Edmund Chilmead refers in the preface to *The History of the Warres* (of which no trace appears to remain). Holcroft's translation of the *History of the Warres* is, in stylistic terms, stiff and archaic, whereas the English translator of *The Secret History of the Court of the Emperor Justinian* produces a highly readable translation full of contemporary, idiomatic English expressions – at one point, for instance, General Belisarius goes 'creeping about the streets of *Constantinople* alone, without authority, or attendance, melancholy, dejected, and expecting every step to be knocked on the head'.[25] The 1674 *Secret History* contains the same expurgations as the 1623 Latin translation and the 1669 French translation, and it seems likely that the English translator was working from both of these texts as he composed the *Secret History*. Compared with these two earlier versions of the *Anekdota*, however, *The Secret History of the Court of the Emperor Justinian* is a decidedly downmarket publication. While the French and Latin texts are handsome folios published by royal privilege, which clearly advertise the name of the translator on the title page, the *Secret History* is a small octavo volume that contains an anonymous translation. Can this difference be attributed to the fact that it is intended as a seditious text, putting Procopius's iconoclastic rhetoric to work in the context of Stuart England?

Perhaps. But before arriving at such a conclusion, we need to consider some significant evidence to the contrary. Although the translator of the *Secret History* is not identified in the text, and no candidate has been put forward in recent scholarship, we may have a clue as to his or her identity in the bookseller whose name is found on the title page of this work. *The Secret History of the Court of the Emperor Justinian* was 'printed for *John Barkesdale* Bookbinder, over against the Five Bells in *New-Lane* and *Shooelane*'. According to the *English Short Title Catalogue*, the *Secret History* is Barkesdale's first foray into the publication, rather than the binding, of texts. The *Secret History* is the only work that Barkesdale (or Barksdale, as his later imprints are spelled) published in 1674. Between 1675 and 1685, however, Barkesdale brought out fourteen titles, ten of which are by a scholar, Church of England clergyman, and probable relative of his named Clement Barksdale. Indeed, between 1675 and 1680, John Barkesdale only sold works by Clement. If we look at Clement Barksdale's career for the decade between 1675 and 1685, we find a similar dependence on John. During this period, Clement Barksdale published twenty works, eleven of which were sold by John – many more than Clement gave to any other publisher during this decade.[26] Since the careers of John and Clement Barksdale were so closely intertwined during the decade beginning in 1675, Clement Barksdale is a likely candidate for translator of the *Secret History*.

If Clement Barksdale did translate the *Secret History*, his involvement might qualify the idea that this text should be seen as part of an oppositional political campaign. Over the course of his career, Barksdale published in a variety of genres: original poetry, such as *Nympha Librethis: or, The Cotswold Muse* (1651); religious tracts – particularly on local ecclesiastical disputes – and sermons; compilations of brief lives, gathered in four volumes as *Memorials of Worthy Persons* (1661–4); and translations, especially from Latin texts, and particularly of the works of Hugo Grotius. The common theme that unites his literary productions, however, is the promotion of religious toleration. In his third volume of *Memorials of Worthy Persons*, he includes not only 'the Lights of *our own Church*' – that is, the Church of England – but also several 'of the *Roman* or *Genevian* Perswasion, thinking They might not be unsociable *here*, whose holy Souls, I believe ... rest in peace'.[27] Barksdale may have been attracted to Procopius's vigorous condemnation of Justinian's religious bigotry and his promotion of religious orthodoxy combined with religious toleration, rather than his iconoclastic attitude towards the Empire's leading figures.[28] And if this is the case, then perhaps we should interpret the *Secret History* as a response to the persecutory ecclesiastical policies that were implemented during the reign of Charles II, rather than to this monarch's constitutional ambitions.[29] Given that the Latin and French translations of Procopius attracted no opposition from the state, that John Barkesdale seems not to have been anxious about putting his name to the first English translation of this text, and that the text may be a plea for religious toleration as much as an attack on arbitrary government, we need perhaps to question whether *The Secret History of the Court of the Emperor Justinian* can really be regarded as the foundation of the association between secret history and Whig politics in late seventeenth-century England.

The publication of Procopius's *Secret History* in English in 1674 does initiate an association between Whig politics and secret history, but not necessarily because this was the intention of the translator or publisher. The clearest evidence for the emergence of such an association is the fact that the English translation of Procopius was reissued, in 1682, with a new title: *The Debaucht Court: or the Lives of the Emperor Justinian, and his Empress Theodora the Comedian*. This text was published by Richard Baldwin, whose career as a bookseller had taken off the previous year at the height of the Exclusion Crisis, when he published scores of texts in support of the Exclusionist, or Whig, cause. Baldwin's name, especially when coupled with an inflammatory title, was almost certainly enough to raise suspicions that the 'Lives of the Emperor Justinian, and his Empress Theodora the Comedian' were designed as a reflection upon the 'Debaucht Court' of Charles II.

Readers who approached the *Secret History* looking for parallels between Justinian's Court and that of Charles would not have searched in vain. The English translation of the *Anekdota* contains verbal echoes of phrases common in contemporary political discourse. Where the French translation of the *Anekdota* criticizes Justinian's tyrannical power (*pouvoir tyrannique*), the English text attacks those who attempt to 'govern in an Arbitrary way', the unusual capitalized adjective highlighting a key word in early Whig polemic.[30] Justinian is also described several times as 'easie [of] accesse'[31] – a phrase often applied ambivalently to Charles to signal both the informality of his Court compared with the stiffness and rigour of Louis XIV, and also his sexual availability and subjection to his mistresses.[32] At a more general level, Procopius's emphasis on the power of women at Justinian's Court echoes the concern of many contemporaries about the power of Charles's mistresses – especially Louise de Kéroualle, Duchess of Portsmouth, who was commonly regarded as a French spy. The fact that Nell Gwyn, another of Charles's mistresses, began her public life in the theatre like the Empress Theodora must have strengthened this association. Procopius details Justinian's determination to plunder both the public and private purses, commenting that 'in all his affairs, *Justinians* cheif designs was getting of Money, by what means was possible to gain it'[33] – a situation that resonates with Charles's disputes with Parliament over Bills of Supply during the Third Dutch War.[34] Finally, during the reigns of both Charles and Justininan, a devastating plague was interpreted by many as a form of judgement upon a corrupt leadership. Seventeenth-century readers habituated to looking for parallels between the lives of great historical figures would have had no difficulty in spotting Charles II in Procopius's portrayal of Justinian, particularly if those readers were already sympathetic to the Whig cause.[35] In the increasingly fraught political atmosphere of the late 1670s and early 1680s, it is hardly surprising that Whig readers perceived *The Secret History of the Court* as a text that appeared to give voice to their dissatisfaction with Charles II's debauched Court and his pretensions to arbitrary rule, even if this was not the original intention of its translator.

By the early 1680s, then, *The Secret History of the Court of the Emperor Justinian* had been co-opted into a Whig literary campaign against the absolutist ambitions of the Stuarts. So why does it matter that, prior to the publication of *The Debaucht Court* in 1682, the *Anekdota* was not necessarily regarded as a politically seditious text, and that the earliest translations of this work cannot be tied down to a particular party political stance? Perhaps the most important reason is that the tendency to assume that there is an intrinsic connection between secret history and radical Whig politics is symptomatic of a more general propensity in recent scholarship to oversimplify secret history's political and formal complexities. Too often, secret history has been subsumed into teleological narratives of political or literary history: just as secret history is assumed to be an overtly Whig form from the very first, so it is passed over as a stepping stone on the way to more sophisticated forms of literature such as the novel. By acknowledging that the first translations of Procopius's *Anekdota* were not necessarily intended as seditious texts we can build up a more nuanced – and, I suggest, more accurate – picture of the form as it emerged during the late seventeenth century. By challenging teleological critical accounts of secret history, many of this genre's rhetorical peculiarities become visible. If we turn to consider the kind of formal model that Procopius's *Anekdota* represents for later secret historians, we find significant correspondences between this text's reception history and its literary characteristics.

Procopius's *Anekdota* as a Literary Model for Whig Secret History

The appeal that Procopius's *Anekdota* held for Whig polemicists during the late seventeenth century was the result of more than just a set of coincidences between the character of the Emperor Justinian, as portrayed by Procopius, and contemporary Whig perceptions of Charles II and his Court. The formal qualities and historiographical strategies of the *Anekdota* also resonated with the aims of the political opposition during the late 1670s and early 1680s. Two aspects of Procopius's narrative in particular proved significant. The first was Procopius's revelation of salacious secrets of state, designed both to attack the personal dignity of the Empire's rulers and also to undermine the idea that the absolute ruler's secrets are inviolable. The second was the revisionist impulse of Procopius' *Anekdota* which, Procopius explicitly states, is designed to supplement and challenge his earlier account of Justinian's reign in *The History of the Wars*.

In the *Anekdota*, Procopius promises to provide his readers with secret information that supplements and revises earlier accounts of the history of Justinian's reign – in particular, his own *History of the Wars*, which Procopius was probably finishing at the same time as he was writing the *Anekdota*.[36] At the opening of the *Anekdota*, Procopius suggests that his *History of the Wars* is an accurate chronicle of the events of Justinian's reign:

> What hapned in the *Roman* Empire, in its Wars with the Barbarous Nations, I suppose I have exactly described, and the order which I have observed, is so just, every Action and Accident is to be found with its proper, and due Circumstances, both of time and of place.[37]

Yet in spite of his initial emphasis on the accuracy and completeness of *The History of the Wars*, Procopius immediately proceeds to reveal its imperfections, informing his readers that 'in my first History of all, I was obliged to omit the

Motives and Causes of such Actions and Events as I related there', out of fear of Justinian's repressive regime.[38] The defining characteristic of secret history as modelled by Procopius, then, is that it brings new information to light in order to revise pre-existing versions of the past.

According to Procopius, the true 'Motives and Causes' behind public events are almost always the personal whims and sexual appetites of the Empire's leading figures. Early in his narrative, for instance, he claims that Belisarius made the Roman army retreat from battle because of the arrival of his wife, Antonina, so that Belisarius 'seemed to prefer his own private interest, before the benefit of the Empire'.[39] Procopius explicitly states that 'this was one thing which I durst not communicate in the History which I published [i.e. *The History of the Wars*], as not thinking my self safe, if I should chance to be discovered'.[40] Elsewhere, Procopius observes that the Empress Theodora sent 'one of her Creatures called *Peter*' as an ambassador to Amalasontha, Queen of the Goths, 'as I mentioned in my other Books'.[41] But he also notes that, when he recorded this fact in his earlier histories, 'I durst not speak what I knew to be true' – that is, that Theodora ordered Peter to murder Amalasontha, believing that Amalasontha's 'quality as Queen, her singular Beauty, her excellent Wit, and above all, her admirable Wisdom ... would have some effect (to [Theodora's] diminution) upon the unconstant nature of her Husband'.[42] Throughout the *Anekdota*, Procopius reveals that the public events of Justinian's reign were the result not of calculated military and political stategy, as he had suggested in his *History of the Wars*, but rather of personal weakness in the rulers of the Empire. In a characteristically sweeping statement, Procopius claims that 'the inroads the *Persians*, the *Saracens*, the *Selavonians*, and other of the *Barbarous* Nations made upon the Empire' – the subject of his entire eight-volume *History of the Wars* – were 'caused only by the ill conduct of the Emperor'.[43]

In the *Anekdota*, Procopius adapts the conventions of perfect history – that is, the kind of explanatory history that he had composed in *The History of the Wars* – to create a form of historiography fit to describe a regime unworthy of more elevated historiographical models. In spite of the protestations of early modern commentators against Procopius's sexual anecdotes and prurient style, there is a kind of decorum in Procopius's gossipy history, in which glimpses into Justinian's bedchamber take the place of political analysis. As he describes a Court dominated by women and a country enslaved to the appetites of its rulers, so Procopius revises a form of historiography designed to relate the achievements and analyse the political motives of great men so that it better sorts with his disreputable subject matter. The stylistic differences between *The History of the Wars* and the *Anekdota* act as an index of the corruption of Justinian's regime.

The revisionist character of the *Anekdota* also casts light on the role that historians play in upholding or challenging the regimes that they describe. At the beginning of the *Anekdota*, Procopius expresses his hope that, although political circumstances make it too dangerous to publish his narrative immediately, the *Anekdota* might, nonetheless, serve as a warning to future generations. As he puts it: 'who would have abhorred the debauches of *Semiramis*, the effeminacy of *Sardanapalus*, and the cruelties of *Nero*, had not great Men undertaken the History of their times, and transmitted it to posterity[?]'.[44] Like the *Bibliotheca historica* of Diodorus Siculus, where Procopius probably read about 'the debauches of *Semiramis*' and 'the effeminacy of *Sardanapalus*', and the histories of Tacitus or Suetonius, where he would have found 'the cruelties of *Nero*' recorded, the *Anekdota* conveys to posterity the wicked deeds of tyrannical rulers. Procopius's seditious narrative is, however, of a different order from these earlier histories. The *Anekdota* is an attack not only upon Justinian, but – more importantly – upon the version of Justinian's reign transmitted to posterity by Procopius's earlier history of his own times, *The History of the Wars*. The lesson offered to posterity by the *Anekdota* is, then, a broader one than may at first appears to be the case. The *Anekdota* is not just exemplary history designed to warn arbitrary rulers about the likely outcome of their tyranny. It also teaches readers to exercise scepticism towards histories of their authors' own times. The iconoclastic tendencies of the *Anekdota* extend beyond the rulers that this narrative condemns to the earlier history that it revises.

Procopius's *Anekdota* bequeaths to later secret historians not only a self-conscious approach towards the claim to disclose secret intelligence, but also a capacious definition of the term 'secret'. Procopius does reveal some information that might be regarded as genuine secret intelligence as he reports on events that took place in very private locations. For instance, he recounts a story in which Belisarius enters a cellar and discovers his wife, Antonina, in a compromising position with their adopted son, Theodosius.[45] And he relates stories told to him by Justinian's servants, who claim that their master changes his shape in the privacy of his own bedchamber, proving that he is a demon rather than a man.[46] Not all of the information that Procopius passes on to his readers, however, falls into the same 'classified' category as this secret intelligence. Indeed, Procopius often emphasizes the fact that Justinian's tyranny was not hidden from sight, but was highly public. At one point, for instance, he observes that 'there hapned so great a contagion quite thorow [Justinian's] Dominions, that few or none escaped who were infected, and few or none escaped without infection: But as to the Tyranny of *Justinian*, there was scarce a Subject of the whole *Roman* Empire but had had some experiment of it'.[47] Later on in his narrative, Procopius affirms that 'the whole world was ... depressed with extream sadness, as well publick Societies, as particular persons, every Man passing his time without any Diversion, and groaning under his Misfortune, as heavy and immoveable'.[48] Expressions such as 'the whole world' and 'every Man' may be hyperbolic, but they also emphasize the very public nature of Justinian's tyranny. Far from providing his readers with privileged intelligence, Procopius fills much of his narrative with stories about Justinian and Theodora's outrages that would have been only too familiar, he suggests, to contemporary readers.

The public nature of Procopius's secrets clearly disturbed some of his early modern commentators. In his critique of Nicolaus Alemannus's translation of Procopius, Thomas Ryves asserts that Alemannus's decision to call his work a secret history is absurd: 'thefts, murders and crimes, many have called "hidden", Ryves contends, 'but no one has ever called "secret".'[49] He implies that, although they were hidden from public view, these crimes were not unknown to Procopius's first readers. The difficulties involved in depicting well-known misdemeanours committed by kings or ministers as part of a secret history continue to inspire attacks on this form throughout the seventeenth century. *The Blatant Beast Muzzl'd* complains that the author of *The Secret History of the Reigns of K. Charles II and K. James II* 'stuffs out his Book with Matters *publickly carried*, and which (as he says) a whole *kingdom loudly complained of*.' These secrets 'made such a noise, that every one must needs *hear* of them, whether they would nor no.'[50] The '*Publick Secrets*' of which this secret history consists are, according to *The Blatant Beast Muzzl'd*, no secrets at all.[51] It is indeed difficult to reconcile the received notion that secret history attacks arbitrary government by exposing secrets of state with the fact that both Procopius's 'original' secret history and the works of his imitators often impart very little information that might reasonably be described as secret.

In addressing the question of Procopius's secret intelligence, it is important to remember that *Anekdota* translates not as 'secret history' – a phrase that comes from the title of the 1623 Latin translation, *Arcana Historia* – but rather as 'unpublished', or 'unpublished things'. The Greek title (whether or not it was added by Procopius) thus suggests that the most significant fact about the material contained in the *Anekdota* is not that it was unknown to its first readers, but rather that it had not previously been recorded in a public, publishable format. The polemical force of the *Anekdota* derives both from the *arcana imperii* that it passes on to its readers and also from the medium in which the contents of this text – whether genuine or open secrets – is presented. The *Anekdota* thus offers to later writers a capacious definition of the term 'secret'. Thomas Ryves and *The Blatant Beast Muzzl'd* may have condemned them for it, but secret historians clearly believed that information might be regarded as secret because it is unspoken, unrecorded or unpublished, rather than because it is unknown. In the era of print, the importance of medium to the rhetorical strategies of secret historians becomes even greater than it was for Procopius. The highly public, popular medium of print contrasts starkly with the private, underhand dealings of the political elite. Whether or not early modern practitioners of this form really provide their readers with secret intelligence, the fact that they publish the private counsels and sexual misdemeanours of monarchs and ministers in printed form constitutes a politically charged act of revelation.

Conclusion

The complexity of the model that the *Anekdota* presents to later secret historians can be seen in its openness to competing interpretations of the key term, 'secret'. In recent scholarship, it has usually been assumed that this adjective refers to the quality of the information contained in the text. Procopius's employment as secretary to Justinian's leading General, Belisarius, gave him privileged access to *arcana imperii*. By disclosing the sexual and political secrets of the Empire's leading figures, Procopius not only humiliates those in power at a personal level, but also violates the aura of mystery surrounding the throne, which constitutes one of the foundations of absolute rule. At one level, at least, secret history is a genre that brings to light previously undiscovered intelligence about the private, underhand dealings of monarchs and ministers, and uses the revelation of those secrets to attack arbitrary government.

This interpretation of the adjective 'secret', however, is challenged by many commentators in the early modern period who apply the term not to the information contained in Procopius's narrative but to the text of the *Anekdota* itself. The fact that Procopius suppressed the *Anekdota* immediately after composition and that it remained concealed for over a thousand years encouraged more conservative critics to suggest that it was – and in some respects ought to remain – a secret text. Commentators including François de la Mothe le Vayer in France and Edward Gibbon in England clearly took pleasure in the privileged access that they, as members of the republic of letters, enjoyed to the more titillating aspects of Procopius's narrative.

Early modern secret historians capitalized on a third interpretation of the term 'secret' that emerges from the *Anekdota*. This interpretation is more rhetorical than positivist: it depends less on the actual quality of the information contained in the text (that is, whether or not a piece of intelligence is actually unknown to its readers), and more on the medium in which that information is contained. Procopius puts into written and thus publishable form information about Justinian and Theodora's tyranny that had previously remained unuttered out of fear of the regime that it condemns. Although much of what Procopius writes was, as he observes himself, already known to his contemporaries, it had been made a secret – albeit an open one – through the repression experienced by Justinian's subjects. Even though Procopius never made his narrative public property, the fact that he committed his knowledge to writing at all constitutes a crucial shift of medium. For later secret historians, the medium of print provides still greater opportunities to highlight the difference between the public milieu in which they operate – a metonymic representation of their candour and openness – and the silence and repression that characterize absolute rule. The paradox of the printed secret is, then, less paradoxical than it might, at first, appear. Importantly, this breadth of definition of the term 'secret' enables polemicists who did not have direct and personal access to secrets of state to write secret history. In early modern secret histories, the rhetoric of disclosure and the self-conscious use of print to publicize the political and sexual corruption of the Stuart monarchs often takes the place of *arcana imperii*, more strictly defined.

It is impossible to know how widely *The Secret History of the Court of the Emperor Justinian* was read in England during the later seventeenth century, when the vogue for secret history was at its peak. As we will see, several detractors of this form explicitly blame Procopius for the popularity of secret history in later seventeenth-century England. It is clear, however, that the most distinctive conventions of Procopian secret history – its revisionist tendencies and its self-consciousness towards the discourse of secrecy – are evident in secret histories by many Whig writers during the Restoration and early eighteenth century. The next chapter considers the ways in which such writers adapt these characteristics in response to the political circumstances of the reign of William III.

2 SECRET HISTORY AND WHIG HISTORIOGRAPHY, 1688–1702

Although secret history first appeared in England in the 1670s, it was during the 1690s that the form really began to flourish. After the Revolution of 1688–9, Whig polemicists could publish the sexual and political secrets of the Stuart kings with impunity, and large numbers of them seized the opportunity to do so. Between 1688 and the beginning of the eighteenth century, at least twenty-five texts were published bearing the title 'secret history'. Some, such as *The Secret History of the Reigns of K. Charles II and K. James II* (1690), its 'prequel', *The Secret History of the Reigns of King James I and King Charles I* (1690), and *The Secret History of the Four Last Monarchs of Great Britain* (1691) – a compilation of these two texts – are homegrown English secret histories; others, such as *The Cabinet Open'd; or, the Secret History of the Amours of Madam de Maintenon with the French King* (1690), *The Royal Mistresses of France, or, The Secret History of the Amours of all the French Kings* (1695) and *The Court of St. Germains; or, The Secret History of James II* (1695) are translations from French originals. Where *The Secret History of the Court of the Emperor Justinian* had attacked Charles II indirectly, through the figure of the Emperor Justinian, the new wave of secret histories launch an explicit, all-out assault on the sexual and political corruption of the Stuart and Bourbon Courts. They argue that Charles II and James II were little more than puppets of France, manipulated at every turn by the mistresses and money provided for them by the enemy of liberty, Louis XIV.

Hostile contemporary commentators often present the new secret histories of the 1690s as evidence of Whig corruption. In *Ductor Historicus* (1698), Thomas Hearne asserts that, if Procopius was indeed the author of both the respectable *History of the Wars* and the seditious *Anekdota* (which Hearne doubts), then he 'deserves to be branded with the Character of a base contemptible Wretch, since he could *blow Hot and Cold*, as we say, in the same Breath'.[1] The Jacobite Hearne thus implies that Procopius provides a model for Whig hypocrisy. Other critics portray secret history as part of an ongoing, Whig campaign against monarchy of any kind. The historiographer Roger North complains that 'not seldom well penned Libels pass with wonderful Acceptance, by the Name of *secret History*, of which there having been an unhappy Pattern in *Procopius*, others have affected to follow it to a monstrous Height of Lying and Defaming of Kings and Potentates'.[2] The author of *The Blatant Beast Muzzl'd* condemns *The Secret History of the Reigns of K. Charles II and K. James II* for its crypto-republicanism:

> I saw plainly, both by the *Contents*, the *Manner* of it, and the *Timing* [of] it, that this Pamphlet was *calculated* meerly for the *Common-wealthish Meridian*, and directly levell'd at the bespattering all Kings alike (as far as he durst) and the representing them (as himself calls one of them) *The Greatest Knaves in Nature*, out of his Hatred to Royalty and Monarchical Government; which by insinuating thus an *Odium* of them into the People, he studies to undermine.[3]

The Oxford antiquary, Anthony Wood, agreed with these sentiments. On the title page of his copy of *The Secret History of the Reigns of K. Charles II and K. James II*, Wood notes that, 'A grand phanatick, or presbyterian, choos you whether was author of this book'. When the author of this secret history writes about the sufferings of nonconformists under Charles II, Wood makes marginal notes blaming Presbyterians for the execution of Charles I.[4]

More recent commentators on secret history also argue that there is a fundamental continuity between secret history in the 1690s and resistance to royal prerogative throughout the seventeenth century – albeit with more approbation than early modern critics of the form. Annabel Patterson contends that, after the Revolution, secret historians uphold the 'Procopian rationale for *anecdota*', using their chosen form to promote 'the venerable liberal issue of freedom of speech and the press'.[5] Although their opinions of secret history differ, both the seventeenth-century critics of this form and Annabel Patterson agree that there is a high degree of consistency between the purposes of pre- and post-Revolution secret history. All secret history, these writers argue, is aimed at curbing the power of the monarchy, attacking pretensions to arbitrary rule by revealing *arcana imperii* and shattering the aura of mystery that sustains absolute power.

The relationship between pre- and post-Revolution secret history is, however, not quite as straightforward as either Patterson or contemporary detractors of secret history would have their readers believe. The political circumstances of 1674, when *The Secret History of the Court of the Emperor Justinian* was published, were very different from those of the 1690s: in 1674, the threat of arbitrary government was immediate and direct; after 1688, when James II went into exile, it appeared (at least temporarily) to be in abeyance. The apparently strong similarities between Procopius's secret history and those published after the Revolution of 1688–9 are, therefore, deceptive. Unlike *The Secret History of the Court of the Emperor Justinian*, the secret histories of the 1690s are not written with the ultimate aim of ousting the regime that they portray. Although

– like Procopius – the vast majority of secret historians during the 1690s are committed to opposing arbitrary government, the strategies that they adopt in order to assert their political position are more varied, and often more interpretatively challenging, than those put into practice by their model. As the threat of absolutism recedes, so secret history becomes increasingly theoretically sophisticated and self-conscious about its own status as a form of anti-absolutist historiography.

Whig Secret History and Whig Historiography

In the aftermath of the Revolution of 1688–9, many Whig writers use secret history to contrast the skulduggery and corruption that characterized the reigns of the Stuarts with the openness and candour of William and Mary's reign.[6] The author of *The Secret History of the Reigns of K. Charles II and K. James II*, for instance, asserts that the purpose of his secret history is

> to bring the Two Last Reigns upon the Stage, and then let all the World judge of the Furberies and Tyranny of those Times, and the Integrity, Sincerity and Sweetness of Their Present Majesties Reign; since by comparing Them, the most wilfully Blind may be convinced, how infinitely Happy we are, under their present Majesties Government, beyond what we were in the late Reign.[7]

This narrative relates stories of the Stuart kings' tyranny and corruption not in order to oust them from power – William and Mary had already accomplished this – but to celebrate their political demise. The tales of intrigue contained in this secret history become part of a celebration of newfound freedoms rather than a means of opposing existing oppression. This difference in purpose from *The Secret History of the Court of the Emperor Justinian* means that Procopius is not the only model for this post-Revolution secret history. The preface asserts that 'it is one of the Encomiums given to *Suetonius*, That he made Publick to the World, the Vices and Miscarriages of the Twelve *Cæsars*, with the same Freedom with which they were by them Committed'.[8] The fact that, in his *Lives of the Twelve Caesars*, Suetonius writes retrospectively about the crimes of former rulers, rather than about a present regime, seems to make this classical author a more appropriate model than Procopius for a post-Revolution secret historian.

In *The True Secret History of the Lives and Reigns of All the Kings and Queens of Great Britain* (1702), John Baron Somers, a leading Whig minister under both William III and Queen Anne, alludes to *The Secret History of the Reigns of K. Charles II and K. James II* in order to assert the Whig credentials of his own narrative and to celebrate, as the earlier secret history had done, the political effects of the Revolution. In the preface to this work, he writes:

> Some People tell us, that *Truth is not always to be spoken*; which perhaps might be so, while we were under the Arbitrary Government of the late King; but we now live in a Reign, *where Truth does not pass for Treason*: And therefore, as 'twas one of the Encomiums given to *Suetonius*, That he made Publick to the World, the Vices and Miscarriages of the Twelve *Cæsars*, with the same Freedom with which they were once Committed; so I have follow'd his Example in this *Secret History*: for Truth shou'd be bolder than Errour.[9]

In this passage, Somers intersperses quotations from *The Secret History of the Reigns of K. Charles II and K. James II* with allusions to an earlier Whig text: the scaffold oration of the Whig martyr, Algernon Sidney, who was executed for treason in 1683.[10] In his speech, Sidney asserted that he and his listeners 'live in an age, that makes *Truth* pass for *Treason*'.[11] Somers's allusions therefore situate his text within a tradition of Whig opposition to arbitrary government.[12] But they also highlight the profound differences between the circumstances of pre- and post-Revolution Whig writers. Somers adapts Sidney's speech to assert that in 1702, unlike in 1683, truth does *not* pass for treason. Earlier writers who spoke out against tyranny risked their lives to do so; following the Revolution of 1688–9, Somers claims, no author need fear the consequences of exposing *arcana imperii*.[13] While Procopius's *Secret History* attacks a current, absolutist ruler, Whig secret history published after the Revolution of 1688–9 embodies the perceived triumph of the English people over the tyrannical Stuarts. Somers uses his secret history to indicate that secret history is, itself, a sign and token of England's freedom from arbitrary rule.

Somers's *True Secret History* is the epitome of what has been known, since Herbert Butterfield popularized the phrase in the early twentieth century, as the 'whig interpretation of history': that is, a teleological account of the past as a narrative of progress towards the present, especially one which represents the triumph of Protestant, constitutional monarchy over the forces of popery and arbitrary government.[14] Somers traces the progress of Revolution principles throughout English history by recording 'the Arbitrary Designs that were carried on in Each Reign' from William the Conqueror to Charles I. He concludes that 'the nearer we arrive to these Present Times, the greater have been the Struglings for Arbitrary Power; but more especially since the coming in of the Family of the *Stuarts*'.[15] The Revolution of 1688–9, according to this view, represents the culmination of a long history of resistance to absolute rule. When Butterfield condemns historians who 'imagine the British constitution as coming down to us by virtue of the work of long generations of whigs and in spite of the obstructions of a long line of tyrants and tories', he could have been describing exactly the method that Somers adopts in his early eighteenth-century secret history.[16]

The prevalence of the whig interpretation of history in secret histories published during the late seventeenth and early eighteenth centuries is affirmed by another source which appears, initially, to be quite different from Somers's *True Secret History*. During the 1690s, a surge of interest in secret history in France parallels the vogue for this form in England. According to the *Hand Press Book Database* and the catalogue of the *Bibliothèque nationale de France*, the only French texts to bear the title *histoire secrète* before 1688 are the translation of Procopius's *Anekdota* by Leonor de Mauger (published as *Ανεκδοτα, ou Histoire secrète de Justinien* (1669)) and Antoine Varillas's *Anecdotes de Florence, ou, l'Histoire secrète de la Maison de Medicis* (1685, English translation 1686).[17] The 1690s, however, witness a dramatic increase in overtly political works describing themselves as *histoires secrètes* in France. During this decade, at least a dozen different French secret histories were published, most of them bearing imprints that testify to their contraband status.

Almost all French *histoires secrètes* of the 1690s are connected in some way with the market for secret history in England. Some, such as *Histoire secrette du voyage de Jacques II à Calais pour passer en Angleterre* (1696) focus on the amatory and political intrigues of the ousted English monarch, James II. Others are translations from texts originally published in English. *Histoire secrète des regnes des rois Charles II et Jacques II* (1690), for instance, is a translation of *The Secret History of the Reigns of K. Charles II and K. James II*, which was also produced in a Dutch edition. Likewise, *Histoire secrette de la Duchesse de Portsmouth* (1690) was translated from *The Secret History of the Duchess of Portsmouth* (1690) and published in London – presumably with a view to export – by the Whig publisher, Richard Baldwin.[18] Sometimes, French secret histories were translated into English. *La Cassette ouverte de l'illustre Criole, ou, les Amours de Madame de Maintenon* (1690) was translated into English as *The Cabinet Open'd, or The Secret History of the Amours of Madam de Maintenon, with the French King* (1690). Although this work was originally published in France and focuses on the intrigues of the French king, it still shows strong connections with English polemic, since its title alludes to a Parliamentarian publication of the English Civil War period: *The Kings Cabinet Opened* (1645).[19] In *La Cour de St. Germain, ou, les intrigues galantes du roy et de la reine d'Angleterre, depuis leur séjour en France* (1695) – translated as *The Court at St Germains; or, the Secret History of James II* (1695) – English subject matter connects a French text with earlier secret histories that expose the *arcana imperii* of the Stuarts. Through their use of the phrase *histoire secrète*, their interest in the intrigues of the Stuart monarchs, and their claims to expose secrets of state, French secret histories allude closely to the genre that had become popular over the channel after the Revolution of 1688–9. It seems that French polemicists attempt to use secret history to 'import' the success of the English Revolution into Louis XIV's France.

Both John Somers's *True Secret History* and the *histoires secrètes* that became popular in France during the 1690s demonstrate a similar attitude towards the relationship between secret history and the Revolution of 1688–9. In each case, secret history is used not only to reveal the secrets of absolute (or would-be absolute) rulers, but is also held up to the reading public as a form that embodies the successful campaign against arbitrary government in England. Of course, there are profound differences between the ways in which Somers and French polemicists use the association between secret history and freedom from arbitrary rule. Somers's *True Secret History* presents itself as a token of newfound liberty – a sign that the corruption and tyranny of the Stuarts belong in England's past, not its glorious future. The French authors who publish *histoires secrètes* on illegal presses, on the other hand, use secret history in their attempt to attack a current absolute ruler, Louis XIV. In spite of the differences between them, however, both Somers and French secret historians present this form as part of a whig narrative (in Butterfield's sense of that epithet) of English history. For these authors, secret history is the representative historiographical form of post-Revolution Britain.

Challenges to the Whig Interpretation of Secret History

The whig interpretation of secret history is a logical response on the part of English and French campaigners against arbitrary rule to the Revolution of 1688–9. Whether or not the reign of William and Mary really was characterized by more openness and candour than the Stuart era, it was in the interest of Whig polemicists to compare the intrigue and corruption fostered by the would-be absolutist Stuart monarchs with the superior moral and political integrity of William and Mary's Court. These writers suggest that the constitutional settlement that emerged out of the events of 1688 provides a secure vantage point from which the machinations of Charles II and James II can be exposed and contrasted with present political liberties.

The problem with this whig interpretation of secret history's function, however, is that it often fails to ring true to the experience of reading the secret histories published in England during the 1690s. As we have already seen, *The Secret History of the Reigns of K. Charles II and K. James II* promises to 'bring the Two Last Reigns upon the Stage' so that readers might compare them with 'the Integrity, Sincerity and Sweetness of Their Present Majesties Reign'.[20] But the work of comparison must take place entirely in the reader's own mind; within the text itself, we only find stories of political and sexual intrigue and the threat of popery and arbitrary government. Indeed, unlike *The Secret History of the Reigns of K. Charles II and K. James II* and John Somers's *True Secret History*, most secret histories published during the 1690s fail to mention the new monarchs, even in passing.[21] Their focus on the sexual and political machinations of the Stuart kings is unrelenting. Moreover, secret historians use a variety of strategies to create the impression that their texts are illegitimate, even seditious, publications. Secret histories published in the wake of the Revolution of 1688–9 more often appear to be products of an era of political oppression than one of political liberty. In order to give a proper account of secret history during the 1690s, it is vital that we acknowledge those characteristics that jar against the whig interpretation of political history favoured by John Somers and French writers of *histoire secrète*.

Many secret histories published during the 1690s use their title pages to suggest that they are underground, seditious texts. N. N., the author of *The Blatant Beast Muzzl'd*, rails against *The Secret History of The Reigns of K. Charles II and K. James II*, telling his readers that they 'may discern at the first Blush, that it carries in its Fore-Head all the proper Brands of a plain *Libel*. No Author's, Printer's, or Licenser's Name to it; no, not so much as the Name of the Place where it was Printed'.[22] We have already seen that the preface to this secret history declares support for the Revolution settlement and praises the 'Integrity and Sweetness of their present Majesties' Reign', but, as N. N. points out, the initial impression that the text gives its reader is one of seditious intent.

Other English secret histories bear false imprints that make them resemble the illegal *histoire secrètes* published during the 1690s in France.[23] Many French *histoires secrètes*, including *Histoire secrète des regnes des rois Charles II et Jacques II* and *Galanteries des Rois de France depuis le commencement de la monarchie*, were ostensibly produced in Cologne and appear under the famous 'Pierre Marteau' (literally, 'rock hammer') imprint. Others, such as *La Cour de St. Germain; ou les intrigues galantes du roy et de la reine d'Angleterre*, claim to have been produced in St Germain 'chez Jacques le Bon au Chateau de l'Amour'.[24] In England, *The Secret History of the Duke of Alançon and Q. Elizabeth* (1691) adapts this practice when it claims to have been published by 'Will of the Wisp'. It may be that this story about Elizabeth's Machiavellian attempts to exclude the beautiful Roman Catholic Princess Marianna, younger sister of Mary Tudor, from her rightful claim to the throne represents an unusual example of a Jacobite secret history, and that the 'illegal' imprint draws attention to its seditious purpose. It also seems likely, however, that the reference to Will of the Wisp is commercially motivated. It connects *The Secret History of the Duke of Alançon and Q. Elizabeth* with the hugely popular *Secret History of the Renown'd Queen Elizabeth with the Earl of Essex* (1680), which was reprinted at least once in every decade between 1680 and 1800 and which claims to have been printed by 'Will with the wisp at the sign of the Moon in the Ecliptick, Cologne' on every edition up to 1767. *The Secret History of the Renown'd Queen Elizabeth* has no obviously seditious purpose; it is a translation from a French romance entitled *Le Comte d'Essex. Histoire angloise* (Paris, 1677) which, far from being an illegal publication, was printed 'avec Privilège du Roy'.[25] The frisson generated by an appearance of illegality clearly appealed to readers of this particular secret history – and therefore also appealed to those who reprinted and sold it in large numbers. In England, the 'underground' appearance of many secret histories seems designed to sell copies as much as to alert readers to a genuinely oppositional impulse within the text itself.

Commercial motives also complicate a whig interpretation of the erotic content of many secret histories produced in England during the 1690s. In a recent analysis of early modern secret history, Eve Tavor Bannet suggests that the erotic content of many secret histories is a vital element of their polemical Whig agenda, since it reinforces the fact that, under absolute rule, the personal, and especially sexual, favourites of the monarch wield excessive and unconstitutional power.[26] This view of the erotic content of secret history is borne out by comments made in the prefaces to several secret histories of the 1690s. The English translator of *The Royal Mistresses of France*, for instance, asserts that 'I am none of those Enthusiast's [sic] who dream of Fifth Monarchies, but I cannot tell what to think of it, when I find the Women in so fair a way to erect One'.[27] The translator thus defends himself against charges of republicanism and indicts absolutist Court culture by conflating the French Court and the English Republic: in spite of the vast political differences between these two regimes, both are, he suggests, petticoat governments. A similarly misogynistic thread runs through the translator's preface to the French edition of *The Secret History of the Duchess of Portsmouth*, which asserts that 'if [Charles II] acted in a way that so little conformed to his judgement, to his powerful intelligence, to politics, to the interests not only of many nations in general, but also to his own realm, then it was a woman, it was the Duchess of Portsmouth, who drove him to it by means of the love that she had inspired in him, by her machinations, and by her power over his mind'.[28] In these condemnatory descriptions of the gynocentric Bourbon and Stuart Courts, there is perhaps an implicit comparison with the new moral order created by the Revolution of 1688–9. Mary's submissiveness to her husband, William, and parliamentary restraints on royal prerogative represent, metonymically, a restoration of right relations in the political sphere. According to a whig interpretation of secret history's erotic content, then, the Revolution of 1688–9 creates a watershed which allows readers to condemn the sexual and political corruption of the Stuarts while enjoying the political liberty that emanates from the godly Court of William and Mary.[29]

Although this interpretation provides a logical analysis of erotic secret histories, however, it is not entirely supported by the texts themselves. Secret histories of the 1690s often elicit a physical, rather than a rational, response as they titillate their readers by presenting them with erotic scenes of intrigue at Court. *The Secret History of the Duchess of Portsmouth*, for instance, describes an all-night orgy after which the Duchess of Portsmouth and two of her female companions strip naked and play a game of 'question and command' with Charles II:

> [The Duchess] ask'd the Prince whether he would have two Commands and one Question, or two Questions and one Command? the Prince desired one Command and two Questions. She ask'd him first Whether he would not be glad to be so Absolute, as hence-forth to Govern without the Grand Senate, and have no further occasion for them? Next she ask'd, Who he thought the happiest Monarch in the World? The Prince having answer'd to those two Questions as he thought fit, she Commanded him to Dissolve the Grand Senate. Her Command was readily obey'd.[30]

The elliptical technique which demands that readers use their imaginations to supply Charles's answers to the Duchess's questions lends this passage political piquancy, but it also encourages its readers to use their imaginations to a different end: that is, to visualize the lascivious scene created by the Duchess of Portsmouth. Contemporary critics of secret history express their horror not only at its seditious intent, but also at its pornographic tendencies. When *The Secret History of the Reigns of K. Charles II and K. James II* accuses Charles II of preferring 'the Caresses of the expanded nakedness of a *French* Harlot, before the preservation of three Nations,'[31] N. N., author of *The Blatant Beast Muzzl'd*, singles out the gratuitous phrase 'expanded nakedness' for particular condemnation, asserting that the author of this secret history 'hugs his own Harlotry [*sic*] Pleasure' in 'picking out, and pencilling to the Life all the immodest Stories he could either hear, or invent' and 'Expressing them pathetically'. As the adverb 'pathetically' suggests, these '*foul pieces of an exuberant Eloquence*' are designed not only to please the author of this secret history, but also to 'gratifie *his sort* of Readers'.[32]

The titillating quality of secret history serves to challenge the whig interpretation of erotic texts written in this tradition. Instead of providing an opportunity to analyse the difference between pre- and post-Revolution political culture, secret history undermines its reader's ability to judge the past in a rational manner. As one contemporary detractor of secret history asserts, 'there is a sort of Frenzy in writing and reading these Books'.[33] The erotic content of secret history, like the seditious appearance of several texts in this tradition, has obvious commercial advantages in a literary marketplace in which scandal sells. But as they reap the financial rewards of their revelations, so secret historians complicate a neat, whig interpretation of their chosen genre.

Sceptical Secret History

It is difficult to determine positive reasons why erotic secret histories might challenge the kind of whig interpretation of the recent political past that is often expressed in the prefaces to these works. In spite of the accusations of crypto-republicanism that were, from time to time, levelled against secret historians, there is little evidence that the authors of these texts deliberately set out to undermine the institution of monarchy or the Revolution settlement by revealing the bedchamber secrets of the Stuart and Bourbon Courts. Indeed, although erotic secret histories unsettle a logical whig interpretation of this form, they do not encourage any specific, alternative political analysis. We can, perhaps, do little more than conclude that the financial benefits, prurient pleasure and political satisfaction gained by revealing the secrets of the Stuarts is at odds with the idea that secret history allows readers rationally to compare and contrast the political circumstances of pre- and post-Revolution Britain.

There is evidence to suggest, however, that towards the end of the 1690s secret history attained a new degree of sophistication, manifested in a concertedly sceptical approach towards the whig interpretation of recent political history. David Jones's *Secret History of White-hall* (1697) scrutinizes the conventions of secret history to provide an acute analysis of this form of historiography. Jones's observations not only have a profound impact upon the relationship between secret history and the opposition to arbitrary government, but also prefigure some of the more audacious ways in which the conventions of secret history are manipulated during the eighteenth century.

The Secret History of White-hall consists of a series of 131 letters sent to an unnamed English peer by a spy at the French Court. The letters begin in 1676, when (as the title page informs us) the spy took up his post as 'Secretary-Interpreter' to the Marquis de Louvois, Louis XIV's Secretary for War. They end in 1689 with news of the French Court's reaction to the coronation of William and Mary. A brief *Continuation of the Secret History of White-hall* (1697), containing thirty-one letters written between 1689 and 1695, was published later in the same year. In the preface to *The Secret History of White-hall*, Jones describes himself as the 'Methodizer', or editor, of this text rather than the author of the letters that it contains.[34] Recent scholarship has suggested that Jones's claims were invented – an elaborate ruse to conceal his own fictions.[35] In this point, however, Jones was telling the truth. In 1719, John Dunton, a well-known contemporary author and bookseller, asserted that *The Secret History of White Hall* 'owes its *Projection* and *Title to my Pen*, and was compos'd of *Memoirs* that I *purchast* my self from the *Secretary Interpreter* to the Marquiss of *Louvois*'.[36] Elsewhere, Dunton identifies this secretary, or spy, as one Richard Wolley (elsewhere spelled Wooley or Woolley), a minister of the Church of England who had contributed to Dunton's literary review, *The Compleat Library* (1692–4).[37] Wolley's other works suggest that he had, indeed, spent time in France during the period under consideration in *The Secret History of White-hall*.[38] Although the details of the relationship between Dunton, Wolley and Jones are somewhat obscure, it seems that Dunton commissioned David Jones, who already had a well-established career as a popular historian by the late 1690s, to write up Wolley's correspondence into *The Secret History of White-hall*.

Jones's decription of himself as simply a 'Methodizer' of Wolley's letters underestimates the importance of his own preface to *The Secret History of White-hall*. Jones's prefatory observations explore the ethical and epistemological consequences of dealing in secret intelligence by focusing self-consciously on the medium of revelation in this text – the letters of a spy. Jones argues, defensively:

> 'Tis hoped no body will quarrel, that this *Piece* which is entitled by the Name of *Secret History, &c.* should be written in an *Epistolary* way, when it is considered that such a *Form* was indispensably necessary under the Circumstances of the *Author*, and his *Noble Correspondent*, and that there is a very engaging part naturally couched under such a method of bringing *State-Arcana's* to light, by way of *Letters*, which, in the very Notion of them carry something of Secrecy.[39]

Although there are no earlier self-styled secret histories in epistolary form, published letters had been used to expose political secrets in many popular texts from *The Kings Cabinet Opened* during the English Civil Wars to the eight volumes of *Letters Writ by Turkish Spy* (1687–94), a hugely popular history of seventeenth-century Europe told through the letters of Mahmut, a Turkish spy living in Paris.[40] In each of these texts, the motif of a discovered cache of letters gives readers the impression that they are getting direct, unmediated access to secrets. Letters are not only a natural medium for the revelation of secrets, but also one that gives readers the voyeuristic pleasure of peering into hidden places. Moreover, letters seem to tell the truth about secret events because they are private documents, not written for public consumption. Spy letters combine the thrill of acquiring secrets with a sense of authenticity and historical authority.

Yet spy letters are not quite the reliable historical documents that Jones seems to claim they are. The ethical considerations raised by the occupation of a spy present a challenge to the reliability of the evidence contained in *The Secret History of White-hall*. In one of his letters, Richard Wolley notes the kind of people whom the French employed as spies during the Popish Plot:

> I. Atheists and loose-principled Men, who yet could act rarely well the Zealots for that Religion or Cause which they were to espouse.
> II. Such Persons as they found to be conceited of their Parts, and of mercenary Spirits.
> III. Hotspurs for Prerogative, and the Church of *England*.
> IV. The fiercest Spirits of the other Factions.
> V. Some Bigots of the *Roman* Communion that were *English*, and particularly those that had been bred up, or had travelled in their Dominions, and were well Jesuited.
> VI. The leading *Irish* Papists in particular.

VII. Men Ambitious of Greatness, or Idolizers of Money, and that chiefly in *Scotland*.
VIII. Men disgustful or disobliged.
IX. Men of desperate Fortunes, and lost Reputations.[41]

Unsurprisingly, Wolley, who was a clergyman and scholar as well as a spy, does not make any connections between these unsavoury characters and his own position at the French Court. Wolley claims always to have been fervent for the 'Legal Party' – by which he means the Whigs – and Jones informs his reader that Wolley returned to England at the Revolution in 1688, implying that he had nothing to fear from William III.[42] Nonetheless in the preface to *The Secret History of White-hall*, David Jones warns his readers that 'it's no hard matter to imagine what Qualifications were necessary to recommend our Author to the Imployment afore noted, and how far his Out-side must differ from his In-side during his aboad' at the French Court.[43] Jones makes it clear that Wolley had to 'act rarely well the Zealot' for the French and Jacobite cause in order to fit in at the French Court. Even when it serves a good political cause, then, the spy's work depends upon duplicity. The publication of secrets always involves a betrayal of trust, and the more significant the secret, the greater the betrayal involved.[44] The fact that *The Secret History of White-hall* is based on the letters of a spy is key to its claim to historicity, but it also presents a serious ethical challenge to that claim.

The early eighteenth century witnessed a fashion for texts with spy narrators – born, perhaps, of the popularity of secret history and the commercial success of *The Turkish Spy*.[45] In many cases, these spy narrators draw attention to the scepticism that is invariably directed towards the testimony of a spy. In his *Memoirs of Secret Service* (1699), for instance, the government spy Matthew Smith makes an impassioned appeal to his reader, claiming that the government refused to pay him for his intelligence work knowing that, as a spy, he would have no credit to enforce his claims upon them.[46] And in the novel, *The French Spy* (1700), the spy narrator, Jean-Baptist, writes his memoirs from the Bastille where he lies imprisoned without hope of release because he cannot persuade his incarcerators that he is a government agent rather than an enemy of the government.[47] In *The Turkish Spy*, the eponymous spy, Mahmut, demonstrates that spies occupy a world in which all knowledge is uncertain. As time progresses, he reveals his anxiety that he might be the unwitting subject of observation as well as an observer of others. He writes to his friend and physician, Cara Hali, that 'we dare not trust each other too far, nor the very Air into which our Words vanish, after it has help'd to form 'em; lest some sly, envious *Daemon* shou'd catch the transient sound, and reverberate the yet Articulated body of Particules which made it, into some inquisitive ear to ruin us'.[48] At the end of the eight volumes, Mahmut's letters break off after he becomes convinced that the Ottoman authorities are trying to have him assassinated.[49] Instead of instilling in him a sense of superior knowledge and power, Mahmut's access to secret intelligence drives him to feel profoundly insecure.[50] According to *The Turkish Spy* and other spy narratives, secret intelligence does not create a privileged group of insiders who are privy to a secret and, therefore, set apart from those outsiders who are excluded from it.[51] Rather, the discourse of secrecy creates an arena in which no one can be sure of the extent or the accuracy of his or her knowledge.

In *The Secret History of White-hall*, David Jones exploits the psychological consequences of the discourse of spying and secrecy to a political end. Instead of encouraging his readers to feel confidence in the knowledge that the Revolution of 1688–9 had vanquished the threat of popery and arbitrary government, Jones asserts that Jacobite and French forces continue to exert a secret influence upon post-Revolution British politics. Referring to his own secret history, he announces that:

> There is no one *Party*, or sect of Men in *England*, much less the Court exempted, but may draw very seasonable *Informations*, and no less timous *Instructions* herefrom; seeing they have all of them, in their respective turns, though many quite against their Knowledge, been imposed upon by *French Emissaries* and made *Tools* of to serve the Interest of *France*, to the prejudice of themselves, and of their own Country.[52]

At one level, Jones's statement reads like a marketing ploy: Englishmen in every station of life, he suggests, must read this text if they are to fulfil their loyal duty. But this preface is also designed to strike a blow at the kind of self-satisfied political complacency exemplified by a whig interpretation of later seventeenth-century history. The letters that make up *The Secret History of White-hall* warn that even outright resistance to France is futile because of the insidious nature of French influence upon English politics, society, and culture. 'The *French*', one letter informs its readers, 'keep their Correspondence among, and make Tools of Men and Parties most averse to them in their Neighbour-Nations, and whom no manner of Motives would ever be prevalent enough to make instrumental to promote an Interest so hateful to them, did they but know who they wrought for'.[53] Jones's secret history carries his readers toward the conclusion that they have no more freedom under William III than they did under James II, since the real threat to their liberty derives from covert political forces: Louis XIV continually undermines the liberty of English subjects not by overt oppression, but by depriving them of the possibility of political agency.

David Jones's *Secret History of White-hall* is an attack on the whig interpretation of the recent past. Instead of suggesting that the Revolution of 1688–9 provides readers in the 1690s with a safe vantage point from which to contrast the French-inspired intrigues of the Stuart monarchs with the political liberties enjoyed by the British under William III, it argues that the extent of France's continuing secret influence on British life is impossible to gauge. In spite of the accusations made against secret history by contemporary detractors, Jones's text is neither republican in its ideology nor aimed at undermining the authority of William III or the Revolution settlement at a more specific level. Rather, it attempts to harness the epistemic uncertainty generated by the act of revelation in order to instil anxiety into a politically complacent readership, lulled into a false sense of security by texts such as those secret histories that espouse a whig interpretation of England's recent past.

The political strategies of *The Secret History of White-hall* are inseparable from its profoundly self-conscious approach towards issues of form and historiography. In the preface to this text, Jones observes that, although *The Secret History of White-hall* is an epistolary work, 'the *Reader* cannot but observe an Air of History to run in a manner through the whole Composition'.[54] Although epistolarity creates an impression of fragmentation through the passage of time between letters and the disparate subjects addressed in each, there is, nonetheless, a strong sense of narrative coherence in the work as a whole. Jones's revisionist account of recent European history does, indeed, create a narrative out of the intelligence contained in Wolley's letters. Throughout *The Secret History of White-hall*, English political history is portrayed as little more than a digression in an ongoing narrative of French expansionist ambitions. According to Jones, French involvement in English affairs neither began nor ended with the reigns of Charles II and James II; French *agents provocateurs*, he tells his readers, have been the driving force behind English foreign and domestic politics since before the Civil Wars (which were, themselves, the result of French efforts to weaken the English nation). Indeed, this secret history reveals that every major event in English politics during the previous half century – including the Civil Wars, the execution of Charles I, the three Dutch Wars, the Popish Plot, the Exclusion Crisis and the rise of party politics – should be seen in the light of Louis XIV's political aims. Even apparent Whig triumphs like the Revolution of 1688–9 are portrayed as the result of French political influence. A letter written on the eve of William of Orange's invasion informs readers that French secret agents were 'extraordinary busy to countermine whatever Advices have been give the King [James II] for taking a timely Precaution to defend himself'. The letter concludes that 'there is ... in this Case a Wheel within a Wheel, and whatever open Professions of Kindness are shew'd [James II] from hence by a timous Premonition of his Danger, there is as great Care seriously to thwart all by contrary Counsels'.[55] While the whig interpretation of recent political history depicts the Revolution of 1688–9 as a watershed, *The Secret History of White-hall* cites it as evidence of France's ongoing involvement in English domestic politics.

David Jones's alternative account of seventeenth-century European political history exemplifies one of secret history's central characteristics: its self-conscious approach towards the ways in which the revelation of previously undiscovered intelligence can reconfigure existing narratives of the past. Secret history's ability to create new narratives out of fragments or anecdotes had received detailed, if hostile, attention in *The Blatant Beast Muzzl'd*, six years before *The Secret History of White-hall* was published. N. N., the anonymous author of this work, attacks the author of *The Secret History of the Reigns of K. Charles II and K. James II* as a 'man of *Consequences*' – that is, an author who over-interprets the past by inventing false motives to make innocent occurrences seem suspicious.[56] According to N. N., Charles II kept a mistress 'for his Pleasure' and the Duke of York 'took an innocent Nap at Sea', but the secret historian claims that the Duchess of Portsmouth was a French spy and that the Duke of York deliberately attempted to sabotage English military interests as part of a plot to bring in French-style popery and slavery.[57] *The Blatant Beast Muzzl'd* often uses textile metaphors to describe this secret historian's methods: he 'tack[s]' his deductions together with a 'dextrous Confidence' in order to 'make his Tale tell smoothly' and 'twists together (as is his constant fashion) a many [*sic*] little Ends of Falshoods, and not one of them prov'd, which his awkward Fancy casts into a smooth Narrative frame, to patch up an invidious Story, and then thinks his Work is done'.[58] By tacking, twisting, patching and smoothing, secret history uses a thread of narrative to turn anecdotal scraps into a coherent, historical whole.

Jones's revisionist history, in which all events in the recent history of Europe are subsumed into a master narrative of French political ambition, appears to exemplify the process of narrative construction that *The Blatant Beast Muzzl'd* condemns. But in fact, both the metaphors that Jones uses in his text and his self-conscious approach to the business of revelation challenge precisely this idea that secrets create alternative, definitive accounts of the past. In place of a 'smooth Narrative frame', David Jones presents his readers with wheels within wheels, creating a historical paradigm in which the true causes of events are hidden, one behind another, like the springs and cogs inside a complex mechanism. As Jones repeatedly warns his readers about the insidious influence of French *agents provocateurs* upon English politics, he opens up the possibility that there are still further secrets, yet undiscovered, which might undermine his own account of recent political history. This idea is reinforced by the fact that Jones's narrative is intended to revise not pro-Stuart, Tory or Jacobite versions of recent history, but Whig texts with strong connections to the secret history tradition. In the preface to *The Secret History of White-hall*, Jones describes his work as a '*Supplemental Part*, as well for the detecting of past Falsities, as for the perfecting of past Discoveries' in a number of recent historical works, including Sir William Temple's *Memoirs* (1691) and Roger Coke's *Detection of the Court and State of England During the Four Last Reigns* (1694).[59] Temple's *Memoirs* have recently been analysed as a form of secret history by Annabel Patterson, and Coke's

Detection promises its readers 'Many ... Secrets, never before made publick' and proceeds to condemn the 'Usurpations' of 'Kings of the *Scotish* Race' upon the English throne.[60] *The Secret History of White-hall* thus demonstrates that further secrets lie hidden behind those that have already been brought to light in earlier secret histories. But in doing so, it tacitly acknowledges its own potential limitations. In sum, David Jones uses secret history not so much to provide a definitive new narrative of the recent political past as to reveal that all historical narrative, including secret history itself, is vulnerable to revision and reinterpretation.[61]

It seems difficult to reconcile Jones's radical scepticism towards political agency, the possibility of distinguishing between fact and fiction, and the stability of historical narrative, with the ostensibly polemical aims of his secret history. By scrutinizing the principal characteristics of secret history and carrying them to an extreme, Jones appears to undermine any basis for political belief or political action. Is *The Secret History of White-hall* anything more, then, than an exercise in Pyrrhonist historiography or a nihilistic expression of political impotence?

The Secret History of White-hall's extreme historiographical scepticism can be reconciled with secret history's characteristic opposition to arbitrary government by focusing on the figure of the historian. When he undermines the authority of his own narrative, Jones is reacting against the view of historians expressed by his friend and fellow historian, Roger Coke, whose *Detection of the Court and State of England* Jones explicitly claims to revise in *The Secret History of White-hall*. In the preface to his *Detection*, Coke declares that:

> The Historian taking to himself an Absolute Dictatorship, nay, an Authority more than Human, over Times, Persons and Actions; governs Fame, measures Deserts; penetrates Intentions; discloses Secrets, is with an undistinguished Arbitrament over Kings and People; the judge of Ages past, and Master of those to come, Absolves or Punishes, Deceives or Instructs.[62]

With a levelling stroke, Coke proclaims the dominance of the historian over even the most powerful absolute monarch. Coke's assertions echo a view of the historian that underpins much of the Whig secret history published during the 1690s. By recording the wicked actions of the Stuart kings for posterity, secret historians use the power of the press to challenge the tyranny of would-be arbitrary rulers. *The Secret History of White-hall*, however, takes a different approach towards the figure of the historian. David Jones repeatedly refutes the idea that any secret history can ever penetrate the deepest secrets of state. He therefore suggests that the 'arbitrament' of historians is no more permanent than that of kings. While some Whig polemicists use secret history to celebrate the political liberties that arrived in England with the Revolution of 1688–9, Jones implies that this whig interpretation of the recent past is evidence of a dangerous political complacency in a country that is still subject to the insidious influence of

France. Through self-conscious scrutiny of both the discourse of secrecy and revelation and the historiographical forms that it generates, David Jones directs secret history's iconoclastic force against secret history itself. In doing so, he makes *The Secret History of White-hall* a profoundly anti-absolutist form of historiography.

Conclusion

David Jones's *Secret History of White-hall*, published in 1697, provides a new perspective on John Somers's *True Secret History of all the Kings and Queens of England*, which appeared five years later in 1702. In the preface to his history, Somers alludes to Jones's work and reveals that he and Jones share a common source in Richard Wolley, the spy whose letters make up the body of *The Secret History of White-hall*. Somers asserts the veracity of the intelligence contained in his text by claiming that much of it was 'Communicated to me, by the Revernd Mr. W. – Who was a Spy in the *French Court*, and by that means, took Minutes of the most Secret Transactions between *England* and *France* for many Years'.[63] Somers's description of Wolley deliberately echoes the title page of *The Secret History of White-hall*, which declares that the author of the letters that make up this text 'had the perusal of all the *Private Minutes* between *England* and *France* for many Years'. Given Somers's habit of citing earlier Whig secret historians in his *True Secret History*, it seems likely that his allusions to Jones's text are designed to co-opt *The Secret History of White-hall* into a Whig corpus of texts that includes Algernon Sidney's dying speech, *The Secret History of the Reigns of K. Charles II and K. James II* and *The True Secret History* itself.

But although Somers uses allusion to connect his own secret history with *The Secret History of White-hall*, the strategies that the earlier text uses to further its anti-absolutist political agenda are radically different from those of the *True Secret History*. While the *True Secret History* celebrates the triumph of Whiggism at the Revolution of 1688–9, Jones systematically attempts to erode his reader's confidence in the stability of the Revolution settlement. John Somers's *True Secret History* should be read as a deliberate reaction against the kind of secret history written by David Jones in *The Secret History of White-hall*. The lengthy theoretical treatise on secret history that prefaces Somers's text is designed to reinstate the authority and reliability of the historian and the whig interpretation of recent political history – both of which had been comprehensively challenged by Jones in *The Secret History of White-hall*.

David Jones's approach towards the discourse of secrecy and revelation seems counter-intuitive in comparison with that of Somers. Somers uses his own position as a statesman with privileged access to private libraries and firsthand experience of political negotiations to affirm the veracity of the evidence he presents in his secret history and, by extension, the authority of his own interpretation of the recent political past. In doing so, he attempts to raise the prestige of secret history, presenting it as a form of neoclassical historiography well suited to recounting Britain's corrupt past from the perspective of its glorious present. David Jones's approach towards the discourse of secrecy and revelation is quite different. Instead of giving his reader confidence in his authority as a historian, Jones undermines the reliability of his own intelligence by highlighting the duplicitous character of his source: a spy in the French court. And instead of providing a definitive, alternative account of recent European political history, Jones uses the anxieties generated by his spy narrator to undermine the apparent coherence of his – and any other – historical narrative. While Somers's narrative is a celebratory, whig interpretation of British history, Jones's is a sceptical account designed to instil political anxiety in his readers – to make them feel that arbitrary rule is a present threat rather than a defeated force.

It is tempting to dismiss the counter-intuitive aspects of Jones's *Secret History of White-hall* as an aberration – perhaps an intellectual exercise in taking the characteristics of secret history to an extreme conclusion, or a straightforward inconsistency that undermines this text's ostensibly political purposes. Jones's initially perplexing approach towards the discourse of secrecy and revelation is, however, not at all unusual among early eighteenth-century secret historians. Although secret history may at first appear to be a form of writing that reveals genuine secrets in order to attack absolute rulers and strike a blow at the foundations of arbitrary government, practitioners of the form manipulate its conventional claim to reveal secrets in a wide variety of different ways. We have already seen that, rather than simply revealing previously undiscovered information about the reign of the Emperor Justinian, Procopius's *Anekdota* encourages later secret historians to scrutinize the adjective 'secret'. David Jones takes up this challenge as he analyses the literary and political ramifications of claiming to disclose *arcana imperii* in secret history. As subsequent chapters show, the kind of self-conscious, counter-intuitive rhetorical techniques found in *The Secret History of White-hall* actually foreshadow the strategies used in many secret histories and responses to secret history during the early eighteenth century.

3 SECRET HISTORY, THE 'REVOLUTION' OF 1714 AND THE CASE OF JOHN DUNTON

During Queen Anne's reign, Whig writers lost their monopoly on secret history. This period witnessed the publication of several highly popular secret histories by Tory polemicists, including: Ned Ward's *Secret History of the Calves-Head Club* (1703), a compendium of republican drinking songs and anti-republican diatribe which went through a large number of ever-expanding editions during the first few decades of the eighteenth century; *The Secret History of Queen Zarah and the Zarazians* (1705), a *roman à clef* that attacks Queen Anne's Whig favourite, Sarah Churchill, Duchess of Marlborough, which was formerly attributed to Delarivier Manley but is probably by Joseph Browne; and *The Secret History of Arlus and Odolphus* (1710), attributed to Colley Cibber, which reveals the reasons why the moderate Tory, Robert Harley (Arlus), was ousted from his position as Secretary of State in 1708 by the Earl of Godolphin (Odolphus), and how he regained popular and royal favour, returning to power in 1710.[1] Such texts pay no heed to the implicit connections between secret history's claims to reveal the secrets of monarchs and ministers and a Whig political agenda, with its antipathy towards arbitrary government and scepticism towards Court culture. Tory secret history argues that corrupt Whig politicians have as much to hide as the Stuart monarchs ever did.

But the appointment of Robert Harley to the post of Chancellor of the Exchequer in 1710, his swift promotion to Lord Treasurer in 1711 and his fall from power in 1714 were events that reignited Whig interest in secret history. Upon first assuming office in 1710, Harley hoped to form a government that would draw on talent from both the Whig and Tory ranks. Pressure from the Tory backbenches and reluctance on the part of Whigs to cooperate with Harley's policies, however, meant that he found himself at the head of an increasingly hardline or highflying Tory administration. As the Tories strengthened their grip on power, Whig polemicists began once more to publish secret history.

In 1712, John Oldmixon published the first three parts of *The Secret History of Europe*, which deliberately and explicitly evokes the anti-absolutist secret histories of the 1690s in its rhetorical acts of disclosure, the content of its revelations, and its commitment to opposing arbitrary government. The list of contents on the title page of the first volume reveals its resemblance to earlier secret histories: 'the Insincerity of *England, Sweden* and *Holland*, in the Triple League', 'the Close Alliance between *Charles* II. and *Lewis* XVI', and 'the Poisoning of *Madam*', are all stories relating to the secret treaty of Dover, signed between Charles II and Louis XIV in 1670, while 'the Secret Treaty between King *James* and the *French* King' concerns similar attempts made by Charles's brother James to recruit French military and financial assistance and introduce Roman Catholicism into England.[2] But – as Oldmixon makes clear in the second volume – the real target of this work is the modern day Tory ministry led by Robert Harley, now Earl of Oxford and Mortimer. By claiming that, since the reign of Charles II, High Churchmen and Tories had attempted to import popery and slavery into Britain, Oldmixon strives 'to set a Rampant *Faction*' – that is, Harley's ministry, which he portrays as essentially Jacobite in character – 'in their True Light'.[3] Just as John Somers had depicted an ongoing struggle between the forces of Protestant liberty and popish slavery in his *True Secret History* of 1702, so John Oldmixon portrays a fundamental continuity between the Stuarts' attempts to introduce popery and arbitrary government during the seventeenth century and what he perceives to be the primary aim of Queen Anne's Tory ministers: the restoration of the Stuarts to the British throne in the person of James II's son, the Pretender. In 1702, Somers believed that the Revolution of 1688–9 had quashed the threat of arbitrary government in Britain; Oldmixon, however, protests that under Robert Harley's ministry, Britain is once more at risk of submitting to a French yoke.

What was it about Harley's ministry that raised such fears and inspired writers like Oldmixon to reclaim secret history in the fight against arbitrary government? In part, government policies were to blame. Chief among these, as far as Whig secret historians were concerned, was the Tories' attitude towards the War of Spanish Succession. In 1702, Britain and the United Provinces had gone to war against France in an attempt to prevent the installation of a Bourbon monarch on the Spanish throne. By the end of the decade, many Tory supporters – feeling the financial strain of increased taxation, despondency towards the progress of the war and, in some cases, a level of sympathy towards France as the home of the Pretender – were calling for an end to the conflict. These Tories claimed that the Whig ministry under Godolphin and Marlborough was deliberately drawing out the war because of the personal financial benefits that its members gained by it.[4] In response, Whig politicians and polemicists rallied to the cry of 'No peace without Spain', asserting that the Tories' real aim in ending the war was to give France European dominance and, ultimately, to return the Stuart Pretender to the British throne.[5] In 1711, negotiations between the warring nations led to the signing of preliminaries of peace; a congress opened at Utrecht in 1712 to negotiate the terms of the peace, and the main treaties were signed in April 1713, bringing the eleven-year war to a close. Many Whigs remained convinced that the terms of the peace were too favourable towards France and believed that Harley had been involved in underhand negotiations with France that compromised British interests. In order to have the treaty ratified by the House of Lords, Harley persuaded the Queen to create twelve new Tory peers who could be relied upon to support his measures. The Whigs complained that Harley was manipulating the constitution to push through a Tory peace – and feared that it was a prelude to the constitutional changes that might accompany the return of a Stuart king.

Harley's style of political management, as much as his policies, elicited suspicion and led to a renewal of interest in secret history among Whig polemicists during his ministry. Harley was a notoriously secretive politician, who relied heavily on secret intelligence and backstairs negotiations. Between 1704 and 1708, as Secretary of State, he had developed an extensive national network of informants to provide him with intelligence.[6] At times, his use of spies proved highly advantageous – as when he employed Daniel Defoe in Edinburgh to keep him informed about Scottish opponents to the Act of Union, which was eventually passed in 1707. In the same year, however, Harley incurred the political costs involved in the use of spies when William Gregg, a clerk in his office, was caught passing state secrets to France. Although Gregg staunchly and bravely refused to implicate Harley in his treachery – an action which might have saved him from execution – suspicions about Harley's conduct continued to circulate, fuelled by pamphlets and periodical articles about the Gregg affair, well into the period of Harley's term as Lord Treasurer.[7]

At a more personal level, Harley's secretive demeanour earned him the antipathy of many of his Whig contemporaries. In 1706, the Whig Lord Chancellor, William Cowper, observed in his diary that Harley's humour 'was, never to deal clearly or openly, but always with Reserve, if not Dissimulation, or rather Simulation; & to love Tricks even where not necessary, but from an inward Satisfaction he took in applauding his own Cunning'. Cowper concludes, 'If any Man was ever born under a Necessity of being a Knave, he was'.[8] In March 1712, while negotiations were underway at Utrecht to end the War of Spanish Succession, Harley made an appointment with Cowper at St James's, 'he desiring Opportunity to satisfie [Cowper] as to the Protestant Succ[essio]n; that no harm, &c intended it, but the contrary'. Harley's manner undermined his aims, however, since '[he] spake, as always, very dark and confusedly, interlaceing all he said with broken hints of Discoveries he had made'.[9] According to a more recent survey of Harley's career, he was 'devious and secretive ... a political wizard and master of "schemes"'. The 'air of mystery' that surrounded Harley was, in part, 'a natural emanation of his serpentine intelligence and love of intrigue'.[10] Harley's nickname – 'Robin the trickster' – testifies to the common perception of his duplicitous character.[11]

Even Harley's friends and supporters acknowledged that the Lord Treasurer's predilection for secrecy was at best an ambivalent quality. In an analysis of Harley's career written shortly before his fall from power, Jonathan Swift suggests that Harley's secretive demeanour would inevitably breed secrecy in those around him. 'I never thought the Reputation of much Secrecy was a Character of any Advantage to a Minister', Swift remarks, 'because it put all other men upon their Guard to be as secret as he, and was consequently the Occasion that persons and Things were always misrepresented to Him'.[12] Swift's explanation of Harley's own perspective on the use of political secrecy in his *History of the Four Last Years of the Queen* hardly seems designed to vindicate this secretive minister. When accused of exercising too much secrecy in government, Swift explains that Harley 'hath been heard to answer, That he seldom did otherwise without Cause to repent'.[13] The most extensive defence of Harley's use of secrecy as a political tool is found not in Swift's fleeting comments on the subject, but in Daniel Defoe's secret histories, including *The Secret History of the October Club* (1711) and *The Secret History of the White-Staff* (1714–15), which are explored in detail in Chapter 6. In these works, Defoe argues that Harley's secret negotiations with the Jacobites were a means of neutralizing their power – and that any observers who failed to realize this were taken in by Harley's ruse, just as the Jacobites were. Whig commentators, however, were unimpressed by such arguments. They continued to assert that Harley's secrecy was a sign of his underhand dealings with the Pretender and a symptom of his admiration for arbitrary government.

Harley's fall from power just before the Queen's death in August 1714 and the relatively peaceful transition of power from the Stuart to the Hanoverian dynasty over the course of the following year gave new impetus to Whig secret historians. In the wake of George I's accession to the throne, many secret historians sought to highlight the parallels between this Protestant 'revolution' and that of 1688. *A Secret History of One Year* (1714) asserts that 'the Circumstances of the Revolution of 1688, and the Turn of Affairs which has now happen'd in *Great Britain*, since the Death of the late Queen, are founded on such a visible Analogy of Causes and Effects, that they may well bear the same name, viz. THE REVOLUTION'.[14] In both 1688 and 1714, a four-year threat of arbitrary government inspired by French absolutism was crushed by the arrival of a foreign but Protestant monarch to protect British political liberties. *A Secret History of One Year* is an appeal for clemency towards the ousted leaders of the former ministry: it holds up the example of William's mercy towards former supporters of James II in the year after his arrival on the throne as a model of prudent government. Such a moderate position is, however, unusual among contemporary secret histories; more often, secret historians use the analogy between 1688 and

1714 to vilify Harley's ministry and triumph over its downfall. According to William Stoughton's *Secret History of the Late Ministry* (1715), Harley and his Tory colleagues attempted 'at every Step ... from the Time of their fatal Admission to Power' to 'bring in Popery and Slavery into [*sic*] these Nations, in the Establishment of their despicable Pretender'.[15] Stoughton declares his hope that the 'late *Glorious Revolution*' – as he terms the Hanoverian accession – 'shall terminate both in his and their Destruction'.[16] The fact that Harley and St John were impeached on charges of treachery in April 1715 made the possibility of their 'Destruction' a very real one – and gave an additional incentive to Whig secret historians determined to reveal the secrets of their underhand dealings with France.

Secret histories published during 1714–15 promote a whig interpretation of the recent political past, contrasting the era of political liberty during which they appear with the corruption and threatened tyranny of the Stuart reigns that they describe. John Oldmixon's *Arcana Gallica; or, the Secret History of France for the Last Century* (1714), which reveals France's persistent attempts to achieve European domination and to spread the absolute power of the French king, is dedicated to the son of William Bentinck, first Earl of Portland, chief adviser to and favourite of William III. Oldmixon thereby reminds his readers of the 'Glorious *Deliverance* ... to which they owe the Present Happy Government, and the hopes of the Future'.[17] Stories of French machinations are thus set in the context of the triumph of political liberty and the Protestant succession in Britain. Likewise, the dedication of the fourth part of Oldmixon's *Secret History of Europe* (1715), addressed to the Hanoverian Prince of Wales, draws attention to the victory of liberty over the forces of popery and slavery that are exposed in this secret history itself. Hanoverian Whig secret history subscribes to the whig interpretation of history much more consistently than its predecessors of the 1690s. Indeed, the fact that secret history published during 1714–15 focuses on the machinations of ministers, not monarchs, itself bears testimony to the success of Whig efforts to curb royal prerogative. By Queen Anne's reign, it is clear that ministers, rather than the monarch, run the affairs of government. Secret histories of the late ministry implicitly reveal the extent to which power had been devolved to Parliament by 1714.

Political factors were not, however, the only force to motivate the renewed popularity of secret history in the wake of the accession of George I. Secret historians may have celebrated the arrival of the Hanoverians upon the British throne from a political perspective, but they also hoped to profit by it. In his *Secret History of the Happy Revolution in 1688* (1715), the Whig agitator Hugh Speke belatedly demands a reward for services rendered to William III and the Protestant cause. Speke makes the extraordinary claim that, as an undercover agent, he was a 'Principal TRANSACTOR' in the Revolution of 1688–9 since he offered military advice to William III and convinced James II to flee to France. Speke asks George I to consider 'how far his mean Services contributed to the Advancement of the Interests of the *Revolution*, and how far that became the *Basis* and Foundation of the present most happy Settlement of the Imperial Crown of these Realms in the August House of *Hanover*'.[18] In effect, Speke suggests that the Hanoverian accession would have been impossible but for his efforts. He claims that under the crypto-Jacobite, Tory ministry that held sway during Queen Anne's reign, his contributions to the cause of political liberty were by no means appreciated; he therefore appeals to George I for financial recompense for secret services in the Protestant cause.

Other Whig polemicists during the early years of George I's reign aimed to benefit from the impact that they expected the Hanoverian accession to have on the market for secret history. *The Secret History of the Chevalier de St George* (1714) returns to the warming pan scandal that surrounded news of the birth of James II's son in 1688. Like many Whig pamphlets during the late 1680s and 1690s, this tract alleges that the Pretender, or 'Chevalier de St George', was not the true son of James II and his consort, Mary of Modena, but that he had been smuggled into the birthing chamber in a warming pan in order to provide James with a male heir. The author and publisher of this secret history appear to have believed that, if stories about Stuart machinations had sold well in the aftermath of 1688, secret historians might prosper once again as a result of the 'revolution' of 1714. A belief in the marketability of secret history probably also prompted a second edition of David Jones's *Secret History of White-hall* in 1717. Whig polemicists attempted to make financial as well as political capital out of the analogy between 1688 and 1714. They clearly hoped that the popularity of Whig secret history might be renewed by the second revolution, just as it was strengthened by the first.

The Case of John Dunton

John Dunton is chief among the early Hanoverian secret historians both in his enthusiasm for Revolution principles and his desire to turn political zeal to financial advantage. During the final years of Harley's ministry and the first years after George I's accession to the throne, Dunton published: *Neck or Nothing* (1713), including 'the *True Character* or *Secret History* of the PRESENT MINISTRY'; *The Court-Spy; or Detection of Such Secret, Odd, and Uncommon Transactions in Church and State, as Are Wholly Omitted by Other News Writers* (1713); *Queen Robin: or the Second Part of Neck or Nothing, Detecting the Secret Reign of the Four Last Years* (1715); *The Shortest Way with the King: or, Plain English Spoke to His Majesty... Containing, The Secret History of King George's Reign* [1715]; *The Hanover-Spy: or, Secret History of St James's* (1718); and *The State-Weather-*

cocks or, New Secret History of the Most Distinguished Favourites Both of the Late and Present Reign (1719). Although not every one of these texts is explicitly called a 'secret history', each of them signals their affiliation with this tradition through key words like 'spy', 'detection' and 'secret'. In all of these texts, Dunton seeks to expose the machinations of those who threaten British Protestantism and political liberty with the forces of popery and arbitrary government. Like so many other Whig polemicists of the early Hanoverian era, Dunton emphasizes the connections between the reign of James II and Harley's Tory ministry, and between the revolutions of 1688 and 1714, in order to bolster both the Whig political cause and his own career as a secret historian.

Dunton's oeuvre provides a fascinating case study in secret history because it reveals the way in which this form's characteristic rhetoric of disclosure functions in the absence of anything that might be described as genuine intelligence. Indeed, in many of his secret histories, Dunton makes rhetorical gestures of revelation without providing his readers with any information at all. *The Court-Spy*, for instance, claims to expose active Jacobite cells in Southwark, which were plotting to bring back the Pretender. Dunton asserts, proudly, that 'the *Jacobite-Plot* to introduce the Pretender was never fix'd on particular Persons, but in this *Narrative*'.[19] Yet Dunton's 'intelligence' is lacking in vital details. His young female informant, for instance, claims to know 'several Places in —, where they catechize and teach their Destructive Principles', and that she is acquainted with 'five Popish Priests, whose Names are Mr. E—, Mr. T—, Mr. R—, Mr. M— and Mr. V—'.[20] Instead of particularity, Dunton here gives his reader names so syncopated that they are indecipherable. Dunton's promise to provide his readers with 'a particular Discovery of [the Jacobites'] *Treasonable Words and Practices*' results in similar disappointment. His Jacobites utter platitudes: 'That the Queen had no Right to the *Throne*. That they hop'd to say Mass in all the Churches, in a little time', and, 'that they expected the Prince of *Wales* (for so they call the *Pretender*) at the Beginning of Winter'.[21] *The Court-Spy* has all the trappings of secret history – an undercover narrator who claims to have privileged access to political secrets coupled with a vigorously anti-Catholic and anti-French political stance – but it provides no information that could be mistaken for genuine intelligence.

Dunton's hyperbolic rhetoric of disclosure coupled with an absence of intelligence is evident once more in *The Hanover-Spy* (1718). In this text, Dunton promises his readers 'a sort of Living History, and not a Dull Collection from The Secret Histories already publish'd'.[22] He affirms that *The Hanover-Spy* is an 'Experimental Secret History' and repeats three times that this text contains 'such Secrets both in Church and State as I have been Privy to, or can Prove by Persons now Living at Court'.[23] The adjectives 'living' and 'experimental' suggest that Dunton's intelligence derives from his own experiences, yet Dunton proceeds to reiterate accusations that had been the mainstay of Whig secret histories during the 1690s and of anti-Stuart, Exclusionist literature since the early years of the Restoration: that the Stuart kings, '*abjur'd the Reformed Religion,* (which tho a great Secret hitherto, I positively affirm to be Matter of Fact) and became Reconciled to the Church of *Rome*';[24] that they resolved to destroy the Church of England, '(which tho' a *surprizing Secret,* yet I assert is a Real Truth)';[25] that the fire of London in 1666 was a Catholic plot, '(which Secret I receiv'd from a Person of undoubted Credit, and dare affirm it for Truth)';[26] and that Charles II refused to countenance excluding his brother from the line of succession, 'not out of Love to his Person, but *Affection to Popery* (a Secret which has hitherto lain conceal'd) which he knew that Gentleman would introduce and establish'.[27] The idea that James II's Catholicism was a 'great Secret' is absurd, while rumours concerning Charles's religion had circulated since at least the early days of the Restoration and had been mentioned in almost every Whig secret history since the 1690s. Conspiracy theories about Catholic involvement in the Fire of London had, likewise, circulated widely ever since 1666. In all of these cases, Dunton claims to disclose information which had, in actual fact, been public knowledge or common gossip for decades. Dunton's parenthetical references to the secrets revealed in his text stretch the definition of a 'secret' beyond breaking point.

Dunton's claim to write 'a sort of Living History, and not a Dull Collection from The Secret Histories already publish'd' is further compromised by the fact that his secret histories are full of allusions to and quotations from earlier texts in this tradition. In *The Court-Spy,* for instance, Dunton reworks the self-conscious references to spying and secrecy found in the preface to *The Secret History of White-hall*. In Chapter 2, we saw that David Jones, the author of *The Secret History of White-hall,* uses his spy narrator to induce scepticism and anxiety in his readers as he reminds them that 'it's no hard matter to imagine what Qualifications were necessary to recommend our Author to the Imployment afore noted [i.e. a spy in the French Court], and how far his Out-side must differ from his In-side during his aboad there'.[28] The preface to Dunton's *Court-Spy* likewise asserts that

> 'Tis a high Point of Credulity to believe he [i.e. the Court-Spy] will be true to me, *whom I endeavour to make false where he owes his Faith*, nor are Men of ordinary Parts (as I hinted before) fit for *Court-Spies; the Art of carrying Two Faces under one Hood,* and conversing as a Friend with them, whom as an Enemy he studys to ruin; of corrupting others to betray their Trust, and to tread with him the same Paths of Danger for Advantage (when Discovery brings certain Death, and no less certain Shame) asks a *practis'd Machivilian* verst in all Kinds of Subtilties and Guiles.[29]

Dunton reveals later in this tract that his informant for this work is not the Jacobite turncoat that he describes here, but rather one William Clark, a Dissenting minister from Shadwell. Dunton, a staunch believer in the Revolution principle of religious toleration, presents Clark as evidence of the loyalty and patriotism of the Dissenters. But to criticize Dunton for his inaccuracy here is to miss the point of this allusion. Dunton's preface is designed not to provide a genuine description of *The Court-Spy*, but rather to connect this text with the tradition of spy narrators in secret history epitomized by *The Secret History of White-hall*.

Dunton reworks not only the self-conscious attitude towards spies and spying that we find in *The Secret History of White-hall*, but also the mechanistic metaphor of wheels within wheels that Jones explores in this earlier secret history. In the *Court-Spy*, Dunton remarks that his own narrative will help to reveal '*Treasonable Practices*' among Harley's ministry, 'For in the *Wonders of Providence* we often see *a Wheel within a Wheel*, and that little Engines often set great Engines at work'.[30] In *The Secret History of White-hall*, the metaphor of a 'wheel within a wheel' is used to refer to French political machinations.[31] As we saw in Chapter 2, this metaphor is a crucial element of Jones's distinctive brand of anti-absolutist historiography. Again, Dunton's allusion to the phrase in *The Court-Spy* is somewhat incongruous since in this text it refers to Dunton's own participation in the fight against Jacobitism rather than (as in *The Secret History of White-hall*) French skulduggery. The verbal echoes of *The Secret History of White-hall* in Dunton's *Court-Spy* do not sustain a close and careful comparison between the ways in which particular images and ideas are used in each text. Rather, they are designed to bring the general political context of the earlier text to bear on the later one. Just as *The Secret History of White-hall* warns its readers about the ongoing threat posed by French and Jacobite forces, so Dunton's *Court-Spy* constitutes an attempt to save a '*Frenchified Nation from impending Ruin*'.[32]

Dunton continues to allude to secret histories of the 1690s after the accession of George I, but his citations from earlier texts now contrast the dark days of Queen Anne's reign with the glorious new Hanoverian regime. Shortly after the Revolution of 1688–9, *The Secret History of the Reigns of K. Charles II and K. James II* had promised to 'bring our Late Monarchs Reigns upon the Stage', and, 'let all the World judge of the Furberies and Tyranny of those Times, and the Integrity, Sincerity and Sweetness of Their Present Majesties Reign; since by comparing Them, the most wilfully Blind may be convinced, how infinitely Happy we are, under their present Majesties Government, beyond what we were in the late Reign'.[33] In *Neck or Nothing* (1713) Dunton suggests that only those who are 'wilfully blind' could fail to see the treacherous intent behind the peace of Utrecht.[34] In *The Shortest Way with the King* (1715), on the other hand, Dunton promises to provide 'The Secret History of King *George*'s reign' and to 'INTRODUCE ... *the Secret Reign of the Monarchs of* Great-Britain, *for the last Sixty Years*, that so by comparing your Majesty's Reign with that of your Predecessors, it may make it appear that *Great-Britain* is now Blest with one of the best of Princes (I'le not except *the Glorious* William) that ever sway'd the *British*

Scepter'.[35] Dunton's allusions to *The Secret History of the Reigns of K. Charles II and K. James II* become still more overt in *The Hanover-Spy* (1718), where he declares that:

> It is one of the Encomiums given to Suetonius, That he made Publick to the World, the Vices and Miscarriages of the Twelve Cæsars, with the same freedom with which they were by them Committed.[36]

Not only does Dunton lift this distinctive sentence verbatim from the preface to *The Secret History of the Reigns of K. Charles II and K. James II*, but exactly the same sentence had also been cited by John Somers in his *True Secret History of the Lives and Reigns of All the Kings and Queens of England*.[37] We have already seen that the preface to Somers's *True Secret History* uses allusion to create a canon of anti-absolutist, Whig texts and to celebrate the triumph of Revolution principles.[38] Dunton's allusion to an allusive text is likewise designed to situate his own secret history within a tradition of literary resistance to popery and arbitrary government and to herald the arrival of a new, Hanoverian era of political liberty.

The fact that Dunton's secret histories are full of commonplace accusations and allusions to earlier secret histories confounds his claim that *The Hanover-Spy* is 'a sort of Living History, and not a Dull Collection from The Secret Histories already publish'd' and an 'Experimental Secret History ... of such Secrets both in Church and State as I have been Privy to, or can Prove by Persons *now living at Court*'. It is tempting to dismiss such claims as an attempt to dupe unsuspecting readers into parting with their money for nonexistent secrets of state. Rather than regarding these assertions as straightforwardly duplicitous, however, we should instead consider them as a form of allusion: the idea of the spy who gathers intelligence at Court is central to secret histories such as *The Secret History of White-hall* – a fact that Dunton acknowledges in formulaic titles such as *The Athenian Spy*, *The Court-Spy* and *The Hanover-Spy*. Aware that secret histories theoretically contain information that is new, true and iconoclastic, Dunton deploys the rhetoric of disclosure without the substance of secret intelligence to back up his claims in a bid to present himself as heir to an outspoken political and literary tradition.

Dunton's assertions are not only allusive, but also highly ironic. When he protests that *The Hanover-Spy* is 'not a Dull Collection from The Secret Histories already publish'd', he actually alerts his readers to the true provenance of much of his ostensibly secret intelligence in previously published secret histories. Throughout his career, Dunton relies heavily upon irony as a rhetorical device. In *A Satyr Upon King William; Being the Secret History of His Life and Reign* (1703), for instance, he promises to '[set] K. *William* in a new Light' by exposing 'Invisible Faults in his Conduct as no Man ever saw but my self' in order to give 'a Secret History of his Life and Reign'.[39] Published the year after William's death, this secret history initially appears to be a Tory or Jacobite reworking of the Whig secret histories of the 1690s, with William III taking the place of the Stuart kings in the earlier texts. The joke in Dunton's satire, however, is that the secret historian fails to uncover any damning secrets about William's reign. He concludes, 'I must so far Satyrize my own Satyr, as freely to own, were K. *William* any thing else but a Man, I shou'd think him Perfect'.[40] Dunton deploys the same kind of heavy-handed, satirical irony in *Seeing's Believing: or, K—ng G—rge Prov'd a Us—per; and His Whole Reign One Continu'd Act of Cr—ty and Op—n* (1716), an attack on Jacobitism that masquerades as a Jacobite text, which was published in the wake of the Jacobite uprising of 1715, as well as *The Shortest Way with the King* (1714), a panegyric on George I that alludes, in its title, to Defoe's satirical tract, *The Shortest Way with the Dissenters* (1702).[41] In order to understand Dunton's use of irony in his Hanoverian secret histories, however, we need to look not only to these overtly satirical texts, but also to the rhetorical strategies that Dunton develops in his Athenian productions – a set of largely apolitical texts that gained popular and commercial success during the period immediately before Dunton began to write political secret history.

The *Athenian Mercury*, published twice a week between 1691 and 1697, nurtures in its readers qualities that are vital to Dunton's use of irony in his later secret histories: curiosity and a strong sense of group identity. The *Athenian Mercury* invites its readers to address questions on any topic – from love to theology, literature to astronomy – to the Athenian Society, who would publish readers' letters and their own responses in the pages of the *Athenian Mercury*.[42] Dunton's tendency to rhetorical inflation is evident in the idea of the Athenian Society which, far from being the numerous body implied by titular allusion to the Royal Society, consisted only of Dunton and his two brothers-in-law, the mathematician Richard Sault and the clergyman Samuel Wesley. Nonetheless, the informative and entertaining ways in which these three men answered a wide variety of questions sustained this popular periodical for a six-year run and gave rise to several collected volumes of *Athenian Mercury* papers entitled the *Athenian Oracle*.

According to Dunton, the defining characteristic of readers of the *Athenian Mercury* is their curiosity and their love of novelty. The 'Athenian' epithet is biblical. It refers to St Paul's questioners in the Areopagus at Athens, who 'spent their time in nothing else, but either to tell, or to hear some new thing'.[43] But Dunton's readers are also distinguished by their willingness to take part in Dunton's publishing venture by sending in their questions to the Athenian Society. The most innovative and distinctive characteristic of the *Athenian Mercury* is its question-and-answer format, which makes readers an integral part of the publication rather than its passive recipients. The group identity of Dunton's ideal Athenians is predicated upon their shared curiosity and their enthusiastic involvement in Dunton's project.

The *Athenian Mercury* folded in 1697 – perhaps a victim of the expansion of the periodical press that was caused by the permanent lapse of the Licensing Act in 1695.[44] For the next two decades Dunton made valiant but increasingly desperate efforts to revive Athenianism in texts including: *Athenae Redivivae: or The New Athenian Oracle* (1704), *The Athenian Catechism* (1704), *The Athenian Spy* (1704, 1706, 1709, 1720), *Athenian Sport; or, Two Thousand Paradoxes Merrily Argued* (1707), *Athenianism; or, The New Projects of Mr. John Dunton* (1710), *Athenian News: or, Dunton's Oracle* (1710), and *The Athenian Novelty, or, a Universal Entertainment for the Lovers of Novelty* (c. 1717). Many of these Athenian texts aim to arouse their readers' curiosity by promising to disclose novelties and secrets, including secrets of state, secrets of the heart and secrets of nature. There is, however, invariably a wide gap between the promises that Dunton makes in the paratexts – that is, the title pages and prefaces – of his works, and their content. The 'two thousand paradoxes' advertised on the title page of *Athenian Sport*, for instance, turn out to be just 134 in number. Likewise, *Athenianism: or, The New Projects of Mr. John Dunton* offers, on its title page, 'six hundred distinct treatises (in prose and verse) written with his own hand'. In fact, this text contains just twenty-four different 'projects' (by which Dunton means miscellaneous poems and tracts, rather than plans or ideas) of which several (including *A Satyr upon King William* and a poem entitled 'The Dissenting Doctors') are reissues of earlier publications rather than genuine novelties. Dunton's hyperbolic promises are coupled with relentless repetition of certain key words: 'Athenian', 'novelty', 'news', 'project', 'spy' and 'secret'. Dunton's rhetorical strategy in his later Athenian texts is a travesty of the successful formula that he had developed in *The Athenian Mercury*. Where *The Athenian Mercury* engages its readers' curiosity by treating diverse questions concerning a broad range of subjects, Dunton's later Athenian publications attempt to arouse public interest by making wild paratextual promises that remain unfulfilled. And instead of encouraging a sense of Athenian group identity by soliciting contributions from readers, Dunton expects his readers to recognize and respond in quasi-Pavlovian fashion to the key words that he repeats across his Athenian texts. Dunton's ideal Athenians are willing to subscribe to the concept of Athenianism – with its emphasis on curiosity and novelty and its characteristically hyperbolic rhetoric – without requiring any of the substance that its promises of revelation imply.

Yet the most peculiar aspect of Dunton's Athenian rhetoric is that it appears, in large part, to be ironic. Michael Mascuch observes that, 'reading through the variety of Dunton's imprints one gets the impression that a good deal of his discourse was produced with a wink and a nudge, as if it was part of some elaborate but half-baked swindle'.[45] The ostentation with which Dunton breaks his promises and repeats Athenian key words does indeed suggest that, rather than attempting to dupe his readers, he actually anticipates their indulgence of, or even complicity with, his bizarre rhetorical strategies. Dunton seems to expect that his readers will find the conventions of Athenianism amusing or endearing rather than disappointing, frustrating or deceitful. Moreover, he is determined that they should recognize Dunton himself as the origin of Athenianism. In his later Athenian tracts, Dunton frequently advertises his own name in the titles of his works (as in *Athenianism; or, The New Projects of Mr. John Dunton* (1710) and *Athenian News: or, Dunton's Oracle* (1710)) and repeatedly describes the Athenian project as 'entirely Mr. *Dunton's* Thought'.[46] Dunton's ambition was to create a group of readers who relish being Athenians to such an extent that they respond – by buying Dunton's texts – to the rhetoric of Athenianism without requiring any interesting content at all. Dunton thus reworks the way in which we might expect the rhetoric of revelation to function. A promise to reveal secrets might reasonably be interpreted as an attempt to encourage readers to feel that they belong to a privileged group of people who are 'in the know' as a result of their reading. Dunton's hyperbolic gestures of disclosure, on the other hand, represent an attempt to create a sense of group identity among readers predicated upon their recognition of and complicity with Dunton's ironic, Athenian gestures of disclosure.

Strange as this tactic may seem, recent research into the reception of fiction during the late seventeenth and early eighteenth centuries renders it more plausible than it might, at first, appear. In a study of deception in eighteenth-century literary and political culture, Kate Loveman reveals that the practice of telling tall tales was a vital aspect of shoring up bonds of sociability in early modern coffee-house culture. Participants in what Loveman terms 'lying games' made up bizarre and often improbable stories, while others questioned them about the particulars, hoping to force them into inconsistencies or self-contradictions. Respondents might also add their own appendices to the tall tales, furthering the jest. In this ludic culture, according to Loveman, 'people win status through perceiving and correctly interpreting the ironies of a story and through the sociable use they make of this understanding: the best way to further the pleasure of the group is not to announce that the tale is a fraud, but ostentatiously to feign credulity, ask quibbling questions and supply additional stories'.[47] Although Dunton's Athenian texts are not the same kind of invented, jesting stories that Loveman identifies as central to coffee-house culture during the early modern period, Dunton appears to have hoped that his 'revelations' about amatory intrigues, the motions of the universe, points of theological controversy and literary debates would elicit a response similar to the one that these oral narratives commonly attracted. In effect, Dunton's ironic Athenianism is a kind of lying game. Instead of calling his bluff, readers are expected to indulge or rally Dunton and create a strong sense of sociable group identity in the process. Just as *The Athenian Mercury* turned the oral business of asking and answering questions into a textual forum that retained vestiges of real sociability, so the Athenian spin-offs attempt to textualize central features of the oral culture out of which they emerge and in which they participate.

We can use the peculiar conventions of Dunton's ironic Athenianism to analyse the rhetorical strategies of Dunton's secret histories. In works like *The Court-Spy* and *The Hanover-Spy*, Dunton makes extravagant promises of secrets to come, only to provide his readers with a series of quotations from and allusions to secret histories of the 1690s surrounded by key words such as 'discovery', 'detection', and 'spy'. In these texts we also find Dunton emphasizing his own position as an author and, at least ostensibly, a revealer of secrets. It seems that Dunton expects readers to react to his secret histories in the same way as the Athenians respond to his Athenian publications. Rather than feeling privileged because the secrets contained in the text put them 'in the know', the ideal readers of Dunton's secret histories are delighted, rather than disappointed, by Dunton's distinctive combination of hyperbolic, revelatory rhetoric and repetitious key words. But while the sense of group identity that Dunton encourages in his Athenian productions has a purely commercial end, in Dunton's secret histories it is politically inflected. The ideal readers of Dunton's secret histories respond positively to his promises of revelation not because they are lovers of curiosity, but because they associate Dunton's gestures of disclosure with the Whig tradition of literary opposition to arbitrary government. In these texts, Dunton attempts to cultivate a group of loyal readers who value the political connotations of the claim to reveal secret intelligence more than the substance of that intelligence. His aims in doing so are, of course, financial as well as political. Since his readers associate the claim to reveal secrets with a tradition of Whig writing, so Dunton hopes they will respond by supporting this noble cause either by buying his texts or, in the case of Whig grandees, by offering him patronage or a pension. Dunton's ironic claims to reveal secrets are not designed to provide readers with intelligence, but rather to draw attention to Dunton's own credentials as a champion of Revolution principles.

The title page of *The Hanover-Spy* confidently declares this work to be Dunton's 'TENTH successful Attempt to detect the Enemies to King GEORGE, and his Illustrious House, at the Hazard of his Life and Fortunes'. Dunton cannot, however, have been measuring that success in financial terms. He spent much of the eighteenth century 'living incognito' – his flamboyant euphemism for hiding from creditors.[48] In spite of his enthusiasm for the genre, Dunton's secret histories seem not to have sold well.[49] They also failed to gain him political patronage in spite of his repeated supplications to prominent Whig dedicatees, including James Stanhope, James Craggs, and Joseph Addison. In a begging letter written to the Earl of Sunderland in June 1718, Dunton complains that that he had ventured his '*Neck for Nothing*' by publishing Jacobite secrets.[50] The negative response that Dunton received from both potential patrons and the public is hardly surprising given the total lack of secrets in his texts. Nonetheless, Dunton was not silenced by rejection. Indeed, the most interesting aspect of Dunton's career as a secret historian is the way in which he responded to his secret histories' failure to bring him any financial reward.

In his analysis of the reasons why his secret histories failed to sell, Dunton resolutely refuses to acknowledge that an absence of intelligence may have been responsible for the public's lack of interest in them. Rather, he ascribes his shortage of success to political factors. In *The Hanover-Spy*, Dunton writes not only a secret history of monarchical conspiracy against Protestantism and political liberty, but also 'The Secret History of *Whiggish Ingratitude*: or, The Case and Sufferings of Mr John Dunton'.[51] Here, he blames the Stanhope–Sunderland administration for their failure to respond appropriately to Dunton's revelatory gestures. Instead of rewarding Dunton as a courageous, outspoken zealot for the Protestant cause, they simply ignore him. In *The State-Weathercocks; or, A New Secret History of the Most Distinguished Favourites Both of the Late and Present Reign* (1719), Dunton once more promises to reveal '*the Secret Reasons,* why the Author of *Neck or Nothing*, has gone *Five Years* unrewarded, for his *Distinguisht Services* to his King and Country'.[52] Both *The Hanover-Spy* and *State Weathercocks* use secret history's characteristic rhetoric of disclosure to draw attention to Dunton's own personal, financial predicament. But Dunton also makes his private affairs an index of public corruption. Throughout his career as a secret historian, Dunton stressed the personal danger that he experienced as a result of his determination to expose Jacobite secets. A few years into the reign of George I, however, he asserts that his straightened circumstances are not the result of a Jacobite conspiracy against him or the forces of arbitrary government threatening to silence all outspoken Whigs, but rather the 'Pride, Avarice, and Ingratitude' of the 'pretended Whigs' of the Stanhope–Sunderland ministry.[53]

Since the vogue for secret history in England had begun after the Williamite Revolution of 1688–9, it ought also – according to Dunton's logic – to have flourished after the Hanoverian 'revolution' of 1714. The Court Whigs of early Hanoverian Britain, however, refused to act their parts in Dunton's analogical narrative of British political history. In 1716, under a Whig ministry led by Lord Townshend, Parliament repealed the Triennial Act of 1694 – previously a mainstay of Whig belief in the power of the people in Parliament – and passed in its place an Act of Parliament which ensured a seven-year electoral cycle.[54] Moreover, having been impeached and committed to the Tower in 1715, Robert Harley was not executed, '*Neck or Nothing*' fashion. Indeed, he was cleared of all charges against him in June 1717 – at the instigation of none other than Robert Walpole, who had chaired the Committee of Secrecy responsible for preparing the original case against Harley.[55] By the end of the second decade of the eighteenth century, the Hanoverian Whigs were apparently no longer committed to the Revolution principles that had fired Dunton since the 1690s. They had become, in words from the title of one of Dunton's secret histories, 'State Weathercocks', turning in the wind blowing from the Court. Ironically, it was the triumph of Whiggism, rather than of Jacobitism and the Pretender, that finally undermined Dunton's attempts to adapt the conventions of seventeenth-century secret history to the political situation of early Hanoverian Britain.[56]

Conclusion

Dunton's secret histories provide an important example of the ways in which the conventions of this tradition can be made to function in the absence of genuine secret intelligence. Unlike David Jones, who used the letters of a French spy as the basis of his secret histories, or John Somers, who had personal access to secrets of state through his position in the highest ranks of government, Dunton had no access to *arcana imperii*. The apparent obstacles to Dunton's participation in the secret history tradition only serve, however, to cast light upon his self-conscious engagement with the conventions of this form. Dunton's texts display many of secret history's most distinctive characteristics: they promise to reveal secrets; they associate the act of revelation with the fight against tyranny and arbitrary government; they even reflect self-consciously upon the use of a spy narrator and the ethical and epistemological difficulties that secret intelligence raises. But Dunton couples his extravagant promises to reveal previously unpublished intelligence with information that seems destined only to disappoint his readers. Instead of particular information about Jacobite plots, Dunton provides stereotypical portrayals of Jacobite activists and indecipherable, syncopated references to people and places. And in the place of promised revelations about threats to Protestantism and the Hanoverian dynasty, Dunton quotes from and alludes to secret histories from the 1690s – all the time protesting that his 'discoveries' about the corruption of the Stuart kings are genuine secrets, never before published. This rhetorical strategy may, at first, appear to be little more than profiteering. But the ostentatious way in which Dunton draws attention to the contrast between his revelatory gestures and the meagre quality of the information contained in his text suggests that he wanted readers to notice the mismatch between rhetoric and substance and regarded it as an important aspect of his their encounter with his texts.

Dunton was not alone among eighteenth-century secret historians in drawing attention to the absence of secrets in his secret histories. In *Arcana Gallica*, John Oldmixon asserts:

> I do not pretend in the following *History*, to publish the Secrets of Cabinets, and the *Arcana*'s of Council. It wou'd be a Ridiculous Impertinence to endeavour to impose these Facts on the *Reader* for *Novelties* never seen before. But this I may venture to affirm, he has never seen them in our own Language, and they are all taken from Books which never durst appear in *France*.[57]

Oldmixon uncovers information made 'secret' by the language in which it is recorded and the repressive censorship regime in France. By gathering and translating *arcana imperii* from proscribed French texts, he makes the rhetorical gesture of disclosure that characterizes secret history. In *The Secret History of Europe*, Oldmixon interrogates the concept of revelation once more when he acknowledges that the facts in his history 'are not pretended to be such Anectdotes, as are no where else to be met with', but rather 'separate Pieces, and some of very different Natures, which probably would never have fallen into the Hands of one Man'.[58] The *arcana* of this text can be found in other printed works but have never previously been brought together. In this secret history, Oldmixon acts the part of a compiler, rather than a discoverer, of secrets. Conscious that he does not have privileged access to secrets of state, Oldmixon adapts and reinterprets secret history's rhetoric of disclosure, continuing to support the work of revelation as part of the fight against arbitrary government.

Oldmixon's self-conscious response to the motif of revelation is a logical reworking of the secret history tradition. Aware of the ideological and historical connections between the discourse of revelation and the fight against arbitrary government, Oldmixon finds a way to 'discover' material for his readers even though he has no immediate and direct access to the inner workings of contemporary political life. By comparison, Dunton's approach towards secret history is much more counter-intuitive. Instead of acknowledging the absence of conventional intelligence in his text openly, he draws attention to it by means of hyperbolic gestures of revelation. His aim is not to persuade his readers by providing them with information about past and present threats to British political liberties, but to create for himself a persona based upon the revelation of secrets to which his ideal readers would respond by affirming his political vision and buying his texts. Dunton implies that, because his readers are united with him in their opposition to popery and arbitrary government, they are therefore prepared to indulge, or even enjoy, his wild revelatory gestures and vitriolic but unspecific attacks upon Jacobites, Robert Harley and the Pretender. Dunton thus appears to regard the absence of intelligence in his secret histories as an important aspect of his polemical strategy rather than a potential obstacle to the positive reception of his texts. This strategy having failed to gain him either the patronage for which he had hoped or any degree of commercial success, Dunton once more performs a counter-intuitive rhetorical move. Refusing to acknowledge that the failure of his texts might be the result of their lack of secrets, Dunton portrays his own dire financial situation as an indictment of contemporary political culture. In effect, he blames the ministerial Whigs under George I for failing to foster a political environment in which secret history might thrive. Dunton consistently relies more heavily on the concept and the rhetorical conventions of secret history than on the substance of his texts for polemical effect. As such, his career affirms the importance of adopting a rhetorical approach towards secret history's central gesture of disclosure.

SECTION 2
SECRET HISTORY IN THE EIGHTEENTH CENTURY: VARIATIONS AND ADAPTATIONS

Section 2 explores a series of eighteenth-century texts that fall outside the core tradition of anti-absolutist, Whig secret history but which engage closely with its rhetorical conventions. Spy narrators, sexual and political scandal, and a self-conscious approach towards the discourse of revelation – among other characteristics – act as points of connection between these texts and secret history. All of the texts under consideration in this section adapt the conventions of secret history in ways that are politically inflected, but the parties and causes that they support are often very different from the Whig origins of secret history. As its conventions are appropriated by writers of different partisan persuasions, secret history becomes a battleground in the party conflicts of early eighteenth-century Britain.

Chapters 4 and 5 address two very different sorts of text written during Queen Anne's reign: respectively, Delarivier Manley's scandalous *romans à clef*, *The New Atalantis* (1709) and *Memoirs of Europe* (1710), and Joseph Addison and Richard Steele's polite periodical, *The Spectator* (1711–14). Chapter 4 demonstrates the ways in which Manley reworks the conventions of Whig secret history to create a distinctively Tory version of this form. More particularly, it shows that Manley uses secret history to encourage a sense of party identity and cohesion among the disparate, factional Tories in the run up to the critical electoral year of 1710. Chapter 5 reveals that *The Spectator* appropriates and parodies many of the characteristic rhetorical devices of secret history as part of its attempt to reform the reading public according to a model of polite sociability. This chapter argues that, in spite of *The Spectator*'s persistent protestations of political neutrality, its engagement with secret history nonetheless carries partisan overtones: Addison and Steele use a backdrop of secret history to contrast the polite virtues of friendship and discretion, associated by them with the Junto Whigs, with the culture of secrecy and intelligence embodied by their political opponent, the Tory Lord Treasurer, Robert Harley.

Chapters 6 and 7 turn to consider texts published during the reign of George I by writers better known in modern scholarship for their contribution to the development of the novel. Chapter 6 begins by exploring Daniel Defoe's *Secret History of the White Staff* (1714–15). In this secret history, Defoe uses a traditionally anti-absolutist literary form to defend Robert Harley, who stood accused by the new Whig ministry of conspiring to bring about arbitrary government in Britain. Since Harley was a notoriously secretive minister who had already been the subject of Whig secret histories, Defoe's decision to use secret history in his defence was a bold and unorthodox polemical move. This chapter traces the distinctive approach towards the relationship between secrecy, narrative and power that Defoe develops in his *Secret History of the White Staff* through to his later novels, *Moll Flanders* (1722) and *Roxana* (1724). It argues that the generic shift from secret history to novel constitutes a political statement about the triumph of Whiggism during the decade after the Hanoverian accession. Chapter 7 focuses on Eliza Haywood's politically ambivalent *roman à clef*, *Memoirs of a Certain Island Adjacent to the Kingdom of Utopia* (1725–6). In spite of Haywood's known affiliation to opposition literary circles, *Memoirs of a Certain Island* appears to offer a panegyric upon the Prime Minister, Robert Walpole. However, this chapter argues that Haywood uses *Memoirs of a Certain Island* to launch a self-reflexive, satirical attack upon the secret history tradition. By doing so, she challenges and ultimately undermines her apparently hypocritical praise of Walpole and affirms her own position as an oppositional political writer.

In each of these variations and adaptations, secret history is used as a vehicle by which writers define their own political position against that of an implicit opponent. Delarivier Manley's *New Atalantis* and *Memoirs of Europe* and Daniel Defoe's *Secret History of the White Staff* appropriate the conventions of Whig secret history in order to garner support for Tory causes. (In Manley's case, her support for the Tories is unqualified; Defoe's secret histories are written in support of Harley, who had led a Tory ministry during Queen Anne's reign but who remained critical of the concept of party.) These writers seize Whig literary territory, leaving the contours of secret history visible but using this form to express ideas that would have horrified contemporary Whigs. The use of a Whig form to bolster a Tory cause is, therefore, rhetorically significant. Defoe and Manley turn secret history into a microcosm of the partisan struggles of the early eighteenth century. The literary conquest of Whig secret history depicts, metonymically, the political victory that Manley desired for the Tory party in 1710 and that Defoe hoped to achieve on behalf of his moderate Tory patron, Robert Harley, over the ministerial Whigs in 1715.

While Defoe and Manley appropriate the conventions of secret history, the contributors to *The Spectator* and Eliza Haywood actively reject them. These writers – very different from one another in almost all other respects – share a sense that secret history belongs to a political culture that is in urgent need of reform. In the last years of Queen Anne's reign, *The Spectator* associates secret history with a culture of intelligence epitomized by the Lord Treasurer, Robert Harley; during the early 1720s, Haywood connects it with the stagnant political culture engendered by Robert Walpole's ministry. Although their targets differ, both *The Spectator* and Haywood absorb the conventions of secret history in order to parody them. They portray secret history as the representative form of a debased culture of contemporary politics.

Whether they seek to appropriate secret history or to satirize it, the early eighteenth-century writers of Section 2 reveal important points of continuity between the core tradition of Whig secret history and later variations and adaptations of this form. Most crucially, secret history's self-conscious approach towards the act of revelation persists in all of the eighteenth-century texts under consideration. Indeed, the political aims of these texts become visible as their authors reflect upon secret history's claim to expose the secrets of those in power. The characteristic that sets Whig secret history apart from other late seventeenth-century forms of polemical writing ensured its continued evolution as it spread through other genres during the politically turbulent years of the early eighteenth century.

4 DELARIVIER MANLEY AND TORY USES OF SECRET HISTORY

Delarivier Manley's *Secret Manners and Memoirs of Several Persons of Quality, of Both Sexes. From the New Atalantis, an Island in the Mediterranean* (1709), more commonly known as *The New Atalantis*, is arguably the most notorious exposé of corruption in high places to be published during the early decades of the eighteenth century. The narrative opens with a meeting between two allegorical figures: Virtue and her daughter Astrea, the personification of justice who, according to classical mythology, lived on earth during the Golden Age but withdrew to the sky when the mortals around her grew wicked and corrupt. In *The New Atalantis* Astrea returns to earth 'to see if Humankind were still as defective, as when she in Disgust forsook it', and lands on 'an *Island*, named *Atalantis*, situated in the *Mediterranean Sea*' – a thinly disguised representation of Britain.[1] Accompanied by Virtue, Astrea resolves to 'go to the *Courts*, where *Justice* is profess'd, to view the Magistrate, who presumes to hold the Scales in my Name, to see how remote their profession is from their Practice; thence to the *Courts* and *Cabinets* of *Princes*, to mark their *Cabal* and *disingenuity*; to the *Assemblies* and *Alcoves* of the Young and Fair to discover their Disorders and the height of their Temptations'.[2] Astrea's intention to peer into the secret spaces (cabinets and alcoves) of powerful figures in order to reveal the discrepancy between public profession and private practice effectively promises readers a secret history of contemporary Britain.

The connections between *The New Atalantis* and earlier secret histories are affirmed by a third allegorical figure – Intelligence – who acts as a guide to Astrea and Virtue on their tour of the vices of Atalantis. As 'first Lady of the *Bedchamber* to the *Princess Fame*', Intelligence is Manley's reworking of the popular motif of the spy narrator who reveals secrets from inside a Court setting.[3] The proverbial unreliability of Fame and the fact that Intelligence 'is but rarely concerned' with truth gesture towards the epistemic difficulties raised by secret history.[4] And, as we will see, Manley uses her discoveries to re-plot familiar narratives of recent political history – again developing one of secret history's most distinctive features. Although *The New Atalantis* uses the phrase '*Secret* ...

Memoirs' on its title page rather than 'secret history', some contemporaries elided the two, referring to Manley's work as a 'Secret History of Secret Memoirs'.[5]

There are, however, significant differences between Manley's *New Atalantis* and earlier texts in the secret history tradition. Chief among these is the fact that Manley is a Tory. The targets of her revelations are, for the most part, prominent Whigs: ministers, including the Whig Junto; members of the royal household, most notably the Duchess of Marlborough; and a large cast of Whig MPs, judges, authors and prominent local activists. Like the earlier Tory polemic, *The Secret History of Queen Zarah and the Zarazians* (1705), Manley's *New Atalantis* argues that Queen Anne has been enslaved by a cabal of tyrannical Whigs. The idea of political slavery is common in Whig polemic, which frequently warns readers about the popery and slavery that the French seek to impose upon their free, Protestant neighbours. Manley's appropriation of this concept is, however, in keeping with the practice of other Tory propagandists during the middle years of Queen Anne's reign. In *A Letter to the Examiner* (1710), for instance, Henry St John condemns Britain's 'Subjection to the Will of an Arbitrary *Junto*', the 'Tyranny' exercised by the 1708–10 Whig ministry in general and the Duchess of Marlborough in particular, and the 'Slavery' into which Queen Anne was forced during this ministry.[6] Where Whig secret history militates against the slavery and tyranny threatened by Tories, Jacobites and France, Tory polemicists attempt to persuade their readers that the real threat to political liberty comes from the duplicitous and corrupt Whigs whose grip upon the Queen allows them to attain a form of arbitrary rule.[7]

Another important difference between *The New Atalantis* and earlier secret histories is, at first glance, less easy to spot. This difference is rhetorical, and it concerns the relationship that Manley constructs between the implied author and reader of her text. Whig secret historians present their readers as ignorant dupes of corrupt and mendacious public figures. The secret historian, in their view, is an agent of political enlightenment – exposing to public view the chicanery that those in power would rather keep concealed. Secret history is intended to put its readers in the know, to bring them into a secret from the excluded position that they previously occupied. Manley, on the other hand, reworks secret history's characteristic rhetoric of disclosure in order to cultivate an impression of shared understanding or even complicity between her implied author and reader. Over the course of this chapter, I explore the variety of ways in which Manley achieves this effect and analyse its political significance. I hope to demonstrate that Manley's adaptation of secret history's key conventions must be understood in the light of the Tory party's efforts to regain power during the years 1709 and 1710.

On Harley's resignation from the post of Secretary of State in 1708, the final vestiges of the Tory-dominated ministry of 1702 disappeared. The Tory party during the later part of Queen Anne's reign was an uneasy alliance of various factions, including Jacobites and High-flyers (the High Church wing of the Tories), Williamite or Hanoverian Tories who attempted to reconcile a belief in the central constitutional role of royal prerogative with the results of the Revolution of 1688–9, and those who – like Robert Harley – rejected the entire concept of party as divisive and destructive. By contrast, the Whigs had formed themselves into a relatively coherent party unit that, according to Geoffrey Holmes, possessed 'not only an unbroken unity of front but an underlying solidarity of purpose'.[8]

Manley registers her sense of the difference between the two parties in a discussion of literary patronage. In her autobiographical narrative, *The Adventures of Rivella; or, The History of the Author of the Atalantis* (1714), Manley's narrator condemns the Tories as 'a Party most Supine, and forgetful of such who served them' with no inherent sense of loyalty to others of their political stamp:

> The most severe Criticks upon *Tory* Writings were *Tories* themselves, who never considering the Design or honest Intention of the Author, would examin [sic] the Performance only, and that too with as much Severity as they would an Enemy's, and at the same Time value themselves upon their being impartial, tho' against their Friends: Then as to Gratitude or Generosity, the *Tories* did not come up to the *Whigs*, who never suffer'd any man to want Incouragement and Rewards if he were never so dull, vicious, or insignificant, provided he declar'd himself to be for them; whereas the *Tories* had no general Interest, and consequently no particular, each Person refusing to contribute towards the Benefit of the whole.[9]

Manley's attack on the ungrateful but impartial Tories treads a fine line between praise and blame. She approves of the Tories' integrity, even as she attacks their ingratitude. Whig patrons, on the other hand, paradoxically express most gratitude toward those writers who are characterized by the absence of that virtue. In *Memoirs of Europe, Towards the Close of the Eighth Century* (1710), Manley has Catiline (Thomas Wharton, a member of the Junto and prominent Whig patron), praise the writer Stelico (Richard Steele) to his fellow Whigs in terms which build on her portrayal of Steele in *The New Atalantis* as Monsieur L'Ingrate:

> They call him in Contempt, a Bread-Writer, a sorry half *Sesterce* Fellow; but his Pen is generally acceptable; he pleases those whom he stings; a commodious useful Hireling, stops at nothing, goes through thick and thin: He cants admirably, and pretends to Vertue, but is as ingrateful and unfair as one cou'd desire.[10]

At a personal level, Manley suggests that Steele's success reveals the corruption and hypocrisy of Whig patronage, while she figures herself as the victim of Tory ingratitude. But Manley's reflections on gratitude also function as a commentary upon the design of her own secret histories. While Whig secret history elicits its readers' anxiety and scepticism, Manley encourages a mode of reading based, if not on gratitude, then certainly on generosity. Moreover, Manley writes secret history that is, itself, generous towards a wide range of Tory opinion. In *The New Atalantis* and *Memoirs of Europe*, Manley reworks secret history's characteristic rhetoric of disclosure in an attempt to accommodate the political sympathies of both High Tories, many of whom retained a strong degree of sympathy or even loyalty towards the House of Stuart and the Pretender, and also Hanoverian Tories, who accepted the Revolution settlement and supported the Protestant succession. Manley thus appropriates a fundamentally Whig form of historiography in an effort to unite the Tory party and make it a force fit to challenge a Whig ministry sustained, as she saw it, by coherent internal organisation and a clear sense of the benefits of partisan propaganda.

Objections

In order to make the case for Manley as a Tory secret historian, I will need to overcome several recent scholarly arguments about secret history in general and Manley's writings in particular. The first of these arguments challenges the idea that there is, or can be, such a thing as Tory secret history. The second denies that Manley's satirical *romans à clef* are partisan, Tory polemic.

In *Early Modern Liberalism*, Annabel Patterson slights what she describes as 'Tory appropriations' of an essentially Whig literary tradition, arguing that while Tory writers may have borrowed the name 'secret history' for their polemics, they did not inherit the 'ethical rationale' of earlier secret histories: 'to outsmart the government in its control of information' as part of a campaign in support of 'the venerable liberal issue of freedom of speech and of the press'. Patterson, like Whig secret historians, seems to regard a predilection for arbitrary government (and therefore secrecy) as a central element of Tory ideology so that, by exposing the secrets of monarchs and governments, Tory secret history is inevitably divided against itself. In her analysis of early modern secret history, therefore, Patterson briefly mentions 'Tory repartee' to an essentially Whig form – a category that includes Manley's *romans à clef* – only in order to dismiss it from her enquiry.[11]

While Patterson queries the existence of Tory secret history in general, other critics challenge the idea that Manley's narratives, in particular, can be described as Tory polemic. Ros Ballaster, for instance, argues that, 'rather than engaging with and reworking contemporary ideological debates with politically charged meanings' like Aphra Behn, who gave party-political overtones to the issue of vow-breaking in her amatory fictions, 'Manley focuses on specific and personal satire in her "key" novels'.[12] Manley's *romans à clef* attack particular 'real world' people rather than abstracted qualities or ideas, unlike contemporary allegorical tales such as Jonathan Swift's *Tale of a Tub* (1704). Even John Arbuthnot's 'John Bull' pamphlets of 1712, which claim to have been 'publish'd ... by the author of the NEW ATALANTIS', mix personal satire upon ministers (especially the Earl of Godolphin and the Duke and Duchess of Marlborough) with general satire: John Bull represents England while his mother denotes the Anglican Church.[13] The personal satirical mode of *The New Atalantis* was noted and defended by Manley herself in the preface to the second volume of this work, where she asserts that 'our *Great Fore-Fathers* in *Satire*, ... not only flew against the *general* reigning Vices, but pointed at *individual* Persons, as may be seen in *Ennius, Varro, Lucian, Horace, Juvenal, Persius*, &c'.[14] The individuals whom Manley satirizes in her secret histories were, for the most part, prominent Whigs. But she also attacks some leading Tories, including Henry St John and the suspected Jacobite, John Sheffield, Duke of Buckingham. The variety of Manley's targets has led some commentators to suggest that she was more interested in making money by spreading scandal than in scoring political points, or that, in the words of her recent editors, she 'intended to offend as many different persons as possible, with only partial regard to partisan concerns'.[15]

One way of reconciling personal satire with Tory ideology is to suggest that, during the rage of party, personal satire becomes political in distinctively partisan ways. Mark Knights argues that Tory historiography of this period repeatedly personalizes history in order to '[stress] that ideology was merely a cover for selfish motives'.[16] Knights focuses on Ned Ward's *Secret History of the Calves-Head Club* (1703), a collection of republican drinking songs and anti-republican commentary.[17] In this work, Ward seeks to show that Whig invocations of religion and Revolution principles are nothing more than hypocritical covers for the political ambition of individual Whigs. According to Knights, Whig historians emphasize the role of divine providence or Revolution principles as the prime motives behind historical change, while Tory historians draw attention to ways in which the Whigs manipulate these ostensibly ideological concerns for personal gain. If Tory historiography presents individuals rather than ideology as the driving force behind history, then perhaps Manley's use of personal satire is characteristically partisan.

The importance of the 'personal', however, is also a prominent feature of Whig secret history during the later seventeenth century. Eve Tavor Bannet, in an essay on secret history collected in the same volume as Knights's analysis of Tory historiography, makes this point clearly. Bannet argues that Whig secret historians of the 1690s typically ascribe the motives behind historical change to the characters of monarchs (Charles's easiness, James's weakness) or the machinations of those who surround the monarch, especially self-interested mistresses and favourites. Bannet therefore argues that Whig secret historians use personal satire to highlight the corruption that ensues when men govern, rather than laws.[18] The importance of personal attacks upon monarchs and mistresses to the tradition of Whig secret history must qualify any easy association of the 'personal' aspects of historiography with Tory ideology. In order to make the case for Manley's *romans à clef* as a distinctively Tory form of secret history, it is clearly necessary to look at, but also beyond, her deployment of personal satire as a polemical form.

Old Stories

The claims that Manley makes about the intelligence that she offers in her secret histories are fundamentally different from those of Whig polemicists of the 1690s. The defining characteristic of Whig secret history is its claim to provide readers with new, previously undiscovered intelligence. In *The Adventures of Rivella*, however, Manley makes a very different assertion about the quality of the intelligence contained in her most famous secret history. Defending her decision to reflect on individuals by writing personal satire in *The New Atalantis*, Manley declares that she neither invented slanderous stories (as her enemies did about her), nor reflected upon those who were truly virtuous but, rather, that 'she did but take up old Stories that all the World had long since reported'.[19] In *Memoirs of Europe*, Manley has one of her principal narrators, the Count de St Gironne, articulate similar sentiments:

> Methinks 'tis hard, and I have often wonder'd at it, why that Man shou'd be thought uncharitable, a Satyrist, or Libeller, who but repeats with his Pen what every Body fearlessly reports with their Tongue: Is it because the Reproach is more indelible? ... I wou'd have every one tender even how they repeat any thing disadvantagious of another, 'till he were very well assur'd not only of the Truth, but that the Mat[t]er of Fact were no longer a Secret.[20]

St Gironne's observations form a commentary upon Manley's own secret history.[21] The intelligence contained in her narratives, she suggests, already circulates in the public sphere; it is 'secret' only insofar as it concerns illicit subjects, and not because it is unknown to the public. Through St Gironne and her autobiographical persona, Rivella, Manley asserts that her secret histories are textualized versions of oral gossip – that is, open secrets rather than genuinely undiscovered intelligence

There are, of course, legal reasons why Manley may have chosen to represent her scandalous narratives as nothing more than a collection of 'old stories'. Manley had been arrested on suspicion of having committed seditious libel following the publication of the second volume of *The New Atalantis* in 1709.[22] She therefore had good reason to play down the seditious potential of the information contained in her texts. But if we overemphasize Manley's legal motives for describing her tales as 'old stories', we risk ignoring what she may have been attempting to achieve, in rhetorical terms, by making such a claim. It is, of course, impossible to gauge exactly how much Manley's early readers would have known about the individuals she satirizes in *The New Atalantis* and, therefore, to assess the credibility of her claim to publish nothing but 'old stories'. Nonetheless, many of the allegations that Manley makes against public figures were commonplace political gossip during the first decade of the eighteenth century.[23] For instance, it was widely rumoured that Sarah Churchill, Duchess of Marlborough, had had illicit affairs with Sidney, Earl of Godolphin and Charles Talbot, Duke of Shrewsbury, and that Shrewsbury, who remained unmarried until he was well into his forties, was a womanizer.[24] Derision of Shrewsbury's Italian wife, Adelaide Paleotti, who was 'so *wonderful* as ... to fill the *Court* and *Kingdom* with *Admiration*, tho' I do not tell you of what sort was that *Admiration*', was widespread among both Whigs and Tories, as Manley's own phrasing suggests.[25] Other allegations – for instance, that the Duchess of Marlborough was attempting to wrest sovereignty away from the Queen, or that the Duke of Marlborough aspired to a royal title – were frequently rehearsed in Tory propaganda.[26] While it remains impossible to tell in a positive sense what the first readers of *The New Atalantis* would already have known about the public figures that the narrative portrays, it does seem that many of the stories that make up this narrative were precisely the kind of 'old stories' to which Rivella alludes.

The tales that Manley tells in *The New Atalantis* are not only 'old stories' in the sense of open secrets; they are also 'old stories' because of their historical setting. Although it was published in 1709, the action of *The New Atalantis* is ostensibly set just after the death of Prince Henriquez [William III, who died in 1702]. Indeed, many of the episodes in the first volume take place during the reign of Sigismund [Charles II] and the Prince of Tameran [James II]. Manley takes the name Tameran from *Hattigé, ou les Amours du Roy de Tamaran* (1676; English translation, 1680), a *roman à clef* which satirizes the affair between the Duchess of Cleveland, represented by Hattigé, and Charles II, depicted as the King of Tamaran. Such intertextual relationships intensify the sense of belatedness that surrounds Manley's tales, as Manley represents James II using an invented name strongly associated with his older brother, taken from a text that was published during Charles II's reign.[27]

The first lengthy episode in *The New Atalantis* roots the action of this narrative in past reigns, as it recounts the love affairs of Count Fortunatus [John Churchill, Duke of Marlborough] with the Duchess de l'Inconstant [Barbara Palmer, Countess of Castlemaine and Duchess of Cleveland] and Jeanitin [Sarah Jenyns, afterwards Sarah Churchill, Duchess of Marlborough].[28] John Churchill married Sarah Jenyns (or Jennings) in 1678. This story is not only set during the reigns of Charles II and James II, it also retreads ground that had been covered by an earlier Tory *roman à clef* – *The Secret History of Queen Zarah and the Zarazians* – only shifting the emphasis from the Duchess of Marlborough's political ambitions to the Duke of Marlborough's treachery. The action of this narrative skips forward to the Revolution of 1688–9, when Fortunatus's treachery in love (he jilts the Duchess in order to marry Jeanitin) is made analogous to his political treachery, as he abandons the Prince of Tameran to support Prince Henriquez.[29] Intelligence cuts off the story of Fortunatus with the accession of the new Princess [Anne], asking only, 'what may he not expect? What will he not perform?'.[30] While Tory readers may have been ready to supply a scathing answer based on their own views of Marlborough's ascendancy at Court during the reigns of William III and Anne, not to mention his management of the War of Spanish Succession, it is significant that Manley does not, at this point in *The New Atalantis*, give an account of Marlborough's more recent career as Captain General of the British forces. By breaking off this section of her narrative with the accession of Anne in 1702, Manley gives the impression that her secret history is not designed to provide its readers with up-to-date intelligence.

A sense of belatedness is sustained throughout the first volume of *The New Atalantis*. In the second lengthy episode in this volume – the story of the Duke and Charlot – Manley attacks Hans Willem Bentinck, first Earl of Portland, William III's favourite who died in 1709, the year in which *The New Atalantis* was published. Nor is the belatedness of *The New Atalantis* simply a result of those stories that concern monarchs and courtiers. Throughout the narrative, Manley alludes to infamous court cases which had been settled years earlier: the dispute over the inheritance of the second Duke of Albemarle, mentioned twice by Manley, was concluded in 1698;[31] Anne Gerrard, Countess of Macclesfield, mentioned three times in volume 2 of *The New Atalantis*, had been divorced by her husband, the second Earl of Macclesfield, in the House of Lords in 1698;[32] the trial of the barrister Spencer Cowper (brother of the Whig Lord Chancellor, William Cowper) for the murder of Sarah Stout, which is represented by Manley as the story of Mosco and Zara at the end of volume one of *The New Atalantis*, took place in 1699 and 1700.[33] Not all of the stories in *The New Atalantis* allude to events of former reigns: the account of the Prado [Hyde Park], for instance, contains cameos of aristocrats and party grandees who were in the public eye at the end of the first decade of the eighteenth century. Nonetheless, Manley relates so many well-known scandals of the late seventeenth century – particularly in the early part of her narrative – that she gives the whole work a strong historical flavour.

The familiarity of much of the scandalous content of *The New Atalantis* means that the relationship between the implied author and the implied reader of this text forms a commentary upon the relationship between the narrator, Intelligence, and her addressees, the goddess Astrea and her mother, Virtue.

Upon first meeting with Virtue and Astrea, Intelligence confides in them that, 'between Friends, the King of this Island is just dead; 'tis yet a mighty Secret, but I must make what haste I can to divulge it'.[34] The secrets of *The New Atalantis* are 'genuine' secrets to the *ingénues*, Astrea and Intelligence, but to the politically engaged reader they are open secrets, common gossip or just historical fact, not previously undiscovered intelligence.

Not only are Virtue and Astrea ignorant compared with Manley's readers, but they are also questionable judges of the intelligence that they receive. The story of the Duke and Charlot, one of the first episodes that Intelligence relates in *The New Atalantis*, provides a case in point.[35] The Duke falls in love with his young and virtuous ward, Charlot, and rapes her, after which they embark upon an illicit affair. Charlot confides in her friend the Countess, a young widow, who promptly steals the Duke's affections from Charlot and eventually marries him. The remainder of Charlot's life, according to Intelligence, becomes 'one continu'd Scene of Horror, Sorrow and Repentance'.[36] The 'moral' that Intelligence draws from this appalling tale is little more than a platitude: 'She dy'd a true Landmark: to warn all believing Virgins from shipwracking their Honour upon (that dangerous Coast of Rocks) the Vows and pretended Passion of Mankind'.[37] Astrea immediately takes up the theme, commending Intelligence's judgement and observing that the story has another moral: 'That no Woman ought to introduce another to the Man by whom she is belov'd; if that had not happen'd, the Duke had not possibly been false'.[38] In early editions of Manley's narrative, this moral and an extended commentary that follows it are highlighted by a series of inverted commas in the margin of the text – marks which seem to denote the sententiousness and gravity of Astrea's remarks (in a manner similar to the contemporary 'pointing hand' symbol). But Astrea's verdict is trite at best, pernicious at worst, and at the end of Astrea's speech, Manley has a disembodied narrative voice contemptuously observe that, 'having done moralizing upon that Story, they [Astrea and Virtue] follow'd the Lady *Intelligence* into the Palace'.[39] Instead of foreclosing the reader's interpretative faculties, Intelligence and Astrea's reductive judgements seem designed to provoke in the reader an alternative judgement.[40] Manley thus creates an impression of complicity between implied author and implied reader based on their shared scepticism of the heavily ironized narrators. Moreover, in satirizing Astrea and Virtue, Manley launches a subtle attack upon the Whig tradition of secret history. The disreputable but knowledgeable narrator, Intelligence, who reveals the secrets of the kingdom to her ignorant but ostensibly virtuous and authoritative companions reflect the dubious narrators and putatively moral readers of secret history. If three female figures who form the narrative frame of *The New Atalantis* are a kind of archetype of Whig secret history, Manley's satirical secret history both appropriates and attacks earlier texts in this tradition.

Roman à Clef

The New Atalantis is a *roman à clef* – a style of writing in which historical personages are represented under the guise of invented names. At least one contemporary commentator drew a distinction between *roman à clef* and secret history proper: the author of *The Blatant Beast Muzzl'd* highlights the difference between 'The *Arcadia* and *Argenis*' – that is, Sir Philip Sidney's *Arcadia* (1580, published 1590) and Sir John Barclay's *Argenis* (1621) – which, 'by the help of a *Clavis*, may have much Truth cover'd under those Poetical Veils' and *The Secret History of the Reigns of K. Charles II and K. James II*, which 'profess[es] to contain nothing but *Real Verities*'.[41] In fact, several self-styled secret histories did represent contemporary politics under the veil of the romance-style settings and names that are typical of *roman à clef*. *The Secret History of the Duchess of Portsmouth* (1690), which depicts Louise de Kéroualle, Duchess of Portsmouth, as 'Francelia' and Charles II as 'the Prince of the Isles', and *The Secret History of Arlus and Odolphus* (1710) – that is, the secret history of Harley and Godolphin – are just two examples of the use of *roman à clef* as a vehicle for the revelation of political secrets. Disguised names add an element of piquant concealment to texts whose purpose is to reveal secrets.

Manley's *New Atalantis* superficially resembles these secret histories that conceal in order to reveal, but it differs from them in two significant respects. First, the historical personages whom Manley conceals under invented names are much better hidden than in most contemporary secret histories: readers really do have to work (or acquire a published key) in order to deduce the referents of her stories, who are much more diverse and numerous than those found in other *roman à clef* style secret histories. Second, Manley is highly self-conscious about the complex rhetorical relationship that *roman à clef* helps to construct between the implied author and reader of her narrative.

Several contemporaries of Manley, as well as more recent readers of early eighteenth-century literature, offer analyses of the nature and function of *roman à clef*. Jonathan Swift notes in *The Importance of the Guardian Considered* (1713) that, 'we have several Ways here of abusing one another, without incurring the Danger of the Law':

> First, we are careful never to print a Man's Name out at length; but as I do that of Mr. St—*le*: So that although every Body alive knows whom I mean, the Plaintiff can have no Redress in any Court of Justice. Secondly, by putting Cases; Thirdly, by Insinuations; Fourthly, by celebrating the Actions of others, who acted directly contrary to the Persons we would reflect on; Fifthly, by Nicknames, either commonly known or stamp'd for the purpose, which every body can tell how to apply.[42]

Swift clearly regards the romance-style names – or 'nicknames' – of *roman à clef* as little more than a convenient way of evading actions for libel.[43] But the idea that Manley coins invented names simply in order to avoid arrest has been effectively challenged in recent literary criticism. Catherine Gallagher argues that Manley's allegorical references to contemporary figures are 'so transparent that one can hardly call them disguises of political purpose at all. Rather ... they *indicate*, although in a supposedly arbitrary way, illicit political intentions'.[44] According to Gallagher, Manley uses invented names not to stave off charges of libel, but rather to draw attention to herself as both a politically dangerous woman and a 'flamboyantly scandalmongering hack'.[45]

Other contemporary commentators focus on the effect that *roman à clef* has on its readers, rather than on the intentions of its author. In the preface to the French translation of *The Secret History of the Duchess of Portsmouth*, the translator of this work outlines the functions and the effects of invented names:

> The use of false names, in my view, makes this story more appealing. One does not always want to see things wholly disclosed. This is especially true of works of wit, which give greater pleasure when some mystery remains, things are only fleetingly glimpsed, and the authors imply more than they say. This no doubt makes their works more delicate and agreeable. The reader sometimes enjoys seeking and divining and it is no small pleasure to him if, while not hiding things so well that they are genuinely difficult to find, one seems only partly to conceal them, so that the reader has the satisfaction of discovering them by the exercise of his own wit.[46]

The translator of the *Secret History of the Duchess of Portsmouth* attributes the pleasure of reading *roman à clef* to the fact that it offers its readers an intellectual challenge as it asks them to crack a code.

Neither Gallagher nor the translator of *The Secret History of the Duchess of Portsmouth*, however, suggests that invented names provide a way of cementing a relationship *between* the implied author and the implied reader of a *roman à clef*.[47] By drawing attention to her own status as a purveyor of scandal in the way that Gallagher suggests, and by making her readers work to interpret the identities of the individuals represented in her *roman à clef*, Manley encourages her readers to become complicit in the scandalous revelations made by the 'author of the Atalantis'.[48] Manley's use of *roman à clef* has a similar effect to her retelling of old stories. Scandalous *roman à clef* requires that readers be already 'in the secret' of a character's real identity in order that they can discover the secrets about them that are contained in a story. If those stories are already well known, the overall effect is of the author signalling to her readers their shared understanding, rather than giving them a series of genuinely shocking revelations.

But what if Manley's readers did not understand whom she intended to signify by the romantically-named characters of her narrative? It is easy enough to identify Sigismund as Charles II, Jeanitin as Sarah Jenyns and Stelico as Steele from the familiarity of their stories or the resemblance of their real names to their romance names – and if any readers were in doubt they could easily check their identifications against printed keys.[49] But what of the characters who were not named in keys, such as the lawyer's clerk 'Alexis', whom Ros Ballaster identifies as one Henry Pierce, a friend to the husband of the poet, Sarah Fyge Egerton, or characters such as 'Berintha', named in the keys as Lady Erney or Ernle but otherwise obscure – presumably in her own time as well as today?[50] Faced with potential difficulties such as these, a rhetorical approach towards the idea of revelation becomes particularly important. I suggest that Manley creates an impression of shared understanding or complicity through her use of *roman à clef* regardless of whether or not readers actually managed to apply the romance names of her narrative correctly. In order to illustrate this idea, it is helpful to turn to turn briefly to a contemporary work which also uses a combination of obscurity and revelation to forge a sense of intimacy between author and reader: Jonathan Swift's *Journal to Stella*.

The text that has become known as *The Journal to Stella* is a collection of letters that Swift wrote daily to two friends, Esther Johnson and Rebecca Dingley, who remained in Dublin while Swift lived in London between 1711 and 1713. In these letters, Swift often drops political 'hints' to his correspondents. These 'hints' appear to reveal secrets, although Swift's mode of expression is extremely obscure:

> I dined with Stratford at lord Mountjoy's, and I'll tell you no more at present, guess for why; because I am going to mind things, and mighty affairs ... that you shall know one day, when the ducks have eaten up all the dirt.[51]
>
> I was early this morning with Mr. secretary St. John about some business ... I was forwarding an impeachment against a certain great person.[52]
>
> I dined with Ld Treasr [Robert Harley] at 5 a Clock to day, & was by while He & L—d Bol— was at Business; for it is fit I should know all that passes new because – &c.[53]
>
> I dined with Ld Tr and thô the Business I had with him is something agst Thursday when the Parlmt is to meet, & this is Tuesday yet he put it off till to morrow, I dare not till you what it is, lest this Lettr should miscarry or be opend.[54]

The circumspection with which Swift writes to his Dublin friends is often attributed to his suspicion of the post office; in the introduction to his edition of the *Journal to Stella*, Harold Williams observes that, 'justifiably apprehensive that his letters to the ladies in Dublin might be opened [Swift] was led, on occasion, to convey his meaning by distant hints'.[55] Others have noted that, in spite of his hugger-mugger style of expression, Swift rarely imparts any 'genuine' political intelligence to Johnson and Dingley.[56] In these accounts, Swift's circumlocution is regarded in purely practical, rather than rhetorical, terms.

There are, however, other ways in which we might interpret Swift's attempts to create an impression of disclosure or revelation even without passing on any real secret intelligence. In part, his political hints are part of his characteristic self-aggrandizement; he uses them to tease and to assert his own importance to his correspondents. But they also create an impression of intimacy between distant parties: even when his hints are almost indecipherable, Swift often writes as though these two women, far away from the political world of London, understand what he is talking about and share his political knowledge – although often this is clearly not the case.[57] Indeed, Swift repeatedly suggests in the *Journal* that obscurity is intimate while clarity is impersonal.[58] Commenting on his cramped, ill-formed handwriting, Swift writes, 'methinks when I write plain, I do not know how, but we are not alone, all the world can see us. A bad scrawl is so snug, it looks like a PMD'.[59] PMD is Swift's code for himself and his two correspondents and, with its multiple referents compacted into just three initials, it too looks 'snug'. In fact, many of the code words which make up Swift's little language are 'snug'-sounding because they are vowel-less and difficult to pronounce. The consonontal clusters 'Pdfr' (which denotes Swift) and 'Ppt' (Esther Johnson) seem to belong more to the silent page than to the oral domain – particularly when compared to the open, Italianate sounds of 'Presto' and 'Stella', which Swift's early editor, Deane Swift, substituted as alternatives. Perhaps when he gives his political 'hints' to Johnson and Dingley, Swift is trying to give the impression of cramped, indecipherable intimacy that characterizes his textual relationship with them.

There are, of course, profound differences between the *Journal to Stella* and Manley's secret histories. Swift may have intended, eventually, to use his letters as the basis for a history of England under Queen Anne, but the letters themselves are, first and foremost, private documents.[60] Manley's *romans à clef*, on the other hand, are scandalous texts which circulated on the open marketplace. Nonetheless, these texts were composed in a similar political climate by writers who were acquainted with one another and who worked for the same party.[61] Moreover, both Swift and Manley use the rhetoric of political secrecy to cultivate the impression of an intimate relationship between author and reader, and each of them does so in order to overcome considerable distances between these two parties: the geographical distance between London and Dublin, in the case of the *Journal to Stella*, and the figurative distance created by the medium of print in the case of Manley. Whether or not Manley's first readers knew the identities of the historical figures to whom she was referring, her use of invented names creates, in itself, the appearance of shared understanding. Manley may have deployed *roman à clef* to draw attention to her persona as a scandalmonger, as Catherine Gallagher argues, and her invented names may have been designed to engage her readers' intellect, as contemporary commentators suggest. But Manley's use of *roman à clef* also fosters a sense of complicity between the secret historian and her readers. Whereas Whig secret historians emphasize the gap that exists between the ignorant reader and the knowledgeable secret historian, and use this gap to induce anxiety in their readers, Manley's manipulation of the tradition of *roman à clef*, like Swift's political hints, bespeak a peculiar form of rhetorical intimacy.

Rewriting History

Through her use of *roman à clef*, Manley reworks secret history's distinctive motif of revelation. But in *The New Atalantis* Manley also appropriates and adapts another of secret history's key characteristics: its claim to rewrite received narratives of the recent political past. In the history of Utopia – a lengthy section of volume 2 of *The New Atalantis* – Manley re-plots the events of recent British history. Her method and purpose in doing so are, however, quite different from those of her Whig predecessors. Whig secret historians implicitly or explicitly claim that their discoveries of secret intrigues in high places revise and undermine official accounts of recent political history. They self-consciously highlight the role that historians and historical narratives play in supporting or challenging corrupt regimes. In the history of Utopia, on the other hand, Manley ostentatiously fictionalizes recent British history, thus increasing the hermeneutic demands of her text. Not only are Manley's readers obliged to penetrate the romance guises through which Manley portrays historical figures, but they also have to work out the political significance of Manley's reconfiguration of the past.

Utopia, according to *The New Atalantis*, is an island in the Adriatic – far removed from Atalantis itself, which is putatively located in the Mediterranean. The geographical relationship between the islands Utopia and Atalantis metaphorically represents the tangential relationship between the histories of Utopia and Britain.[62] The history of this island is a fictionalized but recognizable version of recent British political history. In Utopia, the regal line of descent passes along the female, rather than the male line. The history of Utopia begins with the story of Princess Ormia, ruler of Utopia, who attempts to undermine the country's constitution by making her young son heir to the throne ahead of her two older daughters, the Duchess of Venice and the Lady Olympia. This is, of course, a representation of the political crisis caused by the birth of a son to James II and Mary of Modena in 1688, which demoted the Protestant Princesses Mary (Duchess of Venice) and Anne (Olympia) in the order of succession. By making gender, rather than religion or questions of sovereignty, the crux of the constitutional crisis, Manley allows her readers to amuse themselves at the spectacle of James II in petticoats while also highlighting the importance of gender politics within contemporary high politics.[63]

But the gender of her protagonist is not all that Manley changes in the history of Utopia. The Duke of Venice [William III] invades Utopia in order to defend his wife's right to the throne. Princess Ormia is forced to flee, and both she and her infant son perish at sea while she makes pathetic and contrite lamentations for her arbitrary ambitions and thirst for power. The fact that Manley depicts James II in the form of a woman allows her to key into traditional notions of feminine vulnerability in order to elicit sympathy for Ormia, even as she acknowledges her political failings. And if the Duke of Venice appears to be fighting in a just cause when he removes Ormia from the throne, he is recast as a villain when the Duchess of Venice [Princess Mary] usurps the throne of her older sister, Olympia [Princess Anne]. Manley makes Anne's character older than Mary's, thus reversing the real order of succession. In doing so, she probes the theme of usurpation without suggesting directly that William and Mary usurped the throne of Mary's father, James II. Moreover, she allows poetic justice to prevail by meshing historical fact with her fictional story: the Duchess of Venice dies an untimely death and, because Utopia does not allow men to rule alone, the throne is returned to its rightful occupant, Olympia. After Mary died in 1694, of course, William reigned alone until his death in 1702. By presenting a fictional version of British political history in the history of Utopia, Manley is able to celebrate the reign of Queen Anne while also acknowledging, albeit indirectly, the painful internecine conflict that brought her to the throne.

Once Olympia is on the Utopian throne, Manley's focus shifts away from dynastic struggles and towards party politics. Hope at the installation of a rightful monarch soon gives way to dismay as Olympia becomes completely subject to her corrupt favourites and courtiers, including Madam de Caria [Sarah Churchill, Duchess of Marlborough] and her lover, Count Biron [the Earl of Godolphin]. Olympia is gradually undeceived by Don Geronimo [Robert Harley] and the virtuous Hillaria, who represents Abigail Masham, a cousin of both Robert Harley and the Duchess of Marlborough who supported the Tory cause and increasingly came to replace her cousin, the Duchess, in Queen Anne's affections and confidence.[64] Just as she realizes her mistake in trusting Madam de Caria and Count Biron, Olympia dies in childbirth, leaving a daughter to the care of her husband [George of Denmark], Don Geronimo and Hillaria. At this point in the story, Manley leaves historical fact behind her and enters the realm of Tory fantasy. She removes inconvenient historical facts – such as the death of George of Denmark in 1708, the year before *The New Atalantis* was published – from her account of Utopian history and writes with apparent prescience about events that had not yet happened, including the Tory return to power in 1710 and the death of the Queen.[65]

The overtly fictional version of British history that Manley composes in her history of Utopia appears, to some extent, to be a form of self-defence. While the first volume of *The New Atalantis* is characterized by a sense of belatedness, in the history of Utopia, Manley reflects upon contentious constitutional issues that were current during the reign of Queen Anne. If challenged, Manley could presumably claim that her satire was no reflection upon the Queen or her ministers because the histories of Utopia and Britain are different from one another in significant points.

But, once again, if we focus too closely upon the possible legal reasons behind Manley's fictionalization of British history, we risk missing its rhetorical force. Manley uses the history of Utopia to appeal to and accommodate a wide range of Tory opinion on British constitutional affairs. A central element of Manley's strategy is her representation of the death of Olympia. In one respect, Olympia's death allows Manley to comment upon the failing fortunes of the Tory party in 1709. Ros Ballaster suggests that 'Anne's capitulation to Marlborough and Godolphin [in 1708] must have seemed like a symbolic death, that left the queen a child in the hands of Whig interests'.[66] But the death of Olympia also allows Manley to reflect in more subtle ways upon the state of contemporary British politics. After Olympia's death, Count Biron [Godolphin] moves from Utopia to Atalantis where he becomes a favourite of Prince Henriquez [William III]. As the action of her narrative moves from one island to another, Manley's chronological account of British history is disrupted. Manley's narrator, Intelligence, concludes her account of Biron [Godolphin] by reminding her readers that Henriquez [William III] has recently died, and observing that, 'whether he [that is, Biron] will have the like Success with the new *Empress* is yet a *quære*?'.[67] But this new Empress also represents Anne, only in another allegorical guise. The reader appears to be moving in circles as the narrative has already related Godolphin's 'success' with Queen Anne, represented as Olympia, via the history of Utopia. Manley suggests that Utopia's past and Atalantis's future is Britain's present. Her reader experiences a sense of *déja vu*, of history repeating itself without any sense of progress or improvement. Ongoing corruption leads not just to a sense of stagnation but of decline and decay – motifs which Mark Knights identifies as characteristic of Tory historiography of this period.[68]

If Manley's account of the death of Olympia reflects Tory pessimism during the dark days of 1709, however, then it also makes room for more optimistic predictions about the future. Although Olympia dies, she leaves behind a child in the capable (Tory) hands of Don Geronimo [Robert Harley] and Hillaria [Abigail Masham]. Manley's account of the death of Olympia [Queen Anne] and the accession of a new monarch in Utopia is, from one point of view, a harmless Tory fantasy – an attempt to compensate in the fictional realm for what was, from a Tory perspective, the desperate political reality of 1709. But Olympia's death in this episode is more than simply symbolic. Given Anne's failing health, her imminent demise was a near certainty. Since Anne had no direct heir (her son, the Duke of Gloucester, having died in 1700) it had been decreed by the Act of Settlement of 1701 that the British crown would descend to the Protestant

Hanoverians, rather than the Catholic Stuarts, after her death. But as Anne's reign progressed, speculation about the possibility of a Jacobite uprising and the return of the Pretender intensified.[69] In this political climate, Manley's decision to kill off Olympia and place the crown of Utopia on the head of her newborn child is extremely significant, since this child – unlike all of the other characters in the history of Utopia – has no clear historical referent. Manley thus gives her readers an opportunity to inscribe upon her narrative their own interpretation of Britain's future: Olympia's baby could represent either the House of Hanover or, alternatively, the House of Stuart.

Manley's representation of the flight of Princess Ormia [James II] may hint that she guides her readers more towards a pro-Stuart than a pro-Hanoverian reading of this narrative. The sentimental portrayal of the death of Princess Ormia suggests a degree of sympathy with, if not loyalty towards, the exiled king.[70] Manley represents the Duke and Duchess of Venice [William and Mary] as usurpers, rather than occupiers of a vacant throne, albeit that the rightful monarch in this narrative is Olympia [Anne], not Ormia [James II].[71] Whether or not Manley's narrative contains a Jacobite inflection is, however, less important than the fact that it accommodates both Hanoverian and Jacobite readings. At a time when the Tory party was becoming increasingly divided against itself, Manley wrote a secret history capable of appealing to and comprehending a broad spectrum of Tory opinion.

In the rewritten political history of Britain that Manley creates in the story of Utopia, we see an important development of the two features of Manley's reworking of secret history's conventions that have already been addressed in this chapter: her use of old stories and of *roman à clef*. In all three aspects of *The New Atalantis*, Manley combines the rhetoric of disclosure with a strong sense of the familiar. She teases her readers by concealing historical figures behind romance names and by reconfiguring the events of recent political history, but these devices also create a sense of shared understanding and complicity between the implied author and implied reader of her text. In the history of Utopia, Manley takes this rhetorical strategy a step further. By leaving the identity of Olympia's baby unexplained, Manley allows her readers to choose what kind of secret she is revealing. The fact that her secret history conceals at the same time as it discloses gives it the potential to act as a cohesive force, uniting the disparate factions of the Tory party. In *Memoirs of Europe*, published the year after *The New Atalantis*, Manley builds on this method, producing an extraordinarily sophisticated piece of Tory propaganda out of rhetorical techniques taken from Whig secret history.

Memoirs of Europe (1710)

Like *The New Atalantis*, *Memoirs of Europe* is a *roman à clef* which combines tales of amorous intrigue with partisan propaganda designed to attack prominent Whigs and Whig ideology. Contemporaries often regarded the two volumes of *Memoirs of Europe* as the third and fourth volume of *The New Atalantis*.[72] There are, however, significant differences between *Memoirs of Europe* and its predecessor, particularly in terms of the narrative structure of each work. The episodic structure of *The New Atalantis* reflects the perambulations of its itinerant, allegorical narrators around the island of Atalantis. Each episode is discrete and Manley gives the historical figures who appear more than once in her narrative a different invented name each time they appear.[73] The narrators of *Memoirs of Europe*, on the other hand, are a group of diplomats and nobles who sit together and recount stories that form the vehicle for Manley's *roman à clef*. These narrators revisit particular subjects of interest in their conversations as the narrative progresses, giving *Memoirs of Europe* a structure much more akin to the 'interlace' structure of both English chivalric and French heroic romances than the episodic narrative structure of *The New Atalantis*. Chief among the subjects discussed by the narrators of *Memoirs of Europe* are the political and sexual intrigues of the Court of Constantinople, which represents the Stuart Court. Earlier polemicists had used the connections between Constantinople and Ottoman absolutism to satirize the Stuarts' attempts to attain arbitrary rule,[74] Manley, however, alludes to a period before Constantinople's fall to the Ottomans, which took place in 1453. By engaging closely with the history of Christian Byzantium during the late eighth century, Manley attacks Whig 'tyranny' in early eighteenth-century Britain.

The history of Constantinople in *Memoirs of Europe* begins with the reign of Constantine Copronymus, who represents James II. Entranced by the beauty of a young woman called Irene – identified in the keys as Sarah Churchill, Duchess of Marlborough – Constantine marries her to his son, Leo Augustus [William III]. Irene and Leo have a son, called Constantine Porphyrogenetus [Queen Anne]. Irene so completely dominates her son that, after Leo's death, she effectively becomes the ruler of Constantinople. She then marries the successful but corrupt General Stauratius (also spelled Stauracius) [John Churchill, Duke of Marlborough]. Irene commits a fatal error, however, when she forces her son, Constantine, to marry Theodecta [Abigail Masham]. Just as Sarah Churchill introduced her cousin, Abigail Masham, to Queen Anne, only to find Masham supplanting her in Anne's affections, so Theodecta opens Constantine's eyes to the perfidious influence of his mother, Irene. In many respects, then, the history of Constantinople bears a striking resemblance to the history of Utopia that Manley relates in volume 2 of *The New Atalantis*. The aim of both stories is to attack the ambition of Whig grandees and the ascendancy that they had gained over the Queen and to celebrate the incipient return of the Tories to power. Manley's method in both narratives is to rewrite history, radically altering the relationships between the major figures of English high politics over the previous three decades as well as the genders of key players such as James II and Queen Anne.

The ways in which Manley reconfigures history in *Memoirs of Europe* are, of course, politically significant. By making William III into the son of James II, Manley writes the Revolution of 1688–9 out of history altogether, refusing to address this most divisive of political issues. By turning the Duchess of Marlborough into the wife of William III and mother of Queen Anne, Manley satirizes Sarah Churchill's ambition. At a more ideological level, Manley may also be attacking the devolution of royal power that took place with the Revolution settlement by representing a series of marriage alliances between those characters who depict royalty (such as William III and Anne) and those who represent commoners (such as Sarah Churchill, Duchess of Marlborough, and Abigail Masham). Finally, by making Anne into a weak, male monarch, Manley uses a reversal in gender to highlight the political chaos that ensues when a subject comes to rule over her monarch.

There is, however, an important difference between the way in which Manley rewrites history in the Utopia section of *The New Atalantis* and in *Memoirs of Europe* – a difference that casts light upon Manley's approach towards secret history. In her history of Utopia, Manley invents the romance narrative that turned James II into a woman called Ormia who drowned at sea with her baby, that made Anne the older sister of Mary, and that forced William III from the throne after the death of his wife. In *Memoirs of Europe*, however, the narrative that forms the vehicle for Manley's *roman à clef* – the history of Constantinople – is drawn from a pre-existing printed source: the fourth volume of *The Roman History* (1704) – an anonymous continuation of the two-part *Roman History* published by Laurence Echard in 1695 and 1698.[75] No previous research into *Memoirs of Europe* – probably the least studied of all Manley's *romans à clef* – has noted the extensive debt that it owes to *The Roman History*.[76] By exploring in some detail the relationship between these two texts, we can see Manley building on the ways in which she had manipulated secret history's conventions in *The New Atalantis* to create a *roman à clef* that celebrated increasing Tory success during the year 1710 and sought to make the Tory party into a coherent, united political force.

The title page of *Memoirs of Europe* claims that this text is a translation of a medieval narrative written by 'Eginardus, Secretary and Favourite to Charlemagne'.[77] But Manley alerts her readers to the genuine source for much of her narrative when she notes, in the preface, that '*Mr. Echard's* Continuators, speak of easie *Constantine*'s Reign, much to the same purpose as *Eginardus*'.[78] In its broad historical outlines, Manley's account of the Court of Constantinople rarely deviates from its source, yet the disingenuousness of Manley's claim that *The Roman History* is 'much to the same purpose' as *Memoirs of Europe* quickly becomes clear. Manley supplements and changes aspects of *The Roman History* to make her account more salacious than that found in her source. *Memoirs of Europe* thus reads like a secret history of the public version of events that we find in *The Roman History*.[79]

The most significant of the changes that Manley makes to her source concerns the conjugal relationships of the Emperor Constantine Porphyrogenetus [Queen Anne]. *The Roman History* relates that the Empress Irene forced her son, Constantine, to divorce his first wife, the Empress Mary, in order to marry Theodecta, so as to cause divisions among the clergy.[80] Manley, however, makes Constantine's second marriage bigamous.[81] The bigamous marriage is a leitmotif that runs throughout Manley's oeuvre. It has biographical resonance for Manley, who claimed to have been an unwitting party in a bigamous marriage to her cousin, John Manley.[82] By adapting *The Roman History* in this way Manley is, as it were, setting her personal stamp on this story. But Manley's decision to turn a passing reference to a royal divorce into a story about bigamy also signals the second principal difference between *The Roman History* and Manley's *Memoirs of Europe*. Manley's account of Constantine's second marriage – like all of her borrowings from Echard's continuator – is designed to reflect upon contemporary British politics.

Manley's account of the bigamous marriage of the Emperor Constantine is a thinly veiled attack both on particular Whig grandees and on Whig ideology more generally. The Patriarch Tarasius [Gilbert Burnet, Bishop of Salisbury], who is in league with the Empress Irene [Sarah Churchill, Duchess of Marlborough], defends the practice of bigamy in terms that recall arguments used to justify the Revolution of 1688–9. In 1688, supporters of William of Orange had argued that, although obedience to the monarch was a fundamental, constitutional duty, in certain cases of great necessity – as when arbitrary government was threatened – resistance was justified.[83] Tarasius adapts this idea, insisting 'that tho' second Marriages (the first Wife still alive) were in themselves expressly forbidden, and unlawful; yet in Cases of great Necessity, such as the utter Extinction of the Race of *Leo Iscaurius* [James I] for want of Heirs (which *Caesar* could not have from [his first wife] *Mary* the *Armenian*, whose Constitution was destroy'd by Diseases) they might be dispens'd with; or rather Dispensations were lawful, as Inclination and Necessity suggested'.[84] The priest Tarasius thus describes the law against bigamy as 'a Law, and no Law, binding, or not binding, sometimes to be kept, sometimes to be broken, as Conscience or Desire would prompt'.[85] Tarasius's attitude towards the law represents an indictment of Whig ideology. In the aftermath of the Revolution, prominent Whig polemicists had attempted to undermine Jacobite claims to be the 'loyal' party by insisting that true loyalty consists of obedience to the law rather than fidelity to the person of the monarch.[86] By revealing the Whigs' hypocritical attitude towards the law that they pretend to revere, Manley sets about destroying their claims to be the 'legal' party.

But Manley does more, here, than simply engage in a debate over Whig justifications of the Revolution of 1688–9, or, indeed, a debate over disputed terms such as 'loyal' or 'legal'. In Tarasius's speech, Manley adapts Whig resistance theory to reflect upon constitutional anxieties that were current during the reign of Queen Anne. While, at the Revolution, Whigs argued that the prospect of arbitrary government created a 'case of great necessity', in *Memoirs of Europe*, Tarasius claims that the absence of a legitimate heir has the same effect. Although Mary of Armenia (as wife of Constantine) apparently represents Prince George of Denmark, the fact that Mary was childless with a 'Constitution was destroy'd by Diseases' connects her more closely with Anne who had lost many children through miscarriage and early death and who, by 1710, was obese and suffering from gout.[87] Manley's satire is not, however, simply a personal attack on Queen Anne. Problems of succession plagued the Stuart monarchs, from Charles II, who died without legitimate issue, to James II, whose son was popularly regarded as suppositious, to Mary and Anne, who died childless. In this passage, Tarasius conflates Anne's reign with political arguments that were current during the early 1680s, when a divorce between Charles II and his childless wife, Catherine of Braganza, seemed to some a more palatable option than the accession to the throne of Charles II's Catholic brother, James Duke of York.[88] While Charles II managed to resist calls for a divorce, however, Constantine succumbs to Tarasius's sophistic arguments. There is a sense here that, by limiting the royal prerogative in 1688, the devious Whigs created a constitutional weakness which they were able to exploit during Anne's reign. Manley puns on the word 'constitution' to imply that both Anne's body natural (in the figure of Mary of Armenia) and her position within the body politic (in the figure of Constantine) leave Britain vulnerable to Whig corruption. Moreover, by conflating constitutional arguments from across the later Stuart period, Manley once again creates a sense of history repeating itself, and of the inescapable influence of Whig depravity upon public life.

In the light of this analysis, we can see that critics who accuse Manley of writing only personal – not partisan – satire underestimate the complex nature of her *roman à clef*. Many of the characters that Manley takes from *The Roman History* refer both to particular individuals and to more abstract concepts. Mary of Armenia, for instance, represents George of Denmark or Queen Anne at a personal level but, because Tarasius's speech so strongly recalls the constitutional arguments of the 1680s, she also represents, in a broader sense, the Stuart regime. By the same token, Constantine signifies not only Queen Anne, but also the British constitution, 'espoused' first to one, then to another monarch. The flexibility of her hermeneutic scheme allows Manley not only to satirize the Whigs, but also to accommodate a wide range of Tory opinion. Both Whig and Tory theorists had represented the events of 1688 in terms of divorce.[89] By making Constantine's marriage bigamous, however, Manley suggests that no such definitive breach had taken place, since marriage ties still bind Mary of Armenia (the Stuarts) to Constantine (the British constitution) in spite of the advent of a usurper bride. If this reading suggests Manley's inclination towards Jacobitism by privileging the political aspects of Manley's *roman à clef* over its personal referents, however, then the more personal elements of Manley's allegorical scheme add nuance to such a politicized reading. Although Constantine's bigamous marriage takes place at the instigation of the corrupt Empress Irene (Sarah Churchill, Duchess of Marlborough), his second wife, Theodecta, represents not the dangerous forces of Whiggism, but rather Abigail Masham, to whom (under the guise of 'Louisa of Savoy, Countess of Angoulesm') Manley dedicated volume two of *Memoirs of Europe*. Instead of condemning Theodecta as a bigamist, Manley celebrates her personal virtue and her political wisdom. Indeed, Theodecta opens Constantine's eyes to the evils of the Empress Irene. Manley's portrayal of Theodecta thus suggests a pragmatic, Williamite Tory reading of British political history, in which good political results emerge from fundamentally objectionable circumstances.[90] Indeed, Manley's depiction of the events of 1688 – in which Mary of Armenia [the Stuart kings] with a 'Constitution ... destroy'd by diseases' is supplanted in the royal household by the virtuous Theodecta – recalls Whig propaganda celebrating the replacement of a debauched Court (Manley perhaps implies that Mary of Armenia's diseases, which prevent her from having children, are sexually transmitted) with a virtuous and godly one.[91] Far from acting as a simple reference to her own situation as a cast-off woman, Manley's use of the bigamous marriage motif is complex in its political connotations and generous in its appeal to Tory readers of all stripes.

Memoirs of Europe not only provides a commentary upon the recent political past, however, but also functions as a prediction about Britain's future. It is widely recognized that *Memoirs of Europe* is a more optimistic work than *The New Atalantis* and that it reflects Tory success in the general election of October 1710.[92] But the subtleties of Manley's *roman à clef* only become apparent when *Memoirs of Europe* is read in conjunction with *The Roman History*. In the preface to volume 2 of *Memoirs of Europe*, Manley openly encourages her readers to compare her text against that of her source. Commenting on the putative author of *Memoirs of Europe*, Manley observes:

> EGINARDUS had an Opportunity (as Ambassador at *Constantinople*) to give us, after the Life, the Persons he represents. He seems to have took particular regard to *Stauratius* [John Churchill, Duke of Marlborough], doubtless, because he was the first Person of the Empire. Whether *Eginardus* surviv'd *Stauratius* may be a Question; I incline to believe he did not, being silent upon his End, which was very Remarkable; for as the *Historians* tell us, *The Empress having discover'd his Designs against her Imperial Dignity, would not reward his Ambition as it deserv'd; in Consideration of his former Services, she punish'd him no otherwise than by forbidding all Men to keep him Company, or speak to him: Which moderate Carriage made him so asham'd of his Offence (wandering and alone, shun'd by all the Empire as the Monument of Ingratitude) that he dy'd of Grief, unlamented.*[93]

The italicized section of this passage denotes a direct quotation from volume 4 of *The Roman History*.[94] One reason why Manley invokes Echard's continuator's account of Stauratius's death here is in order to predict the downfall of the Duke of Marlborough. When the second volume of *Memoirs of Europe* appeared in November 1710, Marlborough still held his post as Captain General of the British forces in spite of the fact that his key political ally, the Earl of Godolphin, had been ousted from his position as Lord Treasurer in August of the same year. But Manley's allusion to Stauratius's demise does more than simply predict the downfall of a prominent Whig. It also alerts her reader to the fact that, in *The Roman History*, the story of the Court at Constantinople continues beyond the truncated version found in *Memoirs of Europe*. Moreover, she hints – through her allusion to the downfall of Stauratius – that the ending of volume 4 of *The Roman History* forms a kind of prophecy upon the future of British politics. I suggest that the intertextual relationship between *Memoirs of Europe* and *The Roman History* is so strong that the ending of Echard's continuator's narrative actually forms an integral aspect of Manley's secret history. Indeed, it could be argued that, while *Memoirs of Europe* acts as a secret history of Constantine's reign found in *The Roman History*, the conclusion of volume 4 of *The Roman History* functions as a secret history of Manley's narrative.

When we read in *The Roman History* beyond the point in the story at which *Memoirs of Europe* ends, we can perhaps see why Manley chose to break off her adaptation of her source during the reign of Constantine. In *The Roman History*, Constantine's reign ends when he is abducted on the order of his mother, Irene, and imprisoned in the imperial palace, where he dies in agony after his eyes are gouged out by Irene's henchmen. Echard's continuator declares his horror at this deed, but he also observes a kind of providential decorum in Constantine's death:

> The Reader may observe, in the Death of this Prince, the visible Footsteps of Divine Justice and the Punishment he deserv'd for the innocent Blood he had spilt during his Reign, particularly that of his Uncles, who lost their Eyes by his Order Five Years

before upon the same Day of the same Month, and in the same Chamber; yet doth it by no means excuse the Inhuman Treason of his inexorable Mother, who Sacrific'd her only Son to her Ambition and Revenge.[95]

If read as part of Manley's allegorical scheme, then this passage from *The Roman History*, like the death of Olympia [Anne] in the Utopia section of *The New Atalantis*, apparently represents Anne's symbolic demise at the hands of the Whigs. Indeed, in *The Roman History* the tyrannical Empress Irene goes on to exterminate every living descendant of Leo Iscaurius [James I] and ultimately gains the imperial throne for herself. The hint of poetic justice in *The Roman History* may, however, have spoken to the political concerns of Manley's contemporaries. It seems possible that the emphasis which Echard's continuator places on Constantine's treacherous behaviour towards his uncles serves to recall Anne's betrayal, in the minds of the Jacobites at least, of her own family during the Revolution of 1688–9. In *Memoirs of Europe*, Manley portrays Constantine as the victim of a forced, bigamous marriage. She uses *The Roman History*, however, to suggest that although Anne owed passive obedience to her royal father, she committed an act of active disobedience which ultimately served to weaken her own constitutional position.

The tyrannical reign of the Empress Irene is the penultimate rather than the final episode in volume 4 of *The Roman History*. This volume ends positively, as Echard's continuator relates the bloodless revolution by which the glorious and virtuous Charlemagne claimed the imperial throne at the invitation of the Pope, thus becoming the first Holy Roman Emperor. Manley's decision to make Eginardus, who was Charlemagne's secretary, the putative author of *Memoirs of Europe* suggests that she intended Charlemagne to cast a shadow over the action of her narrative. Her prefatory comments, which speculate that Eginardus may have died before Stauratius (and, therefore, the Empress Irene), are contradicted by *The Roman History*, which makes it clear that Eginardus did, in fact, live to see the accession of Charlemagne to the imperial throne.[96] Manley thus uses the figure of Eginardus both to suggest a degree of continuity between the action of *Memoirs of Europe* and that of *The Roman History* and also to highlight the difference between the tumultuous political situation that Manley depicts in *Memoirs of Europe*, and the peaceful future towards which Constantinople [Britain] is heading – albeit outside the parameters of Manley's narrative.

But because he lies outside the scope of Manley's narrative, Charlemagne remains a highly ambiguous figure as far as Manley's allegorical scheme is concerned. From a party-political perspective it is possible that the new beginning ushered in by Charlemagne's reign reflects recent Tory successes at the polls and in government. Between May and November 1710, when the two volumes of *Memoirs of Europe* were published, the Tories not only won a resounding general election victory, but the Whig ministry led by Godolphin, Marlborough, and the Whig peers known as the Junto was replaced by peers led by Robert Harley. On the other hand, Queen Anne's poor state of health in 1710 meant that a change of monarch seemed imminent. Charlemagne could, therefore, also represent whichever British monarch would come to reign after both Anne's weak regime and the tyrannical 'rule' of the Whigs had come to an end. If this is the case, then Manley leaves it to her readers to determine which British monarch is represented by the figure of Charlemagne. It is possible that, backed by the Pope and crowned Holy Roman Emperor, Charlemagne gestures towards the return of the Stuart Pretender. But it seems as least as likely that Charlemagne, who comes from outside the family of Leo Iscaurius (James I – that is, the Stuarts), denotes the advent of the House of Hanover. Like Olympia's newborn baby in the Utopia section of *The New Atalantis*, who has no obvious historical referent and admits of – indeed, encourages – a variety of interpretations, the shadowy figure of Charlemagne, who exists only outside Manley's narrative, encourages her readers to complete in their own words the story which *Memoirs of Europe* begins.

Conclusion

In *The New Atalantis* and *Memoirs of Europe* we find many of the rhetorical trappings of secret history: spy narrators, *roman à clef*, tales of sexual and political intrigue, condemnation of corrupt favourites, impressionable monarchs, tyrannical rulers, and revised versions of recent political history. But while Whig secret history uses these devices to impress upon its readers their ignorance of the machinations of those in power and the vital role that secret historians play in bringing political secrets to light, Manley puts them to a different end. She uses old stories, *roman à clef* and reconfigured narratives of the recent past to create a sense of implied reader and implied author working together to invest her secret histories with meaning. Manley thus uses the conventions of secret history to cultivate a sense of shared understanding or complicity between the 'author of the Atalantis' and her readers. Moreover, this sense of complicity extends to readers from across the Tory spectrum – both those who were inclined to sympathize with the Jacobite cause, and those who were committed to the Hanoverian succession. The flexibility of Manley's *roman à clef* makes *The New Atalantis* and *Memoirs of Europe* generous texts designed to unite Tories in opposition to the tyrannical Whigs of Queen Anne's reign. Far from being narrow, *ad hominem* attacks upon contemporary Whig grandees, Manley's *romans à clef* are sophisticated, polemical texts designed to galvanize the Tory party into a renewed sense of unity and political purpose.

Does Manley's reworking of secret history's conventions undermine the traditional association between secret history and the Whig political cause? Emphatically, it does not. Manley remodels the conventions of secret history in response to the particular and immediate political situation faced by the Tories in 1709–10, rather than as an expression of the mainstays of Tory belief such as the need to strengthen the Church of England or the benefits of making peace with France. Manley's appropriation of the characteristics of secret history resembles the ways in which Whigs and Tories tussled over key words such as 'loyal' and 'legal' throughout the rage of party.[97] 'Loyal' remained a word that Tories associated with their emphasis on the importance of royal prerogative, while Whig polemicists argued that true loyalty was obedience to the laws – even when those laws were violated by the king. Likewise, Whigs styled themselves the 'legal party' while Tories claimed that their support for Exclusion and then for the Revolution as a *de jure* change of government was a violation of the constitution. Each party thus made polemical capital out of appropriating a discourse commonly associated with the other side. But in each case, it is vital that readers should recognize the act of appropriation. Much more than stating that Tories value the laws and that Whigs are loyal, polemicists who appropriate idioms associated with the political opposition attempt to deny that the characteristics that each side associates with itself are, in fact, representative of that party. Manley does the same thing with secret history. While Whig polemicists use secret history to claim that they are the party of candour and free speech, and that the Tories are all crypto-Jacobites who would bring back the Pretender, popery and arbitrary government, Manley turns the tables to assert that the Whigs of Queen Anne's reign are every bit as tyrannical as they claim the Stuart monarchs to have been and that, in fact, it was their Revolution of 1688–9 that allowed them to gain such ascendancy. The status of *The New Atalantis* and *Memoirs of Europe* as – in Annabel Patterson's dismissive words – 'Tory repartee' to an essentially Whig tradition is, therefore, vital to understanding the rhetorical strategies of these polemical works. Manley keeps the formal structures used by her political opponents in sight even as she inhabits them and turns them to her own political advantage. Paradoxically, she affirms the connections between secret history and Whiggism by choosing this form as a vehicle by which to attack the Whigs and bolster the Tory cause.

5 SECRECY AND SECRET HISTORY IN *THE SPECTATOR* (1711–14)

At first, it is difficult to imagine that *The Spectator*, Joseph Addison and Richard Steele's most successful and influential periodical, has anything to do with secret history. In *Spectator* 10 (12 March 1711), Mr Spectator – the ostensible author of *The Spectator* papers – explicitly contrasts his polite periodical with the kind of intelligence-based, factional and partisan discourse epitomized by secret history.[1] He cites Francis Bacon's observation that 'a well-written Book compared with its Rivals and Antagonists, is like *Moses*'s Serpent, that immediately swallow'd up and devoured those of the *Aegyptians*', and concedes:

> I shall not be so vain as to think, that where the SPECTATOR appears, the other publick Prints will vanish; but shall leave it to my Readers Consideration, whether, Is it [*sic*] not much better to be let into the Knowledge of ones-self, than to hear what passes in *Muscovy* or *Poland*; and to amuse our selves with such Writings as tend to the wearing out of Ignorance, Passion, and Prejudice, than such as naturally conduce to inflame Hatreds and make Enmities irreconcilable?[2]

As a printed text circulating on the literary marketplace, *The Spectator* superficially resembles contemporary partisan, news- or intelligence-based publications. Just as Moses's serpent swallowed those of the Egyptians in the book of Exodus, so Mr Spectator hopes that his publication will eclipse these impolite or even dangerous genres of print. The *Spectator* repeatedly satirizes intelligence-based literary culture. It describes, for instance, '*a News-Letter of Whispers*' which appeal to readers 'first, as they are private History, and in the next place, as they always have in them a Dash of Scandal' and gives an account of 'Modern News-mongers and Coffee-house Politicians' who 'oblige the Public with their Reflections and Observations upon every Piece of Intelligence that is sent us from abroad'.[3] Mr Spectator renounces partisan intelligence of all sorts when he asserts that his periodical 'has not in it a single Word of News, a Reflection in Politicks, nor a Stroke of Party'.[4]

Mr Spectator's allusion to the story of the serpents is significant, however, because while it highlights the differences between *The Spectator* and contemporary intelligence-based publications, it also reveals that they share certain characteristics. Mr Spectator himself suggests that *The Spectator*'s place in the marketplace for print connects this periodical with the impolite publications that he attacks; after all, he envisages poaching readers of factional literature and turning them into polite consumers of *The Spectator*. This chapter argues that *The Spectator* actually has more in common with intelligence-based texts – and with secret history in particular – than may at first appear to be the case. In Mr Spectator, Addison and Steele create a figure who is taciturn, spy-like and who publishes secrets. But *The Spectator*'s resemblance to secret history is, in large part, ironic. Instead of claiming to reveal *arcana imperii* in the vein of the secret historian, Mr Spectator exposes the personal secrets of his correspondents or, more often, flirts with the idea of disclosure in order to highlight his own discreet refusal to reveal any secrets at all. Mr Spectator's parodic resemblance to the narrators of secret history is a form of negative campaigning against an impolite, socially corrosive culture of intelligence, but Addison and Steele also use the figure of Mr Spectator as part of a more positive attempt to rehabilitate the discourse of secrecy. Through *The Spectator* papers, these writers emphasize the central contribution that secrecy makes to certain polite forms of social intercourse: the key Spectatorial virtues of discretion and friendship. Moreover, in spite of its protestations to the contrary, *The Spectator*'s engagement with the discourse of secrecy is not entirely free from partisan motives. I suggest that, read in the political context of the latter years of Queen Anne's reign, Addison and Steele's promotion of polite uses of secrecy bears high political connotations. Specifically, *The Spectator* contrasts the negative culture of intelligence embodied by the Tory Lord Treasurer, Robert Harley, Earl of Oxford, against the positive, polite, sociable uses of secrecy epitomized by the Junto Whigs.

Spying and Secrecy in *Spectator* 439

The *Spectator*'s approach towards secrecy and intelligence involves ideas about the publication of secrets, personal conduct, and high politics. We can see all three concepts in play in *Spectator* 439 (24 July 1712), in which Mr Spectator launches a forthright attack upon secret intelligence. This paper provides a useful point of entry to *The Spectator*'s engagement with contemporary discourses of secrecy and revelation.

Spectator 439 opens with a motto taken from book twelve of Ovid's *Metamorphoses*:

> Hi narrata ferunt aliò: mensuraque ficti
> Crescit; & auditis movus adjicit auctor.

In *The Mottoes of The Spectators, Tatlers, and Guardians Translated into English* (1735), Thomas Broughton translates these lines as: 'Some carry Tales; each in the telling grows, / And every Author adds to what he knows'.[5] In both Ovid and *Spectator* 439, the image of the Palace of Fame – 'a General Rendezvous of Speeches and Whispers' – is used to represent the fundamental unreliability of intelligence. Here, coherent information is transformed into 'a confused Hubbub of low dying sounds.'[6]

The association between fame and unreliable intelligence was commonplace during the early eighteenth century. As we saw in the previous chapter, Delarivier Manley's narrator, Intelligence, is First Lady of the Bedchamber to Princess Fame and much more interested in scandal than truth.[7] In a contemporary translation of Ovid's *Metamorphoses*, to which Addison contributed, John Dryden explicitly connects Fame's palace with contemporary news culture. The palace is 'built of Brass, the better to diffuse / The spreading Sounds, and multiply the News' – where 'multiply' connotes both the work of the printing press and also the way in which intelligence invariably produces several competing accounts rather than univocal truth. According to Dryden, Fame's palace is 'A Mart for ever full; and open Night and Day'; that is, a place in which secrets are traded and bartered and where economic considerations outweigh truth.[8] In the context of Mr Spectator's repeated rejections of news, scandal and partisan intelligence, *Spectator* 439 seems at first to be a self-referential attempt to distinguish between *The Spectator* and the contemporary intelligence-based offerings of the print marketplace, in much the same vein as *Spectator* 10.

But this paper takes an unexpected turn when Mr Spectator makes it clear that his target is not the addiction to news or debased literary culture that characterizes the partisan public sphere, but the high political uses of intelligence and the work of spies. Mr Spectator suggests that Courts are 'to the Governments which they superintend, as *Ovid's* Palace of Fame, with regard to the Universe'. His analogy acknowledges the power of Courts, but also highlights its unsteady foundations. Indeed, he goes on to berate spies in terms that elucidate the reasons why intelligence is invariably untrustworthy:

> A Man who is capable of so infamous a Calling as that of a Spy, is not very much to be relied upon. He can have no great Ties of Honour, or Checks of Conscience, to restrain him in those covert Evidences, where the Person accused has no Opportunity of vindicating himself. He will be more industrious to carry that which is grateful, than that which is true. There will be no Occasion for him, if he does not hear and see things worth Discovery; so that he naturally inflames every Word and Circumstance, aggravates what is faulty, perverts what is good, and misrepresents what is indifferent. Nor is it to be doubted but that such ignominious Wretches let their private Passions into these their clandestine Informations, and often wreak their particular Spite or Malice against the Person whom they are set to watch.[9]

Spies and intelligencers are a prosaic version of Fame's palace. Whether rumours about secrets are filtered through people or texts, they are unlikely to provide their recipients with anything like reliable information.

The main function of *Spectator* 439, however, is not to condemn spies and intelligencers *per se*, but rather to ridicule those who rely upon their information. Absurd, secretive characters who operate in bad faith are a staple topic of *The Spectator*. *Spectator* 148 (20 August 1711), for instance, introduces the Whisperer, who tries to pass off stories that 'all the town knows' as secrets in order to win friends.[10] According to the newsletter projector of *Spectator* 457 (14 August 1712), 'the great Incentive to Whispering is the Ambition which every one has of being thought in the Secret, and being looked upon as a Man who has Access to greater People than one would imagine'.[11] In *Spectator* 439, the message to readers is rather more forthright: only 'Vulgar souls' rely upon the 'clandestine Informations' of a spy. The examples that Mr Spectator cites to prove his point are, however, amusing even as they illustrate a serious point. Dionysius's Ear – an ear-shaped funnel that allowed the Sicilian tyrant, Dionysius, to listen in secret to his prisoners' conversations – betrays such foolhardy cowardice that 'a *Cæsar* or an *Alexander* would rather have died by the Treason, than have used such disingenuous Means for the detecting of it'.[12] In another story, a Cardinal kicks his 'Impudent Scoundrel' of a spy out of the room for telling him – at his own insistence – the low public esteem in which he was held. And finally, Mr Spectator recounts an anecdote about Richard Weston, first Earl of Portland, who is tormented after he insists on finding out Queen Henrietta Maria's opinion of him – an opinion that is, of course, very low. Dependence upon intelligence is not only a risky political strategy, but also evidence of weak character. In *Spectator* 439, Mr Spectator elicits his readers' contempt for those who use intelligence to discover public opinion.

Mr Spectator's condemnation of intelligence combines a self-referential promotion of polite literature over the customary mix of gossip, news and anecdote that filled the contemporary print marketplace with a reader's guide to personal conduct: 'A Man who in ordinary Life is very Inquisitive after every thing which is spoken ill of him', concludes Mr Spectator, 'passes his Time but very indifferently'.[13] But his use of high political examples – Dionysius of Syracuse, the Earl of Portland, and a Cardinal – to illustrate the negative consequences of intelligence may have caused readers to reflect on the use of intelligence in their own Court and government. We have already seen that Robert Harley, Earl of Oxford, was notorious for his secretive demeanour and his interest in political intelligence. Harley may have received from his spies and intelligencers precisely the kind of personal information about himself that, according to *Spectator* 439, betrays weakness of character. In one of his letters to Harley, the spy, Daniel Defoe, writes:

> If you'l allow the Vanity of the Expression, *If I were a Publick Minister* I would if Possible kno' what Every body Said of me ... Please Sir to give me leav, tho' the words shock my Soul as I write them and I believe them to be Impotent Forgerys, yet to Repeat Them that you may Make use of them as you See Cause.[14]

Joseph Addison would not, of course, have known the contents of Defoe's letters to Harley, but could he have had in mind this notoriously secretive minister who cared deeply about public opinion when he wrote *Spectator* 439?[15]

Addison certainly had personal experience of Harley's secretive style of political management. While Harley was occupied as Secretary of State for the Northern Department in establishing a national intelligence network, Addison was serving under Lord Sunderland as Undersecretary of State for the Southern Department. In a letter sent to his patron, Lord Manchester, after Harley's dismissal from his post in 1708, Addison notes that Harley and his friends had engaged in 'schemes to undermine most of our Great officers of State and plant their own party in the room of 'em', and he goes on to condemn 'so wily a secretary'.[16] Contemporaries clearly feared Harley's predilection for secrecy, but they also ridiculed it. The Whig Lord Chancellor, William Cowper, observes that Harley's 'Discourse was either obscure & broken hints, or imposing and absurd to the Highest Degree'.[17] He registers his contempt for the Lord Treasurer as well as concern about his policies.[18] When Mr Spectator condemns characters who find out, to their own cost, what others think of them, he may also be calling to mind Queen Anne's chief minister.

Spectator 439 epitomizes the most important aspects of *The Spectator*'s attack upon secret intelligence. It begins by highlighting the unreliability of news, gossip, anecdotes and secrets and appears to represent a conventional attempt to convince readers to reject the kinds of publication – such as secret history – that tout such contraband goods. But it goes on to focus much more closely on the ways in which secret intelligence reflects upon those who use it, both in the private and the political spheres. This subtle shift in direction allows Mr Spectator to evoke contemporary party-political debate while ostensibly advising readers about their own personal conduct. As we turn to consider the ideas expressed in *Spectator* 439 in the context of the rest of this periodical, we will see that spying and intelligence are a vital part of Addison and Steele's campaign to distance *The Spectator* and its readers from the culture of secrecy that permeated contemporary political and social life.

Spectatorship

Spying and intelligence are crucial topics for *The Spectator* not only because they represent, metonymically, the social ills that this polite periodical seeks to challenge, but also because they help to define its central conceit: spectatorship. Within *The Spectator*, spying becomes the negative image of Mr Spectator's politer form of ocular activity. Whereas the spy is treacherous and spying connotes danger for both the watcher and the watched, the spectator is a passive observer who attains a degree of detachment from the subject of his gaze. In *Spectator* 286 (28 January 1712), one of Mr Spectator's correspondents assures him that 'the Unchaste are provoked to see their Vice expos'd, and the Chaste cannot rake into such Filth without Danger of Defilement; but a meer SPECTATOR, may look into the bottom, and come off without partaking in the Guilt'.[19] In spite of this correspondent's confidence in the difference between spying and spectatorship, however, the relationship between these two activities is not always characterized by straightforward opposition. As we shall see, *The Spectator* papers themselves subtly draw attention to the ways in which the categories of spy and spectator collapse into one another.

The use of 'ocular' titles in seventeenth century periodicals was commonplace by the time Addison and Steele came to write *The Spectator*. Roger L'Estrange's Tory *Observator* (1681–7), John Tutchin's Whig periodical of the same title (1702–10), Ned Ward's *London Spy* (1698–1700), Defoe's *Review* (1704–13) and Swift's *Examiner* (1710–11) provide precedents for the title of Addison and Steele's publication. The *Spectator* differs from these earlier periodicals, however, not only in matters of politics (Ward and L'Estrange were diehard Tories; Defoe's *Review* and *The Examiner* are written from a more moderate, Harleian Tory point of view) but also in the nature of the ocular activity implied by their titles. Mr Spectator claims that he 'behold[s] all Nature with an unprejudic'd Eye'.[20] Although he occupies the same printed medium as factional 'observators' and 'examiners' as well as the spy narrators and intelligencers who populate contemporary secret history, Mr Spectator highlights the difference between their intrusive or even aggressive way of looking at the world and his own detached, polite perspective.

Only twenty numbers into *The Spectator*'s first run, however, a correspondent who signs herself 'S. C.' challenges the idea of the polite detachment of the spectator when she attributes a social phenomenon which she terms 'staring' to the popularity of Addison and Steele's periodical. She writes:

> There never was (I believe) an acceptable Man, but had some awkward Imitators. Ever since *The* SPECTATOR appear'd, have I remarked a kind of Men, whom I choose to call *Starers*; that without any regard to Time, Place, or Modesty, disturb a large Company with their impertinent Eyes.[21]

In spite of her initial description of Mr Spectator as 'acceptable' and her implication that staring is a travesty of spectatorship, S. C. also suggests that Mr Spectator himself may be responsible for encouraging 'impertinent Eyes'. Her implicit criticism of Mr Spectator grows stronger in her next sentence: 'Spectators make up a proper Assembly for a Puppet-Show or a Bear-Garden; but devout Supplicants and attentive Hearers are the Audience one ought to expect in Churches'.[22] The impudence of the starers, S. C. suggests, is tantamount to spectating – not, here, an innocent, unprejudiced, detached activity, but rather one that is offensive in its vacuousness and its association with places of low social resort.

S. C.'s opinion of spectating is borne out by other contemporary references to this practice. In *The London Spy*, Ned Ward provides many examples of aggressive but vacuous spectators, including those at Bartholomew Fair, where the eponymous spy describes 'a mix'd Multitude of Longing Spectators' who 'were waiting with Impatience the beginning of the Show; looking upon one another as simply as a Company sat down at Table, that waits with an hungry Appetite an Hour for their Dinner'.[23] Such spectators are controlled by their physical desires rather than their rational faculties – by their desire to consume, rather than their capacity for taste or judgement. In fact, Mr Spectator himself uses this derogatory sense of 'spectator' in one of his earliest papers when he complains that 'Mortals who have a certain Curiosity without Power of Reflection' peruse his papers 'like Spectators rather than Readers'.[24] He defends himself at the end of this paper by 'admonish[ing] the World, that they shall not find me an idle but a very busy Spectator'.[25] Yet according to S. C.'s letter, starers themselves are a kind of busy spectator. Instead of being passive spectators like the 'Assembly for a Puppet-Show or a Bear-Garden', they are active and aggressive; the impolite, unthinking qualities of the spectator are combined here with impudence. The ambivalence of Mr Spectator's name challenges the idea that impartiality and detachment underlie this periodical's polite social agenda.

Mr Spectator expands upon the concept of spectatorship in *The Spectator* by referring to his essays as 'speculations'. Both 'spectatorship' and 'speculation' imply a degree of separation from worldly affairs. As Mr Spectator states in the very first *Spectator* paper:

> I live in the World, rather as a Spectator of Mankind, than as one of the Species; by which means I have made my self a Speculative Statesman, Soldier, Merchant and Artizan, without ever medling with any Practical Part in Life. I am very well versed in the Theory of an Husband, or a Father, and can discern the Errors in the Oeconomy, Business and Diversion of others, better than those who are engaged in them.[26]

Mr Spectator does not act the part of a statesman, soldier, merchant or artisan, but thinks (or speculates) his way into these roles. The concept of speculation underscores the sense of detachment that allows Mr Spectator to observe and judge the world around him. Yet the etymological connection between spectating and speculating complicates the idea of Mr Spectator as a detached, contemplative figure. In Latin, a *specula* is a look-out tower. In its literal sense, speculation is 'the exercise of the faculty of sight; the action, or an act, of seeing, viewing, or looking on or at; examination or observation'.[27] The transferred use of the word 'speculation' to mean contemplative or cognitive activity was always more common than its literal meaning and, during the early eighteenth century, the literal sense was rapidly slipping out of use.[28] Nonetheless, in a periodical entitled *The Spectator* that is so concerned with ways of looking and that is written by authors who possessed an extensive classical education, it is likely that the word 'speculation' connotes both Mr Spectator's meditations and the visual activity that gives rise to them.

This etymological strand of enquiry adds a new dimension to the concept of spectatorship when we consider that, in Latin, *speculator* means spy.[29] According to the *OED*, 'speculator' in the late seventeenth and early eighteenth centuries could be construed as 'a watchman, sentry, or look-out'.[30] In his *Dictionary*, Samuel Johnson defines 'speculator' as, 'a spy; a watcher'.[31] Indeed, while Johnson contends that 'speculation' in the literal sense of 'sight' was obsolete by the mid-eighteenth century, 'speculator' still had currency as a synonym of spy, even if it was a rare usage of this word.[32] Mr Spectator is never referred to explicitly as a 'speculator' in *The Spectator*. Yet he is – as he points out on several occasions – a 'speculative' man, and in *Guardian* 71 (2 June 1713), which we will consider in more detail shortly, Addison uses the term 'Speculative Men' explicitly to refer to spies.[33] The etymology of the word 'speculator', then, points in two directions: one the one hand, towards abstract thinking and social detachment, and on the other, towards espionage with all its attendant connotations of duplicity and bad faith. Addison and Steele prioritize the first of these meanings in their explicit depiction of Mr Spectator, but the less respectable connotations of the etymon, 'speculator', resonate throughout *The Spectator* papers. Mr Spectator is a contemplative social commentator whose 'speculations' are based on the intelligence he gathers from places where only a spy can go.[34]

At least one later eighteenth-century writer drew the attention of his readers to the spy-like nature of Mr Spectator's observations. In his novel, *The Adventures of Peregrine Pickle* (1751), Tobias Smollett parodies Mr Spectator's more sordid characteristics in his character named Misanthrope, who declares:

> I now appear in the world, not as a member of any community, or what is called a social creature; but merely as a spectator, who entertains himself with the grimaces of a jack-pudding, and banquets his spleen in beholding his enemies at loggerheads. That I may enjoy this disposition, abstracted from all interruption, I feign myself deaf; an expedient by which I not only avoid all disputes, and their consequences, but also become master of a thousand little secrets, which are every day whispered in my presence, without any suspicion of their being overheard...
>
> In consequence of my rank and character I obtain free admission to the ladies, among whom I have obtained the appellation of the Scandalous Chronicle; and as I am considered (while silent) in no other light than as a footstool or elbow chair, they divest their conversation of all restraint before me, and gratify my sense of hearing

with strange things, which (if I could prevail upon myself to give the world that satisfaction) would compose a curious piece of secret history, and exhibit a quite different idea of characters from what is commonly entertained.[35]

Many of Mr Spectator's traits, and even the language that he uses to describe them, are parodied in the character of the Misanthrope. Although Mr Spectator claims membership of a club and asserts that 'Man is said to be a Sociable Animal' (or, 'social creature', as the Misanthrope puts it), he is a silent, secretive character who gathers intelligence in underhand ways (indeed, he admits to having been 'taken up for a Jesuit' as a result of his 'profound Taciturnity').[36] Mr Spectator, like the Misanthrope, apparently occupies an ambivalent position between vacant voyeur and prurient inquisitor. Indeed, while the Misanthrope's inertia prevents the publication of his 'curious piece of secret history', Mr Spectator does publish the intelligence that he gleans about those who fall under his gaze. By citing secret history explicitly, Smollett draws attention to the proximity of *The Spectator* to the impolite discourses found in secret histories and scandal chronicles from which it attempts to distance itself.[37]

Smollett's parody of *The Spectator* may be an amusing caricature of some of the more impolite aspects of this periodical's principal narrator. He is, however, picking up on parallels and analogies to which Mr Spectator draws his readers' attention in his own papers. Far from distinguishing his own behaviour from that of the speculators whom he condemns, Mr Spectator actually highlights the spy-like ways in which he gathers intelligence about his readers and their acquaintance. In an early number he boasts, 'I ... enter into all Companies, with the same Liberty as a Cat or other domestick Animal, and am as little suspected of telling any thing that I hear or see'.[38] Elsewhere, he informs his reader that he uses social 'spies', permitting 'a she Slanderer or two in every Quarter of the Town, to live in the Character of Coquets, and take all the innocent Freedoms of the Rest, in order to send me Information of the Behaviour of their respective Sister-hoods'.[39] Mr Spectator is, it seems, both spy and spy-master, willing to gather secret intelligence about his contemporaries in a variety of different ways.

But if Mr Spectator reveals the similarities between his own publication and contemporary secret histories and scandal chronicles through the figure of the spy narrator, then he also emphasizes the significant differences between these two kinds of publication. Instead of publishing factional intelligence or salacious exposés of sexual and political intrigue, Mr Spectator gives his readers moral advice and topics for polite conversation. Indeed, one of the reasons for his drawing attention to the fact that he receives scandalous intelligence is to highlight his decision *not* to publish it. In *Spectator* 4 (5 March 1711), Mr Spectator tells his readers that his refusal to speak sharpens his other senses, giving him 'a more than ordinary Penetration in Seeing' – even into the secret thoughts of those around him. Nonetheless, he promises that 'whatever Skill I may have in Speculation' – that is, in seeing with overtones of spying – 'I shall never betray what the Eyes of Lovers say to each other in my Presence'.[40] Unlike Manley's Intelligence, who moves invisibly among the citizens of Angela (or London) and betrays any secrets she can discover, Mr Spectator promises a degree of discretion in his dealings with his potential readers.

In a very late *Spectator* paper, published in the second series of 1714, Mr Spectator elaborates on the idea that he routinely withholds secrets:

> I have often thought, that if the several Letters, which are Written to me under the Character of SPECTATOR, and which I have not made use of, were published in a Volume, they would not be an unentertaining Collection. The Variety of the Subjects, Stiles, Sentiments and Informations, which are transmitted to me, would lead a very curious, or very idle Reader, insensibly along, through a great many Pages. I know some Authors, who would pick up a *Secret History* out of such Materials, and make a Bookseller an Alderman by the Copy.[41]

The idea for this paper, written by Thomas Tickell, actually derives from a paper that Addison had contributed to another periodical, *The Guardian*, a year earlier.[42] In *Guardian* 134 (14 August 1713), Addison proposes to set up a particular room in Button's coffeehouse, the regular meeting-place of his literary coterie and the address to which contributions to *The Guardian* were sent, for 'the several Packets of Letters and private Intelligence which I do not communicate to the Publick', either because they are full of 'Lewdness and Ribaldry' or because they are too violently polemical. Although inappropriate for publication in *The Guardian*, 'these Manuscripts will in time be very Valuable, and may afford good Lights to future Historians who shall give an Account of the present Age'.[43] Here, Addison gently satirizes both his correspondents and his own publishing project, but he also underscores the fact that the material printed in *The Guardian* has been adjusted for a public forum. The publication of such material could, indeed, turn a polite periodical into a secret history; withholding this sort of information highlights the difference between these two kinds of text.

The fact that *The Spectator* refuses to reveal secrets becomes a running joke in this periodical. In *Spectator* 252 (19 December 1711), Mary Heartfree – who, like the ageing libertine Will Honeycomb, can read 'the secret language of the eyes' in the glances of theatregoers – promises Mr Spectator, in her next letter, 'a Present of secret History, by translating all the Looks of the next Assembly of Ladies and Gentlemen into Words, to adorn some future Paper'.[44] Mary Heartfree's letter is, of course, held up for public ridicule; the implication is that she has fundamentally misunderstood the aim of this periodical. Her use of the phrase 'secret history' signals to every polite reader the reason why Mr Spectator does not take her up on her offer. Nonetheless, foolish correspondents who offer Mr Spectator secret intelligence become a standard feature of *The Spectator*, from the projector who plans to set up a scurrilous 'news-letter of Whispers' in *Spectator* 457 (14 August 1712), to Thomas Quid-Nunc, the newsmonger of *Spectator* 625 (26 November 1714). Mr Spectator satirizes these characters in order to encourage his readers' complicity with his own views on secret intelligence. Only a reader who lacks the perspicacity to understand Mr Spectator's rhetorical strategies could really mistake *The Spectator* for a scandal chronicle.

Mr Spectator repeatedly invokes the rhetoric of disclosure in ironic fashion. In one paper, he admits to 'laying open the *Arcana*, or secrets of Prudence to the Eyes of every Reader'.[45] In another, he refuses to explain the capital letter that ends each paper, citing the example of 'an ancient Philosopher, who carried something hidden under his Cloak' who, when asked what it was that he concealed, replied, '*I cover it ... on purpose that you should not know*'.[46] In fact, the capital letters denote the authorship of each of the papers: C, L, I, and O for Addison – as Steele himself explains in the final number of *The Spectator*'s first run – and R and T for Steele.[47] These 'Amulets or Charms' do conceal a sort of secret, but it is far from being, as Addison claims, 'Cabbalistical'. Mr Spectator's satire of intelligence and intelligencers turns a dangerously divisive social force into subjects for his readers' amusement. As he flirts with the discourse of revelation and with the idea of exposing his readers' vices, he affirms the politeness of his own use of secret intelligence.

Spying and Secrecy in *The Guardian* (1713)

Just as Delarivier Manley's *Memoirs of Europe* refined and clarified the rhetorical techniques that Manley had developed in a much more diffuse way through her earlier satire, *The New Atalantis*, so *The Guardian* – a sequel to *The Spectator* – distils the connections between secrecy, spying and politeness that are a recurrent topic of *The Spectator* papers. By exploring ideas of spying and secrecy in *The Guardian*, the ways in which *The Spectator* appropriates and parodies impolite discourses to a polite end are cast in sharper relief.

The *Guardian*'s interest in spies and spying first becomes evident in number 71 (2 June 1713) of this periodical. Like *Spectator* 439, *Guardian* 71 denounces the figure of the spy: 'hated both by God and Man, and regarded with the utmost Contempt even by such as make use of him'.[48] At first, *Guardian* 71's denunciation of spies appears to be a conventional topic for a periodical concerned with inculcating politeness among its readership. The way in which this paper addresses the concept of spying is, however, particularly significant because of the unusual terminology which Nestor Ironside – *The Guardian*'s equivalent of Mr Spectator – applies to it. In this paper, Nestor Ironside explains that a 'great Man's Spy' is commonly known as a 'Lion'. He gives two possible explanations for this curious term. He notes that 'Lion' was the surname of a barber who acted as a spy for Sir Francis Walsingham, Principal Secretary under Elizabeth I, by extracting secrets as he washed the hair of his clients. Lion thus 'became an inexhaustible Fund of private Intelligence'.[49] The other explanation is that the term 'lion' derives from the statues of lions situated outside the Doge's palace in Venice. Nestor Ironside says of these lions:

> Those who have a Mind to give the State any private Intelligence of what passes in the City, put their Hands into the Mouth of one of these Lions, and convey into it a Paper of such private Informations as any way regard the Interest or Safety of the Commonwealth. By this means all the Secrets of State come out of the Lion's Mouth. The Informer is concealed, it is the Lion that tells every thing. In short, there is not a Mismanagement in Office, or a Murmur in Conversation, which the Lion does not acquaint the Government with. For this Reason, say the Learned, a Spy is very properly distinguished by the Name of Lion.[50]

The Lions of Venice appear to turn the nasty act of informing on one's neighbours into a public service. The anonymity they provide, however, means that the act of informing also smacks of treachery. Nestor Ironside concludes that 'Hangmen and Executioners are necessary in a State, and so may [be] the Animal I have been here mentioning; but how despicable is the Wretch that takes on him so vile an Employment?'[51]

Yet in spite of Nestor Ironside's unequivocal condemnation of 'lions' in *Guardian* 71, just a month later he made the figure of the lion an integral aspect of *The Guardian*'s social existence and, indeed, an emblem for the periodical itself. Shortly after taking up the editorship of *The Guardian* from Richard Steele in July 1713, Joseph Addison reintroduced the subject of the lion in *Guardian* 98 (3 July 1713). In this paper, Nestor Ironside announces:

> [I]t is my Intention to erect a Lion's Head in Imitation of those I have described in *Venice*, through which all the private Intelligence of that Commonwealth is said to pass. This Head is to open a most wide and voracious Mouth, which shall take in such Letters and papers as are conveyed to me by my Correspondents, it being my Resolution to have a particular Regard to all such Matters as come to my Hands through the Mouth of the Lion ... Whatever the Lion swallows I shall digest for the Use of the Publick. This Head requires some Time to finish, the Workman being resolved to give it several Masterly Touches, and to represent it as Ravenous as possible. It will be set up in *Button*'s Coffee-house in *Covent-Garden*, who is directed to shew the Way to the Lion's Head, and to instruct any young Author how to convey his Works into the Mouth of it with Safety and Secrecy.[52]

As we have already seen, the lions' heads in Venice are symbols of the underhand dealings and treachery of informers and spies. By encouraging them to post their offerings through the lion's mouth, Nestor Ironside appears to place his readers in the position of the 'lions' or spies whom he derides in *Guardian* 71. The relationship between the lion at Button's coffee house and its Venetian predecessors is, however, a development of the relationship between *The Spectator* papers and the partisan news, gossip and secret history that they seek to displace. Just as Mr Spectator parodies his disreputable forerunners and thus attempts to neutralize, by means of satire, the moral threat that they pose to the reading public, so the lion of *Guardian* 98 mimics, in satirical fashion, both the Venetian lions and the spies who are named after them. Addison inserts the word 'Author' very late in his decription of the lion's head at Button's coffeehouse – making it clear at last that the offerings for the lion's head should not be tattling stories but literary works. The *Guardian*'s lion gathers fodder for Addison's coterie at Button's, not Courts or ministers. The *Guardian* attempts to undermine the culture of intelligence in the print marketplace and political not simply by providing an alternative, polite mode of discourse, but by basing the form of its polite offerings on the underhand, scurrilous kinds of disclosure that it seeks to counteract.

The *Guardian*'s parodic approach towards 'lions' challenges one recent critical interpretation of the ways in which Addison and Steele's periodicals go about the business of encouraging politeness. Scott Paul Gordon argues that Mr Spectator's impolite methods of gathering intelligence constitute a 'voyeuristic gaze, that disciplines subjects by observing them'.[53] He suggests that *The Spectator* is a kind of invisible eye, which keeps readers in fear that their foibles and misdemeanours will be exposed in print. Gordon's Foucauldian analysis of *The Spectator* resonates in interesting ways with contemporary efforts to connect Addison and Steele's periodicals to the Reformation of Manners movement. In a letter to *The Guardian*, one of Nestor Ironside's correspondents writes:

> LYONS being esteemed by Naturalists the most generous of Beasts, the noble and Majestick Appearance they make in Poetry, wherein they so often represent the Hero himself, made me always think that Name very ill applied to a Profligate set of Men, at present going about seeking whom to Devour: And though I cannot but acquiesce in your account of the Derivation of that Title to them, it is with great Satisfaction I hear you are about to restore them to their former Dignity, by producing one of that Species so publick Spirited, as to Roar for Reformation of Manners.[54]

This correspondent's allusion to 'Reformation of Manners' attempts to ally *The Guardian*'s rehabilitation of the lion to the work of the Societies for the Reformation of Manners, which became popular during the reign of William and Mary and thrived during the early eighteenth century.[55] The Societies encouraged people to inform upon their neighours' immoral behaviour, sometimes by issuing blank booklets for recording instances of vice. Their advocates believed that 'the Name of an *Informer* is now become much more *Glorious* among *wise* and *good Men*, than it was grown *Contemptible*, by the *ill Practices* of *some* in our dayes; And that it does therefore appear truly *Honourable*, for Persons of the *greatest Quality* to give *Informations* in these Cases, for the Service of the most High God'.[56] Not only Scott Paul Gordon in the twenty-first century, then, but also the proponents of the Societies for Reformation of Manners in the eighteenth, suggest that Addison and Steele's periodicals rehabilitate the work of informing by encouraging the public exposure of vice.

In spite of superficial similarities between periodicals such as *The Spectator* and *The Guardian* and the Societies for the Reformation of Manners, however, their techniques for encouraging social reform are quite different from one another. While the Societies eagerly and sincerely solicited intelligence about moral depravity from the neighbours of those who committed it, *The Spectator* and *The Guardian* adopt a much more sceptical and often ironic attitude towards the business of informing. Their ambivalence is hardly surprising: many contemporaries attacked the Societies for their use of underhand tactics and their hypocritical godliness. Daniel Defoe asserts that 'the Office of an Informer has something so Infamously Officious in it, from the Proper suspition of its being done meerly for a Reward; and from the late Infamous Practice of such People upon the Innocent, that Honest Men are always backward in it', while Ned Ward describes 'A Modern *Reformer* of Vice: Or, a Reforming *Constable*' as 'a man most commonly of a very Scandalous Necessity, who has no way left, but *Pimp* like, to Live upon other Peoples *Debaucheries*'.[57] Indeed, *The Spectator* papers themselves indulge in satire aimed at the ulterior motives that reformers might have for chasing after vice. In *Spectator* 8 (9 March 1711), 'one of the Directors of the Society for the Reformation of Manners' lacks any self-consciousness as he writes, exultantly, that he is 'very well acquainted with all the Haunts and Resorts of Female Night-Walkers'. Although this correspondent describes Mr Spectator as a '*Fellow-Labourer*', Mr Spectator chooses to keep his distance, commenting laconically that this letter 'will give the Reader as good an Entertainment as any that I am able to furnish him with'. At the end of his paper he resolves to reserve judgement upon masquerades – one of the Society's bugbears – until he has had the opportunity to visit one of these 'Midnight Entertainments' himself.[58]

So although *The Spectator* and *The Guardian* encourage readers to inform on those around them, they turn their correspondents' letters into occasions for self-directed irony and their readers' polite amusement. By parodying the apparatus of informing – whether the furtive behaviour of a spy or the use of a lion to receive anonymous tip-offs – they make these devices vehicles for polite wit. Instead of reforming their readers by threatening them with public exposure, these periodicals use irony and parody to encourage them to 'distinguish themselves from the thoughtless Herd of their ignorant and unattentive Brethren.'[59]

Discretion and Friendship

The *Guardian* and *The Spectator*'s parodic appropriations of the discourses of spying, secrecy and revelation are one method by which they attempt to harness the corrosive social effects of the culture of intelligence and turn it into an instrument of polite social reform. In *The Spectator*, however, Addison and Steele also attempt to rehabilitate the discourse of secrecy in a more positive way. In a number of papers, they suggest that secrecy is an intrinsic aspect of two key Spectatorial concepts: discretion and friendship.

In *Spectator* 225 (17 November 1711), Mr Spectator argues that discretion is the single most important social virtue:

> Though a Man has all other Perfections, and wants Discretion, he will be of no great Consequence in the World; but if he has this single Talent in Perfection, and but a common share of others, he may do what he pleases in his particular Station of Life.[60]

Mr Spectator claims that there is a clear method for attaining this virtue. Discretion, he suggests, consists in the ability to separate out (or keep discrete) those thoughts which are appropriate for public conversation from those which ought to remain hidden:

> I have often thought if the Minds of Men were laid open, we should see but little Difference between that of the Wise Man and that of the Fool. There are infinite *Reveries*, numberless Extravagancies, and a perpetual Train of Vanities which pass through both. The great Difference is, that the first knows how to pick and cull his Thoughts for Conversation, by suppressing some, and communicating others; whereas the other lets them all indifferently fly out in Words.[61]

Without this ability to 'pick and cull' that which should remain concealed from that which may be exposed to public view, discretion is impossible. Mr Spectator expands upon this idea in *Spectator* 228 (21 November 1711), published four days after his paper on the subject of discretion. Here, he portrays a class of people called 'the Inquisitive' who, like 'the Whisperer' of *Spectator* 148 (20 August 1711) and the newsletter projector of *Spectator* 457 (14 August 1712), live only to pass on intelligence. Although not intentionally malicious, the blankness of the minds of the Inquisitive can have the same effect as malevolence:

> As the Inquisitive, in my Opinion, are such meerly from a Vacancy in their own Imaginations, there is nothing, methinks, so dangerous as to communicate Secrets to them; for the same Temper of Inquiry makes them as impertinently communicative: But no Man though he converses with them need put himself in their Power, for they will be contented with Matters of less Moment as well.[62]

The Inquisitive are entirely undiscerning. As one of Mr Spectator's correspondents puts it in a later paper, 'they have a Relish for every thing that is News, let the matter of it be what it will; or to speak more properly, they are Men of a Voracious Appetite, but no Taste'.[63]

As in the case of 'speculation', an etymological approach towards the concept of discernment proves illuminating. 'Discernment' shares a Latin etymon, *discernere*, 'to separate', with the adjectives 'discrete' and 'discreet' – both verb and adjectives connote the ability to distinguish between objects and to evaluate their relative worth.[64] Cultural questions of taste and politeness are thus firmly linked to the moral virtue of discretion. But there is also a close connection between discretion and the practices of secrecy. Indeed, the Latin word *secretus* denotes both the adjective 'secret' and the past participle of *secernere*, which also means 'to separate' or 'to set apart'.[65] The ability to separate, to judge, and to keep secret are, Mr Spectator suggests, central to discretion. He thus attempts to resituate the practices of secrecy, which had been degraded by a culture of intelligence, within a positive cultural and moral framework.

Discretion is not, however, an appropriate mode of behaviour in all social circumstances. Crucially, Mr Spectator insists that discretion – and its attendant association with the proper uses of secrecy – has no place between friends. In *Spectator* 68 (18 May 1711), devoted to the subject of friendship, Mr Spectator asserts that, in the presence of his friend, 'a Man gives a Loose to every Passion and every Thought that is uppermost, discovers his most retired Opinions of Persons and Things, tries the Beauty and Strength of his Sentiments, and exposes his whole Soul to the Examination of his Friend'.[66] Likewise, although *Spectator* 225 celebrates the virtue of discretion, it also observes that 'Discretion ... has no place in private Conversation between intimate Friends. On such occasions the wisest Men very often Talk like the weakest; for indeed the Talking with a Friend is nothing else but *thinking aloud*'.[67] Both *Spectator* 68 and *Spectator* 225 underline the crucial role that secrecy plays in connecting discretion with friendship: friendship both permits and is defined by a relaxation of the public rule of discretion (that is, the preservation of secrets) in favour of the free exchange of ideas, opinions and information (that is, the absence of secrets).

In both of these papers, Mr Spectator affirms his ideas about secrecy, friendship and discretion by alluding to a rather obscure source: the Wisdom of the Son of Sirach, a section of the book of Ecclesiasticus, which is found among the apocryphal rather than the canonical books of the Bible. Passing briefly over Montaigne, Bacon and Cicero, whose essays on friendship form the backbone of the humanist tradition of writing on this subject, Mr Spectator asserts that 'whoso discovereth Secrets loseth his Credit, and shall never find a Friend to his Mind'. He goes on to exhort his reader to 'love thy friend, and be faithful unto him; but if thou bewrayest his Secrets, follow no more after him', and concludes by insisting that, 'as for a Wound it may be bound up, and after reviling there may be Reconciliation: but he that bewrayeth Secrets, is without Hope'.[68] Mr Spectator promotes Ecclesiasticus as a scriptural source of apothegmatic wisdom to rival more familiar works by revered classical and fashionable modern essayists.[69] Piety is not, however, the only reason why he does so. It also seems significant that Ecclesiasticus – unlike other writers on friendship – specifically cites the betrayal of secrets as the cause of an irrevocable breach of friendship and implies that friendship is defined by the free exchange of what would otherwise be regarded as secret information. *Spectators* 68 and 225 demonstrate the central position that secrecy occupies in Addison's moral and social vision. They emphasize the fact that secrecy need not be the preserve of spies and intelligencers. Moreover, they suggest that, by turning secrecy into a divisive social and political force, mercenary peddlers of secrets travesty the positive role that secrecy plays in fostering the virtues of discretion and friendship.

It is perhaps significant that, at the time when Addison was writing *Spectators* 68 and 225, friendship was an idea strongly associated in the political sphere with the Whig Junto.[70] The five Whig peers who made up the Junto – Somers, Halifax, Wharton, Orford and Sunderland – were invariably portrayed by both their political supporters and enemies as a group of friends. Towards the end of the eighteenth century, Edmund Burke celebrated the 'great connexion of Whigs in the reign of Queen Anne' who 'believed that the only proper method of rising into power was through hard essays of practised friendship and experienced fidelity' and were, therefore, 'not afraid that they should be called an ambitious Junto'. Burke asserts that Addison, 'who knew their sentiments', complimented the Junto 'upon the principle of this connexion' in lines from his poem, *The Campaign* (1705): 'On the firm Basis of Desert they rise, / From long try'd Faith, and Friendship's Holy Ties'.[71] The Junto's basis in friendship was the subject of comment throughout Queen Anne's reign. On 20 November 1708 the third Earl of Shaftesbury wrote to Robert Molesworth that Somers 'is bound to the party of Friends with whom he rose' – that is, the Junto.[72] Opponents of the Junto regularly accused these peers of acting as an impenetrable clique.[73] In *Examiner* 31 (1 March 1711), Jonathan Swift satirically numbers the Junto (whom he describes as the '*High-Flying Whigs*') among other 'Societies of Men [who] are in closest Union among themselves' because they are 'engag'd in some *evil Design*' or because they 'labour under one *common Misfortune*', such as banditti, highwayman, thieves, papists and Presbyterians.[74] More recently, Geoffrey Holmes has identified the Junto's pre-eminent political organization as, in great part, the product of frequent personal contact.[75] Four of the Junto peers and many of their political supporters – including Addison and Steele – were members of the Kit-Cat Club, a gathering of prominent Whigs of which the printer, the elder Jacob Tonson, was secretary.[76] In an attack on Richard Steele's anti-Jacobite tract, *The Crisis* (1714), a clergyman identified only as B. R. suggests that Steele's dedication of the tract to the clergy of the Church of England was misplaced, since 'the *Junto*, the Kit-Cat, and Beef-Stake are yet in Being'.[77] Although the context for this assertion is a polemic, the fact that B. R. elides a political clique with two sociable societies suggests the extent to which the Junto's foundation in the friendship of its members was widely recognized.

By contrast with the Junto, Robert Harley is frequently caricatured in contemporary propaganda as secretive to the point of cunning. Although Harley and Jonathan Swift belonged to the same prominent political and social clubs, Swift nonetheless claims that Harley 'certainly did not value, or did not understand the Art of acquiring Friends; having made very few during the Time of his Power, and contracted a great number of Enemies'. Swift's criticism of Harley's unfriendliness is ambivalent; he goes on to use it as evidence of Harley's incorruptability: 'Some of us used to observe, that those whom he talked well of, or suffered to be often near him, were not in a Scituation of much Advantage; and that his mentioning others with Contempt or Dislike, was no Hindrance at all to their Preferment'.[78] Other contemporaries portray Harley more straightforwardly as both unfriendly and untrustworthy. Following a dinner in January 1706 at which Harley – then Secretary of State – attempted to woo several members of the Junto and other prominent Whigs, Lord Cowper recorded an anecdote which sums up Whig scepticism towards Harley's professions of friendship:

> S[ecretar]y Harley took a Glass, & drank to Love and Friendship & everlasting Union, & wish'd he had more Tockay to drink it in (we had drank two Bottles, good, but thick). I replied, his White Lisbon was best to drink it in, being very Clear. I suppose he apprehended it (as I observ'd most of the Company did) to relate to that humour of his, which was, never to deal clearly or openly, but always with Reserve, if not Dissimulation, or rather Simulation; & to love Tricks even where not necessary, but from an inward Satisfaction he took in applauding his own Cunning.[79]

Harley's attempts to promote himself as a potential friend to the Whigs as well as the Tories clearly failed to have the desired effect upon his audience.

'Cunning' is a word which recurs in contemporary analyses of Harley's behaviour. Abel Boyer describes Harley as the 'cunning Treasurer' in his analysis of the last four years of Anne's reign.[80] In a character sketch written shortly after the change of ministry in 1710, Thomas Wentworth, Lord Raby, claims that Harley is 'generally allowed as cunning a man as any in England' who 'has been always employing spies and inspectors into every office to have a general information of everything'. He suggests that Harley procured the change of ministry by 'cunningly pretending only to clip the power' of Marlborough and Godolphin in order to produe the support of moderate Whigs.[81] Donald Bond, the recent editor of the *Tatler*, suggests that the portrait in *Tatler* 191 (29 June

1710) of Polypragmon, 'the Cunning Man' whose 'greatest Cunning is to appear cunning', was widely interpreted by contemporaries as a satire on Robert Harley.[82] In a less oblique character portrait of Harley written shortly before this minister's fall from power in 1714, Jonathan Swift expresses his concern that 'too great an Affectation of Secrecy, is usually thought to be attended with those little Intrigues and Refinements which among the Vulgar denominate a Man a great Politician, but among others is apt whether deservedly or no, to acquire the Opinion of Cunning: A Talent which differs as much from the True Knowledge of Government, as that of an Attorney from an able Lawyer'.[83] And in his *History of the Four Last Years of the Queen*, composed during Harley's ministry and repeatedly revised during Swift's lifetime but not published until 1758, Swift was more explicit, observing that 'an Obstinate Love of Secrecy in this Minister seems at a distance to have some Resemblance of Cunning; For, He *is* not only very retentive of Secrets, but *appears* to be so too; which I number among his Defects'.[84] Although Swift denies that Harley is cunning, the fact that he takes pains to defend him against the charge suggests its prevalence in contemporary political discourse.

In this connection, it may be significant that Addison takes great pains in *Spectator* 225 to distinguish discretion from cunning. Mr Spectator sets out a long list of comparisons between discretion and cunning – for instance, 'Discretion points out the noblest Ends to us, and pursues the most proper and laudable Methods of attaining them: Cunning has only private selfish Aims, and sticks at nothing which may make them succeed' and 'Discretion is the Perfection of Reason, and a Guide to us in all the Duties of Life: Cunning is a kind of Instinct, that only looks out after our immediate Interest and Welfare'. He concludes: 'In short, Cunning is only the Mimick of Discretion, and may pass upon weak Men, in the same manner as Vivacity is often mistaken for Wit, and Gravity for Wisdom'.[85] *Spectator* 225 is ostensibly an essay about the private virtue of discretion but, when read in the context of contemporary partisan debate, it acquires additional political resonance. During *The Spectator*'s publication run, the power of the Junto was eclipsed by the Tories under Robert Harley.[86] In a factional political climate, Mr Spectator's discrimination between secrecy as an aid to friendship and secrecy as the basis of cunning could easily have been applied to, or read as a reflection upon, the Junto's and Harley's very different styles of political management. In spite of *The Spectator*'s protestations of political neutrality, it seems at least possible that its ostensibly moral and social critique of the concept of secrecy contains traces of contemporary high political battles.[87]

Ultimately, however, it is more important to *The Spectator*'s moral and political purpose that partisan connotations are suppressed than that they are noticed. Central to *The Spectator*'s inculcation of politeness among its readers is the fact that this periodical applies to itself the rule of discretion that it advocates to its readers. In the opening paragraph of *Spectator* 68, Mr Spectator observes that, although 'one would think that the larger the Company is, in which we are engaged, the greater Variety of Thoughts and Subjects would be started in Discourse', in fact, 'we find that Conversation is never so much streightened and confined as in numerous Assemblies'. He goes on to note that 'when a Multitude meet together upon any Subject of Discourse, their Debates are taken up chiefly with Forms and general Positions; nay, if we come into a more contracted Assembly of Men and Women, the Talk generally runs upon the Weather, Fashions, News, and the like publick Topicks'. Only 'as Conversation gets into Clubs and Knots of Friends' does it '[descend] into Particulars, and [grow] more free and communicative'.[88] Mr Spectator's observation is prescriptive as well as descriptive. The virtue of discretion demands that, in public and mixed assemblies, 'publick Topicks' not only do, but should prevail. It is noteworthy that while topics such as the weather, fashions, and news might be described as trivial, Mr Spectator attaches to them the more value-neutral adjective, 'publick'. And Mr Spectator's prescription applies not only to the literal public assemblies in which his readers might participate, but also to the virtual public assembly that is *The Spectator* itself. Early in *The Spectator*'s first run, Mr Spectator informs his readers that his periodical has 'Three-score thousand' daily readers, including women and men from a variety of social backgrounds.[89] The accuracy (or otherwise) of Mr Spectator's estimate is less important than the message that he was sending to his readers by emphasizing the scale and breadth of his readership: *The Spectator* is a public forum, in which the rule of discretion should be observed.

We can see discretion at work in the manner in which *The Spectator* addresses contentious, impolite topics. Mr Spectator consistently – and often ostentatiously – steers his essays away from the factional gossip that make up intelligence-based publications like secret history and towards more polite, general or publick topics. For instance, he begins *Spectator* 45 (21 April 1711), which was written when the preliminary negotiations towards ending the War of Spanish Succession were underway, by asserting:

> There is nothing which I more desire than a safe and honourable Peace, tho' at the same time I am very apprehensive of many ill Consequences that may attend it. I do not mean in regard to our Politicks but to our Manners. What an Inundation of Ribbons and Brocades will break in upon us? What Peals of Laughter and Impertinence shall we be exposed to? For the Prevention of these great Evils, I could heartily wish that there was an Act of Parliament for Prohibiting the Importation of *French* Fopperies.[90]

Mr Spectator appears here to teeter on the edge of the impolite, partisan discourse that he proscribes from the pages of *The Spectator*. In 1711, Whigs inside and outside parliament were campaigning vociferously against peace negotiations which, they believed, would both weaken British trading interests and leave Europe vulnerable to French domination. But Mr Spectator evokes a contentious, partisan issue in order to draw attention to its unsuitability for the pages of *The Spectator*, teasing his readers as he moves from factional to moral debate. In doing so, he makes his own periodical a model of the polite, discrete uses of secrecy that he consistently encourages in his readers.

Conclusion

The *Spectator* demonstrates that not all early eighteenth-century Whigs were delighted by the iconoclastic connotations of secret history's rhetoric of disclosure. Like many Whigs, Addison and Steele associated a culture of secrecy and intelligence with the political style of that most secretive and cunning Lord Treasurer, Robert Harley. But instead of portraying secret history as a means of countering Harley's power by disclosing his secrets, they depict this revelatory form as a product of the same, intelligence-based culture that Harley epitomises – part of the problem, rather than of the solution. The *Spectator* acts as an antidote to this culture of suspicion and intelligence, bearing out Samuel Johnson's assessment of this periodical in his *Life of Addison* (1781):

> It has been suggested that the Royal Society was instituted soon after the Restoration, to divert the attention of the people from publick discontent. The Tatler and The Spectator had the same tendency: they were published at a time when two parties, loud, restless, and violent, each with plausible declarations, and each perhaps without any distinct termination of its views, were agitating the nation; to minds heated with political contest, they supplied cooler and more inoffensive reflections.[91]

Not only does *The Spectator* supply 'cooler and more inoffensive reflections' to its readers, but it does so by appropriating and reworking the conventions of the polemical literature that sustained party conflict. Addison deliberately cultivates a resemblance between Mr Spectator and the spy narrators that populate secret histories, and he hints to his readers that *The Spectator* may contain secret intelligence akin to that of a secret history. He does so, however, in order to demonstrate the difference between *The Spectator* and contemporary intelligence-based publications.

Although its political aims are very different from either John Dunton's anti-Harley secret histories or Delarivier Manley's *romans à clef*, *The Spectator* shares with these texts a key rhetorical device: each couples the rhetoric of disclosure with an absence of intelligence. Although taciturn, underhand and voyeuristic, Mr Spectator is not a spy; in the place of political intelligence, *The Spectator* contains moral advice and topics for polite conversation. By challenging the dominance of a culture of intelligence in the literary marketplace, *The Spectator* pits the virtue of discretion against the jealousy and suspicion that pervaded the political climate of the last four years of the reign of Queen Anne.

6 DANIEL DEFOE: HARLEYITE SECRET HISTORY AND THE EARLY NOVEL

In his extensive study of early modern secret history, Michael McKeon argues that the first years of the reign of George I are a 'watershed' in the history of this form, as well as in English public affairs. He remarks that events such as the end of the War of Spanish Succession, the death of Queen Anne, and the accession of George I 'would seem to have made mandatory the disclosures of secret history'. But he also observes, albeit 'with some uncertainty', that, at this time, revelatory, satirical forms of polemic such as secret history and poems on affairs of state suddenly lost popularity. McKeon suggests that, while poems on affairs of state completely disappeared after the Hanoverian accession, secret history did survive this watershed, albeit in a much modified form. The decades after 1714, McKeon argues, witness the 'ongoing "privatization" of the secret history, that is, the gradual shift of normative weight from the public referent to private reference – more precisely, the gradual absorption of the public realm's traditional priority and privilege by the realm of private experience'. In McKeon's analysis, this shift is registered by the incorporation of the conventions of secret history, hitherto a public, polemical form, into the private, domestic form of the novel.[1]

That the Hanoverian accession creates a historical watershed is not, of course, an observation unique to studies of secret history. If the popularity of poems on affairs of state and polemical secret history does indeed wane after this date, then it may seem to bear out J. H. Plumb's argument that the 'growth of political stability' took place quite suddenly after 1715.[2] The idea that secret history is no longer relevant or useful under an oligarchic, one-party regime and that, deprived of a political outlet for secret history, writers recycle its conventions in a non-polemical, novelistic context is an attractively neat narrative.

Contrary to McKeon's assertions, however, new secret histories do appear after George I's accession to the throne. As we saw in Chapter 3, the death of the Queen and the advent of the new Hanoverian regime precipitated a wave of secret histories by Whig polemicists – including John Oldmixon, Hugh Speke, John Dunton and the anonymous authors of texts such as *A Secret History of One Year* (1714) and *The Secret History of the Chevalier de St George* (1714) –

which must at least qualify the idea that the events of 1713–15 failed to generate polemical secret history. It is, however, the career of Daniel Defoe, secret historian and novelist, that most thoroughly compounds the 'watershed' account of secret history during the early eighteenth century.

Daniel Defoe had a professional interest in the practice of secrecy. Between 1703 and 1714 he served as a spy for the government. From 1704 until 1708, and again between 1710 and 1714, Defoe received his commissions from Robert Harley, at first in his capacity as Secretary of State for the Northern Department, and later as Lord Treasurer. The relationship between Defoe and Harley is, as we will see, vital to understanding Defoe's career as a secret historian, but Defoe's interest in secrecy extends beyond his role as Harley's spy. As a political propagandist, satirist and novelist, Defoe frequently kept his identity as an author secret, both for rhetorical effect and personal safety. Given the time and effort that he invested in practising secrecy, it is no surprise that the concept of secrecy should be a major preoccupation in many of the texts that Defoe produced throughout his lengthy writing career.

In the letters that he wrote to his employers while serving as an intelligence agent, in the secret histories that he published to defend Robert Harley after his fall from power in 1714 (most notably, *The Secret History of the White-Staff*, published 1714–15) and also in his novels, *Moll Flanders* (1722) and *Roxana* (1724), Defoe scrutinizes the politics and ethics of secrecy in both public and private life. Instead of simply using his narratives as vehicles for reflecting upon the concept of secrecy, however, Defoe presents the concept of narrative – that is, a sequence of selected events re-presented in a particular, significant order – as a central element in understanding the practice and the rhetoric of secrecy. Defoe suggests that secrets *are* narratives, created by rearranging the events of the past and/or supplementing those events with fictional interpolations in order to form a narrative of concealment. And if narrative is a vital tool in the creation of secrets then it is also a hermeneutic device necessary to their exposure, since secrets can only be kept hidden by preventing those who would discover them from reconstructing a coherent narrative of what really happened. In Defoe's texts, both the concealment and the disclosure of secrets are underpinned by a self-conscious, analytical approach towards the narratological foundations of secrecy.

This chapter emphasizes the consistency of Defoe's narratological approach towards the concept of secrecy throughout his career, but it also explores the different ways in which his ideas manifest themselves across a range of texts. The chapter begins by examining Defoe's relationship with Robert Harley through their correspondence and the secret histories that Defoe wrote to defend Harley after his fall from power in 1714. Defoe's choice of secret history as the genre in which to write a defence of Harley is noteworthy, in the secret histories of John

Oldmixon and John Dunton, Robert Harley is portrayed as a would-be agent of arbitrary government and the Stuart Pretender. Defoe, on the other hand, uses secret history in an attempt to clear Harley of these charges against him. Crucial to Defoe's efforts is his self-conscious scrutiny of secret history's key formal conventions, especially its claim to re-plot and revise pre-existing narratives of the recent political past.

The second part of the chapter turns to consider the ways in which Defoe remodels his narratological approach towards the concept of secrecy in the novels *Moll Flanders* and *Roxana*. Recent criticism has pointed out the close connections between *Roxana*, in particular, and the tradition of secret history, but it has tended to focus on parallels between the content of each kind of text – sexual scandal in high places and titillating scenes of amorous intrigue.[3] In this chapter, however, I demonstrate that the most significant connections between Defoe's novels and his secret histories are found in their distinctive attitude towards the relationship between secrecy and narrative form. In tracing a movement from secret history to the novel this chapter confirms, to some extent, Michael McKeon's arguments about the privatization of secret history during the early eighteenth century. But it also argues that the public, polemical character of late-Stuart and early-Hanoverian secret history continues to resonate in subtle and oblique ways within the ostensibly private or domestic forms of Defoe's novels.

Defoe and Harley

Defoe's attitude towards secrecy in politics is different from that of almost every other writer in the secret history tradition. In secret histories from *The Secret History of the Court of the Emperor Justinian* (1674) to John Dunton's *State-Weathercocks; or, a New Secret History of the Most Distinguished Favourites Both of the Late and Present Reign* (1719), political secrecy is invariably associated with the *arcana imperii* that sustain absolute monarchy. Even Tories like Delarivier Manley tend to associate secret activities with political and sexual corruption. In secret histories of all political persuasions, secrecy is almost universally regarded as a symptom of underhand, corrupt modes of government.

Defoe's letters to Robert Harley, on the other hand, consistently betray his enthusiasm for political secrecy. In a particularly significant letter sent during the summer of 1704, Defoe asserts that 'Intelligence is the Soul of all Publick bussiness [*sic*]', and that, 'As Intelligence Abroad is So Considerable, it follows in Proportion That The Most usefull Thing at home is Secrecy'. He complains that, 'Tis plain the French Out do us at These Two Things, Secrecy and Intelligence', and proceeds to lament, 'How Many Miscarriages have happen'd in England for want of Silence and Secresy!'[4] Interspersed with these apothegmatic comments on the value of secrecy is Defoe's design for a national and international intelligence network. He outlines the need to place spies at Court and around the country. He also affirms the necessity of employing spies in Scotland, where Defoe himself would later serve as an agent, and France, Britain's enemy in the War of Spanish Succession.

In describing his plan for a French intelligence network, Defoe has recourse to a literary exemplar:

> It Reminds me of a Book in Eight Volumes Published in London about 7 or 8 yeares Ago Call'd Letters writ by a Turkish Spye – The books I Take as They are, a Meer Romance, but the Morall is Good, A Settl'd Person of Sence and Penetration, of Dexterity and Courage, To Reside Constantly in Paris, Tho' As tis a Dangerous Post he had a Larger Allowance than Ordinary, Might by One happy Turn Earn all the money and the Charge be well bestow'd.[5]

It seems likely that Defoe's reference to Giovanni Paolo Marana's *Letters Writ by a Turkish Spy* (1687–94) is self-serving, and that Defoe envisaged himself as the 'Settl'd Person of Sence and Penetration, of Dexterity and Courage' whom he praises to Harley. But this letter is also significant for what it tells us about Defoe's attitude towards spies and intelligencers. We have seen that the spy narratives of the 1690s and *The Spectator* emphasize the unreliability and treachery of the spy, concurring with Jonathan Swift's estimation of spies as 'the most accursed, and prostitute, and abandoned race, that God ever permitted to plague mankind'.[6] In his autobiographical *Appeal to Honour and Justice* (1715), however, Defoe asserts that his work as a spy in Scotland was 'far from being unfit for a Sovereign to direct, or an honest Man to perform'.[7] Defoe's references to *The Turkish Spy* suggest that, as early as 1704, Defoe is making heroes out of secretive characters, and blurring the boundary between the literary representation of secrets and the political practice of secrecy.

Chief among Defoe's secretive heroes was none other than Harley himself. We have already seen that Whig opponents of Harley's ministry, from the Lord Chancellor William Cowper to writers like John Dunton and Joseph Addison, believed that Harley's secretive behaviour was symptomatic of a wider sympathy for the politics of secrecy, embodied in the absolutism of the French Court. In 1711, Harley had authorized secret negotiations between Queen Anne's Secretaries of State, the Earl of Dartmouth and Henry St John, and Nicolas Mesnager, a French diplomat, which eventually brought the War of Spanish Succession to an end in 1713 with the Treaties of Utrecht.[8] It appeared to Whig proponents of the war that Harley's ministry of 1710 to 1714 consisted of a series of secret and treacherous machinations designed to undermine the British constitution and the liberty and property of its subjects. It is hardly surprising, therefore, that almost as soon as George I came to the throne, his newly-appointed Whig ministry began to prepare the case for Harley's impeachment. Defoe's *Secret History of the White-Staff*, a defence of Harley's political conduct while Lord Treasurer (or White Staff), was published in three parts in 1714 and 1715, during which time Harley was impeached on charges of treason and other crimes and misdemeanours and confined to the Tower.[9]

It was probably Harley's reaction to his impeachment, as much as the impeachment itself, that provoked Defoe into writing secret history in his former patron's defence. While Henry St John (by this time Viscount Bolingbroke) fled to France in order to escape the charges against him, Harley took up his seat in the House of Lords and appeared to remain impervious to the panic among the Tory ranks during this period of crisis.[10] In his *History of the Four Last Years of the Queen*, composed in 1713 but not published until 1758, Jonathan Swift describes Harley's character in terms that seem to predict Harley's response to his impeachment:

> There is One Thing peculiar in his Temper, which I altogether disapprove, and do not remember to have heard or met with in any other Man's Character: I mean an Easiness and Indifference under any Imputation, although he be ever so Innocent; and, although the strongest Probabilities and Appearances are against him. So that I have known him often suspected by his nearest Friends for some Months in Points of the highest Importance, to a degree that they were ready to break with him, and only undeceived by Time or Accident.[11]

Swift may have disapproved of Harley's temperamental peculiarities, but his discussion of them is designed to vindicate this much-suspected minister. Nonetheless, Harley sought to have this passage removed from Swift's *History*.[12] Indeed, in spite of having assisted Swift in the early stages of his history's composition, Harley gradually withdrew his support for the publication of the *History of the Four Last Years*. It is tempting to assume that the same character trait that Swift describes in this passage – Harley's refusal to defend himself under the gravest imputations – also led to the prohibition of this vindicatory history.[13]

The History of the Four Last Years was supposed to serve as an 'official', or at least sanctioned, account of Harley's final ministry; Defoe's *Secret History of the White-Staff* covers the same period from a very different perspective. The phrase 'secret history' in the title of this work connects it with contemporary Whig exposés of Harley's secrets. As tracts such as William Stoughton's *Secret History of the Late Ministry* (1715) and John Dunton's *Queen Robin: or the Second Part of Neck or Nothing, Detecting the Secret Reign of the Four Last Years* (1715) reveal, Whig polemicists relished the prospect of unearthing Harley's secrets. The title of Defoe's *Secret History of the White-Staff* likewise suggests that this tract deliberately sets out to reveal Harley's secrets against his will.[14] Deliberately or not, Harley helped to affirm this impression by taking out an advertisement denouncing Defoe's secret history in the *London Gazette* on 9 July 1715.[15] In part, he was forced to do so because several of Defoe's Grub Street antagonists accused Harley either of writing the pamphlets himself, or of co-authoring them with Defoe.[16] Yet Harley's denunciation of *The Secret History of the White-Staff* affirms, either unwittingly or by design, the portrait that Defoe paints of him throughout his secret histories.[17] Defoe implies that he is obliged to publish Harley's secrets because this secretive minister refuses to give an account of his own past actions.

Defoe's attitude towards Harley's ministry was, however, very different from that of most of his contemporaries. While Whig secret historians like Stoughton, Oldmixon and Dunton published damning revelations about Harley's secretive dealings with France and the Pretender, Defoe claimed that his own disclosure of previously undiscovered intelligence about Harley would vindicate this much reviled minister. Moreover, *The Secret History of the White-Staff* argues that the real threat to British liberties during the last four years of Anne's reign came not from France, the Pretender or Robert Harley, but rather from the jealousy and resentment of, on the one hand, the 'displaced Party' – that is, the Junto Whigs and the Earl of Godolphin – and, on the other, the High Tory 'October Club'. Harley's main opponents are named in *The Secret History of the White-Staff* as Francis Atterbury, Bishop of Rochester ('the Mitre'), and Simon Harcourt, Lord Chancellor ('the Purse'), who, 'acting upon Principles of absolute Government, pushed at establishing their Party in a Power or Capacity of Governing by the Severity of the Law; to say no farther'.[18] Harley's efforts to act 'in a medium between all the extreams of Parties' are represented as the only way to guarantee the liberties established by the Revolution of 1688–9 in a political milieu characterized by party rage.[19] Defoe claims that, during Queen Anne's reign, each faction strove to gain total domination not only of the other party, but also of the Queen and the entire nation. The real threat to political liberty at this time came not from the Jacobites but from the more extreme elements of the mainstream parties.

Defoe's portrayal of Harley's methods for pursuing a moderate course between the extremes of party challenges secret history's conventional association of political secrecy with corruption and tyranny. According to Defoe, Harley realized that 'nothing but close Measures, Moderation, Temper, and Time, could carry the point'.[20] The idea that 'close Measures' are a way of ensuring freedom from oppression sits uneasily with secret history's association of secrecy with arbitrary government. In *The Secret History of the White-Staff*, Defoe encourages his readers to look at Harley's love of secrecy from a new perspective. Instead of explaining away Harley's secretiveness and reticence, acknowledging them to be faults as Swift had done, or suggesting that they are evidence of Harley's treachery in the vein of contemporary Whig secret historians, Defoe argues that secrecy and dissimulation are honourable political tactics when they are used for the benefit of the commonwealth.

To substantiate Defoe's arguments about the political benefits of secrecy, *The Secret History of the White-Staff* focuses on Harley's relationship with the Jacobites, expanding upon ideas that Defoe had already articulated in *The Secret History of the October Club* (1711), which was published while Harley was still in power.[21] Defoe claims that Harley's apparent intriguing with Jacobites was, in fact, a form of dissimulation vital to the preservation of the British constitution. By luring Scottish Jacobites to London with promises of places and pensions, for instance, Harley was able to neutralize the threat that they posed as long as they remained in Scotland. In *The Secret History of the White-Staff*, one Jacobite Lord addressing another makes it clear that the Jacobites rather than the British public were the real victims of Harley's secrecy:

> My Lord ... you are moved indeed at this [i.e. Harley's] Treachery, and so am I also; but you don't see all the Wheels of this Machin[e]; we are all trick'd and bubbl'd from the Beginning; the Policy of this damn'd *Staff* has ruin'd us all; and we are wheedled in to be the Instrument of our own Disappointment, by a Management [of] which none of us had Penetration enough to take notice.[22]

Since Harley was in the Tower charged with treason when this secret history was published, Defoe's description of Harley as a traitor to the Jacobites, rather than the Crown, is particularly poignant. Defoe implies that any readers who believed Harley's actions to have been treacherous were duped by his convincing act, just as the Jacobites were. The masterstroke of Defoe's propaganda campaign is his tacit suggestion that those readers who refuse to believe his version of events actually reinforce the explanations that they seek to deny by confirming the success of Harley's anti-Jacobite smokescreen.

In his effort to overturn secret history's conventional argument that political secrecy is evidence of treachery, Defoe appropriates and reworks the rhetorical figures and tropes with which secret history typically exposes the secrets of those in power. We have already seen that earlier secret histories promise to uncover the 'secret Springs' behind familiar political events, and to reveal to their readers that political history is a set of 'wheels within wheels' – a complex series of interlocking events, many of which remain hidden, visible only in their effects.[23] Throughout his secret histories, Defoe also deploys mechanistic metaphors – wheels, engines and springs – in his analysis of the function of secrecy in political life. *The Secret History of the White-Staff*, for instance, represents Harley's struggle against the 'several Springs and Wheels, Engines and Arts' by which the extreme members of both political parties opposed one another and him.[24] In *The Secret History of the October Club*, on the other hand, Defoe uses mechanistic metaphors to describe Harley's own strategy for controlling the Jacobites, which was only gradually understood by men of more moderate political principles:

> When they saw the Wheel within the Wheel; when they saw the Scheme Work, and that the Engineers of the State Gradually and Wisely dropt all their first appearances and acted upon the same Revolution Foundations that others had done before them, all those Fears [concerning Harley's apparently Jacobite sympathies] vanish'd at once.[25]

The idea of Harley as chief engineer of the machine of state, a controller of wheels within wheels, recurs in *Minutes of the Negotiations of Monsr Mesnager* (1717), Defoe's last explicit defence of Harley.[26] Published in the year of Harley's release from the Tower, *Minutes of the Negotiations* provides an account of the negotiations between France and Britain that led to the Peace of Utrecht from a French perspective. The first-person narrator, a fictionalized version of the French plenipotentiary Nicolas Mesnager, describes Harley's distaste for party politics and his desire to employ men of all political persuasions as a 'Design' to create 'a middle Party of NEUTERS, that should have acted by his Schemes, and under Direction, *as Wheels in a Watch*, perfectly passive, except *as wound up* or *screwed down* by the Engineer, *who was to be himself*'.[27] Defoe uses mechanistic tropes so frequently that he seems to be displaying them ostentatiously, as though to affirm his position within the secret history tradition. But his use of imagery common to secret history actually reveals the distance between his own texts and the Whig tradition within which he is writing.

In most secret histories of the late seventeenth and early eighteenth centuries, 'secret springs' and 'wheels within wheels' are used to denote the intricate complexity of state affairs and, therefore, of political history. Defoe, on the other hand, uses these mechanistic metaphors to assert Harley's supremacy as the single, arch-controller of contemporary politics. In *Minutes of the Negotiations of Monsr Mesnager*, the narrator describes Harley as 'the First moving Cause of every Thing, without being really concerned in any of the Particulars'.[28] By representing Harley as the *primum mobile* of the political universe, Defoe brings together the language of Ptolemaic astronomy and the mechanistic figures that characterize secret history; wheels within wheels merge with the celestial spheres. Defoe is also drawing here on the commonplace metaphor of providence as the first mover, the original secret spring or centremost wheel, which governs all earthly affairs. In expounding Ezekiel's vision of a 'wheel within a wheel'[29] the moralist Richard Allestree makes a standard exegetical move when he asserts that 'the wheel within [a wheel] is the wheel of Gods Providence, that turns about the wheels of all outward things, be they never so low and mean'.[30] Indeed, the author of one contemporary devotional work suggests that God's providence might be imagined in terms of a wise man who '[carries] on his designs, and intended purposes by others, in such a secret, close, and covert way and manner, as that, those his subservient Agents, although they chiefly act as from him, and for him, shall imagine and think the while, they act all along for themselves; and that there were no other secret spring, or engine that moved them, than their own Affections'.[31] For Defoe, this analogy works the other way around: if providence manages agents without letting them know the purpose of their work, then the adept political manager should do likewise.[32]

In some respects, Defoe's attitude towards political secrecy and the management of political secrets appears to betray a sympathy for absolute rule, albeit according to the will of a chief minister rather than a monarch. Defoe suggests that Harley's capacity to keep his secrets inviolate should be praised rather than feared. The contrast between Whig secret history's use of mechanistic metaphors and Defoe's could hardly be greater. When Whig secret historians represent political history as a complex, interlocking set of wheels within wheels, they gesture towards the idea that the forces of history operate independently of key players – even apparently all-powerful monarchs. Defoe, on the other hand, represents Harley as a force analogous to providence in a manner that recalls the kind of parallels between God and the King found in the work of seventeenth-century divine right theorists.[33] There is, however, a crucial difference between the discourse of secrecy in Defoe's secret histories and the ways in which secrecy is used to uphold arbitrary power. Michael McKeon has shown that arbitrary government is dependent upon what he calls 'tacit' secrets of state: by refusing even to acknowledge that secrets of state exist, arbitrary rulers maintain an aura of impenetrable secrecy.[34] Defoe, on the other hand, renders political secrecy 'explicit' (to use McKeon's term) by revealing the strategies that Harley uses to maintain control over secrets of state. Indeed, the thorough and consistent way in which Defoe articulates Harley's methods for preserving political secrets across a number of different texts amounts to a coherent method for keeping intelligence secret.

Defoe's analysis of the relationship between secrecy and power focuses particularly closely upon the relationship between political managers and their agents. He takes it for granted that all political managers need agents in order to do their business and keep them informed.[35] The way in which those agents are managed is vital to keeping political secrets. Harley – at least, as Defoe portrays him – is a master of the art of managing his agents. Defoe also notes, however, that many of his contemporaries fail to understand Harley's skill in this respect. In *Minutes of the Negotiations of Monsr Mesnager*, the French plenipotentiary, Mesnager, observes that, while Harley is 'affable and courteous, easy of Access' in private company, his behaviour 'in publick Business' is very different:

> There his Discourse is always reserved, communicating nothing, and allowing none to know the whole Event of what they are Employed to do; his Excess of caution makes Business hang on his Hands, and his Dispatches were thereby always both slow and imperfect; and it is said, he scarce ever sent any Person abroad, though on Matters of the greatest Importance, but that he left some of their Business to be sent after them.[36]

Mesnager's tone is undoubtedly critical – even mocking – as he describes Harley's excessively cautious approach towards political secrets. His criticisms resonate with those of Jonathan Swift, who numbered procrastination and poor communication among Harley's worst defects.[37] But when read in the context of Defoe's other writings, Mesnager's criticisms actually expose this French plenipotentiary's poor judgement rather than Harley's failings as a political manager. In fact, the tactics that Mesnager derides are precisely those that, in Defoe's estimation, make Harley an exceptionally good manager of secrets.

The idea that no agent should be allowed 'to know the whole Event of what they are Employed to do' finds expression in several of Defoe's letters to Harley. In the summer of 1704, Defoe advises Harley to employ 'Two Trusty Agents' to gather information from every region in Britain, but he also insists that these agents 'Not kno' who they Serv Nor for what End'.[38] On another occasion he informs Harley that, 'By my Brother any thing you please to Convey to my Wife will Come Safe, But Rather by Bill than in specie, and Seal'd because Sir I have Learnt in all these things to make Agents without Accquainting them with Perticulars'.[39] Likewise, in *The Secret History of the White-Staff*, Defoe asserts that Harley duped the Jacobites into believing that he was in their interest, so that, 'by being made to entertain that Dream, [the Jacobites] hamstringed their Cause, and suffered themselves, both within Doors and without, to be made the Instruments and Agents to make that impossible, which they fancied they were bringing to pass'.[40] Moreover, Defoe makes it clear that when Harley experienced political difficulties during his final ministry, it was due to his inability to follow these principles. At the beginning of *The Secret History of the White-Staff*, Defoe observes that

> as ... Prime Ministers cannot be suppos'd to act by their own Hands, or advise by their own Councils in all things they do, or in every Branch of their Administration; so we often find that they have their more immediate Agents, by whom they not only may be said to commit great part of the Management, but who oftentimes possess their Councils so entirely as to overrule them in many things, and at last top upon their masters, and become independent of them.[41]

Defoe uses the word 'council' in two different senses in this passage. The first instance has connotations of the modern word 'counsel' – that is, advice.[42] The second time the word appears, however, it carries a now obsolete sense: a confidence or secret.[43] By sharing secrets or 'councils', Defoe suggests, a manager risks empowering his agents. If real political control is to be achieved, the two conditions outlined by Mesnager must be met: first, agents must be (at least to some extent) the dupes of their political masters; and second, managers must spread their intelligence between agents, trusting no single agent with an entire commission.

These two pieces of advice, which are reiterated in various forms throughout Defoe's letters and secret histories, have their foundation in Defoe's narratological conception of the relationship between secrecy and political control. By spreading intelligence among agents and by ensuring that those agents are dupes who remain unaware of the true nature of their employment, a political manager like Harley is able to prevent his agents from reconstructing the narrative of their employer's secrets. In effect, Defoe's narratological approach towards secrets is designed to prevent agents from becoming potential secret historians. Defoe's methodologically self-conscious secret histories discuss the fact that secret historians use narrative as a hermeneutic device in order to uncover political secrets. As he attempts to demonstrate who was really to blame for the political turbulence of the years from 1710 to 1714 in *The Secret History of the White-Staff*, Defoe suggests that 'we shall be led to the Persons by the Chain of the Enquiry', since 'such Affairs as these hang upon one another, by a long Train of second Causes, which leads us to discover one by another'.[44] In an earlier part of *The Secret History of the White-Staff* he describes Harley as 'the Clue we are to trace in this *Secret History*', where the word 'clue' retains its original, literal sense of a ball of thread used to find the way out of a labyrinth or maze.[45] Since political secrets are composed of narratives that conceal the truth, the work of the secret historian is to trace clues and follow chains of enquiry – that is, to create narrative sequences – in order to reconstruct an account of what really happened.

Defoe's observations about the relationship between secrecy and narrative have a tangible impact upon the shape of his secret histories. For instance, they help to explain why *The Secret History of the White-Staff* barely mentions the peace of Utrecht and makes no mention at all of the illicit negotiations between the Tory ministry and Mesnager, in spite of the fact that these secret dealings were the basis of treason charges against Harley. It seems at first glance that Defoe attempts to defend his former patron by skirting around these controversial events in his secret histories. In his *Detection of the Sophistry and Falsities of the Pamphlet, Entitul'd the Secret History of the White-Staff* (1714), John Oldmixon mocks the fact that Defoe's secret history says 'not a word' about the peace.[46] But in the secret history that Oldmixon is attacking, Defoe asserts that the peace negotiations are 'exotick in Nature, to the Relation which is now in hand'.[47] The reason why there is no account of the peace negotiations in *The Secret History of the White-Staff* is that, according to Defoe, Harley was not involved in these contentious events. By emphasizing his narratological approach to the tumultuous political history of Anne's reign, Defoe turns an apparently defensive omission of damning evidence into a positive denial of wrongdoing.

There is, however, a paradox at the heart of Defoe's attitude towards the secrets of Harley's final ministry. Defoe suggests that Harley manages to prevent political agents from becoming secret historians within the context of a secret history that traces Robert Harley as a 'clue' through the labyrinthine political history of Queen Anne's reign. Defoe had to find a way to reconcile his claim to reveal Harley's secrets with his assertion that Harley is a supreme manager of political intelligence. He does so by drawing attention to the physical form and publication history of his text.

The Secret History of the White-Staff is not a single work, but rather three texts, which appeared at the end of September 1714, 27 October 1714, and 29 January 1715.[48] Although the content of each of these three parts is very similar, Defoe attempts to give his readers the impression that none of them deals adequately with the complex history of Harley's ministry. He asserts at the beginning of the second part of this secret history that 'it will be needful to give a brief Recapitulation of a Circumstance or two, which is but hinted lightly at in the first part, in order to preserve the Connection of the historical Relation of things, and, with the greater Clearness, to introduce the Matters which are behind'.[49] Defoe's choice of the preposition, 'behind', gives the impression that he is clearing away obstructions to get to the truth, restructuring a sequential, linear narrative out of the secrets that are concealed one behind another. Yet this method is clearly not conclusive. In part 3 of this secret history, Defoe asserts that 'many secret Histories [of the period under consideration] are yet behind untold, which it were very useful to have made known', and he ends this final part of his narrative by stating that 'there are yet several large Fields that are not mentioned, or entred into, and which have some *Arcana* of publick Matters to bring to light, before the History of the *White-Staff* can be said to be compleat'.[50] Defoe's protestations sound suspiciously like an advertisement for future parts of *The Secret History of the White-Staff*. But in this case, sequential publishing is significant to Defoe's argument about Harley and secrecy. No secret history of Harley can ever prove definitive, Defoe implies, because of Harley's capacity to keep his secrets concealed.

Although the tripartite structure of Defoe's secret history supports Defoe's arguments in this text, a surprising intervention in the publication history of *The Secret History of the White-Staff* reveals Defoe's recognition of a more sceptical readership who might look askance at his claims to produce ever more secret accounts of the past. On 4 January 1715 – after the publication of the first and second parts of *The Secret History of the White-Staff*, but before the third had appeared – Defoe published a text with a most intriguing title: *The Secret His-*

tory of The Secret History of the White-Staff, Purse and Mitre (1715). Although he wrote them all, Defoe attempts to put as much distance as possible between his secret histories and this *Secret History of the Secret History*. He claims that *The Secret History of the Secret History* was written by 'a Person of Quality' and he also uses a different publisher for this text from the publisher who had produced *The Secret History of the White-Staff*.[51]

In *The Secret History of the Secret History*, an honest Quaker tells a 'Person of Quality' that he knows the true story behind both Defoe's secret histories of Harley and the antagonistic responses to them:

> The same People employing other Hands, have been the Editors not only of the Books themselves, but also of several of the Answers to these Books, causing the deceiv'd People to Dance in the Circles of their drawing, while these have enjoy'd the Sport of their own Witch-craft.[52]

Although this passage implies that the conjuring booksellers take pleasure in their occult arts, there are, of course, more mercenary reasons for their underhand practices. The Quaker asserts that the publication of party polemic is not ideologically driven, but is, instead, a response to consumer demand:

> These Persons do not Consult the Side, or Party on which, or in whose behalf the said Books may be suppos'd to plead; but the great Thing, which they regard, is that the said Books *may Sell*; and if they find it sells, so as to answer their Design, they go on, perhaps, to employ the same Persons to write an Answer, or Answers thereto.[53]

The Quaker alleges that William Pittis, a High Tory polemicist who had attacked Defoe's pamphlets in *The History of the Mitre and Purse* (1714), had written both Defoe's secret histories and the hostile responses to them, at the instigation of the notorious Grub Street bookseller, Edmund Curll.[54] What could Defoe's motives have been for writing this secret history, which effectively undermines all of the arguments in favour of Harley that Defoe presents in *The Secret History of the White-Staff*?

In part, *The Secret History of the Secret History* is an attempt to pour water on the party-political conflagration that threatened to consume *The Secret History of the White-Staff*. In *The Secret History of the White-Staff*, Defoe declares that 'the *Rage of Parties*, well was it call'd by that Name in Her Majesty's Speech, ran to so fearful an Extreme, that neither Side could be said to stick at any thing to offend, or to defend'.[55] Defoe's scornful attack on party rage reflects Harley's own antipathy towards party politics, expressed most coherently in the pamphlet *Faults on Both Sides* (1710).[56] But in spite of Defoe's protestations about the evils of party politics, *The Secret History of the White-Staff* was attacked by adversaries from both sides: the staunch Whig, John Oldmixon, quickly published *A Detection of the Sophistry and Falsities of the Pamphlet, Entitul'd the Secret His-*

tory of the White-Staff (1714) in two parts, while the Tories attacked Defoe and Harley through *Considerations on the Secret History of the White-Staff* (1714), *A History of the Mitre and Purse* (1714) and William Pittis's *Queen Anne Vindicated from the Base Aspersions of Some Late Pamphlets* (1715).[57] In the context of these contentious, partisan publications, *The Secret History of the Secret History of the White-Staff* can be read as Defoe's final attempt to undermine the rage of party that he held responsible for Harley's downfall. By claiming that *The Secret History of the White-Staff* and its antagonists are nothing more than a series of elaborate fictions designed to earn a crust for party scribblers, Defoe attempts to convince his readers that the foundations of secret history are financial rather than political. In doing so, he sacrifices his defence of Harley to a distinctively Harleyite cause: the opposition to party politics.

Defoe's aims in *The Secret History of the Secret History of the White-Staff* are not, however, entirely ideological. This strange text is also a manifestation of Defoe's profound, theoretical interest in the relationship between secrecy and narrative. By suggesting that behind every secret lies another, deeper, darker, as-yet-undiscovered mystery, Defoe indulges in the kind of self-reflexive scrutiny of the discourse of revelation that we have already seen in texts such as David Jones's *Secret History of White-hall*. The epistemic instability occasioned by the rhetorical act of disclosure is encapsulated in the repetitive title and the perplexing argument of *The Secret History of the Secret History of the White-Staff*. But while earlier texts in the secret history tradition connect secret history's promise of unending historical revisionism with the fight against arbitrary government, Defoe's self-conscious interest in the discourse of revelation completely undermines his political aims. His exploration of the relationship between secrecy and the hermeneutic function of narrative ultimately proves to be at odds with his attempt to defend Robert Harley. *The Secret History of the Secret History*'s claim that Defoe's earlier secret histories had 'no Substance, or Foundation in the matters of Fact' is just the last in a long series of self-destructive rhetorical gestures found throughout his secret histories.[58] We have already seen that Defoe refuses to address the grounds for the treason charges that had been brought against Harley during his impeachment, and that he repeatedly claims that his narrative is incomplete. Defoe thus leaves open the possibility that any new intelligence could condemn as well as vindicate Harley.

Defoe's critics were quick to point out *The Secret History of the White-Staff*'s failings as a piece of propaganda. They alerted readers to factual errors and inconsistencies in Defoe's account of the four last years of the Queen's reign.[59] More recently, Paula Backscheider has commented that 'it was unlike [Defoe] to be such an inept defender, or to open so many new lines of attack to his opponents'.[60] She suggests that Defoe believed that Harley would return to power and that a show of loyalty was likely to be more advantageous in the long run than a detailed justification of Harley's actions. A different explanation is provided by Geoffrey Sill, who acknowledges that, if this text is taken as a historical account of the events of Harley's ministry, it can only be regarded as a 'tissue of lies'.[61] He argues instead that *The Secret History of the White-Staff* is a type of classical tragedy in pamphlet form, in which Harley, a heroic emblem of political moderation and tolerance, falls victim to the forces of party tyranny.[62] But for Defoe, Harley is more than an emblem of moderation and tolerance; he is also an exemplary model of the management of political secrets, and as a result he provides Defoe with an opportunity for exploring the relationship between secrecy, narrative and political power. In the end, Defoe's fascination with this triadic relationship seems to have overtaken even his desire to defend his patron. It also allowed him to explore the discourse of revelation once more in a very different generic context: the novel.

Secrecy and Narrative Form in Defoe's Novels

Shortly after relating his famous discovery of a single footprint in the sand, Robinson Crusoe exclaims, 'how strange a Checquer Work of Providence is the Life of Man! and by what secret differing Springs are the Affections hurry'd about as differing Circumstance[s] present!'[63] Several pages later, when Crusoe discovers the remains of a cast-away ship off the coast of his island, he refers to the 'secret moving Springs in the Affections' which make him yearn for a companion.[64] Crusoe's use of this well-worn metaphor underlines the profound loneliness of his circumstances on the island, not least because of its association with the secret histories that Defoe had been engaged in publishing five years earlier. In Defoe's secret histories, the 'secret springs' metaphor suggests the complexity of the political machine and the society that it governs. In *Robinson Crusoe*, on the other hand, the same metaphor denotes Crusoe's intense introspection, and the intricate workings of the human mind.[65] As the 'secret springs' metaphor shifts context from secret history to the novel, it appears to signal the watershed to which Michael McKeon refers in his account of secret history during the early eighteenth century. Crusoe's use of secret history's most characteristic trope to describe his own emotional condition apparently indicates the privatization of the conventions of secret history. Alone on his island and deprived of a public existence, Crusoe has little need for secrecy and the secret springs of the affections entirely replace those that drive public life. In his later novels, *Moll Flanders* and *Roxana*, however, Defoe steers a path between the extreme introspection of the secret springs of Crusoe's mind and the public context of the secret springs of secret history. In these novels, secrecy is a central element, even a precondition, of social existence.

The plots of *Moll Flanders* and *Roxana* are full of secrets. Moll and Roxana keep secrets from their husbands, their children, their confidants, and the law. But the nature of their secrets reflects the generic differences between these novels about the lives of two private citizens and the tradition of polemical secret history with which Defoe engages in *The Secret History of the White-Staff*. Although Roxana consorts with princes and peers, and thus comes closer to being a public figure than the low-born thief, Moll Flanders, the secrets that she keeps with and from her lovers have no obvious or direct bearing upon public life. Nor are the differences between the discourse of secrecy in Defoe's novels and secret histories confined to the nature of the secrets contained in these texts. In his novels, Defoe's use of a first-person narrative voice creates a confessional tone. For the most part, Moll and Roxana give the impression that they are telling their readers their secrets without reserve.[66] The relatively open relationship that Defoe constructs between the narrators of his novels and their implied readers differs starkly from the secretive manner in which the protagonists of these novels behave towards the characters with whom they interact. As narrators of their own stories, Moll and Roxana disclose their secrets to their readers; as characters in those stories, they do all they can to conceal their secrets from the husbands, children, confidants and legal authorities who have a vested interest in discovering them. So while Defoe's secret histories are third-person narratives which expose the secrets of unwilling subjects, *Moll Flanders* and *Roxana* disclose their own secrets voluntarily.[67] In spite of these differences, however, there are also significant similarities between the discourse of secrecy in secret history and in Defoe's novels. In particular, Defoe's distinctive approach towards the relationship between secrecy and narrative dictates the formal structure of both kinds of text.

While Defoe's secret histories are concerned with the function of secrecy in high politics, *Moll Flanders* and *Roxana* explore the role of secrecy in private life through a discussion of the politics of friendship. Towards the end of her narrative, Moll Flanders embarks on a lengthy digression on the subject of secrecy and friendship:

> Let them say what they please of our Sex not being able to keep a Secret; my Life is a plain Conviction to me of the contrary; but be it our Sex, or the Man's Sex, a Secret of Moment should always have a Confident, a bosom Friend, to whom we may Communicate the Joy of it, or the Grief of it, be it which it will, or it will be a double weight upon the Spirits, and perhaps become even insupportable in itself; and this I appeal to all human Testimony for the Truth of.[68]

In her friendless condition, Moll scrutinizes what Robinson Crusoe describes as the 'secret moving Springs in the affections' which he feels upon discovering a cast-away ship off the shore of his island. These introspective secret springs lead

Crusoe to reflect that, 'in all the Time of my solitary Life, I never felt so earnest, so strong a Desire after the Society of my Fellow-Creatures, or so deep a Regret at the want of it'.[69] Both Moll Flanders and Robinson Crusoe appear to suggest that the desire to share secrets is fundamental to friendship, and that friendship is an essential aspect of human existance.[70]

Although both Moll Flanders and Robinson Crusoe long for a companion, however, the similarities between their psychological self-analysis and their need for friendship should not obscure the differences between their sentiments. While Crusoe yearns for the society of a companion, Moll has a politician's attitude towards the relationship between secrecy and friendship: her wish for a confidant emerges out of her knowledge of how to keep a secret. Moll's self-conscious awareness of the fragility of the human mind and the deleterious effects of secrecy upon it lead her to assert that, without an outlet for confession, the 'weight' of a secret becomes 'insupportable'; that is to say, the body refuses to conceal what the mind or reason would keep hidden. She cites the example of those men and women who reveal secret crimes, 'such as secret Murther in particular', in their sleep, 'tho' the Consequence would necessarily be their own Destruction'.[71] Her desire for a friend in whom she can confide is, therefore, a vital part of Moll's political management of her secrets. In *The Spectator*, Addison suggests that secrecy is a morally ambivalent quality, redeemed only by its capacity to seal friendships.[72] *Moll Flanders*, however, presents something of an opposite view, portraying friendship as a convenient way of keeping secrets. By providing an outlet for the unbearable pressure of concealment, 'a Confident' or 'a bosom Friend' ensures that the bearer of a secret can maintain the integrity of his or her intelligence.

The cathartic function of confession is a central element of Moll's political approach towards secrecy and friendship. It is, however, only the first step towards the efficient management of secrets. A secondary function of confession is its capacity to turn friends or confidants into agents. At one point in her narrative, Moll laments the fact that she had 'no Body to whom I could in confidence commit the Secret of my Circumstances to [*sic*], and could depend on for their Secresie and Fidelity'.[73] Her concern here is not to have someone with whom she can divide the psychological burden of her secrets, but rather to find a manager for her financial affairs: "Tis evident Men can be their own Advisers, and their own Directors, and know how to work themselves out of Difficulties and into Business better than Women', Moll asserts, 'but if a Woman has no Friend to Communicate her Affairs to, and to advise and assist her, 'tis ten to one but she is undone'.[74] When she asserts that 'to be Friendless is the worst Condition, next to being in want, that a Woman can be reduc'd to', Moll is describing not the personal loneliness of a Robinson Crusoe, but rather a kind of political vulnerability: without friends, she is forced to operate without agents.[75] Later in her story, Moll confesses a secret to her friend whom she calls 'the Governess', acknowledging that 'to conceal it, was to deprive myself of all possible Help, or means of Help, and to deprive her of the Opportunity of Serving me'.[76] And when Moll confesses her secret sins to the chaplain or Ordinary of Newgate – an act which initially, at least, seems born of a spiritual rather than a political desire to reveal her secrets – she nonetheless manages to turn her confessor into her agent. Moll reports that when the Ordinary visited her shortly before she was due to be executed 'he shew'd me that his time had been employ'd on my Account; that he had obtain'd a favourable Report from the Recorder to the Secretary of State in my particular Case, and in short that he had brought me a Reprieve'.[77] Through her confession, Moll accrues worldly as well as spiritual advantages.

Moll reveals her political acumen in the way in which she manages her agents as well as her secrets. Crucially, she never gives too much away. Even her principal confidant, the Governess, is not told anything more of Moll's circumstances than is strictly necessary to give her 'the Opportunity of serving me'.[78] Moll's approach towards secrecy and friendship is informed by the idea, expressed by Defoe in several letters and his secret histories, that no political agent should be allowed 'to know the whole Event of what they are Employed to do'.[79] Like Defoe as he portrays himself in his letters to Harley, and like the version of Harley that Defoe presents to his readers in his secret histories, Moll Flanders attempts to gain political leverage by creating agents without letting them fully into the secret of her affairs. She reveals herself to be a political manager of secrets, regardless of the fact that her secrets are significant in a private rather than a public context. In this respect, her approach towards the relationship between secrecy and friendship contrasts starkly with another of Defoe's secretive first-person narrators: Roxana.

Both *Moll Flanders* and *Roxana* explore the connections between secrecy and friendship. But while Moll controls her secrets by spreading intelligence among a number of different agents, Roxana has a single chief confidante who participates in her story from beginning to end. According to Roxana, Amy is 'not only ... a Servant, but an Agent; and not only an Agent, but a Friend, and a faithful Friend too'.[80] The climactic rhetorical movement from 'Servant' to a 'Friend' in Roxana's description of Amy draws attention to the difference between her attitude towards secrecy and friendship and that of Moll Flanders. While Moll uses the limited disclosure of secrets to turn friends into agents and servants, Roxana keeps no secrets from Amy, turning a loyal servant by degrees into a dangerous friend. So intimate is the relationship between Amy and Roxana that Amy has sometimes been described as Roxana's *alter ego*, a kind of projection of Roxana's own psychological condition.[81] But this approach to Amy's character obscures the importance of her role as Roxana's agent. An agent is, of course, any person who acts on behalf of or as a proxy for another, and Roxana informs her reader that Amy 'was my Steward, gather'd in my Rents, *I mean my Interest-Money*, and kept my Accompts, and, *in a word*, did all my Business'.[82] But Amy is also Roxana's secret agent or spy. At several points in her narrative, Roxana sends Amy on what she calls 'commissions' to gather intelligence about Roxana's former lovers and enemies as well as the family that she leaves behind after she has herself been abandoned, destitute, by her first husband.[83] Amy's function as Roxana's agent is a neglected and illuminating aspect of this, Defoe's last novel.

In *Moll Flanders* and in his secret histories, Defoe draws attention to the fact that the relationship between an agent and an employer must be based on sound narratological principles if secrets are to remain inviolate. He observes that employers should prevent their agents from constructing a full and accurate reconstruction of the narrative of a secret by witholding from them the true nature of their employment. To this end, he observes that intelligence must always be spread between agents rather than entrusted to a single person. In *Roxana*, Defoe depicts what might happen if an employer were to fail to grasp these principles and, therefore, to misunderstand the relationship between secrecy, narrative, and power.

Roxana only registers an awareness of the problems inherent in her attitude towards secrecy at the end of her narrative.[84] Throughout the final third of the novel, Roxana is pursued relentlessly by her estranged daughter, Susan, who attempts to persuade Roxana to acknowledge their true relationship. Amy, who grows increasingly infuriated by Susan's importunities, offers to murder Roxana's troublesome daughter. Although Roxana wishes to be rid of Susan, she is horrified by Amy's suggestion, and dismisses Amy from her service. But shortly after she has turned Amy away, Roxana comes to reflect 'that *Amy* knew all the Secret History of my Life; and had been in all the Intriegues of it, and been a Party in both Evil and Good', and that 'it must be only her steddy Kindness to me, and an excess of Generous Friendship for me, that shou'd keep her from ill-using me in return for it; which ill-using me was enough in her Power, and might be my utter Undoing'.[85] When Defoe puts the phrase 'secret history' into Roxana's mouth here, it seems initially to function as shorthand for the illicit sexual intrigues in which she engages throughout her narrative. But it also draws attention to the reasons why Amy has power over Roxana. When she realizes that Amy is in a position to 'publish' or make public a full narrative of Roxana's life, Roxana begins to grasp the relationship between secrecy, narrative, and power. Her new understanding is registered by a second use of the phrase 'secret history' soon after she has dismissed Amy. In Amy's absence, Roxana puts her friend the Quaker in charge of her financial affairs, but she is keen to inform her reader that 'you must not understand me as if I let my Friend the QUAKER into any Part of the Secret History of my former Life', since 'it was always a Maxim with me, *That Secrets shou'd never be open'd, without evident Utility*'.[86]

Roxana's axiomatic assertion about the management of secrets chimes with the ideas about secrecy that run through Defoe's letters, secret histories and *Moll Flanders*. But Roxana's behaviour throughout this narrative reveals that she has frequently failed to live up to her own strictures.[87] The fact that Amy remains a constant presence throughout the majority of this narrative reveals the lack of sophistication with which Roxana approaches the management of her secrets. And although Roxana's tone in this passage is cool and collected, the atmosphere of the final section of *Roxana* becomes increasingly dark and hysterical. Roxana learns to be self-conscious in her management of secrets too late, by which time her own secret history has slipped out of her control.

Roxana's naivety with regard to the management of secrets is evident in her repeated praise of Amy's faithfulness.[88] When, at the beginning of their story, Amy refuses to leave Roxana in spite of her destitution, Roxana acknowledges her 'Kindness and Fidelity' and frequently thereafter reflects upon Amy's faithful temper.[89] Yet it is precisely Amy's constant presence at Roxana's side that undermines Roxana's ability to manage her secrets. Amy acts as a narrative thread which connects together Roxana's various incarnations, from her marriage to a brewer, through her liaison with a jeweller, a European prince, an English peer and, finally, a respectable Dutch merchant. Just as Robert Harley is the 'clue' that Defoe follows through the labyrinthine politics of Queen Anne's reign in *The Secret History of the White-Staff*, so Amy is the clue that Roxana's estranged daughter, Susan, follows to discover the identity of her mother.

Susan's reading of her own past underscores the hermeneutic function of narrative. Susan appears in Roxana's story when Amy discovers her among the maids at the London house where Roxana is living a dissolute existence as the mistress of an English peer. Torn between the wish to raise her daughter out of the condition of a servant and the desire to prevent Susan from knowing about her mother's debauchery, Roxana commissions her agent Amy to provide Susan with a substantial income, but without letting Susan know its source. A chance meeting, however, allows Susan to discover that Amy, whom Susan had previously known only as Roxana's head servant, is the provider of her new wealth. This coincidence causes Susan to attempt to deduce the true relationship between herself, Amy and Roxana. Susan's knowledge of her past 'all consisted of broken Fragments of Stories, such as the Girl herself had heard so long ago, that she herself cou'd make very little of it'.[90] Yet she is able to piece together a plausible account of the reasons for Amy's conduct because she knows that 'her Mother had play'd the Whore; had gone away with the Gentleman that was Landlord of the House; that he married her; that she went into *France*; and as she had learn'd in my Family, where she was a Servant, that Mrs *Amy* and her Lady *Roxana* had been in *France* together; so she put all these things together, and joining them with the great Kindness that *Amy* now shew'd her, possess'd the Creature that

Amy was really her Mother'.[91] The clumsy, paratactic clauses in which Defoe relates Susan's deductions reflect the difficulty that Susan experiences in reconstructing her fragmented past into a narrative whole. Susan follows the 'clue' that is Amy to the wrong conclusion. Her method is, however, strongly reminiscent of secret history. In his secret histories, which repeatedly draw attention to the fact that much information about Harley's ministry is 'yet behind untold', Defoe highlights the fallibility of the technique that Susan uses to piece together the story of her own past in *Roxana*.

By acknowledging the importance of secret history to the plot of *Roxana*, it becomes possible to approach some of the more perplexing formal elements of this novel with new insight. Chief among these is the ending of *Roxana*. Just as Susan attempts to construe her own identity by deductive means when Roxana refuses to acknowledge her, so, by the end of her narrative, Roxana is obliged to infer what has happened to her importunate daughter from the available circumstantial evidence. Amy murders Susan 'off stage', underscoring Roxana's total loss of control over the narrative of her own life. Nonetheless, Roxana clearly holds herself responsible for Susan's death, and she reports in the novel's final sentence that 'the Blast of Heaven seem'd to follow the Injury done the poor Girl, by us both; and I was brought so low again, that my Repentance seem'd to be only the Consequence of my Misery, as my Misery was of my Crime'.[92] This bleak conclusion understandably disturbed *Roxana*'s first readers. Throughout the eighteenth century, publishers added new endings, most of which made Roxana into a Christian penitent on the model of *Moll Flanders* and the tradition of spiritual autobiography to which both novels clearly owe debts.[93] In his study of the influence of spiritual autobiography on Defoe's novels, G. A. Starr also expresses his bafflement at the abrupt and unedifying ending of Defoe's final novel. He suggests that Defoe may have intended to bring Roxana to an eventual repentance like her predecessor, Moll Flanders, 'but at some point decided to let her spiritual development complete its natural course, and end with the distinct prospect of damnation'.[94] Alternatively, he suggests that Defoe's decision to write *Roxana* as a first-person narrative was a 'crippling tactical error' since, by making Roxana a commentator on her own life, Defoe 'not only deprived her reflections of much of their intrinsic validity but made her entire character extremely ambiguous'.[95]

The disconcerting conclusion of *Roxana* is intrinsically connected to the overall structure of this novel. While *Moll Flanders* is composed of a sequence of discrete, apparently unconnected episodes, the plot of *Roxana* is much more 'joined up'. As Lincoln Faller puts it:

> No single event in Roxana's life can be freely considered by itself as, for instance, a comparable event in Moll's. Not everything Roxana does leads to her doing some-

thing else, but the ligatures between her actions are a good deal more developed than in any of Defoe's other novels, or in contemporary fiction generally.[96]

The narrative structure of each novel appears to be a sign of the soteriological status of its particular narrator. Although the penitent Moll Flanders laments that she 'had a past life of a most wretched kind to account for, some of it in this World as well as in another', that past life never catches up with her during the course of her episodic narrative.[97] Roxana, on the other hand, is tied down by providential and narratological ligatures. The narrative chains that prevent Roxana from putting the past behind her are analogous, if not causally connected, to the inescapability of her reprobate status.

Questions of salvation provide one explanation for the differences in narrative structure between *Moll Flanders* and *Roxana*; the influence of secret history on these novels can, however, be made to account for the shape of their plots in a rather more worldly way. Put simply, Moll is a proficient manager of secrets because she understands the relationship between secrecy and narrative, while Roxana does not manage her secrets well because she fails to comprehend this relationship. In fact, Roxana's attempts to guard her secrets are often the cause of, rather than the solution to, her problems because they create narrative connections between the various episodes of her life. For instance, following her unexpected sighting of her first husband, the Brewer, among the Gendarmes in Paris, Roxana reports:

> I found out a Fellow, who was completely qualified for the Work of a Spy, (for *France* has Plenty of such people,) this Man I employ'd to be a constant and particular Attendant upon his Person and Motions; and he was especially employ'd, and order'd to haunt him *as a Ghost*; that he should scarce let him be ever out of his Sight; he perform'd this to a Nicety, and fail'd not to give me a perfect Journal of his Motions, from Day to Day; and whether for his Pleasures, or his Business, was always at his Heels.[98]

The activities of this spy are later taken up by Amy, whom Roxana sends to France with 'four Articles of Confidence in Charge to enquire after, for me': her husband in the Gendarmes, two of her former lovers, and a Jewish merchant who had tried to have Roxana arrested after the death of her lover, the Jeweller.[99] Roxana's determination to keep an eye on her past makes it much more difficult for her to escape and contain it. The fact that she repeatedly revisits earlier episodes in her life is a symptom of her wrongheaded approach to the relationship between secrecy and narrative. Items from Roxana's past – for instance, her Turkish dress and, indeed, Amy herself – repeatedly appear in the present, creating connections between Roxana's various guises or incarnations. At the end of the narrative, Defoe portrays Roxana not simply as an unregenerate woman heading for damnation, but also as a woman whose worldly, if not her eternal, fortune could have been improved had she managed her secrets better.

Roxana's mismanagement of her secrets contrasts with Moll's expert control over her past. When Moll spots Jemmy, the highwayman whom she had previously married in Lancashire, with a group of men at an inn immediately following her marriage to a London banker, her reaction is to hide herself away, only 'peeping at them' from inside her room.[100] She expresses relief when she realizes that Jemmy has gone down a different road from the one she intends to travel, since, 'had they gone towards *London*, I should have been still in a fright, least I should meet him on the Road again, and that he should know me'.[101] Likewise, when she arrives back in Virginia with Jemmy at the end of her narrative, she is at pains to keep her new husband away from her old family, including her former husband, whom she had discovered to be her brother upon her first arrival in Virginia. There are, of course, practical reasons for Moll's discretion: in each case, the concealment is designed to hide an act of bigamy. Nonetheless, Moll's apparently instinctive methods for self-preservation have a firm basis in Defoe's theories about the political management of secrets. Moll is consistently careful to eradicate the temporal and spatial connections between episodes in her life that would allow any of her acquaintance to piece together a full narrative of her past. By keeping the component parts of her life's story discrete, she prevents this narrative from being made public against her will. She thus ensures that when her 'secret history' is published, it takes the form of a confessional pseudo-autobiography rather than a scandalous, third-person exposé. Of course, *Roxana* is also a first-person narrative; in spite of Roxana's concerns, her life's story is made public neither by Susan nor by Amy, but by Roxana herself. Nonetheless, the fact that 'the secret history of Roxana' is published by Roxana rather than Susan or Amy is due to the fact that Amy does not breach her fidelity to her mistress, and not at all to Roxana's management of her secrets.

Although the soteriological status of the two narrators may, in part, account for the episodic plot of *Moll Flanders* and the ligatured plot of *Roxana*, then, Defoe also hints at other, more immediate reasons for the structural differences between his two novels. As Moll Flanders herself puts it, providence 'ordinarily Works by the Hands of Nature' and 'makes use here of ... natural Causes to produce ... extraordinary Effects'.[102] The relationship between secrets, narrative and power in Defoe's last two novels governs the plots of these works and reveals the impact of his early relationship with Robert Harley upon his later career as a novelist.

Secret History to the Novel: a Politicized Reading

By absorbing the conventions of secret history, *Moll Flanders* and *Roxana* apparently bear testimony to Michael McKeon's argument about the 'privatization' of secret history in early Hanoverian Britain. These novels transfer the ideas about the relationship between secrecy, narrative, and power that Defoe develops in his letters and secret histories to a private context, exploring the ways in which they affect the politics of friendship rather than high politics. Instead of signalling a retreat from political engagement, however, this movement of the discourse of secrecy from the public to the private domain can, itself, be read as a political statement. In *Roxana* in particular, Defoe not only absorbs the ideas about secrecy, narrative and power that he had developed in the secret histories that he published a decade earlier, but he also alludes explicitly to this polemical form in a number of ways – through Roxana's sexual intrigues with British peers and European nobles, by putting the phrase 'secret history' in her mouth on two separate occasions, and by adapting the narrative structure of secret history within a novelistic context. By alluding to secret history in a novel, Defoe invites his readers to compare these two literary forms. And by encouraging those readers to consider the differences between secret history and the novel, I suggest, Defoe sends his readers a message about political change during the early eighteenth century.

Key to this interpretation of *Roxana* is the fact that, in this novel, at least two time schemes are superimposed upon one another. Roxana begins her novel by claiming to have come to England as child of about ten years old with her Huguenot parents in 1683, which would make the ending of the novel roughly coincide with the year of publication, 1724.[103] Much of the action of this novel, however, evokes the Restoration Court. The title page of the first edition of *Roxana* declares that the narrator was 'known by the Name of the Lady Roxana, in the Time of King Charles II'. At a masquerade, Roxana dances with a masked nobleman who, rumour has it, is the Duke of Monmouth.[104] The air of courtly sexual licence that pervades this narrative also alludes in a more general way to the Stuart Court. Roxana engages in sexual intrigues with prominent noblemen: she has a lengthy affair with a European prince, lives a life of decadence and luxury in Courts of Europe, and, on her return, embarks on an eight-year affair with an English peer.

Paul K. Alkon, among others, has suggested that Defoe's 'double time scheme' is deliberately unsettling. He argues that Defoe uses it to draw satirical connections between the Hanoverian Court and that of Charles II:

> If the scene is put entirely in the eighteenth century, the satiric force of comparisons with a notoriously dissolute period vanish [*sic*], although *Roxana* would still be a devastating picture of eighteenth-century high life. Conversely, the implicit satirical

meanings would either vanish or diminish in power if *Roxana* had been set entirely in the seventeenth century. Readers would in that case be less inclined to connect her depravity with eighteenth-century manners.[105]

This reading of the double time scheme as a focus of satire is supported by the fact that the title-page, which declares that this novel was set during the time of Charles II, also reveals that Roxana was known as 'the Countess of Wintelsheim in Germany', which may represent an allusion to George I's German mistresses, Melusine von der Schulenburg and Sophia Charlotte von Kielmansegg. Nonetheless, I believe that satire of the Hanoverian Court was not Defoe's only or even his primary intent in using a double time scheme in *Roxana*. Instead, the double time scheme draws the reader's attention to the relationship between Defoe's novel and the tradition of secret history to which it alludes.

The Restoration setting of much of *Roxana* creates strong connections between this novel and the secret histories of the 1690s, which expose the secrets of Charles II's Court. Roxana's relationships with a European prince and an English peer of the realm evoke texts such as *The Secret History of the Duchess of Portsmouth* (1690) and *The Cabinet Open'd; or, the Amours of Madam de Maintenon with the French King* (1690), which focus on royal mistresses in order to peer at monarchs in a state of undress. In its highly self-conscious approach towards the narratological impact of secrecy, however, *Roxana* is much closer to Defoe's own *Secret History of the White-Staff*, which takes the revisionist tendencies of earlier secret history to a new level of sophistication. So while the character, Roxana, gestures towards Whig secret history of the 1690s, the structure of the novel, *Roxana*, alludes to Defoe's Harleyite secret histories of the early Hanoverian period. In *Roxana*, then, we find not two time schemes superimposed upon one another, but three: Defoe combines content that recalls Whig secret histories of the 1690s with a narrative structure that alludes to his Harleyite secret histories of 1714–15, in a novel that evokes the Court culture of the 1720s.

This triple time scheme allows Defoe to draw attention to the ways in which the conventions of secret history are adapted over time and also, perhaps, to imply some of the reasons behind those changes. By 1724, when *Roxana* was published, the political conditions that had inspired secret history over the course the previous half-century were barely discernible any longer. In particular, the royal prerogative was diminished to such an extent that the sexual intrigues of kings, courtiers, and their mistresses had become curiosities and matters for entertainment, rather than issues of national security. Under these circumstances, Defoe implies, the conventions of secret history can safely be absorbed into the novel because secret history's iconoclastic rhetoric of disclosure is no longer needed in the political sphere. Defoe's career confirms Michael McKeon's belief that the conventions of secret history are transferred to 'private' contexts in the novels of the 1720s. But it contradicts his idea that this kind of privatization marks the end of secret history's polemical function. Instead of denoting a retreat from political engagement, the generic shift from secret history to the novel that takes place in Defoe's career between 1714 and 1724 may, itself, be read as a political statement about the triumph of Whiggism under the Hanoverian monarchs.

There are, of course, limits to what *Roxana* can tell us about Defoe's political opinions during the 1720s.[106] It is impossible, for instance, to assess in detail Defoe's attitude towards Robert Walpole's ministry – a ministry which forms the target for secret histories by John Dunton and, as we will shortly see, Eliza Haywood – from his reworking of the conventions of secret history in his novels.[107] And there are also limits to what secret history can tell us about Defoe's novels. The conventions of secret history cannot, for instance, fully account for the heady combination of fear and excitement that *Moll Flanders* and *Roxana* generate in their readers, nor is it necessary to have a detailed understanding of Defoe's sophisticated ideas about the relationship between secrecy, narrative and power in order to feel the affective impact that these ideas can make. Indeed, the sense of political security that emerges out of the contrast between the political context of 1714–15 in which Defoe's secret histories were published and that of the 1720s is strikingly at odds with the hysteria and terror that dominate *Roxana*'s plot. Nonetheless, by understanding Defoe's contributions to the evolution of secret history, it becomes possible to analyse in greater depth the complex characters and narrative structures of his mature fictions. The relationship between *The Secret History of the White-Staff*, *Moll Flanders* and *Roxana* casts new light both on the internal characteristics of Defoe's novels and also on the political implications of genre during the first three decades of the eighteenth century.

Conclusion

We saw in Chapter 3 that Harley's fall and impeachment, the accession of George I to the British throne, and the transfer of nearly all ministerial posts to Whig incumbents was portrayed by many Whig polemicists as a Revolution analogous to the events of 1688. The new wave of secret histories that followed the 'Revolution' of 1714 promise to expose the treacherous secret intrigues of Harley's Tory ministry, which had governed throughout the last four years of Queen Anne's reign. In the midst of this revival of Whig secret history, Defoe published a text that – on the title page at least – resembles those of Whig polemicists such as John Oldmixon, William Stoughton and John Dunton. But *The Secret History of the White-Staff* radically departs from the aims and the assumptions of its contemporaries. While Whig polemicists represent Harley as a corrupt politician whose intrigues with France threatened British constitutional freedoms, Defoe depicts him as a political moderate valiantly attempting to liberate Britain from the tyranny of party politics. He argues that Harley's predilection for secrecy guaranteed British political liberties rather than threatening them. However, Defoe's self-conscious approach towards the discourse of revelation in *The Secret History of the White-Staff* ultimately undermines his attempts to defend Harley. By alerting his readers to the fact that secrets are made up of ever-smaller groups of wheels within wheels, he challenges the idea that he or any other secret historian can provide a definitive account of Harley's ministry. In *The Secret History of the Secret History of the White-Staff* Defoe takes the discourse of revelation to its fullest, sceptical conclusion, destabilizing the arguments of his own Harleyite secret histories as well as the polemics of his opponents.

We see the narratological basis of Defoe's approach towards secrecy at work once more in his novels of the 1720s. In *Moll Flanders* and *Roxana*, the political management of secrets – albeit in a private context – is one of the main foundations of both character and plot. The connections that I have traced between *The Secret History of the White-Staff* and Defoe's novels of the 1720s represent a new way of analysing the relationship between secret history and the novel. Recent literary criticism has focused on the importance of secret history to developments in the concepts of fact and fiction during the late seventeenth and early eighteenth centuries. It suggests that the epistemological instability occasioned by the discourse of secrecy and revelation fed into a more general concern with the foundations of knowledge that led, ultimately, to the emergence of the novel. Other research argues that the novel absorbs the motifs and conventions of secret history into tales of private life and domesticity – and sheds secret history's polemical associations in the process.[108] While these approaches towards secret history have been invaluable in helping to elucidate some of the complexities of the early eighteenth-century novel, they do not tell the whole story of secret history's influence upon later, more overtly literary, narrative forms. Daniel Defoe – perhaps the most sophisticated secret historian and novelist of the first three decades of the eighteenth century – provides us with a different way of thinking about the relationship between these two genres. For Defoe, the idea that secrets are narratives underpins both his secret histories and his novels of the 1720s. Regardless of whether he is dealing in ostensibly factual or fictional material, the same sense of secrecy as a structural principle applies. And as he alludes to secret history through the structure of his novels, Defoe allows the political connotations of this generic shift to emerge from his stories of private life.

7 ELIZA HAYWOOD: SECRET HISTORY, CURIOSITY AND DISAPPOINTMENT

At the same time as Defoe was probing the relationship between secret history and the novel in *Moll Flanders* and *Roxana*, one of his most prolific contemporaries – Eliza Haywood – was also writing works that also engage with both generic traditions. Between 1722 and 1727, Haywood published a number of works that bear the title 'secret history', including: *The British Recluse; or, Secret History of Cleomira, Suppos'd Dead* (1722); *The Masqueraders; or Fatal Curiosity: Being the Secret History of a Late Amour* (1724); *The Arragonian Queen: A Secret History* (1724); *Mary Stuart, Queen of Scots: Being the Secret History of Her Life and Reign* (1725), and *The Secret History of the Present Intrigues of the Court of Caramania* (1727). Haywood's second set of collected works carries the title *Secret Histories, Novels & Poems* (1725) and a third, projected set of collected works was advertised as *Secret Histories, Novels &c.* in 1726, although it was never published.[1]

Haywood's approach towards the relationship between secret history and the novel differs markedly from that of Defoe. While Defoe reworked the conventions of secret history in *Roxana* in such a way as to draw attention to the generic differences between the novel and secret history, it is hard to differentiate, in formal terms, between Haywood's self-styled 'secret histories' and her other novels, romances and histories. Indeed, the full title of Haywood's early story, *The British Recluse; or, Secret History of Cleomira, Suppos'd Dead. A Novel*, suggests Haywood's lack of concern to discriminate between genres. Moreover, there is little apparent difference between the generic category of *The Masqueraders*, which bears the 'secret history' epithet on its title page, and its two companion pieces, *The Fatal Secret: or Constancy in Disress* (1724) and *The Surprize; or, Constancy Rewarded* (1724), which do not. Haywood's early twentieth-century biographer, George Frisbie Whicher, asserts that that many of Haywood's short romances 'were described on the title-page as secret histories, while others apparently indistinguishable from them in kind were denominated novels', and infers that 'the writer attached no particular significance to her use of the term [secret history], but employed it as a means of stimulating a meretricious interest in her stories'.[2]

Haywood's more overtly historical works that bear the title 'secret history' also have strong generic affiliations with romance-inspired amatory fiction. For instance, although it claims to reveal material never before published, *Mary Queen of Scots* is a romanticized, popular version of stories found in Samuel Jebb's *De vita et rebus gestis serenissimæ principis Mariæ Scotorum Regnæ* (1725), and has no obvious contemporary political resonance.[3] Even *The Secret History of ... the Court of Caramania*, a thinly veiled allegory of the affair between George II and his mistress, Henrietta Howard, Countess of Suffolk, which is usually regarded as one of Haywood's more scandalous works, is not overtly polemical in the same way as most earlier texts in the secret history tradition, even though it depicts the erotic intrigues of the monarch and his mistress. Instead of seeking to expose the precarious foundations of arbitrary government by displaying the monarch in a state of undress, Haywood weaves a love story around the unglamorous new monarch.[4] While Defoe's earliest forays into secret history are overtly political in character and his allusions to secret histories in his novels can be interpreted in a political light, Haywood's self-styled secret histories appear at first to share nothing with the polemical, Whig tradition except for a general interest in sexual intrigue and a name.[5]

But although many of Haywood's narratives appear to have little in common with polemical secret history, two important texts published in 1724 and 1725 demonstrate that at least some of Haywood's output was both self-conscious in its engagement with the discourse of secrecy and revelation and, as a result of this self-reflexive impulse, politically inflected. Although *Memoirs of a Certain Island Adjacent to the Kingdom of Utopia* (1725–6) and *A Spy upon the Conjurer* (1724) are not explicitly called 'secret histories', their titles nonetheless signify their close relationship with this tradition. The title of *Memoirs of a Certain Island* gestures towards Delarivier Manley's adaptation of Whig secret history, *The New Atalantis*, the full title of which is *Secret Manners and Memoirs of Several Persons of Quality, of Both Sexes. From The New Atalantis, an Island in the Mediterranean*. Contemporaries were quick to draw parallels between the two texts. Both Aaron Hill and Alexander Pope, for instance, refer to *Memoirs of a Certain Island* as the 'New Utopia', presumably basing their shortened version of Haywood's title on Manley's.[6] The anonymous author of *The Neuter: or, A Modest Satire on the Poets of the Age* (1733) declares, in her dedication to Lady Mary Wortley Montagu, that 'in *the New Eutopia* and things of that Nature [Haywood] had endeavour'd to copy Mrs. Manley's Vice, without her merit'.[7] The title of *A Spy upon the Conjurer*, with its subtitle, *All Discover'd*, alludes to secret history through the motif of the spy narrator (on which Manley also draws in the figure of Intelligence) and the rhetoric of revelation and disclosure. Although the 'conjurer' in Haywood's narrative is a deaf-mute fortuneteller named Duncan Campbell rather than a political figure, the verb 'to conjure' signifies, in the early eighteenth century, both 'to summon by magic' and also 'to conspire' or, literally, 'to swear together'.[8] The title page of this text thus hints that its revelations might be political in character. In both *Memoirs of a Certain Island* and *A Spy upon the Conjurer,* Haywood appropriates and reflects upon secret history's formal conventions.

As she engages with secret history, Haywood – like the other eighteenth-century authors discussed in this study – adapts its rhetorical conventions to a political end. The nature of Haywood's modification of this tradition is, however, significantly different from that of her predecessors and contemporaries. While most secret histories claim to provide their readers with previously undiscovered intelligence (whether or not they live up to the expectations they generate), and draw attention to the novel, scandalous or titillating quality of the intelligence they provide, Haywood uses the rhetorical trappings of secret history to present her readers with intelligence that appears to be deliberately disappointing. This chapter explores the political implications of Haywood's decision to manipulate secret history in this way. It argues that Haywood uses the failure of secret history, rather than its success, in order to indict the oligarchic political culture of the mid-1720s.

Biographical Contexts

Before analysing the ways in which Haywood adapts secret history to the political circumstances of the Walpole era, however, I want to posit a possible explanation for the fact that her approach towards secret history becomes particularly self-conscious, apparently quite suddenly, during the years 1724–5. Key to this development is the breakdown of Haywood's relationship with the Hillarian circle, a literary coterie that gathered around the poet, Aaron Hill, during the early 1720s.[9] Haywood's personal and literary rivalry with fellow Hillarian, the poet Martha Fowke Sansom, put her position within the coterie under pressure. From 1722 onwards, Haywood painted a series of damning *roman à clef* portraits of Sansom which attack both her literary ineptitude and her personal immorality – blows which Sansom returned in a violent description of Haywood as a 'scorpion', 'devil' and 'tygress' in her autobiography, *Clio*, which was written during the early 1720s but not published until 1752.[10] Haywood represents another Hillarian, the poet and aristocrat manqué, Richard Savage, as Sansom's villainous agent.[11] Haywood's campaign against Sansom reached its climax in the first volume of *Memoirs of A Certain Island*, in which she depicts Sansom as the lecherous Gloatitia and Savage as a traitor to the friendship that he had once professed for Haywood.[12] Aaron Hill's patience with the feud within his coterie ran out with the publication of Haywood's *Memoirs*. In the issue of Hill's periodical, the *Plain Dealer*, published on 26 October 1724 – just a month after the publication of Haywood's *roman à clef* – he condemns Haywood as 'the *Unfair* Author of the NEW UTOPIA'.

Haywood's breach with the Hillarian circle meant that she was deprived of an important source of professional encouragement. Both Aaron Hill and Richard Savage had written complimentary verses on Haywood's novels *Love in Excess* (1719) and *The Rash Resolve* (1724), and the Hillarian circle was one of the only literary coteries in early eighteenth century London actively to encourage female artistic endeavour.[13] As her relationship with the Hillarians gradually dissolved, Haywood lost the prospect of patronage either directly from Aaron Hill or through the reputation of the circle. She began to make the transition from coterie writer to lone literary businesswoman playing the market for fiction.[14]

This change in circumstances had a number of effects on Haywood's writing career. It led to an enormous increase in her rate of production and publication and it also prompted qualitative changes in the kinds of work that she produced. Between 1719 and 1722 Haywood published just one or two titles a year. In 1723, she published four, including her play, *A Wife to Be Lett*. Several of these publications – including Haywood's highly successful early novel, *Love in Excess* – were beautifully produced texts which targeted, and received much praise from, a culturally sophisticated readership. As Kathryn King remarks, Haywood 'seemed destined for an enviable place at the literary table' following the publication of *Love in Excess* and *Letters from a Lady of Quality to a Chevalier* (1720). Yet King goes on to observe that 'for some reason', these prestigious publications 'were followed by a string of cheaply produced, short amatory tales and secret histories'.[15] In 1724, Haywood published thirteen volumes of mainly amatory fiction, followed by eleven in both 1725 and 1726: on average, Haywood was producing a volume nearly every month during this three-year period.[16] King notes that 'published in rapid succession and printed in crowded lines on thin paper, these "Haywoods" were clearly targeted at a less culturally aspiring readership. Although the reasons for the development are uncertain it is clear that by 1725 there existed two Haywoods, one elegant and the other scandalous'. King clearly suspects that Haywood's first obviously scandalous *roman à clef*, *Memoirs of a Certain Island*, had something to do with this change in Haywood's career path, but she does not explain its significance.[17] *Memoirs of a Certain Island* is crucial both because it strikes the final blow to Haywood's relationship with the Hillarian circle and because it is the product of Haywood's self-conscious reflections upon her newly assumed role of secret historian.

As Haywood's output increased, so did her desire to exploit her reputation as an author of secret history. The growing importance of secret history to Haywood's self-presentation is evident in the titles of the two sets of collected works that she published in 1724 and 1725. Either Haywood or her publishers, Daniel Browne and Samuel Chapman, decided to call her first four-volume collection *The Works of Mrs Eliza Haywood* – a neoclassical title that evokes the prestigious 'Haywood' who wrote *Love in Excess* and was praised by the Hillarians. The only story published in these volumes to bear the title 'secret history' is *The British Recluse*, in which the phrase is found in the subtitle. In *The Masqueraders; or, Fatal Curiosity. Being the Secret History of a Late Amour*, which was published as a separate in the same year as *The Works*, the phrase 'secret history' is demoted still further, appearing only as an explanatory tag rather than as part of the title proper. It is surprising, then, that when Haywood's second four-volume collected works was published the following year, bearing the same stationers' imprint as *The Works*, it appeared under the racy title, *Secret Histories, Novels and Poems* (1725). This change in title is the more striking because the content of the two sets of collected works is broadly similar: *Secret Histories, Novels & Poems* republished seven titles that had appeared in *The Works*, and added just five, only one of which (*The Masqueraders*) carries the subtitle 'secret history'. The new prominence of the phrase 'secret history' is perhaps attributable to the recent publication of *Memoirs of a Certain Island*, which was published in September 1724 (albeit bearing a 1725 imprint).[18] If Haywood's experiment with secret history helped to precipitate her rift with the Hillarians, then this breakdown in relations with her coterie also seems to have fuelled Haywood's cultivation of the scandalous persona of a secret historian. *Memoirs of a Certain Island* and *A Spy upon the Conjurer* are the result of Haywood's increasingly professional attitude towards the business of writing, but they also represent a moment of extreme self-consciousness towards the form that brought her commercial success. Although Haywood's career was long and diverse, therefore, this chapter focuses closely on *A Spy upon the Conjurer* and *Memoirs of a Certain Island* as the two works that most clearly illustrate Haywood's sophisticated approach towards secret history.[19]

Memoirs of a Certain Island (1725–6)

Crucial to a critical interpretation of Haywood's *Memoirs of a Certain Island* is the first location that Haywood's narrator, Cupid, visits on his tour of the eponymous island. The Enchanted Well is a spring controlled by a necromancer called Lucitario, who convinces the residents of Utopia to make offerings to statues that he has erected of the goddesses Pecunia and Fortuna. Lucitario tells the Utopians that their money will turn the water into gold, but there is nothing magical about the Enchanted Well, and Lucitario makes a handsome profit out of this piece of deception. The prominent position of the Well in this narrative has led to speculation that Haywood began to compose *Memoirs of a Certain Island* in the wake of the South Sea Bubble crisis of 1720, when overinvestment in the South Sea Company led to a devastating stockmarket crash.[20] The Well is, however, more than just a topical reference. It functions as a metonym for the avaricious citizens who congregate around it. Over the course of this narrative, Cupid repeatedly returns to the Well to tell the stories of the people gathered there. Haywood portrays them as 'bubbles' – not only Lucitario's dupes, but also vacuous characters whose seductive, glittering surfaces barely hide their empty moral and intellectual centres. In this respect, the Enchanted Well is not just the focal point of the narrative structure of *Memoirs of a Certain Island*, but also a symbol that epitomizes the satiric purpose of this *roman à clef*.

The importance of the Enchanted Well within *Memoirs of a Certain Island* appears to indicate that it was published as a politically oppositional narrative. Robert Walpole's ministry was commonly held to be responsible for encouraging the overinvestment which led to the South Sea Bubble, and Walpole himself earned the nickname 'Skreen-Master General' or simply 'The Skreen' for his efforts to cover up government corruption in its wake.[21] In spite of the Bubble, however, Walpole enjoyed a period of tremendous political success and prosperity between 1724 and 1726.[22] Like her forebear, Delarivier Manley, Haywood was a Tory writer who used publications such as her play, *Frederick, Prince of Brunswick-Lunenburgh* (1729), and her political romance, *The Adventures of Eovaai* (1736), to express overt hostility to Walpole.[23] *Memoirs of a Certain Island* – Haywood's first foray into political secret history – seems to indicate her strengthening oppositional stance. It appears, then, that *Memoirs of a Certain Island*, like earlier secret histories, attempts to reveal the secrets of state upon which a corrupt regime is founded.

There are, however, several problems with this interpretation of *Memoirs of a Certain Island*. According to the key which was printed with the second edition of this *roman à clef*, Lucitario, the necromancer who governs the Enchanted Well, represents James Craggs the elder, a Whig former Member of Parliament who had been instrumental in converting government debt into South Sea stock during 1719.[24] Craggs's suicide in March 1721 was extremely convenient for the ministry: he became a scapegoat who was found to have encouraged the South Sea project for his own gain.[25] By representing Craggs as the architect of the Bubble, Haywood's narrative presents no challenge to the ministerial cover-up operation orchestrated by Robert Walpole; indeed, Haywood's account seems to offer support to the official government line on the crisis.

Even more problematic for an 'oppositional' reading of *Memoirs of a Certain Island* is the way in which Haywood concludes each of the two volumes of this work. At the close of each volume, the narrator, Cupid, encounters the Genius of the Isle in an apocalyptic scene. The Genius intercedes with the angry deity on behalf of those virtuous Britons who are capable of rescuing their nation from utter depravity. At the end of the first volume, the Genius singles out for particular praise Argeno, who is identified in the key as the Duke of Argyll, a leading Walpolean Whig, and Cleomenes, who is identified as Walpole himself.[26] The Genius lauds Cleomenes as a 'greatly noble *Patriot*, whose only Care, whose only Aim, is how to serve his Country ... he despises all those sordid Views by which his Contemporaries are sway'd, looks down on Titles, and chuses to be great in Worth alone'.[27] Not only does the Genius use the term Patriot – by this time associated with the opposition to Walpole – to describe a character who is identified as Walpole in the key, but he goes on to claim that 'no secret Bribes, no Flatteries, no Insinuations, ever mov'd [Cleomenes] to a forgetfulness of what he owes to Heaven, or to his Country', and also to praise his marital fidelity.[28] Walpole's political corruption was legendary, and in 1724 and 1725 Walpole's two mistresses each gave birth to a daughter by the man whom Cupid describes as a votary to Hymen.[29] At the end of volume 2 of *Memoirs of a Certain Island*, the Genius of the Isle asserts that, alongside Argeno and Cleomenes, the Order of the Knights of Fame [the Knights of the Bath] will become saviours of the Island's morals.[30] The Order of the Bath was revived in 1725 by George I at the suggestion of Walpole himself, who used it as a vehicle for dispensing patronage.[31] It seems impossible to reconcile such a celebration of Walpole as a virtuous patriot with the received account of Haywood as a resolutely oppositional political writer.

There are a number of possible solutions to this interpretative conundrum. It could be, for instance, that Haywood was not responsible for the key to her narrative. Although the author of the key provides accurate identifications of Haywood's private acquaintance, it is possible that he or she changes the identities of the public figures depicted in this narrative in an attempt to avoid the recriminations potentially involved in libelling the principal minister of state. It is noteworthy that, while the London edition of *Memoirs of a Certain Island* supports the ministerial line on the South Sea Crash by representing the necromancer, Lucitario, as James Craggs, the key to the Dublin edition of the first volume of this work, published in 1725, glosses Lucitario as 'Mr. W—l—e'.[32] But the Dublin edition nonetheless concurs with the London text in its representation of the virtuous Argeno as the Duke of Argyll, and the patriot Cleomenes as Walpole. Indeed, where the key to the London edition names Cleomenes as 'Mr. W—e', the Dublin text prints Walpole's name in full, creating tension between the opening of this narrative, which condemns Walpole as a conjuring necromancer, and its ending, which portrays him as a moral exemplar. Even if the identities of individual characters are open to dispute, it is more difficult to explain away the laudatory references to the 'Knights of Fame', or Knights of the Bath.

Perhaps, then, we must take *Memoirs of a Certain Island* at face value, as a narrative written in praise of Walpole. If this is the case, it seems probable that Haywood was motivated more by financial than by political considerations. Having lost one potential source of patronage in the form of the Hillarian circle, it could be that Haywood 'sold out' and courted Walpole's ministry for funds. There is no indication among Walpole's papers or correspondence that he had any contact with Haywood, or that Haywood ever wrote to him to solicit financial assistance.[33] Nonetheless, Haywood may have been writing in the hope or expectation of reward from the ministry. If she was making a bid for ministerial patronage in *Memoirs of a Certain Island*, a significant reappraisal of the politics of the early part of Haywood's career would be required.

If Haywood was not being straightforwardly flattering in her description of Walpole, then her apparent panegyric invites a variety of possible readings. It is just possible that she hoped that her praise of Walpole as virtuous, honourable and faithful would influence this dissolute minister for the better. On the other hand, her praise of Walpole might be interpreted ironically: as a means of pointing out the gap between her laudatory description of Cleomenes and Walpole's true character. Alternatively, it could be that she is directing irony at the 'Genius' of an island that is as corrupt as the ministry he praises. But Haywood's readers would have to perform hermeneutic acrobatics to arrive at these interpretations, since Haywood gives no stylistic signals – a change in tone or register, for instance – to indicate her ironic intent. It is possible, however, to sustain a reading of Haywood's praise of Walpole as ironic if we look beyond the localized representation of Walpole as Cleomenes and the Knights of the Bath as the Knights of Fame towards a deeper pattern of irony in *Memoirs of a Certain Island*. Although there are no stylistic signals that she intends to satirize Walpole in this narrative, Haywood does use hyperbole, fast shifts in narrative perspective and a variety of other rhetorical techniques in order to satirize the conventions of secret history. By directing irony at the genre in which *Memoirs of a Certain Island* is written, Haywood challenges the authority of her own narrative and its political conclusions.

The ironic intent that lies behind Haywood's *roman à clef* becomes clearer when we read this work against its model, *The New Atalantis*. Both *Memoirs of a Certain Island* and Manley's *New Atalantis* present their readers with a narrator associated with amorous intrigue: Intelligence in Manley's text; Cupid in Haywood's. There are, however, important differences between the function of the principal narrator of each text. In *The New Atalantis*, the deity, Astrea, descends from heaven and seeks out Intelligence, an inquisitive mortal who narrates tales of amorous intrigue at her request. In *Memoirs of a Certain Island*, the roles are reversed: the god Cupid seeks out and courts an unnamed Stranger whom he leads around the island because, as he puts it, 'I see Curiosity and Expectation in thy Eyes'.[34] In spite of Cupid's faith in the Stranger's curiosity, however, the Stranger remains impassive throughout the narrative: he barely speaks to Cupid and is little more than a cipher for Haywood's implied reader. In *The New Atalantis*, Intelligence's curiosity drives the narrative forward; in *Memoirs of a Certain Island*, Haywood suggests that the reader's own curiosity creates narrative movement. Haywood's adaptation of her model appears initially to indicate that she is confident of her ability to sustain her reader's curiosity and attention. Rather than relying upon a focus within the narrative to move her reader from one scene to the next, the reader's own curiosity is presumed to perform this function.

Throughout *Memoirs of a Certain Island*, however, Cupid is openly at pains to maintain his implied reader's engagement with his narrative. He repeatedly interrupts his interlocutors, cuts short his own stories, and hurries in new scenes of intrigue with remarkable, even unnerving, rapidity. For instance, in one episode the sexual intrigues of Bellario (Eustace Budgell, Joseph Addison's cousin and an occasional contributor to *The Spectator*) are revealed in the form of letters from the women whom he has debauched and ruined.[35] The Stranger, at Cupid's behest, occupies himself with opening these letters but, 'as the Stranger was beginning to open another *Billet*, the God prevented him, by saying, there remains no more of any consequence; beside, too much Time has been already spent on a Subject so trifling as *Bellario*. Let us now turn our Eyes again on that numerous Assembly'.[36] Haywood seems concerned here that her reader may be more discerning than the Stranger, and less inclined to spend time on 'Subject[s] so trifling as Bellario'. She frequently concludes inset stories abruptly and each conclusion is entwined with the promise of further revelation. At the end of one particularly lengthy tale of unrequited love, the narrator asserts rather callously that:

> The broken-hearted *Windusius* had, perhaps, continued longer in these Exclamations, if the God of Love, who knew he had finished his Narration, and was desirous to entertain the Stranger with some other Theme, had not, on a sudden, shewed himself between them, and vouchsafing some words of divine Consolation to his dejected Votary, dismiss'd him; having Intelligences to communicate to the other, which Fate permitted not to be revealed to any but himself.[37]

Cupid's lack of sympathy for his 'votary' is presumably born of Haywood's awareness that Windusius's story had begun forty pages earlier and that, by this time, her reader may expect some novelty. Throughout the narrative, Haywood attempts to invigorate her reader's flagging spirits by swift changes of scene and the promise of secrets to come. But the extent to which Haywood reflects upon her own narrative strategy through Cupid's rather clumsy utterances suggests that she is also attempting to justify her own editorial principles to a potentially disenchanted or even hostile readership.

Haywood's awareness of the difficulty of sustaining her readers' attention may derive in part from the quality of the intelligence contained in her text. While Manley's *New Atalantis* is principally concerned with figures of some public standing, Haywood makes no claims to reveal secrets of state or even to recount well-known, scandalous political intrigues in any detail. Indeed, the most vivid portraits in the first volume of *Memoirs of a Certain Island* are of Haywood's immediate circle, especially Martha Fowke Sansom, Richard Savage and members of Aaron Hill's family.[38] The key to *Memoirs of a Certain Island* provides little help in deciphering the identities of the private individuals whom she represents in her narrative. The middle letters of the names in the key are occluded (for instance, Martha Sansom is represented as Mrs. S—s—m), making the identities of more obscure characters entirely impenetrable.[39] In fact, no key exists for a large section of the narrative.[40] Sometimes the narrative ceases to be *roman à clef* at all, as Cupid indulges in a generalized diatribe on the abuse of contemporary morals.[41] If readers approached Haywood's text expecting to find secrets of state or even particular accounts of contemporary public scandals, they are likely to have been disappointed.

Haywood may have had no choice but to publish such disappointing 'intelligence' in *Memoirs of a Certain Island*. Unlike Manley, who had sufficient contact with figures close to the government for the Earl of Sunderland to accuse her of 'having receiv'd Information of some special Facts, which they thought were above her own Intelligence', Haywood was a political outsider.[42] Perhaps it is Haywood's painful awareness of the substandard nature of her secrets that makes Cupid hurry his readers on through his narrative, and that led Haywood or her publisher to syncopate the key to this narrative as a way of compensating for the lack of excitement in the text itself. But to write off *Memoirs of a Certain Island* as a political and aesthetic failure because of its lack of genuine intelligence is, I suggest, both to misinterpret and underestimate Haywood's rhetorical strategy in this work. Cupid's self-conscious, strenuous efforts to sustain his reader's attention throughout this narrative seem deliberately designed to highlight the difficulty of doing just that. In *Memoirs of a Certain Island*, Haywood not only publishes secret history, but she also analyses the experience of reading it. Her self-conscious narrative draws attention to its own use of the rhetorical trappings of secret history by failing to live up to the expectations that they generate.

A Spy upon the Conjurer (1724)

The idea that *Memoirs of a Certain Island* is deliberately designed both to arouse and to disappoint its readers' curiosity is supported by *A Spy upon the Conjurer*, a text published six months before *Memoirs of a Certain Island*, in which Haywood probes the relationship between secrecy, curiosity and disappointment in narrative form. Although the conspiratorial title evokes the spy narrators of secret history, its political overtones are ironic: Duncan Campbell, the 'conjurer' in question, is not a conspirator but a celebrated, deaf-mute fortuneteller who had arrived in London from Scotland in around 1698.[43] Haywood knew Campbell personally, since she was a member of a literary coterie that met at his house.[44] In spite of this personal connection between Haywood and Campbell, however, *A Spy upon the Conjurer* is not simply a biography of Campbell, but rather a text that reflects Haywood's growing preoccupation with the relationship between secret history, professionalism and politics.

By the early 1720s, Duncan Campbell's fortunes were flagging. Several members of his coterie took it upon themselves to publish his biography as a way of raising funds to ease his financial circumstances. The first such text appeared in 1720 when William Bond published *The History of the Life and Adventures of Mr. Duncan Campbell* (1720). As an aid to Campbell's fortunes, however, it appears not to have been a great success, since in December 1722 the following advertisement for a further biography of Campbell appeared in *The British Journal*:

> In consideration of some Misfortunes, which Enemies and Indisposition have brought on him for these last two Years, the Lady Author [has made] him a Present of 200 Books, printed on Royal Paper, neatly bound and gilt, for the Benefit of himself, by way of Subscription. They will be sent as soon as finish'd to his House in *Exeter-Court* in the Strand, where those who are willing to become Subscribers, are desir'd to send their Names, or what they are pleas'd to contribute, the Design being wholly for his Advantage, he will not presume to set a Price.[45]

Eliza Haywood's *Spy upon the Conjurer* was finally published, eighteen months later, on 19 March 1724.[46] But although Haywood's immediate aim in publishing this text appears to have been to provide Duncan Campbell with financial relief, the enduring interest of this narrative lies in its self-conscious approach towards the experience of reading a text that claims to publish secrets. Instead of simply writing a sequel to a narrative which had raised insufficient funds for Campbell's benefit, Haywood uses the antagonistic relationship between her own text and Bond's *History of the Life and Adventures of Mr. Duncan Campbell* to reflect upon the connections that exist between secrecy, curiosity and the consumption of narrative.[47] In order to understand Haywood's rhetorical strategies in *A Spy upon the Conjurer*, therefore, it is necessary to turn first to William Bond's *History of the Life and Adventures of Mr. Duncan Campbell*.

In his *History of the Life and Adventures*, Bond worries openly that the qualities which make his text appealing to potential readers could also have a deleterious effect upon those readers' morals. In the introduction to this biography, he expresses his desire of 'engaging many curious People of all sorts to be my Readers; even from the Airy nice Peruser of Novels and Romances, neatly Bound, and finely Gilt, to the grave Philosopher, that is daily thumbing over the musty and tatter'd Pieces of more solid Antiquity'.[48] When he appeals to 'curious People of all sorts', Bond hints at the source of his anxiety. Although he needed to arouse curiosity in potential readers order to make his work sell (it was, after all, a fundraiser for Duncan Campbell), *The History of the Life and Adventures* reveals that Bond regarded curiosity as a visceral and dangerous force:

> There is certainly a very keen Appetite in Curiosity; it cannot stay for Satisfaction; it is pressing for its necessary Repast, and is without all Patience. Hunger and Thirst are not Appetites more vehement, and more hard and difficult to be repress'd, than that of Curiosity: Nothing but the *present Now* is able to allay it.[49]

Appetitive curiosity is boundless, irrational and invisible. The italic typeface and capitalization in Bond's text mimics, typographically, curiosity's urgency and excess.

Particularly problematic for Bond is the fact that curiosity's negative effects are closely associated with the two classes of readers – women and antiquarians – that Bond identifies as a likely audience for his narrative. Emphasizing its Latin etymon *cura*, or 'care' (in words like 'curator'), natural philosophers and antiquarians had begun to dissociate curiosity from impious enquiry and feminine prurience.[50] But the recovery effort was slow, and critics of 'modernity' were keen to ensure that the traditional connections between curiosity, femininity and foolishness were upheld. The Scriblerian farce, *Three Hours After Marriage* (1717), presents Dr Fossile – a fictionalized version of Dr Joseph Woodward – as inquisitive, pedantic and impotent.[51] Although Bond's commercial success depended upon his capacity to engage the curiosity of a broad readership composed of both novel-readers and students of antiquity, he also needed to steer a difficult course between the associations of curiosity with prurience on the one hand and pedantry on the other. Bond sums up his dual aim by expressing his desire 'to Entertain the Fancies of the ... gay Tribe, by which means I may entice them into some solid Knowledge and Judgment of Human Nature' and to 'Bribe the Judgment of this ... Grave Class so far, as to endure the intermixing of Entertainment with their severer studies'.[52]

Bond's actual solution to the potential problems caused by arousing excess curiosity in his readers is, however, more complicated than his own assertions suggest. As well as combining entertaining stories with more obviously instructive material, Bond tempers the curiosity of his readers by highlighting the semantic ambiguity of the noun, 'curiosity'. While curiosity as a personal quality is voracious and boundless, curious objects (or curiosities) are, almost by definition, small and delicate. Moreover, objects become curiosities by virtue of being confined, put on display, held up to scrutiny and, most importantly, explained.[53]

In his introductory address to 'curious people of all sorts', Bond swiftly diverts his readers' attention from the pleasure they may derive from reading either 'Novels and Romances' or 'Pieces of more solid Antiquity' – pleasure which is predicated upon the satisfaction of personal curiosity – towards the curious qualities of the objects they read, whether those objects are 'neatly bound and finely gilt' or 'tattered and musty'. Moreover, *The History of the Life and Adventures* is, itself, structured as a cabinet of curiosities. Each of its chapters displays a different aspect of the curious phenomenon that is Duncan Campbell: his life story, his deafness and his gift of the second sight. And in each of his chapter-cabinets, Bond contextualizes Campbell's more extraordinary character traits and powers in such a way as to lessen the force of their impact upon the reader. Campbell's gift of the second sight, for instance, is attributed to the fact that his mother is from Lapland where the second sight is common, so that 'we may the less admire at the Wonders performed by her Son, when we consider this Faculty of Divination to be so derived to him from her, and grown as it were Hereditary'.[54] Here, Campbell's exotic origins are used to 'normalize' apparently unique powers. In addition, Bond cites numerous ancient and modern authorities to suggest that there are perfectly rational explanations for Campbell's use of what Bond terms 'Natural *Magick*'.[55] In fact, Bond appears more astounded by the fact that, as a deaf person, Campbell was taught to read and to write than by his apparently supernatural abilities; Bond's reflections upon Campbell's deafness introduce a long section in which he discusses contemporary theories about the education of deaf children.[56] As a man with the gift of the second sight, Duncan Campbell is likely to arouse a high degree of curiosity in Bond's diverse readership. But Bond turns his text into an exercise in moderating curiosity. By making *The History of the Life and Adventures* a cabinet of curiosities designed to contain and explain the phenomenon that is Duncan Campbell, Bond attempts to channel and regulate this dangerous emotion.

In *A Spy upon the Conjurer*, Haywood attempts to cultivate in her readers precisely the kind of irrepressible, prurient curiosity that Bond had sought to control in his *History of the Life and Adventures of Mr. Duncan Campbell*. While Bond's text opens with a preface written by Duncan Campbell, which authorizes the information contained in this text, the reference to spying in the title of Haywood's text together with its subtitle, *All Discover'd*, lend this later narrative an impression of illegitimacy. Haywood implies that *A Spy upon the Conjurer* is a secret history of Duncan Campbell – that it exposes Campbell's secrets contrary to his desires and that these secrets will supplement and revise Bond's earlier, official account of Campbell's life. The way in which this text was initially marketed reveals, however, that Duncan Campbell probably colluded with Haywood's efforts to make her text appear surreptitious and scandalous.[57] The first advertisement for *A Spy upon the Conjurer* states that Haywood's text was 'Printed for and sold by Mr. Campbell, at the Green-Hatch in Buckingham-Court, White-hall; and at Burton's Coffee-House, Charing-Cross'.[58] In spite of its title, Haywood's text was sanctioned by Duncan Campbell, just as Bond's had been. Yet within days, the advertisements had changed to suppress Campbell's role in the publication and sale of Haywood's work.[59] And while Campbell's name was suppressed, Haywood's was promoted. Although Haywood's name did not appear on the title page of this first issue of her work, *A Spy upon the Conjurer* was reissued later in 1724 with a new title page which added the crucial words, 'Revised by Mrs. ELIZ. HAYWOOD', and removed any reference to Campbell as publisher or bookseller.[60] Haywood's name would have been sufficient to associate this text with the kind of amatory intrigues that were a constituent element of both the romance-inspired narratives that Haywood wrote between 1719 and 1724 and also, by the time the second issue of *A Spy upon the Conjurer* appeared, with more overtly polemical secret history in the form of *Memoirs of a Certain Island*.

Haywood, her publishers and Duncan Campbell himself thus conspired to suggest that Haywood's text is precisely the kind of publication from which William Bond had sought to dissociate his *History of the Life and Adventures*. In his preface to Bond's work, Duncan Campbell praises Bond for refusing to 'divulge the secret Intrigues and Amours of one part of the Sex, to give the other part room to make favourite Scandal the Subject of their Discourse', and he insists that, instead of composing a narrative out of 'patchwork Romances of polluting Scandal', Bond writes stories 'which always terminate in Morals, that tend to the Edification of all Readers of whatsoever Sex, Age, or Profession'.[61] But while Campbell sought to bolster the authority of Bond's text by writing a preface for it, he clearly felt, in the case of Haywood's narrative, that the omission of such authorizing strategies was more likely to have the desired effect upon sales.

If readers bought *A Spy upon the Conjurer* expecting to find a scandalous exposé of Duncan Campbell, however, they would have been disappointed. For all its appearance of illegitimacy and scandal, Haywood's narrative reveals almost no secrets about Campbell at all and is, for the most part, complimentary towards his prodigious powers. And although Haywood's narrative does contain stories about the amorous intrigues of Duncan Campbell's clients, the narrative contains no key. This work is not *roman à clef* in the vein of Delarivier Manley and *Memoirs of a Certain Island*.[62] In fact, Haywood seems more interested in her own narrator, Justicia, than in either Campbell or the secrets of his clients. While the title of Bond's *History of the Life and Adventures of Duncan Campbell* indicates Campbell's central position in this narrative, *A Spy upon the Conjurer* trains the reader's attention on the spy herself. Justicia is prodigiously curious. She listens in on conversations, peers through chinks in doorways, pieces together torn fragments of paper on which Campbell has written predictions, and even steals his letters in order to gain access to the secrets of Campbell's clients. As the narrative progresses, Justicia increasingly ignores the secrets of Duncan Campbell and his clients, and her own intelligence gathering becomes the principal subject of her narrative. While Bond renders curiosity safe by prioritizing the 'object' sense of this word, Haywood emphasizes the ferocious personal curiosity that drives the narrator of her text.

Like William Bond, Eliza Haywood manipulates the conventional association of curiosity with femininity, but Haywood's response to the gendered connotations of this personal quality is predictably different from Bond's. Bond associates curiosity with an absence of rationality and a lack of self-control that he suggests is distinctively feminine. At one point in *The History of the Life and Adventures*, for instance, Duncan Campbell instructs the narrator to burn a prediction that he has written for one of his female clients in order to prevent it from falling into the wrong hands. Curiosity, however, gets the better of the narrator and, unbidden by Campbell, he reads the scrap of paper on which the prediction was written. His retrospective observations on his behaviour reveal the gendered nature of the contemporary discourse about curiosity:

> This shows how a sudden Curiosity, when there is not Time given to think and correct it, may overcome a Man as well as a Woman: For I was never over-curious in my Life; and tho' I was pleas'd with the Oddness of the Adventure, I often blush'd to my self since, for the unmanly Weakness of not being able to step with a Note, from one Room to another, to the Fireside, without peeping into the Contents of it.[63]

Bond portrays the effects of his own curiosity as a weakness, a failing, the result of a lack of reflection. This incident reveals the dangerous power of curiosity to emasculate even the manly author of *The History of the Life and Adventures*.

Haywood, on the other hand, suggests that curiosity demands considerable effort and positive determination on the part of the curious. Indeed, the narrator of *A Spy upon the Conjurer*, Justicia, notes that 'if Mr. *Campbell* had known the Pains I took to find out the Affairs of those who came to consult him, he would have forbid me his House'.[64] She goes on to reflect that, in spite of his great powers of foresight, Campbell fails to detect her secret activities:

> His Art of Divination did not stoop so low as to give him any Idea of the litt[l]e foolish Curiosity I was then possess'd with. Not but he gave me Hints sometimes that I was of an inquisitive Nature; and when I have shew'd myself more forward, than indeed became a Woman who pretended to good Breeding, in pressing into the Company of People who seem'd not desirous of being seen by a Stranger, he would often smile and write to me, *O Woman! Woman! Woman! The Sin of Eve taints thy whole Sex*.[65]

Campbell's attribution of women's inquisitiveness to Eve is conventional, and his misogynistic comments in this context make him seem faintly ridiculous, but they are also significant because several of the qualities ascribed to him by Bond's

History of the Life and Adventures – especially his perfect, unmediated powers of apprehension and even, arguably, his total lack of curiosity about his clients – might be interpreted as quasi-prelapsarian characteristics. In spite of these associations, however, Haywood's *Spy upon the Conjurer* portrays Campbell's perfect insight and his consequent lack of curiosity as a human failing rather than an Adamic virtue. Duncan Campbell quite literally overlooks the spy; his powers of divination do not 'stoop so low', Justicia reports, as to take into account the 'little, foolish', feminine curiosity that drives this narrative. Haywood's *Spy upon the Conjurer* is engendered – that is, produced and denoted as feminine – by its narrator's unlicensed curiosity. And by placing female curiosity at the centre of *A Spy upon the Conjurer*, Haywood highlights the parallels between her narrator's curiosity and the circumstances of her text's creation. The female curiosity that fosters the market conditions in which such a text will sell is replicated by the curiosity of its narrator. *A Spy upon the Conjurer* appears to celebrate the mutually supportive relationship of a curious, feminine readership and a marketplace willing and able to satisfy its demands.[66]

But if Haywood affirms the productivity of female curiosity, she also draws attention to the triviality of its objects. There is a consistent mismatch between the fever pitch of Justicia's curiosity and the kinds of secret that she discovers. For instance, peering through a crack in the door during one of Duncan Campbell's conferences she hears intriguing exclamations: '*O Lord God of Abraham! How wonderful are thy Works!*' and '*Mighty is the Preserver of Isaac! – Strange things doth he reveal!*' Justicia reports: 'my Curiosity getting the better of my good Manners, and resolving, if possible, to inform myself, I pushed open the Door, and rush'd in upon them; pretending I came to look for a Pen.'[67] As it turns out, Campbell's clients 'appear'd not at all concern'd at the Liberty I had taken' having come 'on no secret Affair'. Their exotic ejaculations are explained by their being Jewish, and they have come to Campbell because they have been victims of slander. Justicia concludes abruptly: 'But to make short of my Story, Mr *Campbell* undertook and perform'd the Cure of this Witchcraft, Ill Tongue, or whatever it was that disturb'd this Gentleman.'[68] Justicia can barely stay long enough to utter this offhand comment before she precipitates the reader into the next tale of intrigue. Disappointment at the insubstantial nature of the secrets that she discovers only fuels her curiosity.

Instead of providing its readers with secret intelligence, *A Spy upon the Conjurer* offers them a self-conscious commentary upon the experience of reading for secrets. Indeed, the principal object of enquiry in *A Spy upon the Conjurer* is neither Duncan Campbell nor the secrets of his clients, nor even the narrator, Justicia, but rather curiosity itself. In this text, Haywood reflects upon the market conditions in which secret history flourishes and the rhetorical effects that secret historians need to employ to secure their share of that market. She suggests that secret history is sustained by curiosity that has become unshackled from its object and that proliferates uncontrollably as a result of this separation. Justicia and, it is implied, Haywood's readers take infinitely more pleasure in the fervent pursuit of secrets than in their discovery. Haywood's sense that her readers were willing to chase after secrets with no guarantee of any reward suggests that the kind of secret history they want is a bubble. Just as, in 1720, investors poured money into a financial scheme that was ultimately, and devastatingly, revealed to be nothing but a fiction, so Haywood suggests that readers of her secret histories expend time, energy, and money in chasing after disappointing secrets. Through her analysis of the cycle of curiosity and disappointment that characterizes the chase after secrets, Haywood directs scepticism towards the demands of the literary marketplace at the same time as she satisfies them.

Secret History, Curiosity and Disappointment

Reading Haywood's amatory fiction in the context of contemporary financial developments, Catherine Ingrassia observes that 'Haywood's texts metaphorically and structurally replicate the process of deferral, continuation, and imaginative participation that characterizes speculative investment. The "love" relationship within Haywood's fiction, the perpetual imagining of an end which must never come, mirrors the implicit understanding on which speculative investment depends: the continued deferral of complete repayment until a date which will, of course never arrive'.[69] But while Ingrassia figures women's engagement with the commercial, amatory or literary marketplace as empowering, Haywood's narratives are much more ambivalent about the kinds of speculative investment that curiosity encourages. Indeed, her implied readers' attitude towards the secrets that her texts appear to offer bears an uncomfortable resemblance not only to stock-jobbers, but also to the predatory libertines who populate Haywood's tales of amatory intrigue.

In *A Spy upon the Conjurer* Haywood plays on conventional associations of curiosity with frivolity and femininity. Elsewhere, however, she reveals that curiosity has a much darker, more masculine side. The plot of *Fantomina* (1725), in which a woman changes her guise four times in order to maintain her deceived lover's interest in her, epitomizes the idea that a libertine's sexual interest in a woman lasts only as long as his curiosity; 'enjoyment' is always secondary to the thrill of the chase, and usually results in one woman being abandoned while the libertine begins his pursuit of another. As the narrator of *The Rash Resolve* (1724) puts it: ' – O the Enchantments of *Novelty*! the Delights there are in having something to subdue – the pleasing Fears – the sweet Hopes, – the tender Anxieties – the thousand nameless, soft Perplexities which fill the roving Soul of Man when in pursuit of a *new* Conquest! but *after Possession* are no more remembred –'.[70] In *Memoirs of a Certain Island*, this kind of libertine curiosity is exemplified by the Chevalier Blantier who marries a woman called Olimpia:

> *Olimpia* marry'd – *Olimpia* enjoy'd, there remain'd nothing for [Blantier] to desire; and in the fair *Silenia*, her Sister, he imagin'd there was a hoard of Charms with which he never should be cloy'd. – *Silenia*, who was not the thousandth part so lovely as her Sister, and whom, till he had obtain'd the other, he never sent one single Sigh for, was now the Goddess of his Affections; and the impossibility there seem'd of gratifying his Passion, made it blaze more fierce.[71]

In Haywood's amatory fiction, male curiosity is an autotelic, pathological quality to which female characters repeatedly fall prey.

Yet in spite of the obvious damage that predatory curiosity inflicts upon its female victims, the attitude that Haywood's curious libertines adopt towards women is replicated in the narrative structure of *Memoirs of a Certain Island*. The episodic form of this narrative creates a 'libertine' reading experience for its readers. In each episode, Haywood promises her readers a secret which invariably fails to live up to expectations, leading to further promises and further disappointments. The disappointing nature of Haywood's secrets, coupled with the relentless forward drive of the narrative, gives the impression that secrets, like women in the eyes of a libertine, have little intrinsic value, and that their status as 'curious' objects derives entirely from the personal curiosity of the reader. Haywood suggests that the pleasure of the chase, rather than attainment of an object of curiosity, is the main attraction of a libertine secret history such as *Memoirs of a Certain Island*.

Haywood provides a prophylactic for over-curious readers of her narratives, however, in the form of self-directed irony. Irony is not usually a quality associated with Haywood's amatory narratives. More often, her prose is described as overbearingly sincere, absorbing its readers into a world in which passion overcomes all rational attempts at resistance.[72] Much of Haywood's amatory fiction does fit this description, but from time to time Haywood uses irony to distance her reader from the action of her narrative. For instance, her narrators paraphrase and catalogue lovers' vows in order to highlight their hollow conventionality, as in this passage from *Idalia* (1723):

> A thousand, and a thousand Times he had told her, That he lived but in her Sight: — That he should court Death as a Blessing, if any Accident should deprive him of her: — That the united Charms of her whole Sex besides, would be ineffectual to alienate his Thoughts one Moment from her; — and swore as many Vows of an eternal Constancy, as there were Saints in Heaven to witness them.[73]

The lover's hyperbole is punctured by the narrator's anaphoric conjunction ('that'), which highlights the ironic filter of indirect speech. Far from being consistently florid and hysterical, Haywood's prose can be cursory and elliptical, covering a great deal of ground in as few steps as possible. When she adopts this style, Haywood seems to suggest that there is no need for her to fill in any detail since readers familiar with the conventions of amatory fiction can do it themselves:

> Vast was [his eyes'] Power, and numberless the Conquests they had gain'd! – DALINDA (for so shall I call the present Victim of their force) had not Arguments sufficient to confute the Strenuousness of those he urg'd, and even Reason seem'd to take the part of Love. – In fine, that very Night he completed his Conquest, and got possession of all those Joys the glorious Prize could give.[74]

The words 'in fine' express, perhaps wearily, the conventional nature of Dalinda's seduction. Dalinda is not only the present victim of her lovers' eyes, but also the present victim offered to Haywood's reader. Haywood suggests that, for both the aggressive seducer in this story and for her readers, there have been and will be many more victims like Dalinda. In Haywood's amatory fiction, the ironic effects created by paraphrase and repetition grant their readers brief moments of respite from the torrid, sincere and absorptive prose that dominates her tales. The episodic narratives, *A Spy upon the Conjurer* and *Memoirs of a Certain Island* are, in structural terms, very different from these tightly plotted stories, but they too use repetition to generate ironic distance between reader and narrative. In Haywood's longer texts, however, repetition operates at a structural rather than a local level. The repetitious episodes of *Memoirs of a Certain Island* encourage Haywood's more perceptive readers to distance themselves from the erotic content of this text, and scrutinize the experience of reading this narrative.[75]

Haywood's analysis of the experience of reading secret history can, I suggest, help us to interpret her apparent support for Walpole in *Memoirs of a Certain Island*. By situating Haywood's localized expressions of support for Walpole within the broader context of the self-conscious commentaries on secret history that Haywood wrote in 1724 and 1725, it becomes possible to appreciate the irony with which Haywood invests what appears, at first, to be panegyric. By directing irony at the curiosity that underpins the narrative structure of *Memoirs of a Certain Island* in particular, and the market for secret history in general, Haywood satirizes both the form in which she writes and the political conclusions at which it apparently arrives. The opening of *Memoirs of a Certain Island* assists the ministry in its attempts to conceal government involvement in the South Sea scandal, and the ending of each of the two volumes of this narrative praises Robert Walpole in ecstatic terms. But the self-conscious episodes that fill the space in between these isolated moments of Walpolean adulation present a challenge to the opening and conclusion of the narrative. While the key to *Memoirs of a Certain Island* turns the narrative into a hypocritical bid for ministerial patronage, Haywood's own rhetorical strategies subtly undermine such blandishment.

Haywood's satirical approach towards secret history is not unprecedented. In Chapter 3 we saw John Dunton highlighting the political and commercial failure of his secret histories as part of an attack upon successive Whig ministries during the early years of Hanoverian rule. Dunton points to the fact that his secret histories neither sold well on the commercial marketplace nor attracted literary patronage in order to reveal the impotence of this form under an oligarchic government that has abandoned Revolution principles. Although her Tory sympathies separate Haywood from Dunton, Haywood's approach towards secret history bears interesting resemblances to that of her Whig contemporary. A highly self-conscious attitude towards curiosity underpins the ways in which both of these authors adapt the conventions of secret history. Dunton's inability to sustain his readers' curiosity through his promises of secrets leads him to re-evaluate the political function of secret history in Walpole's Britain. As Haywood explores the rapacious curiosity that underpins the market for texts such as *A Spy upon the Conjurer* and *Memoirs of a Certain Island*, she portrays contemporary politics, society and literary production as intertwined elements of a corrupt and debased public sphere. The fact that, in the mid-1720s, secret history fosters readers who are more interested in the empty pursuit of secrets than in acquiring political knowledge is, according to both Haywood and Dunton, a symptom of the more general deadening effect of oligarchic government upon political culture. Both authors therefore adopt a nostalgic approach towards secret history. Dunton harks back the glory days of the 1690s, when the vogue for secret history provided a literary analogue of the strength of Revolution principles. Haywood, on the other hand, alludes to Delarivier Manley's *New Atalantis* in order to highlight the difference between the era of party rage in which Tory secret history had flourished, and the stultifying political stability of the 1720s in which it withers. Haywood and Dunton – two supremely market-oriented secret historians – reveal the extent to which self-conscious scrutiny of the evolving genre of secret history remains a vital element of this form's polemical strategies.

Conclusion

It is easy to dismiss Haywood's engagement with secret history as superficial. In the titles of her early works and published collections, she elides secret history and other generic categories – novels, histories and romances – with scant regard for the differences between them. But during the first years of her career as a professional, rather than coterie, author, Haywood closely scrutinizes the generic characteristics that make secret history popular and the market conditions in which this form thrives. She satirizes the cycle of curiosity and disappointment that the discourse of revelation generates, mocking her readers' voracious appetite for secrets even as she panders to their desires. It is within the context of her ironic, self-reflexive approach towards secret history's promise to reveal secrets that we should read Haywood's perplexing, apparently pro-Walpole secret history, *Memoirs of a Certain Island*. Haywood situates her praise of Walpole within a form that epitomizes the corrupt, acquisitive society that gathers around the Enchanted Well. Although Haywood clearly hoped to profit from this social and political milieu – both by selling copies of her ostensibly revelatory work and, perhaps, by gaining Walpole's patronage – she criticizes it obliquely, undermining the authority of both the genre in which she chooses to write and the political conclusions at which she appears to arrive.

Although Haywood draws upon the politicized discourses of secrecy and revelation in her works of 1724–5, her contribution to the development of secret history lies as much in the literary as in the political sphere. In *A Spy upon the Conjurer* and *Memoirs of a Certain Island*, Haywood provides a unique analysis of the experience of reading for secrets. As she does so, she suggests that the polemical tradition that she has inherited is bankrupt. Her attack on Walpole in *Memoirs of a Certain Island* is also an attack on secret history itself. Paula Backscheider speculates that 'when a genre begins to wear itself out, to become less relevant and satisfying to the culture, it begins simultaneously to adapt and deconstruct itself. Such periods are marked by rapid and fascinating experimentation and revisionary writings, and Haywood's works are an indispensible part of one of these times'.[76] Encouraged to write secret history as a result of her need to succeed in the literary marketplace, Haywood scrutinizes the conventions of this popular form to portray it as part of the debased culture with which it at first appears to contend.

CONCLUSION

As it claims to peer into the bedchambers and cabinets of princes and ministers, to expose secrets of state, and to revise pre-existing narratives of the recent political past, secret history generates a number of critical assumptions. We might reasonably suppose that secret historians really do – or at least try to – disclose secrets; that these secrets provide an alternative version of history which supplements and undermines previous accounts of the past; that secret historians claim historical authority both for themselves and their narratives; and that the iconoclastic historical method and political rhetoric of secret history creates strong connections between this polemical form of historiography and the Whig opposition to arbitrary government. Such ideas are propounded in the prefaces to several secret histories as well as commentaries on this form that were published during the last decades of the seventeenth century and the first decades of the eighteenth. Secret history appears to be a distinctively English form of historiography. Its proponents claim it as the genre of history best able to represent – that is, both depict and epitomize – the political liberties achieved by the Revolution settlement. Whether the threat to liberty is located in the French Court, the would-be absolute Stuart kings, or – in the early eighteenth century – the backstairs intrigues of Robert Harley's administration, the formal characteristics of secret history appear ideally suited to its professed political aims. There seems to be a straightforward relationship between secret history's claim to reveal secret intelligence, its distinctive formal characteristics, and its partisan purpose.

But it turns out that, of all of the critical assumptions that secret history's characteristic rhetoric of disclosure generates, only the political association between this form and the opposition to arbitrary government is consistently borne out in practice by the self-styled secret histories published over a fifty-year period. In the place of the secrets of state that they promise, many secret histories give their readers a self-conscious analysis of the political and formal repercussions of their claim to get open the closet door of those in power. From Procopius's *Secret History of the Court of the Emperor Justinian* (1674), which suggests that the rhetorical gesture of revelation is as potent as the actual disclosure of state secrets, to John Dunton's Hanoverian secret histories of the late 1710s and early 1720s, which couple ostentatious claims to expose Jacobite conspiracies with a total absence of secrets, secret histories of this period adopt a singularly self-reflexive approach towards the discourse of revelation. As a result, their use of the disclosure of secrets as a polemical strategy is often highly counter-intuitive. Instead of providing their readers with definitive accounts of the recent political past, secret historians such as David Jones and Daniel Defoe highlight the epistemic and narrative instability caused by the claim to expose secrets: secrets cannot be verified, and the act of disclosure makes possible – or even invites – further revelations and competing, alternative versions of the recent past. Secret history thus internalizes the censure of its critics. With its spy narrators and information obtained from gossiping mistresses, secret history regularly confesses itself to be unreliable – the product of treachery and betrayals of trust. It draws attention to its own voyeuristic narrative perspective. It suggests that secret history is not only sexual in its content, but also fecund at a formal level, as the discourse of revelation produces multiple narratives of the past. Attempts to define secret history as a logical or respectable neoclassical form of anti-absolutist historiography are, therefore, a reaction against its prevailing characteristics. Champions of secret history – from John Somers at the turn of the eighteenth century to Annabel Patterson at the turn of the twenty-first – attempt to rescue secret history not only from its association with sexual scandal and the murky political underworld, but also from its bizarre, self-conscious, counter-intuitive approach towards the discourse of revelation.

Secret history's counter-intuitive rhetorical strategies appealed to those eighteenth-century writers who, in a variety of different genres, remodelled the conventions of this polemical form of historiography. In some cases, writers forged new secret histories out of old ideas. Daniel Defoe's *Secret History of the White-Staff*, for instance, resembles *The Secret History of White-hall* in more than name alone. In his Harleyite secret histories of 1714, Defoe draws upon the same sceptical approach towards the relationship between secrecy and narrative form that David Jones had explored nearly twenty years earlier. As successive parts of the tripartite *Secret History of White-hall* expose ever deeper, darker secrets, and *The Secret History of the Secret History of the White-Staff* claims that these secrets are nothing more than a ruse to sell copies, Defoe undermines his reader's confidence in his own revelations and creates the impression that the discourse of secrecy might potentially generate endless new, equally unreliable accounts of the past.

Other early eighteenth-century writers modify the conventions of secret history in texts that bear a less direct relationship with this polemical tradition than those of Defoe. Delarivier Manley's *New Atalantis* and *Memoirs of Europe* promise to expose the secrets of contemporary Whig grandees. But through the retelling and re-plotting of old stories, the use of *roman à clef*, and detailed allusion to pre-existing texts, Manley's narratives cultivate an impression of shared knowledge and complicity between author and reader that differs profoundly from Whig secret history's emphasis on its readers' political ignorance. In *The Spectator*, secret history's spy-like narrators and its claim to expose secrets are parodied in the figure of Mr Spectator, as Addison and Steele attempt to rehabilitate the discourse of secrecy by associating it with discretion and friendship rather than a corrupt, factional and intelligence-based literary and political culture. By the 1720s, John Dunton and Eliza Haywood suggest that the polemical potential of secret history is very nearly exhausted. United in their opposition to Walpole – although differing in their positive political beliefs – Haywood and Dunton adopt a sceptical approach towards their chosen form to give oblique expression to their political ideas. Vital to all of these eighteenth-century adaptations and variations are secret history's political origins as a form of Whig polemic and its literary origins as a highly self-reflexive genre of historiography. The fact that the core tradition of Whig secret history is so self-conscious about the connections between its claim to reveal secrets and its political agenda encourages later writers to innovate with its literary characteristics, reworking them within new social and political contexts.

The elements of extreme self-consciousness and polemical Whig politics are absent from most of the self-styled secret histories published during the later eighteenth century. Only a few secret histories from this period pursue the same kind of oppositional, anti-Court or anti-French political agenda as those published during the 1690s and after the accession of George I to the throne. At a time when France was once more at war with Britain, *A Cabinet Council; or Secret History of Lewis XIV* (1757) republished details of the Assassination Plot against William III and other Jacobite conspiracies of the early eighteenth century, warning its readers that 'though the King, Ministers and Circumstances are changed, the same Spirit presides over French Councils, though at different Periods; and that Louis XV is but what his Predecessor was; the invariable Maxim of both being to divide and conquer'.[1] Although smaller in scope, *The Secret History of the Last Two S-ss-ns of Parliament* (1754), which represents Irish grievances to an oppressive British government, and the much reprinted *Terrae Filius; or Secret History of the University of Oxford* (1721), which depicts Jacobite intrigue within the University, also recall secret history's origins in the opposition to arbitrary government and, in particular, in anti-Stuart polemic during the later seventeenth century.

Much more common during the later eighteenth century is the publication of secrets or anecdota as objects of historical interest without any obvious polemical function. *The Secret History of the Rye-House Plot* (1754), an account by one of the plotters of the assassination attempt against Charles II in 1683, *The Secret History of Colonel Hooke's Negotiations in Scotland, in Favour of the Pretender; in*

1707 (1760), and James MacPherson's two massive volumes of *Original Papers; Containing the Secret History of Great Britain, from the Restoration, to the Accession of the House of Hannover* (1775) print or reprint the kind of information that, during the late seventeenth or early eighteenth centuries, might have had great polemical force. In these texts of the later eighteenth century, however, the purpose of such revelations from times past is the education or entertainment of readers, rather than the desire to convince them of a present political threat. Indeed, by 1770, David Hume was able to assert that 'from the Commencement of the Reformation till the Revolution, there is not any important Secret in the English History'.[2] The eradication of any trace of the rhetoric of disclosure was one aspect of Hume's creation of a philosophical, non-partisan and polite form of historiography for a new era in British history. Over the course of the eighteenth century, the stuff of late seventeenth- and early eighteenth-century secret history becomes matter for readers' curiosity and edification, rather than inflammatory material designed to instil fear and paranoia in a politically engaged readership.

Indeed, by the middle of the eighteenth century, the majority of self-styled secret histories are straightforward amatory fictions, many of which tell stories of aristocratic love intrigues. Lydia Grainger's *Modern Amours: or, a Secret History of the Adventures of Some Persons of the First Rank* (1733), *The Fair Concubine: or, the Secret History of the Beautiful Vanella* (1732) and *Memoirs of the Nobility, Gentry &c. of Thule: or, the Island of Love. Being a Secret History of their Amours, Artifices and Intrigues* (1742–44) use courtly settings only to increase the prurient, voyeuristic interest that these narratives elicit, rather than to attack the kind of Court culture that they represent. The difference between these eighteenth-century courtly exposés and their seventeenth-century predecessors is evident in *The Life, Amours, and Secret History of Francelia, Late D—ss of P—h, Favourite Mistress to Charles II* (1734), a reprint of *The Secret History of the Duchess of Portsmouth* (1690). Whereas the earlier text explicitly claimed that the Duchess of Portsmouth's control over Charles II was evidence of the political consequences of arbitrary government, the eighteenth-century text informs its readers that 'it is no Novelty for a Prince to keep a Mistress or two; and though some sanguine Mortals may blame the Action, yet a Man of Sense will always prudently avoid meddling with State Affairs, especially as they do not relate at all to him, nor is he called upon to give his Opinion'.[3] The eighteenth-century amatory secret histories that use courtly settings seem rather closer in kind to sensational, prurient narratives about criminal women such as *The Incestuous Mother; or, the Secret History of Arabella Holland* (1751) or *The Secret History of Miss Blandy, from her first appearance at Bath, to her Execution at Oxford, April 6, 1752* (1752) than to earlier, polemical secret histories. Indeed, by the middle of the eighteenth century, some texts that call themselves secret histories had distinctly pornographic tendencies: *The Natural Secret History of Both Sexes* (1740), ostensibly by one 'Luke Ogle', bears the subtitle, 'a modest defense of public stews. With an account of the present state of Whoring in these Kingdoms', while *The Secret History of Pandora's Box* (1742) is a celebration of vaginas. In earlier secret histories, erotic descriptions of monarchs and their mistresses are a vital part of an iconoclastic attack upon arbitrary government; by the middle of the eighteenth century, however, the political connotations of eroticism have all but disappeared in many texts that borrow the 'secret history' tag.

There is no equivalent during the later eighteenth century of the cluster of well-known authors, including Manley, Addison, Defoe and Haywood, who appropriated both the literary conventions and the political connotations of secret history in response to the early eighteenth-century rage of party. Perhaps Gothic fiction, with its secretive characters, obscure historical settings and its emphasis on the psychological effects of shocking revelations borrows something from the paranoid atmosphere created by secret history published, in some cases, over a hundred years earlier. But even if it is possible to sustain a politicized reading of individual novels which seem to evoke the secret history tradition, such as Sophia Lee's *The Recess* (1783) or Ann Yearsley's *The Royal Captives; A Fragment of Secret History* (1795), the concentration, variety and inventiveness of those early eighteenth-century authors who rework secret history's rhetorical characteristics to a serve their own, specific, political ends is unique to the early eighteenth century.[4] Texts from Delarivier Manley's *New Atalantis* to Daniel Defoe's *Roxana*, from *The Spectator* to Eliza Haywood's *Memoirs of a Certain Island* speak to one another through their shared engagement with a highly self-reflexive, politicized form of historiography. They testify to the literary flexibility and political utility of secret history's key literary conventions as well as their abiding association with the Whig cause.

Secret history challenges the idea that generic self-consciousness is a sign that the conventions of a particular genre are becoming hackneyed and less useful to their readers.[5] For fifty years after the publication of *The Secret History of the Emperor Justinian*, secret history transfers contemporary fears about political secrecy into narrative form in a highly theorized, self-reflexive manner. The first texts written in this tradition are, in many ways, just as self-conscious as those published decades later. Perhaps this degree of self-consciousness made it inevitable that the fashion for secret history should be relatively short-lived. A genre that relentlessly scrutinizes its own conventions is, to some extent, self-consuming. Moreover, secret history was developed in response to a threat of absolute rule that faded over time. Its strong association with the partisan politics of the late seventeenth and early eighteenth centuries rendered it decidedly old fashioned and out of place in the very different political milieu of mid-eighteenth-century Britain. Nonetheless, secret history provides an invaluable perspective upon the half-decade between the reigns of Charles I and George

I. It embodies and probes the intensely factional political environment within which it is published. By revealing the ways in which literary texts respond to contemporary political developments, it also demonstrates that partisanship acts as a spur to literary innovation. Secret history allows us to experience the dynamic relationship between political and literary culture in late Stuart and early Hanoverian Britain as it explores its own claims to reveal secrets of state.

NOTES

Introduction

1. A. Varillas, *Anekdota Heterouiaka. Or, The Secret History of the House of Medicis*, trans. F. Spence (1686), sig. a4ʳ–a5ʳ.
2. On the secret treaty of Dover, see J. Spurr, *England in the 1670s: 'This Masquerading Age'* (Oxford: Blackwell, 2000), pp. 11–13. For the terms of the treaty see A. Browning (ed.), *English Historical Documents, 1660–1714* (London: Eyre and Spottiswoode, 1953; repr. London: Routledge, 1996), pp. 863–7.
3. On political plots during the later seventeenth century, see R. Greaves, *Deliver Us From Evil: the Radical Underground in Britain, 1660–1663* (Oxford: Oxford University Press, 1986), *Enemies Under His Feet: Radicals and Nonconformists in Britain, 1664–1677* (Stanford, CA: Stanford University Press, 1990) and *Secrets of the Kingdom: British Radicals from the Popish Plot to the Revolution of 1688–9* (Stanford: Stanford University Press, 1992); M. S. Zook, *Radical Whigs and Conspiratorial Politics in Late Stuart England* (University Park, PA: Pennsylvania State University Press, 1999), and P. Hopkins, 'Sham Plots and Real Plots in the 1690s' in E. Cruickshanks, *Ideology and Conspiracy: Aspects of Jacobitism, 1689–1759* (Edinburgh: John Donald, 1982), pp. 89–109. For a broader perspective on conspiracy in early modern Europe, see B. Coward and J. Swann (eds), *Conspiracies and Conspiracy Theory in Early Modern Europe From the Waldesians to the French Revolution* (Aldershot: Ashgate, 2004) and G. S. Wood, 'Conspiracy and the Paranoid Style: Causality and Deceit in the Eighteenth Century', *William and Mary Quarterly*, 3rd series, 39:3 (1982), pp. 401–44.
4. On the warming-pan scandal, see R. Weil, *Political Passions: Gender, the Family and Political Argument in England, 1680–1714* (Manchester: Manchester University Press, 1999), pp. 86–104.
5. E. Gregg, 'Was Queen Anne a Jacobite?', *History*, 57 (1972), pp. 358–75.
6. Secret history thus qualifies Jürgen Habermas's thesis that the 'bourgeois public sphere' was characterised by the rational, free exchange of information between participants (see J. Habermas, *The Structural Transformation of the Public Sphere: A Inquiry into a Category of Bourgeois Society*, trans. T. Burger (Boston, MA: MIT Press, 1989), pp. 27–31). For a fuller discussion of the challenge that eighteenth-century political secrecy presents to Habermas's arguments, see M. A. Rabb, *Satire and Secrecy in English Literature from 1650–1750* (New York: Palgrave Macmillan, 2007), pp. 8–10.
7. M. S. Zook, 'The Restoration Remembered: The First Whigs and the Making of their History', *The Seventeenth Century*, 17:2 (2002), pp. 213–34 (pp. 218–9).

8. M. Knights, *Representation and Misrepresentation in Later Stuart Britain: Partisanship and Political Culture* (Oxford: Oxford University Press, 2005), pp. 272–332; K. Loveman, *Reading Fictions, 1660–1740: Deception in English Literary and Political Culture* (Aldershot: Ashgate, 2008).
9. See, for instance, B. Shapiro, *Probability and Certainty in Seventeenth-Century England: a Study of the Relationships Between Natural Science, Religion, Law, and Literature* (Princeton, NJ: Princeton University Press, 1983) and *A Culture of Fact: England, 1550–1720* (Ithaca, NY and London: Cornell University Press, 2000); D. L. Patey, *Probability and Literary Form: Philosophic Theory and Literary Practice in the Augustan Age* (Cambridge: Cambridge University Press, 1984); M. McKeon, *The Origins of the English Novel, 1600–1740* (Baltimore, MD and London: Johns Hopkins University Press, 1987).
10. Rabb, *Satire and Secrecy*, pp. 67–89, argues that both secret history and satire are concerned with iconoclastic, alternative ways of interpreting the past, but Rabb does not explore the political or historiographical implications of secret history's revisionist tendencies. A. Welsh, *Strong Representations: Narrative and Circumstantial Evidence in England* (Baltimore, MD and London: Johns Hopkins University Press, 1992), demonstrates the self-conscious approach adopted by eighteenth-century writers towards questions of plot and narrative structure, although Welsh focuses on the relationship between literature and the law of evidence rather than contemporary politics and historiography. W. Eamon, *Science and the Secrets of Nature: Books of Secrets in Medieval and Early Modern Culture* (Princeton, NJ: Princeton University Press, 1994), p. 269, suggests that the idea of the 'hunter of secrets' who 'looks for traces, signs and clues that will lead to the discovery of nature's hidden causes' is common in early modern literature about scientific secrets. This metaphor derives from an understanding that secrets can be discovered by tracing a sequence of events which, in turn, implies that secrets are narratives.
11. J. P. Sommerville suggests that although 'absolutism' is not a contemporary term, it is useful for analysing the political systems of many European countries during the early modern period (see J. P. Sommerville, 'Absolutism and royalism' in J. H. Burns (ed.), *The Cambridge History of Political Thought, 1450–1700* (Cambridge: Cambridge University Press, 1991), pp. 347–73, pp. 347–50). Some contemporary Whig polemicists in England believed that the Stuarts were attempting to achieve the kind of absolute power that Louis XIV was believed to enjoy in France. In fact, Louis did not (and perhaps could not) rule in an arbitrary way – that is, solely according to his own will and whim. Nonetheless, the concept of arbitrary power was common in early modern oppositional polemic and so, in this study, I use both 'arbitrary rule' and 'absolutism' to denote the forms of government feared by many late seventeenth- and early eighteenth-century writers.
12. P. H. Wilson, *Absolutism in Central Europe* (London: Routledge, 2000), p. 51.
13. See P. Burke, 'Tacitism, Scepticism and Reason of State' in Burns (ed.), *The Cambridge History of Political Thought*, pp. 479–98.
14. P. S. Donaldson, *Machiavelli and Mystery of State* (Cambridge: Cambridge University Press, 1988), pp. 111–40.
15. Sommerville, 'Absolutism and Royalism', p. 348.
16. The opening of Andrew Marvell's *Account of the Growth of Popery and Arbitrary Government* (1677) brings together the secretive characteristics of both arbitrary government and Roman Catholicism (see A. Marvell, *The Prose Works of Andrew Marvell*, ed. A. Patterson, M. Dzelzainis, N. H. Keeble, and N. von Maltzahn, 2 vols (New Haven, CT and London: Yale University Press, 2003), vol. 2, pp. 225–9.

17. For a more detailed analysis of print in the context of other contemporary technologies of disclosure, see Rabb, *Satire and Secrecy*, pp. 4–5, and McKeon, *The Secret History of Domesticity: Public, Private and the Division of Knowledge* (Baltimore, MD: Johns Hopkins University Press, 2005), pp. 49–64.
18. There is, therefore, a fundamental rhetorical difference between texts that expose secrets to a select audience (manuscript poems on affairs of state, or seditious newsletters, for instance), and secret histories, which make their secrets available to anyone able to purchase or borrow the text in question. Consequently, the texts under consideration in this study are all published texts.
19. For a broader analysis of sexual satire of the Court during the reign of Charles II, see H. Love, *English Clandestine Satire, 1660–1702* (Oxford: Oxford University Press, 2004), and H. Weber, *Paper Bullets: Print and Kingship under Charles II* (Lexington, KY: University Press of Kentucky, 1996).
20. See also Bannet, '"Secret History": Or, Talebaring Inside and Outside the Secretorie' in P. Kewes (ed.), *The Uses of History in Early Modern England* (San Marino, CA: Huntington Library, 2006), pp. 367–88.
21. D. Jones, *The Secret History of White-hall from the Restoration of Charles II down to the Abdication of the Late K. James* (1697; 2nd edn 1717), p. vi. Because of irregularities in pagination in the first edition, all subsequent references (unless otherwise specified) are to the second edition.
22. J. Somers, *The True Secret History of the Lives and Reigns of all the Kings and Queens of England, from King William the First, Called, the Conqueror* (1702), sig. A3^v.
23. F. E. Beasley, *Revising Memory: Women's Fiction and Memoirs in Seventeenth-Century France* (New Brunswick, NJ: Rutgers University Press, 1990), pp. 15–16, suggests that the French *historiographe du roi* under Louis XIV was a post dedicated to producing panegyric narratives of the King's reign in which the monarch's secrets and secrets of state had no place.
24. T. Ryves, *Imperatoris Iustiniani defensio aduersus Alemannum* (1626), pp. 9–10.
25. J. Oldmixon, *Arcana Gallica: or, the Secret History of France, for the Last Century* (1714), p. i.
26. A. Patterson, *Early Modern Liberalism* (Cambridge: Cambridge University Press, 1997), pp. 187–90, 195–8, argues that *An Account of the Growth of Popery* should be considered as a secret history in the vein of Procopius. See also A. Patterson, 'Marvell and Secret History' in W. Chernaik and M. Dzelzainis (eds), *Marvell and Liberty* (Basingstoke: Macmillan, 1999), pp. 23–49. While there are clear correspondences between the *Account* and the tradition of secret history that I am tracing, it will become apparent that the rhetorical strategies deployed by Marvell are actually very different from those used by the vast majority of secret historians from the period under consideration.
27. N. von Maltzahn, 'Introduction' to *An Account of the Growth of Popery and Arbitrary Government* in *Prose Works of Andrew Marvell*, vol. 2, pp. 179–84.
28. J. Swift, *The Conduct of the Allies, and of the Late Ministry, in Beginning and Carrying on the Present War* (1711), p. 60.
29. On Swift's relationship with Harley, and Harley's awareness of the power of print to mould public opinion, see J. A. Downie, *Robert Harley and the Press: Propaganda and Public Opinion in the Age of Swift and Defoe* (Cambridge: Cambridge University Press, 1979).
30. Jones, *The Secret History of Whitehall*, p. v.

192   Notes to pages 9–16

31. Marvell, *Prose Works*, vol. 2, pp. 243–4.
32. Anon., *The Secret History of the Chevalier de St George* (1714), p. 2.
33. J. Dunton, *The Hanover-Spy; or, Secret History of St. James's* (1718), p. 25.
34. W. St Clair, *The Reading Nation in the Romantic Period* (Cambridge: Cambridge University Press, 2004), argues that it is impossible to make any judgements about the reception of any books without such information. My own speculations as to how authors encourage us to read their texts are based upon an analysis of their rhetorical techniques situated in the context of a necessarily partial reconstruction of their literary, political and cultural spheres of operation.
35. J. Oldmixon, *The Secret History of Europe*, 4 vols (1712–14), vol. 1, 'Preface' (no page number or signature).
36. Varillas, *Anekdota Heteroniaka*, sig. A7^v.
37. N. N., *The Blatant Beast Muzzl'd: or, Reflexions on a Late Libel, Entituled The Secret History of the Reigns of K. Charles II and K. James II* (1691), sig. A9^r.
38. N. Lenglet Dufresnoy, *A New Method of Studying History, Geography, and Chronology*, trans. R. Rawlinson, 2 vols (1728), vol. 1, pp. 232–3.
39. J. Swift, *Travels into Several Remote Nations of the World* (1726), book 3, chapter 8, ed. R. DeMaria Jr. as *Gulliver's Travels* (London: Penguin Books, 2001), p. 185.
40. Jones, *The Secret History of Whitehall*, title page.
41. On the growing importance of corroboration and multiple witnessing to contemporary standards of scientific proof, see S. Shapin and S. Schaffer, *Leviathan and the Air-Pump: Hobbes, Boyle and the Experimental Life* (Princeton, NJ: Princeton University Press, 1985), p. 25.
42. Lenglet Dufresnoy, *A New Method*, vol. 1, p. 232.
43. N. N., *The Blatant Beast Muzzl'd*, pp. 14–16.
44. Somers, *The True Secret History*, sig. A3^v.
45. Ibid.
46. Ibid.
47. Jones, *The Secret History of Whitehall*, pp. v–vi.
48. Anon., *The Secret History of the Reigns of K. Charles II and K. James II* (1690), sig. A2^v.
49. 'conuitiorum satyra', Ryves, *Imperatoris Iustiniani defensio*, p. 9.
50. R. Rapin, *Instructions for History, with a Character of the Most Considerable Historians Ancient and Modern*, trans. J. Davies (1680), pp. 54–5.
51. Ibid., p. 60.
52. For a survey of *histoire galante* and related genres in France, see J. deJean, *Tender Geographies: Women and the Origins of the Novel in France* (New York: Columbia University Press, 1991) and E. Harth, *Ideology and Culture in Seventeenth-Century France* (Ithaca, NY and London: Cornell University Press, 1983), pp. 180–220. For an account of the influence of these French modes upon English amatory fiction, see R. Ballaster, *Seductive Forms: Women's Amatory Fiction from 1684–1740* (Oxford: Clarendon Press, 1992), pp. 42–66.
53. 'Si [Charles II] a agi d'une maniére si peu conforme à son Jugement, aux grandes lumieres de son Esprit, à la Politique, aux Interests non seulement de plusieurs Etats en général, mais encore de ses propres Etats, c'est une Femme, c'est la Duchesse de Portsmouth, qui l'y a porté par l'amour qu'elle lui avoit inspiré; par ses ruses, & par le pouvoir qu'elle avoit sur son Esprit', Anon., *Histoire Secrette de la Duchesse de Portsmouth* (1690), sig. *4r.
54. Varillas, *Anekdota Heteroniaka*, sig. a1^{r-v}.
55. Ibid., sig. a1^v.

56. Ibid., sig. a1ᵛ–a2ʳ.
57. Ibid., sig. a2ᵛ.
58. On 'perfect history' during the early modern period, see Shapiro, *Probability and Certainty*, pp. 130–8. On Procopius's debt to Thucydides and, more generally, his use of classical models for his histories of early medieval Christian Byzantium, see A. Cameron, *Procopius and the Sixth Century* (London: Gerald Duckworth & Co., 1985; reissued, London and New York: Routledge, 1996), pp. 37–45, and A. Kaldellis, *Procopius of Caesarea: Tyranny, History, and Philosophy at the End of Antiquity* (Philadelphia, PA: University of Pennsylvania Press, 2004), pp. 9–12.
59. Rapin, *Instructions for History*, p. 59.
60. Rapin's original French reads, 'rien ne touche davantage la curiosité des hommes, que quand on leur découvre ce qui est la plus caché dans le cœur humain, c'est à dire, les ressorts secrets qui le font agir dans les enterprises qui luy sont ordinaries' (R. Rapin, *Instructions pour l'histoire* (Paris, 1677), p. 65).
61. On early modern attitudes towards Tacitus, see P. Burke, 'Tacitism' in T. A. Dorey (ed.), *Tacitus*, (London: Routledge and Kegan Paul, 1969), pp. 149–71.
62. C. de Marguetel de Saint-Denis, seigneur de Saint-Evremond, 'Observations upon Salust and Tacitus' in *Miscellaneous Essays by Monsieur St. Euremont* (1692), pp. 116–27, p. 117.
63. Rapin, *Instructions for History*, p. 25. Both Saint-Evremond and Rapin contrast Tacitus' 'policy'-based explanations with those of other historians (particularly Sallust) who make the character or 'Nature' of major figures the key to understanding the course of historical events.
64. In addition to the points mentioned below, secret history makes no effort to replicate the stylistic density and obscurity characteristic of Tacitean history (see Burke, 'Tacitism', pp. 151–3).
65. P. Hicks, *Neoclassical History and English Culture From Clarendon to Hume* (Basingstoke: Macmillan, 1996), pp. 18–19.
66. The two sides of this ambivalent intepretation of Tacitus are sometimes referred to, respectively, as 'red' and 'black' Tacitism, based on an early twentieth-century analysis: G. Toffanin, *Machiavelli e il 'Tacitismo', la 'politica storia' al tempo della Controriforma* (Padova: A Draghi, 1921). See also Burke, 'Tacitism', pp. 162–7, and Hicks, *Neoclassical History*, pp. 18–19.
67. Rapin, *Instructions for History*, p. 59, italics added.
68. On this aspect of the relationship between secret history and satire, see Rabb, *Secrecy and Satire*, pp. 67–89.
69. Varillas, *Anekdota Heteroniaka*, sig. a2ᵛ.
70. Ibid., sig. a2ʳ.
71. Ibid.
72. Ibid., sig. a4ᵛ.
73. Bannet, '"Secret History"', p. 388.
74. Somers, *The True Secret History*, p. 1.
75. On the relationship between the 'secret springs' and 'wheels within wheels' metaphors, see pp. 139–4.
76. It is interesting that the secret treaty of Dover – a favourite topic of seventeenth-century secret historians – was not one but two treaties. A simulated, but still secret, treaty, which was shown to Charles's leading Protestant ministers, Ashley, Buckingham and Lauderdale, omitted a clause in which Charles promised to declare himself a Roman

Catholic. This clause was contained in an even more secret version of the treaty (see J. R. Jones, *Country and Court: England, 1658–1714* (London: Edward Arnold, 1978), p. 173). The existence of this double treaty appears not to have been known to early modern secret historians, but it neatly exemplifies the belief of many contemporaries that political events were made up of wheels within wheels.

77. N. N., *Blatant Beast Muzzl'd*, (sig. A7^r)
78. Ibid., p. 40.
79. Anon., *An Examen of the New Comedy, Call'd the Suspicious Husband ... To Which Is Added ... A Piece of Secret History* (1747), pp. 49–56.
80. In this respect, my analysis is at odds with Rabb, *Satire and Secrecy*, p. 69, which argues that 'secret history accommodates Tory and Whig, feminine and masculine, and conservative and liberal' and that 'its strategic appeal arises precisely from qualities inclusive of parties and genders'.
81. Anon., *Poems on Affairs of State: from the Time of Oliver Cromwell to the Abdication of K. James the Second* (1697), sig. A3^r, tells its readers that 'from [these poems] we may collect a just and secret History of the former Times'. In *The Blatant Beast Muzzl'd*, sig. A7^v, however, N. N. describes broadside ballads as 'lesser squirting Papers, handed about by malicious Fops' and insists that his target is 'greater and more bulky Pieces', or secret histories.
82. Rabb, *Satire and Secrecy*, p. 69, describes secret histories as 'crass texts' that 'help the satirist by constructing a readership willing to entertain more than one possible meaning to appearances, a readership that could think ironically, that could tolerate the difference between information and truth, and that could read complex satire'. She thus reads secret history in the light of contemporary satire rather than as a complex form in its own right.
83. R. Mayer, *History and the Early English Novel: Matters of Fact from Bacon to Defoe* (Cambridge: Cambridge University Press, 1997), pp. 94–112. K. O'Brien, 'History and the Novel in Eighteenth-Century Britain', in Kewes (ed.), *The Uses of History*, pp. 389–405, pp. 389–405, uses secret history to put forward a different argument from Mayer's: that, while the novel experimented with the rhetoric of historicity, historical writing resisted the incursion of rhetorical techniques borrowed from fiction.
84. McKeon, *Secret History*, pp. 621–717; W. B. Warner, *Licensing Entertainment: The Elevation of Novel Reading in Britain, 1684–1750* (Berkeley and Los Angeles, CA: University of California Press, 1998).
85. M. M. Bakhtin, *The Dialogic Imagination: Four Essays by M. M. Bakhtin*, ed. M. Holquist, trans. C. Emerson and M. Holquist (Austin, TX: University of Texas Press, 1981).
86. On non-literary contexts for the novel, see J. P. Hunter, *Before Novels: the Cultural Contexts of Eighteenth-Century English Fiction* (New York and London: Norton, 1990); L. Davis, *Factual Fictions: the Origins of the English Novel* (New York: Columbia University Press, 1983); McKeon, *Origins of the English Novel*.
87. Brean Hammond suggests that even texts that are not, themselves, novels are, nonetheless affected by the process of 'novelisation' that pervades the literary culture of the late seventeenth and early eighteenth centuries (see B. Hammond, *Professional Imaginative Writing in England, 1670–1740: 'Hackney for Bread'* (Oxford: Clarendon Press, 1997), pp. 107–11 (on Bakhtin and 'novelisation') and pp. 303–7 (for a summary of 'novelisation')).

Notes to pages 23–32   195

88. Rabb, *Satire and Secrecy*, pp. 67–89, does suggest that satire and secret history are connected by the important position that alternative versions of the past occupy in each form.
89. McKeon, *Secret History*, pp. 5–6.
90. Patterson, *Early Modern Liberalism*, pp. 185, 188–9.
91. The vast amount of literature generated by what has become known as 'the linguistic turn' in historical studies is explored at length in J. Tully (ed.), *Meaning and Context: Quentin Skinner and his Critics* (Cambridge: Polity Press, 1988), and summarized in Knights, *Representation and Misrepresentation*, pp. 41–8.
92. For a much fuller account of the vocabulary of partisan struggle, see R. Ashcraft, 'The Language of Political Conflict in Restoration Literature', in *Politics as Reflected in Literature* (Los Angeles, CA: The William Andrews Clark Memorial Library, University of California, 1989), pp. 1–28.
93. Knights, *Representation and Misrepresentation*.
94. See also Loveman, *Reading Fictions*, pp. 5–6.

1 Procopius of Caesarea and the Secret History of the Court of the Emperor Justinian (1674)

1. In this chapter, I refer to Procopius's narrative (in general) as the *Anekdota* and the English translation of this work (in particular) as *The Secret History of the Court of the Emperor Justinian* or simply *The Secret History*.
2. See below, p. 31.
3. Procopius of Caesarea, *The Secret History of the Court of the Emperor Justinian* (1674), p. 2. All subsequent references are to this edition.
4. McKeon, *Secret History*, pp. 470–1; Patterson, *Early Modern Liberalism*, p. 183.
5. Procopius, *The Secret History*, pp. 1–2.
6. '... non ad huius Imperatoris infamiam magis quam ad omnium Regum & Principum iniuriam pertinere videbatur', Ryves, *Imperatoris Iustiniani defensio*, sig. A5ᵛ.
7. In fact, Thomas Ryves complains that Alemannus deliberately mistranslated Procopius so as to strengthen his accusations against Justinian and Theodora. By removing a tag – 'they say' – from his accusation that certain women were forced into sexual relations with their slaves under Justinian's rule, Alemannus turns a rumour in Procopius's original into a fact in his own translation (Ryves, *Imperatoris Iustiniani*, p. 8). But in spite of such local instances of minor misrepresentation, Alemannus does translate most of Procopius's *Anekdota* and retains (even if he strengthens) the iconoclastic tone of the original.
8. Varillas, *Anekdota Heterouiaka*, sig. a1ʳ.
9. Ibid., sig. a1ᵛ.
10. Ibid., sig. d2ᵛ.
11. Ibid., sig. d2ᵛ.
12. F. de la Mothe le Vayer, *Oeuvres*, 2 vols (3rd edn, Paris, 1662), vol. 1, p. 359.
13. On the question of authorship, see Cameron, *Procopius*, p. 16.
14. 'Le nom d'*Anecdotes* monstre que c'est un travail secret, & que son Auteur ne vouloit pas estre divulgué' (la Mothe le Vayer, *Oeuvres*, vol 1, p. 356).
15. Thomas Ryves was strongly critical of the fact that Alemannus's use of the title *Arcana Historia* could lead to this interpretation, declaring: 'So [Procopius] wished this his history to remain in obscurity at the time: so what? Did no one before Procopius? Did no

one after him write such things which would spread with danger to him, which, while still alive, he did not wish to go out into the light? But who, however, is so insane that he would think his writings should accordingly be named "arcana"?' ('At enim hanc suam historiam ad tempus in obscuro manere voluit: quid tum? nemon ante Procopium? Post eum nemo, ea scripsit, quae vivo in lucem exire noluit? sed quis tamen tam mente captus, vt scritpa sua, arcana proinde nominanda esse existimaret?'), Ryves, *Imperatoris Iustiniani*, p. 10.

16. 'L'on m'a envoié de Rome ce que la honte a fait retrancher de la page quarante & uniéme & quarante-deuxiéme des *Anecdotes* imprimées, où Procope fait faire à cette femme [Theodora] des actions de lubricité si estranges, sur tout quand des Oisons alloient en plein theatre chercher des grains de bled où ils devoient le moins estre, que je ne croi pas que personne envie là dessus l'original entier à la Bibliotheque du Vatican, ni qu'on ait jamais ouï parler de semblables abominations' (la Mothe le Vayer , *Oeuvres*, vol. 1, p. 359).

17. J. Jortin, *Remarks on Ecclesiastical History*, 5 vols (1751–73), vol. 4, p. 350.

18. Jortin, *Remarks*, vol. 4, p. 366.

19. E. Gibbon, *The Decline and Fall of the Roman Empire* (1776–88), ed. D. Womersley, 3 vols (Harmondsworth: Penguin, 1994), vol. 2, p. 565.

20. G. Ménage, *Menagiana, ou Les bons mots et remarques critiques, historiques, morales et d'érudition de Monsieur Ménage*, 3rd edn, 2 vols (1715), vol. 1, p. 347. *Menagiana* (first published in 1693) is a posthumous miscellany of the writings and sayings of Gilles Ménage. The third edition of 1715 is the first to include the excised passages.

21. Gibbon, *Decline and Fall*, vol. 2, p. 565.

22. 'silentij velo', Ryves, *Imperatoris Iustiniani*, p. 8.

23. Edmund Chilmead was a mathematician, musician and critic who served as a chaplain at Christ Church, Oxford, during the 1630s. He sided with the royalists at the outbreak of Civil War and subsequently fell on hard times. He supported himself by hosting a weekly musical meeting in London and he also took on paid work as a translator, especially from Greek. An entry in Anthony Wood's *Athenae* Oxonienses notes that Chilmead 'assisted Sir *Hen. Holbroke* [sic] Knt (by whom he had been exhibited to) in his Translation of *Procopius* of *Caeserea* his *History of the Wars of the Emperor* Justinian, in 8 books &c. Lond. 1653 fol. by exactly comparing the *English* with the *Greek*, as it was written by *David Hoeschelius*, who had it out of the Duke of *Bavaria*'s Library' (A. Wood, *Athenae Oxonienses*, 2n edn 2 vols (1721), vol. 2, p. 170). The preface to the *History of the Warres* informs us that Holcroft had recently died and that his translation was published posthumously. The author of this preface takes pains to explain the process of choosing a copy text for this edition in a way that suggests intimate knowledge of the Hoeschelius manuscript, and so Chilmead seems a plausible candidate (see Procopius of Caesarea, *The History of the Warres of the Emperour Justinian in Eight Books*, trans. H. Holcroft (1653), sig. A3ʳ). Chilmead died in 1654, the year after the *History of the Warres* was published.

24. Procopius, *History of the Warres,* sig. A5r. Suidas is a tenth-century lexicographer who mentions the *Secret History* in passing.

25. Procopius, *Secret History*, p. 21.

26. During this decade, eleven of Clement Barksdale's works are sold by John Barkesdale, two have no identified publisher, two are published by Clement Barksdale himself, one is published by Mark Pardoe, and one (a reprint of a tract also published by John Barkesdale) is published by Samuel Lee.

27. C. Barksdale, *Memorials of Worthy Persons. (Lights and Ornaments of the Church of England.) The Fourth Decade* (Oxford, 1663), epistle dedicatory.
28. See Procopius, *Secret History*, pp. 59–62, and Cameron, *Procopius*, p. 66.
29. On religious policy during the reign of Charles II – particularly the Act of Uniformity (1662) and other elements of the 'Clarendon Code' – see J. Spurr, *The Post-Reformation: Religion, Politics and Society in Britain, 1603–1714* (Harlow: Longman, 2006), pp. 144–54.
30. Procopius, *Secret History*, p. 2.
31. Ibid., pp. 68, 78.
32. John Evelyn praised Charles II for being 'Easy of accesse, not bloudy or Cruel', (J. Evelyn, *The Diary of John Evelyn*, ed. E. S. de Beer, 6 vols (Oxford: Clarendon Press, 1955), vol. 4, p. 409); Weber, *Paper Bullets*, pp. 97–9, shows that Charles's 'easiness', particularly as far as sexual access to the royal body was concerned, invited criticism and satire.
33. Procopius, *Secret History*, p. 146.
34. Jones, *Country and Court*, p. 169.
35. On 'parallels' in contemporary literature, see A. Roper, 'Drawing Parallels and Making Applications in Restoration Literature' in *Politics as Reflected in Literature*, pp. 29–65 (pp. 40–7).
36. Cameron, *Procopius*, p. 9.
37. Ibid., p. 1.
38. Ibid., p. 2.
39. Ibid., p. 11.
40. Ibid., p. 11.
41. Ibid., p. 82.
42. Ibid.
43. Ibid., p. 58.
44. Ibid., p. 2.
45. Ibid., p. 66.
46. (pp. 3–4)
47. Procopius, *Secret History*, p. 34.
48. Procopius, *Secret History*, p. 135.
49. 'homicidia, scelera, occulta multi, arcana, nemo unquam appellavit', Ryves, *Imperatoris Iustiniani*, pp. 9–10.
50. N. N., *Blatant Beast Muzzl'd*, p. 20.
51. Ibid., p. 21.

2 Secret History and Whig Historiography, 1688–1702

1. T. Hearne, *Ductor Historicus or, a Short System of Universal History An Introduction to the Study of that Science* (1698), p. 195. In his criticisms, Hearne draws upon la Mothe le Vayer, who describes Procopius as 'soufflant le chaud & le froid' (la Mothe le Vayer, *Oeuvres*, vol. 1, p. 359).
2. R. North, *Examen: or, an Enquiry into the Credit and Veracity of a Pretended Complete History* (1740), p. xi.
3. N. N., *The Blatant Beast Muzzl'd*, sig. A6[r-v].
4. Bodleian Library, Wood 242, p. 31.
5. Patterson, *Early Modern Liberalism*, pp. 185, 189.

6. Of course, William and Mary were not necessarily more open about their policies than the Stuart monarchs. Indeed, one French observer remarked that William's 'chief characteristic is great distrust, so that very few persons, even amongst those who are in office, are acquainted with his secrets' (cited in W. L. Sachse, *Lord Somers: A Political Portrait* (Manchester: Manchester University Press, 1975), p. 146). It was, however, convenient for Whig polemicists to use the issue of secrecy to draw a contrast between the new and the old regime. Moreover, Whig writers were aware that, whatever William's secret will, he would have more difficulty in enforcing it than the Stuarts because of the limitations placed on the royal prerogative by the Revolution settlement in 1689.

7. Anon., *The Secret History of The Reigns of K. Charles II and K. James II*, sig. A2ᵛ. The unusual word 'furberies' – an anglicisation of the French *fourberie*, or 'deception' – gestures towards the French source of the Stuart tyranny that was ousted by William III in 1688. See *OED*, 'fourbery' *obs*.

8. Anon., *The Secret History of the Reigns of K. Charles II and K. James II*, sig. A2ʳ. This slogan confirms the idea that the polemical force of secret history need not derive from the fact that it publishes information that had previously been unknown – that is, 'genuine' secrets – but that it can also come from the fact that secret history puts into public, printed form information that was previously secret because unpublished. The bold 'freedom' with which the Caesars committed corrupt acts is here matched by the public form in which this information is presented to its readers.

9. Somers, *The True Secret History*, sig. A2ᵛ.

10. The reference to Suetonius, the phrase 'Truth is not always to be spoken' and the sentiments that accompany it allude to the preface to *The Secret History of the Reigns of K. Charles II and K. James II*, sig. A2ʳ⁻ᵛ.

11. A. Sidney, *Colonel Sidney's Speech, Delivered to the Sheriff on the Scaffold, December 7ᵗʰ 1683* (1683), p. 1.

12. Somers may have had personal reasons for doing so. He had been impeached for his part in bringing about the first Partition Treaty and, although acquitted in June 1701, he was generally accused of having acted '*in an Arbitrary way; (that is, as they expounded it, not in Concert with the People)*' (J. Swift, *A Discourse of the Contests and Dissensions between the Nobles and the Commons in Athens and Rome* (1701), p. 43). His condemnation of arbitrary government is presumably, in part, an attempt to assert his Whig principles at a time when the Tories had gained the ascendancy in the Commons. On Somers's impeachment and its aftermath, see Sachse, *Lord Somers*, pp. 171–234.

13. That said, no secret history published during William III's reign actually reveals his state secrets. Somers's *The True Secret History* comes to a conclusion with the reign of Charles I, even though Somers promises his reader an account of England's secret history 'to this Present Year 1702' (sig. A2ʳ). At the end of his *True Secret History*, Somers promises his readers a second volume containing the reigns of Charles II to William III, but this second volume does not appear until 1730. In spite of his failure to reveal current secrets of state, Somers's rhetorical posturing is designed to contrast the political freedoms enjoyed by the English people under a limited monarchy with the fear and insecurity that – he claims – they felt when absolute rule seemed to be a genuine and immediate threat.

14. H. Butterfield, *The Whig Interpretation of History* (London: G. Bell and Sons, 1931). On the 'whig' historiography of some early Whig historians, see Zook, 'The Restoration Remembered', pp. 214–15. In this study, I distinguish between whig historiography and the Whig party by capitalizing the latter.

15. (pp. 423–4)

16. Butterfield, *The Whig Interpretation of History*, p. 41.
17. <http://catalogue.bnf.fr> and <http://www.cerl.org/web/en/resources/hpb/main>, accessed 1 October 2008.
18. Richard Baldwin published both the English and French versions of this text. He was also the publisher of the second impression of *The Secret History of the Court of the Emperor Justinian* which appeared under the title, *The Debaucht Court; or, The Lives of the Emperor Justinian, and His Empress Theodora the Comedian* (1682). On Baldwin as a Whig publisher, see L. Rostenberg, *Literary, Political, Scientific, Religious & Legal Publishing, Printing & Bookselling in England, 1551–1700: Twelve Studies*, 2 vols (New York: Burt Franklin, 1965), vol. 2, pp. 369–415, and M. Treadwell, 'London Trade Publishers 1675–1750', *Library*, 6th series, 2 (1982), pp. 99–134.
19. Anon., *The Kings Cabinet Opened; or, Certain Packets of Secret Letters & Papers, Written with the Kings Own Hand, and Taken in His Cabinet at Nasby-Field, June 14. 1645* (1645), consists of a series of letters between Charles I and his French wife, Henrietta Maria, that inform their readers about Charles's absolutist ambitions and his sympathy for the Roman Catholic cause. On *The Kings Cabinet Opened*, see McKeon, *Secret History*, pp. 482–6. On adaptations of the title of this tract during the later seventeenth century, see L. Potter, *Secret Rites and Secret Writing: Royalist Literature, 1641–1660* (Cambridge: Cambridge University Press, 1989), p. 61.
20. Anon., *Secret History of the Reigns of K. Charles II and K. James II*, sig. A2^v.
21. In this respect, secret history is very different from other more overtly celebratory forms, like Williamite panegyric, which owe their existence to the Revolution. On Williamite panegyric, see A. Williams, *Poetry and the Creation of a Whig Literary Culture, 1681–1714*, (Oxford: Oxford University Press, 2005), pp. 93–134, and S. Zwicker, *Lines of Authority: Politics and English Literary Culture, 1649–1689* (Ithaca, NY and London: Cornell University Press, 1993), pp. 178–80.
22. N. N., *The Blatant Beast Muzzl'd*, p. 1.
23. On the marketplace for illegal publications in eighteenth-century France, see R. Darnton, *The Forbidden Best-Sellers of Pre-Revolutionary France* (New York: W.W. Norton, 1995) and J. Popkin and B. Fort (eds), *The Mémoires secrets and the Culture of Publicity in Eighteenth-Century France* (Oxford: Voltaire Foundation, 1998).
24. For a modern perspective on the 'Pierre Marteau' imprint, see www.pierre-marteau.com, accessed 9 January 2009.
25. *Le Comte d'Essex* was, in fact, published in 1678 in the wake of Thomas Corneille's tragedy, *Le Comte d'Essex* (1678) and Mme de Lafayette's novel, *La Princesse de Clèves* (1678), which it imitates stylistically. Backdating the *privilège du Roy* on this title was probably designed to give the impression that it predated (and, perhaps, served as a model for) these works. According to Georges Ascoli, the French version of the *histoire secrète* was translated from an English text, *The History of the Most Renowned Queen Elizabeth and His [sic] Greatest Favourite the Earl of Essex*, which was published in London in 1650, and this claim is reiterated by the recent editor of Corneille's play (see G. Ascoli, *La Grande-Bretagne devant l'opinion française au XVII siècle*, 2 vols (Paris: Libraire Universitaire J. Gamber, 1930), vol. 2, p. 285, and T. Corneille, *Le Comte d'Essex* (1678), ed. W. Gibson (Exeter: University of Exeter Press, 2000), p. XVII). According to the *English Short Ttitle Catalogue*, however, the earliest recorded edition of this particular English title appears in 1700 and it refers to a later edition of *The Secret History of the Most Renown'd Queen Elizabeth, with the Earl of Essex* (1680). Since the style of *Le Comte d'Essex. Histoire angloise* is very close to, and probably imitative of, *La Princesse*

de Clèves, it seems highly unlikely that there was, in fact, an earlier English edition of this work.
26. Bannet, "'Secret History'", pp. 373–6. Bannet's analysis of the political significance of secret history's erotic content provides an important corrective to Annabel Patterson's dismissal of erotic secret history as frivolous, apolitical and somehow not 'real' secret history (see Patterson, *Early Modern Liberalism*, p. 186).
27. C. Vanel, *The Royal Mistresses of France, or, The Secret History of the Amours of all the French Kings, from Pharamond the First Monarch, Anno 418. to this Present Time* (1695), sig. A2^r.
28. 'Si [Charles II] a agi d'une maniére si peu conforme à son Jugement, aux grandes lumieres de son Esprit, à la Politique, aux Interests non seulement de plusieurs Etats en général, mais encore de ses propres Etats, c'est une Femme, c'est la Duchesse de Portsmouth, qui l'y a porté par l'amour qu'elle lui avoit inspiré; par ses ruses, & par le pouvoir qu'elle avoit sur son Esprit' (Anon., *Histoire Secrette de la Duchesse de Portsmouth*, sig.*4r).
29. On the 'godly' nature of the Revolution of 1688–9, see T. Claydon, *William III and the Godly Revolution* (Cambridge: Cambridge University Press, 1996); C. Rose, *England in the 1690s: Revolution, Religion, and War* (Oxford: Blackwell, 1999), pp. 195–209; Williams, *Poetry and the Creation of a Whig Literary Culture*, pp. 121–7.
30. Anon., *The Secret History of the Duchess of Portsmouth* (1690), p. 132.
31. Anon., *The Secret History of the Reigns of K. Charles II and K. James II*, p. 85.
32. N. N., *The Blatant Beast Muzzl'd*, p. 7, italics in original.
33. Lenglet Dufresnoy, *A New Method*, vol. 1, p. 232. The English translator of this work adds, in a footnote to this assertion, that 'this is no where so notorious as in *England*, where these Books swarm, and infect the Minds of the ignorant'.
34. Jones, *The Secret History of White-hall*, p. vii.
35. Robert Mayer states that 'Jones's ... special knowledge resulted from his employment by the Marquis de Louvois as an interpreter' (Mayer, *History and the Early English Novel*, p. 99); Annabel Patterson asserts that 'it is clear that the writer of the preface, the editor of the volume ... and the author of the letters are one and the same' (Patterson, *Early Modern Liberalism*, p. 191).
36. J. Dunton, *The State-Weathercocks: or, a New Secret History of the Most Distinguished Favourites Both of the Late and Present Reign* (1719), p. 31, sig. f4^r. The impetus for Dunton's complaint was the publication of a second edition of *The Secret History of White-hall* in 1717. Dunton claimed that the rights in copy for *The Secret History of White-hall* belonged to him, but that the 'Welsh Knaw-post', David Jones, had sold the letters that made up the original *Secret History of White-hall* to a publishing conger, swindling Dunton out of the hundred guineas that he expected to make from publishing a second edition of this text himself (see Dunton, *The State-Weathercocks*, p. 33, sig. f5^r).
37. J. Dunton, *The Life and Errors of John Dunton, Late Citizen of London* (1705), p. 227.
38. N. Besogne, *Galliae Notitia: or, The Present State of France*, trans. R. Wolley (1691), sig. A5^{r-v}.
39. Jones, *The Secret History of White-hall*, p. vi.
40. G. P. Marana, *Letters Writ by a Turkish Spy*, 8 vols (1687–94). The Turkish Spy was probably written by Giovanni Paolo Marana, a Genoese political exile who sought refuge in Paris. On the disputed authorship of this work, see R. Ballaster, *Fabulous Orients: Fictions of the East in England, 1662–1785* (Oxford: Oxford University Press, 2005), p. 146.
41. Jones, *The Secret History of White-hall*, p. 131.

42. Ibid., pp. 294, iv.
43. Ibid., p. iv.
44. See also Bannet, '"Secret History"', p. 388 and Ballaster, *Fabulous Orients*, p. 155.
45. Forumlaic titles including: Marchamont Nedham's *The Germane Spie: Truly Discovering the Deplorable Condition of the Kingdom and Subjects of the French King* (1691); Anon., *The English Spy: or, The Intrigues, Pollicies, and Stratagems of the French KING with His Secret Contrivances, for Undermining the PRINCES OF CHRISTENDOM, DISCOVERED* (1695); Gatien de Courtilz de Sandras's novel, *The French Spy: or, The Memoirs of John Baptist de la Fontaine*, trans. J. C. M. D. (1700); Ned Ward's journal, the *London Spy* (1699–1700) and Charles Gildon's *The Golden Spy: or, A Political Journal of the British Nights Entertainments of War and Peace, and Love and Politics* (1709) as well as John Dunton's publications, *The Athenian Spy* (1704, 1760, 1720), *The Court-Spy* (1713) and *The Hanover-Spy*, may have been inspired by the popular success of Marana's *Letters Writ by a Turkish Spy*, commonly known as *The Turkish Spy*.
46. M. Smith, *Memoirs of Secret Service* (1699), p. xviii.
47. G. de Courtilz de Sandras, *The French Spy*, p. 351.
48. Marana, *Letters Writ by a Turkish Spy*, vol. 7, p. 344.
49. Ibid., vol. 8, pp. 355–57.
50. Ballaster, *Fabulous Orients*, p. 148.
51. Most discussions of the operations of secrecy in cultural or literary contexts assume that secrecy creates a straightforward binary division between 'insiders', or 'knows', who have access to a secret and 'outsiders', or 'know-nots', who are excluded from it (for this terminology, see S. Bok, *Secrets: on the Ethics of Concealment and Revelation* (Oxford: Oxford University Press, 1984), p. 6, and K. Lochrie, *Covert Operations: The Medieval Uses of Secrecy* (Philadelphia, PA: University of Pennsylvania Press, 1999), p. 93). Sceptical secret history challenges the idea that these two groups are well-defined, discrete categories, emphasizing instead the anxiety that secrecy induces by highlighting the impossibility of knowing whether or not one is truly an insider.
52. Jones, *The Secret History of White-hall* (1st edn, 1697), sig. A7^r-A8^r. The preface to the 1717 edition reads: 'There is no one Party, or sect of Men in *England*, the Court itself not exempted, but may draw very seasonable *Informations*, and no less timous *Instructions* herefrom...' (Jones, *The Secret History of White-hall*, p. viii). The italicization of the word 'party' in the 1697 edition suggests that the author is using it in a narrow sense to implicate political parties rather than simply to denote a group of men. More striking, however, is the much stronger implied criticism of the Court in the 1697 version of this preface, which is toned down in the later version.
53. Jones, *The Secret History of White-hall*, p. 39.
54. Ibid., p. vi.
55. Ibid., p. 318.
56. N. N., *The Blatant Beast Muzzl'd*, p. 31.
57. Ibid., pp. 30–1.
58. Ibid., pp. 32–3, p. 76.
59. Jones, *The Secret History of White-hall*, p. vi.
60. R. Coke, *A Detection of the Court and State of England During the Four Last Reigns and the Interregnum* (1694), sig. A3^{r-v}. The claim to reveal secrets 'never before made public' is made on the title page of the third edition, which was published in 1697.
61. Patterson, in *Early Modern Liberalism*, pp. 160–1, describes anecdotes in Tudor chronicles as 'the symptoms and signals of resistance to the generalizing and ordering impulses,

both in historiography and in the societies history tends to monumentalize' because they are stories which '[refuse] to be absorbed into the unifying texture of grand narrative'. Patterson's sense of the disruptive qualities of anecdotes is also expressed by L. Gossman, 'Anecdote and History', *History and Theory*, 42:2 (2003), pp. 143–68 – although Gossman acknowledges that anecdote can also be used to epitomize as well as to disrupt, and can therefore act as a form of proof which affirms orthodox narratives. Jones's *Secret History of White-hall* uses anecdote (in the sense of 'unpublished thing', rather than the more modern sense of short, apothegmatic story) to create a sense of disruption that has implications for its own status as narrative history as well as more monumental, whig accounts of the recent past.
62. Coke, *A Detection*, sig. A4^v-A5^r. Coke notes that he is quoting here from 'Babtista Nani'. His assertions are lifted from B. Nani, *A History of the Affairs of Europe in this Present Age, But More Particularly of the Republick of Venice*, trans. R. Honywood (1673), sig. b1^v.
63. Somers, *The True Secret History*, sig. A3^v.

3 Secret History, the 'Revolution' of 1714 and the Case of John Dunton

1. On *The Secret History of the Calves Head Club*, see M. Knights, 'The Tory Interpretation of History in the Rage of Parties' in Kewes (ed.) *The Uses of History*, pp. 347–66, pp. 357–63; on the attribution of *The Secret History of Queen Zarah and the Zarazians* to Joseph Browne, not Delarivier Manley, see J. A. Downie, 'What if Delarivier Manley Did *Not* Write *The Secret History of Queen Zarah*?' *The Library*, 5:3 (2004), pp. 247–64.
2. Oldmixon, *The Secret History of Europe*, vol. 1, title page.
3. Ibid., vol. 2, sig. A2^r.
4. Their views were aired in Swift, *Conduct of the Allies*.
5. In *Conduct of the Allies*, p. 69, Swift explores 'how this new Language of *No Peace without Spain*, was first introduced, and at last prevailed among us'.
6. On Harley's spy network during this period, see A. McInnes, *Robert Harley: Puritan Politician* (London: Victor Gollancz, 1970), pp. 77–86.
7. See, for instance, F. Hoffman, *Secret Transactions During the Hundred Days Mr William Gregg Lay in Newgate Under Sentence of Death for High Treason* (1711) and J. Oldmixon, *A Letter to the Seven Lords of the Committee, Appointed to Examine Gregg* (1711).
8. 6 January 1705/6, W. Cowper, *The Private Diary of William, First Earl Cowper, Lord Chancellor of England, 1705–14*, ed. E. C. Hawtrey (Eton: Roxburghe Club, 1833), p. 33. Cowper takes his distinction between dissimulation and simulation from Francis Bacon's essay 'Of Simulation and Dissimulation', in which Bacon distinguishes between the '*Negative*' practice of dissimulation (that is, 'when a man lets fall Signes, and Arguments, that he is not, that he is') and the '*Affirmative*' practice of simulation or 'false Profession' ('when a man industriously, and expressly, faigns, and pretends to be, that he is not'). While dissimulation is an intrinsic aspect of the '*Closenesse, Reservation, and Secrecy*' that Bacon regards as '*both Politick, and Morall*', simulation is 'more culpable, and lesse politicke', and is, as such, a quality that Bacon would have his readers adopt only 'if there be no Remedy' (F. Bacon, *The Essayes or Counsels, Civill and Morall*, ed. M. Kiernan (Oxford: Clarendon Press, 1985), pp. 21–2).
9. Cowper, *The Private Diary*, p. 54

10. E. Cruickshanks, S. Handley and D. W. Hayton (eds), *The History of Parliament: The House of Commons, 1690–1715*, 5 vols (Cambridge: Cambridge University Press for the History of Parliament Trust, 2002), vol. 4, p. 244.
11. See, for instance, J. Dunton, *Queen Robin: or The Second Part of Neck or Nothing, Detecting the Secret Reign of the Four Last Years* (1714), p. 46.
12. J. Swift, *Some Free Thoughts upon the Present State of Affairs. Written in the Year 1714* (Dublin, 1749) in J. Swift, *Political Tracts 1713–1719*, ed. H. Davis and I. Ehrenpreis (Oxford: Basil Blackwell, 1953), pp. 73–98 (pp. 80–1).
13. J. Swift, *The History of the Four Last Years of the Queen* (1758), ed. H. Williams (Oxford: Basil Blackwell, 1951), p. 75.
14. Anon., *A Secret History of One Year* (1714), p. 3. This secret history, once attributed to Defoe, is de-attributed by P. N. Furbank and W. R. Owens, *Defoe De-Attributions: A Critique of J.R. Moore's Checklist*, (London and Rio Grande, OH: The Hambledon Press, 1990), p. 66.
15. W. Stoughton, *The Secret History of the late Ministry; from their Admission, to the Death of the Queen* (1715), sig. a*ᵛ.
16. Ibid., p. 2.
17. Oldmixon, *Arcana Gallica*, sig. A3ʳ.
18. H. Speke, *The Secret History of the Happy Revolution in 1688* (1715), p. 78.
19. J. Dunton, *The Christians Gazette: or, Nice and Curious Speculations Chiefly Respecting the Invisible World* (1713), p. 68. *The Court-Spy* is the title of one section of *The Christians Gazette*, which is, in spite of its title, a single volume rather than a periodical. All subsequent references to *The Court-Spy* are taken from *The Christians Gazette*.
20. Dunton, *Court-Spy*, p. 66.
21. Ibid., p. 66.
22. Dunton, *The Hanover-Spy*, p. xi.
23. Ibid., title page, pp. xi, 23–4.
24. Ibid., p. 25.
25. Ibid., p. 26.
26. Ibid.
27. Ibid., p. 27.
28. Jones, *The Secret History of Whitehall*, p. iv.
29. Dunton, *The Court-Spy*, p. 63.
30. Ibid., p. 70.
31. Jones, *The Secret History of Whitehall*, p. 318.
32. Dunton, *The Court-Spy*, p. 70.
33. Anon., *The Secret History of the Reigns of K. Charles II and K. James II*, sig. A2ᵛ.
34. J. Dunton, *Neck or Nothing: in a Letter to the Right Honourable the Lord —* (1713), p. 5.
35. J. Dunton, *The Shortest Way with the King: or, Plain English Spoke to His Majesty* (1715), title-page, p. 2.
36. Dunton, *The Hanover-Spy*, p. xi.
37. Anon., *The Secret History of the Reigns of K. Charles II and K. James II*, sig. A2ʳ; Somers, *The True Secret History*, sig. A2ᵛ.
38. See above, p. 54.
39. J. Dunton, *A Satyr upon King William; Being the Secret History of His Life and Reign* (1703), sig. b1ᵛ.
40. Dunton, *Satyr upon King William*, b3ᵛ.

41. The ironic nature of Dunton's text is, of course, a good deal more obvious than that of Defoe's: *The Shortest Way* was widely interpreted as a genuine high church attack upon the Dissenters and created a furore once its ironic character was discovered (see P. R. Backscheider, *Daniel Defoe: His Life* (Baltimore, MD and London: Johns Hopkins University Press, 1989), pp. 94–105).
42. On the innovative qualities of the *Athenian Mercury*, see H. Berry, *Gender, Society and Print Culture in Late-Stuart England: The Cultural World of the Athenian Mercury* (Aldershot: Ashgate, 2003), p. 6.
43. 'And they took him and brought him unto Areopagus, saying, May we know what this new doctrine, whereof thou speakest, is? For thou bringest certain strange things to our ears: we would know therefore what these things mean. (For all the Athenians and strangers which were there spent their time in nothing else, but either to tell, or to hear some new thing', Acts 17: 19–21.
44. Berry, *Gender, Society and Print*, p. 24.
45. M. Mascuch, *Origins of the Individualist Self: Autobiography and Self-Identity in England, 1591–1791* (Cambridge: Polity Press, 1997), p. 137.
46. J. Dunton, *Athenae Redivivae: or, the New Athenian Oracle* (1704), sig. A2^r; J. Dunton, *Athenian Spy* (2nd edn, 1706), sig. A4^r.
47. Loveman, *Reading Fictions*, pp. 67–8.
48. See, for instance, J. Dunton, *The Art of Living Incognito, Being a Thousand Letters on As Many Uncommon Subjects* (1700).
49. Dunton reports that his *Life and Errors*, with its 'secret history' of Dunton's errors 'han't bore the Charge of Paper and Print' (J. Dunton, *Dunton's Whipping Post; or, a Satyr upon Every Body* (1706), p. 2). So unsuccessful were Dunton's writing ventures more generally, that Jane Nicholson, the mother of his second wife, Sarah, refused to hand over her daughter's dowry because she was convinced that Dunton would squander it in doomed publishing ventures (see J. Dunton, *The Case of John Dunton, Citizen of London* (1700)).
50. Bod. MS Rawl. 72, f.153.
51. Dunton, *The Hanover-Spy*, p. 1.
52. Dunton, *The State-Weathercocks*, p. ii.
53. Ibid., p. iv. In accusing the ministry of ingratitude, Dunton is inverting party political accusations made by Arthur Mainwaring in the Whig periodical, the *Medley*. On 6 November 1710, the *Medley* charged the new Tory ministry with showing ingratitude towards the Duke of Marlborough, who was in danger of losing his post as General of the British forces. Jonathan Swift responded at length in *Examiner*, 17 (23 November 1710), in which he satirically contrasts the humble rewards given to the greatest Roman generals with the vast sums bestowed on Marlborough (see J. Swift and A. Mainwaring, *Swift vs. Mainwaring: The Examiner and The Medley*, ed. F. H. Ellis (Oxford: Clarendon Press, 1985), pp. 10–12, 49–57.)
54. On the reasons behind the repeal of the Triennial Act in 1716, see Knights, *Representation and Misrepresentation*, pp. 360–75.
55. Walpole's campaign to release Harley was driven by political tactics rather than his conviction of Harley's innocence. It was an element of his opposition to the Stanhope–Sunderland ministry while Walpole was out of office. See J. H. Plumb, *Sir Robert Walpole: The Making of a Statesman* (London: The Cresset Press, 1956), pp. 254–6; B. W. Hill, *Robert Harley: Speaker, Secretary of State, and Premier Minister* (New Haven and London, CT: Yale University Press, 1988), pp. 227–30.

56. On the fate of Revolution principles in early Hanoverian England, see J. P. Kenyon, *Revolution Principles: The Politics of Party, 1689–1720* (Cambridge: Cambridge University Press, 1977), pp. 170–99.
57. Oldmixon, *Arcana Gallica*, p. 1.
58. Oldmixon, *The Secret History of Europe*, vol. 4, 'Preface' (no page number or signature).

4 Delarivier Manley and Tory Uses of Secret History

1. D. Manley, *Secret Memoirs and Manners of Several Persons of Quality, of Both Sexes. From the New Atalantis, an Island in the Mediterranean*, 2 vols (1709), vol. 1, p. 1.
2. Ibid., vol. 1, pp. 8–9.
3. Ibid., vol. 1, p. 18.
4. Ibid., p. 18.
5. R. Steele, *Tatler*, 243 (28 October 1710), in *The Tatler* (1709–11), ed. D. F. Bond, 3 vols (Oxford: Clarendon Press, 1987), vol. 3, p. 248.
6. H. St John, *A Letter to the Examiner* (1710), p. 7.
7. Rachel Carnell provides an insightful commentary upon some of the connections between Manley's *New Atalantis* and Whig secret history that I do not discuss here (see R. Carnell, *A Political Biography of Delarivier Manley* (London: Pickering and Chatto, 2008), pp. 174–80.
8. G. Holmes, *British Politics in the Age of Anne* (London: Macmillan, 1967), p. 246.
9. D. Manley, *The Adventures of Rivella; or, the History of the Author of the Atalantis* (1714), pp. 110–11.
10. D. Manley, *Memoirs of Europe, Towards the Close of the Eighth Century*, 2 vols (1710), vol. 1, pp. 236–7. A 'sesterce' or 'sestertius' is a small Roman coin.
11. Patterson, *Early Modern Liberalism*, p. 186.
12. Ballaster, *Seductive Forms*, p. 117.
13. The title page of J. Arbuthnot, *John Bull Still in his Senses: Being the Third Part of Law is a Bottomless-Pit* (1712), claims that this work is 'Publish'd, (as well as the two former Parts), by the Author of the NEW ATALANTIS'. *An Appendix to John Bull Still in his Senses: or, Law is a Bottomless-Pit* (1712) and *Lewis Baboon Turned Honest, and John Bull Politician* (1712) make the same title-page claims (see, J. Arbuthnot, *The History of John Bull*, ed. A. W. Bower and R. A. Erikson (Oxford: Clarendon Press, 1976), pp. 42, 75, 91).
14. Manley, *New Atalantis*, vol. 2, sig. A5ʳ. On the debate over personal satire during this period see C. Condren, *Satire, Lies and Politics: The Case of Dr Arbuthnot* (Basingstoke: Macmillan, 1997), pp. 33–8 and P. K. Elkin, *The Augustan Defence of Satire* (Oxford: Clarendon Press, 1973), pp. 118–45. Neither Condren nor Elkin discusses Manley's works.
15. D. Manley, *The Selected Works of Delarivier Manley*, ed. R. Carnell and R. Herman, 5 vols (London: Pickering and Chatto, 2005), vol. 1, p. 21. Elsewhere, Carnell puts forward a slightly different argument: that 'although *The New Atalantis* does revise Whig secret histories popular after the Revlolution of 1688-9 through a Tory prism, the work also put on display the hypocrisy and greed of public officials in both parties' (Carnell, *Political Biography*, p. 168).
16. Knights, 'Tory Interpretation of History', p. 353–4.
17. Ibid., pp. 363–9.
18. Bannet, '"Secret History"', p. 384.

19. Manley, *Adventures of Rivella*, p. 110.
20. Manley, *Memoirs of Europe*, vol. 1, pp. 254–5.
21. Ruth Herman speculates, although without supporting evidence, that the Count represents Anthony Hamilton, author of *Mémoires de la vie du Comte de Grammont* (Cologne, 1713) (see *Selected Works of Delarivier Manley*, vol. 3, p. 337). He is not identified as such in contemporary keys, however, and it seems equally possible, as Ros Ballaster suggests, that he has no historical referent (Ballaster, *Seductive Forms*, pp. 141, 146).
22. Manley gives an account of her arrest and questioning in *Adventures of Rivella*, pp. 108–16. See also N. Luttrell, *A Brief Historical Relation of State Affairs from September 1678 to April 1714*, 6 vols (Oxford: Oxford University Press, 1857), vol. 6, pp. 505, 506, 508, 546.
23. Rachel Carnell speculates that Manley was not arrested after the publication of the first volume of the *New Atalantis* (although she was taken up after the second had been published) because 'most of the events about which Manley gossips' in the first volume 'were old news' (Carnell, *Political Biography*, p. 179). Ruth Herman also notes that 'the stories she retells about the really important [political] figures are for the most part already well known. It is obvious that Manley was determined not to store up too much trouble for herself' (R. Herman, *The Business of a Woman: The Political Writings of Delarivier Manley* (Newark, DE: University of Delaware Press, 2003), p. 92). This chapter suggests different reasons for Manley's use of familiar stories.
24. D. Manley, *The New Atalantis*, ed. R. Ballaster (London: Pickering and Chatto, 1991), p. 296.
25. Manley, *New Atalantis*, vol. 2, p. 134. On Adelaide Paleotti, see Manley, *New Atalantis*, ed. Ballaster, p. 278, and D. H. Somerville, *The King of Hearts: Charles Talbot, Duke of Shrewsbury* (London: Allen and Unwin, 1961), pp. 233–36. See also Anon., *A Secret History of the Amours and Marriage of an English Nobleman with a Famous Italian Lady* (1712), which at least evokes even if it does not directly allude to the relationship between Shrewsbury and Paleotti, in spite of Michael McKeon's assertion that 'in this secret history the narration itself is apparently devoid of public reference' (McKeon, *Secret History*, p. 566).
26. W. A. Speck, *The Birth of Britain: A New Nation* (Oxford: Blackwell, 1994), p. 161.
27. On the relationship between *Hattigé* and *The Secret History of Queen Zarah and the Zarazians*, see R. Herman, 'Similarities between Delarivier Manley's *Secret History of Queen Zarah* and the English Translation of *Hattigé*', *Notes and Queries*, 47:2 (2000), pp. 193–6. As noted above, p. 202, J. A. Downie has recently argued that the traditional attribution of *Queen Zarah* to Manley is mistaken.
28. Manley, *New Atalantis*, vol. 1, pp. 20–43.
29. Weil, *Political Passions*, p. 176, suggests that 'Manley breaks down the barrier between sex and politics, not by making sex a metaphor for political power, but by making behaviour in sexual liaisons a test of character and political trustworthiness'.
30. Manley, *New Atalantis*, vol. 1, p. 42.
31. The case of the Duke or Albemarle's inheritance appears in the *New Atalantis*, vol. 1, pp. 167–8 and vol. 1, p. 212.
32. The Countess of Macclesfield appears as the masked woman in labour to whom the midwife, Mrs Nightwork, gives assistance in vol. 2, pp. 8–15 and as a member of the New Cabal named Ianthe in vol. 2, pp. 49, 56.
33. The case of Spencer Cowper appears at vol. 1, pp. 237–44.
34. Manley, *New Atalantis*, vol. 1, p. 19.

35. For a discussion of this tale as an emblem of the relationship between female reading and seduction, see Ballaster, *Seductive Forms*, pp. 132–6.
36. Manley, *New Atalantis*, vol. 1, p. 83.
37. Ibid.
38. Ibid.
39. Ibid., p. 84.
40. As Ros Ballaster puts it, 'interpretation, or judgement, ... is the reader's, not the narrator's, business' (Ballaster, *Seductive Forms*, p. 145). Other examples of inadequate judgements occur at vol. 1, pp. 130, 193, 203, 244, vol. 2, pp. 109–11, 112–3, 195.
41. N. N., *The Blatant Beast Muzzl'd*, sig. A9[r].
42. J. Swift, *The Importance of the Guardian Considered, in a Second Letter to the Bailiff of Stockbridge* (1713), pp. 24–5.
43. For a recent account of the English law of libel during this period, see Knights, *Representation and Misrepresentation*, pp. 261–6. For the relationship between libel and satire, see C. R. Kropf, 'Libel and Satire in the Eighteenth Century', *Eighteenth-Century Studies*, 8:2 (1974–5), pp. 153–68.
44. C. Gallagher, *Nobody's Story: The Vanishing Acts of Women Writers in the Marketplace, 1670–1820* (Berkley and Los Angeles, CA: University of California Press, 1994), p. 98.
45. Ibid., p. 130.
46. 'Les Noms supposez rendent, ce me semble, cette Histoire plus agreable. On n'aime pas toûjours à voir les choses entierement à découvert. Les Ouvrages surtout de l'Esprit plaisent plus lors qu'il y a un peu de mystére, lors qu'on ne fait qu'entrevoir les choses, & que les Auteurs en donnent plus à entendre, qu'ils n'en disent. Cela rend sans doute leurs Ouvrages plus délicats & plus agreables. Le Lecteur se plait quelquefois à chercher & à deviner; & on ne lui procure pas peu de plaisir quand on ne lui cache pas, à la verité les choses en sorte, qu'il lui soit fort difficile de les trouver, mais lors qu'on semble ne les lui cacher en partie, qu'afin qu'il ait la satisfaction de les découvrir tout-a-fait lui meme par son Esprit', Anon., *Histoire Secrette de la Duchesse de Portsmouth*, sig. *5[r-v].
47. Rabb, *Satire and Secrecy*, pp. 6–7, and Loveman, *Reading Fictions*, p. 117, do emphasize the idea that printed secrets, such as the identities of people concealed by *roman à clef*, are a means of forging sociability or intimacy between groups of readers, although not specifically between the implied author and implied reader of a *roman à clef*.
48. Manley was frequently referred to as 'the author of the Atalantis' in contemporary writings, perhaps most notably on the title pages of Arbuthnot's 'John Bull' pamphlets (see p. 89) and her own *Adventures of Rivella*, subtitled, *The History of the Author of the Atalantis*.
49. A key to the first volume was published with the second edition of 1709; a key to the second volume was printed with the first edition.
50. Manley, *New Atalantis*, ed. Ballaster, p. 279.
51. J. Swift, *Journal to Stella*, ed. H. Williams, 2 vols (Oxford: Clarendon Press, 1948; Oxford: Basil Blackwell & Mott, 1974), vol. 1, pp. 136–7.
52. Ibid., vol. 1, pp. 177–8.
53. Ibid., vol. 2, p. 598.
54. Ibid., vol. 2, p. 656.
55. Ibid., vol. 1, p. iii.
56. Irvin Ehrenpreis suggests that Swift often '[hid] information from the ladies unless he knew that a number of courtiers already had it, and it was therefore no true secret. Con-

sequently, he often sounds imprudent when he isn't' (I. Ehrenpreis, *Swift: the Man, his Works, and the Age*, 3 vols (London: Methuen, 1962–83), vol. 2, p. 654).
57. Swift acknowledges, at one point, that Johnson and Dingley cannot understand all of his political hints: 'I am sorry when I came first acquainted with this Ministry, that I did not send you their Names & Characters, and then you would have relisht would [*sic*] I would have writ; especially if I had let you into the particulars of Affairs' (Swift, *Journal to Stella*, vol. 2, pp. 495–6).
58. Michael DePorte observes that 'secrets are a kind of currency with Swift: he imparts them as tokens of affection' (M. DePorte, 'Riddles, Mysteries, and Lies: Swift and Secrecy' in *Reading Swift: Papers from the Fourth Münster Symposium on Jonathan Swift*, ed. H. J. Real and H. Stöver-Leidig (München: Wilhelm Fink Herlag, 2003), pp. 115–31 (p. 122)).
59. Swift, *Journal to Stella*, vol. 1, p. 79.
60. When he fears the downfall of the Tory ministry, Swift observes 'my letters will at least be a good history to shew you the steps of this change' (Swift, *Journal to Stella*, vol. 2, p. 436), perhaps suggesting that he intended to use them as materials towards a history of the four last years of the Queen.
61. Carnell, *Political Biography*, pp. 159–62.
62. Because of its proximity to Atalantis, Utopia has sometimes been associated with Scotland (Manley, *New Atalantis*, ed. Ballaster, p. 295), but the relationship between Utopian and British political history is metaphorical rather than geographical.
63. Manley may also have been remembering, or causing her readers to remember, the fact that James and his older brother escaped from Parliamentarians during the Civil War by dressing as women. On gender politics and high politics in late-Stuart England, see Weil, *Political Passions*.
64. The Duchess of Marlborough eventually surrendered her offices in the royal household in January 1711, at which point Abigail Masham took control of the privy purse (Hill, *Robert Harley*, p. 148).
65. Perhaps Manley's prediction of Harley's return to office – an event that took place in August of the following year – was one of the passages which led Lord Sunderland, in his interrogation of Manley, to accuse her of having 'receiv'd Information of some special Facts, which they thought were above her own Intelligence' (Manley, *Adventures of Rivella*, p. 113).
66. Manley, *New Atalantis*, ed. Ballaster, p. 298.
67. Manley, *New Atalantis*, vol. 2, p. 154.
68. Mark Knights suggests that Tory historians emphasized decay over time in opposition to Whig narratives of progress (Knights, 'Tory Interpretation of History', p. 355).
69. In 1713, for instance, Daniel Defoe published three anti-Jacobite pamphlets, with deeply provocative and ironic titles: *And What if the Pretender Should Come? Or, Some Considerations of the Advantages and Real Consequences of the Pretender's Possessing the Crown of Great Britain* (1713); *Reasons Against the Succession of the House of Hanover* (1713) and *An Answer to a Question That No Body Thinks of, viz. But What If the Queen Should Die?* (1713). Defoe's political opponents failed or refused to see the irony; he was imprisoned on charges of seditious libel (see Backscheider, *Daniel Defoe*, pp. 322–8; M. E. Novak, *Daniel Defoe, Master of Fictions: His Life and Ideas* (Oxford: Oxford University Press, 2001), pp. 421–6.
70. Manley, *New Atalantis*, vol. 2, pp. 142–3.

71. The argument that James II's flight in 1688 was an act of abdication which left the throne vacant was a mainstay of Williamite Tory and moderate Whig defences of the Revolution (see Kenyon, *Revolution Principles*, pp. 10–13).
72. E. Curll, *A Complete Key to the Tale of a Tub* (1710), p. 23, published after the first volume of *Memoirs of Europe*, notes that 'The writing of *second Parts* of Books [is here] merrily expos'd; a common way with the Hackney Authors, when a Piece takes, to write a second Part in Imitation ... A late Instance of which Madam *Manley* has furnish'd us with, in a *second* and *third* Part of her *Memoirs from the New* Atalantis'.
73. For an acute analysis of the way in which Manley gives several invented names to a single historical individual in the *New Atalantis*, see Gallagher, *Nobody's Story*, pp. 123–9.
74. Ballaster, *Fabulous Orients*, pp. 171–6.
75. For an account of Echard's *Roman History*, see R. T. Ridley, 'The Forgotten Historian: Laurence Echard and the First History of the Roman Republic', *Ancient Society*, 27 (1996), pp. 277–315.
76. In her recent edition of *Memoirs of Europe*, Ruth Herman mistakes the identity of 'Mr. Echard', suggesting that Manley was referring to a French historian, Jacques Echard, who, as Herman notes, concluded a history of the Dominicans, *Scriptores Ordinis Praedicatorum recensiti* (1719), which had been started by another French historian, Jacques Quétif (D. Manley, *Selected Works*, p. 331). Herman therefore considers Manley's suggestion that Echard had 'continuators' to be 'a tongue in cheek comment on her part'. Since Jacques Echard's history was not published until 1719, however, it cannot be the history to which Manley is referring in the preface to *Memoirs of Europe*. In her recent biography of Manley, Rachel Carnell describes the Court at Constantinople in *Memoirs of Europe* as 'a clever reconfiguration of actual court and dynastic relations', but does not identify Echard as the source of Manley's story (see Carnell, *Political Biography*, p. 193).
77. Eginardus is more commonly known as Einhard. His major literary legacy is his *Vita Caroli Magni* (*c.* 817–30 AD) or 'Life of Charles the Great', which is closely modelled on the 'Life of Augustus' in Suetonius's *Twelve Caesars*.
78. Manley, *Memoirs of Europe*, vol. 1, sig. A7ᵛ.
79. It is tempting to suggest that Manley is following Procopius in writing a salacious secret history of a pre-existing public history of a Byzantine emperor. In his account of the reign of the Emperor Justinian, however, Echard's continuator draws only on the respectable *History of the Wars* rather than the scandalous and satirical *Anekdota*. There is no evidence to suggest that Manley had read or, indeed, knew of Procopius's *Anekdota*.
80. L. Echard, *The Roman History*, 5 vols (the last three by an anonymous 'continuator') (1695–1704), vol. 4, p. 409.
81. Manley, *Memoirs of Europe*, vol. 1, p. 228.
82. In the story of Delia in the *New Atalantis* (vol. 2, pp. 181–91), Manley recounts the story of her own bigamous marriage to her cousin, John Manley. In her autobiographical *Adventures of Rivella*, p. 29, Manley refers her readers to the story of Delia for an account of her unfortunate marriage.
83. On Whig resistance theory, see L. Schwoerer, 'The Right to Resist: Whig Resistance Theory, 1688 to 1694', *Political Discourse in Early Modern Britain*, ed. N. Phillipson and Q. Skinner (Cambridge: Cambridge University Press, 1993), pp. 232–52.
84. Manley, *Memoirs of Europe*, vol. 1, p. 241.
85. Manley, *Memoirs of Europe*, vol. 1, p. 242.
86. 'To obey the King himself contrary to Law is Disloyalty, and to disobey the King in obedience to the Laws is Loyalty' (S. Johnson, *The Works of the Late Reverend Mr. Samuel*

Johnson, Sometime Chaplain to the Right Honourable William Lord Russel (1710), p. 170); 'The true Etymology of the word *loyalty* (which has been so strangely wrested in the late Reigns) is an entire Obedience to the Prince in all his commands, according to Law; that is, to the *Laws themselves*, to which we owe both an active and passive Obedience' (R. Molesworth, 'Preface' to F. Hotoman, *Franco-Gallia: or, An Account of the Ancient Free State of France*, trans. R. Molesworth (2nd edn, 1721), p. x. Molesworth's preface was reprinted in 1775 as *The Principles of a Real Whig*).

87. We might compare Manley's representation of James II as Princess Ormia in the Utopia section of the *New Atalantis* with her depiction of George of Denmark as Mary the Armenian in *Memoirs of Europe*. Not only does Manley cross-dress both male royals as women, but in each case men are conflated with their wives. It was Mary of Modena, not James II, who carried the Pretender over to France, and it was Anne, not George, whose constitution was weakened by diseases. Manley thus subverts the androcentricity of public history not only by focusing on the private lives of public figures, but also by giving a character who seems to represent a male historical figure characteristics that clearly belong to his female partner.

88. On arguments for divorce rather than Catholic succession, see M. Knights, *Politics and Opinion in Crisis, 1678–81* (Cambridge: Cambridge University Press, 1994), pp. 34–5.

89. Weil, *Political Passions*, pp. 121–41.

90. In the same passage of *Memoirs of Europe*, Manley acknowledges that making a political virtue of an illegal necessity is 'expressly against St *Paul*, who forbids us to do *Evil* that *Good* may come of it' (Manley, *Memoirs of Europe*, vol. 1, pp. 241–2), but this concession seems designed to draw attention to the ironies of her argument, rather than overturning it.

91. Of course, Manley's representation of the events of 1688 in *Memoirs of Europe* differs starkly from that of Whig propaganda in that she portrays the Revolution as the result of a political coup rather than divine providence. On the perceived role of providence in the Revolution of 1688–9, see Kenyon, *Revolution Principles*, pp. 24–6.

92. See, for example, Herman, *Business of a Woman*, pp. 111–12.

93. Manley, *Memoirs of Europe*, vol. 2, sig. A6^v–A7^r.

94. In *The Roman History*, we find, 'His Designs were prevented by a seasonable Discovery to *Irene*, who, in consideration of his former Services, punish'd him no otherwise than by forbidding all Men to keep him Company; which moderate Carriage towards him made him so asham'd of his Offence, that he dy'd for Grief shortly after' (Echard, *Roman History*, vol. 4, p. 413).

95. Echard, *Roman History*, vol. 4, p. 412.

96. '*Eginhard*, who was Secretary to *Charles* the Great, and therefore might reasonably be thought to know more of the Matter than some later Writers, saith his Master was not ambitious of the Title [Holy Roman Emperor], nor would have accepted of it, if he had not been surpriz'd in it by the Pope' (Echard, *Roman History*, vol. 4, p. 416).

97. On party cant and debates about key words in political discourse, see Knights, *Representation and Misrepresentation*, pp. 214–6, 280–98.

5 Secrecy and Secret History in the *Spectator* (1711–14)

1. On early eighteenth-century ideas about politeness, see L. E. Klein, *Shaftesbury and the Culture of Politeness: Moral Discourses and Cultural Politics in Early Eighteenth-Century England* (Cambridge: Cambirdge University Press, 1994). On the *Spectator* as a vehicle

for the inculcation of politeness, see J. G. A. Pocock, *Virtue, Commerce, and History: Essays on Political Thought and History, Cheifly in the Eighteenth Century* (Cambridge: Cambridge University Press, 1985), pp. 236–7, and N. Phillipson, 'Politics and Politeness in the Reigns of Anne and the Early Hanoverians', in J. G. A. Pocock (ed.), *The Varities of British Political Thought, 1500–1800*, (Cambridge: Cambridge University Press, 1993), pp. 211–45, pp. 225–7.
2. J. Addison, *Spectator*, 10 (12 March 1711), in *The Spectator*, ed. D. Bond, 5 vols (Oxford: Oxford University Press, 1965), vol. 1, p. 45. All subsequent references are to this edition. As Donald Bond points out in a footnote, the story of Moses's serpent comes from Exodus 7:10–12, where it is Moses's companion, Aaron, rather than Moses himself, who turns his rod into a serpent before the Pharaoh.
3. Addison and Pope, *Spectator*, 457 (14 August 1712), vol. 4, p. 112; Addison and Pope, *Spectator*, 452 (8 August 1712), vol. 4, pp. 90–1.
4. Addison, *Spectator*, 262 (31 December 1711), vol. 2, p. 517. The absence of news or partisan revelations is a point in which the *Spectator* differs from most contemporary periodicals including its immediate predecessor, the *Tatler*, which printed foreign news under the title 'from St James's coffee-house'.
5. T. Broughton, *The Mottoes of the Spectators, Tatlers, and Guardians Translated into English* (1735), p. 79.
6. Addison, *Spectator*, 439 (24 July 1712), vol. 4, p. 42.
7. See above, p. 90.
8. In the second edition of his poem, *The Temple of Fame* (1715), Alexander Pope is rather more sanguine about Fame's capacity for right judgement. In the early part of this poem, Pope reveals the ways in which Fame upholds the immortal memory of the ancients including Homer, Virgil, Pindar, Horace and Cicero. Later on in the poem, however, he discusses the ways in which rumour operates like the ripples on a pond to alert listeners to new 'neither wholly false, nor wholly true'. In this part of the house of Fame, 'The flying Rumours gather'd as they roll'd, /Scarce any Tale was sooner heard than told; / And all who told it, added something new, / And all who heard it, made Enlargements too' (A. Pope, *The Temple of Fame: A Vision*, 2nd edn (1715), pp. 39–40).
9. Addison, *Spectator*, 439 (24 July 1712), vol. 4, p. 43.
10. Addison, *Spectator*, 148 (20 August 1711), vol. 2, p. 83.
11. Addison [and Pope], *Spectator*, 457 (14 August 1712), vol. 4, p. 113.
12. Addison, *Spectator*, 439 (24 July 1712), vol. 4, p. 44.
13. Addison, *Spectator*, 439 (24 July 1712), vol. 4, p. 44.
14. Daniel Defoe to Robert Harley, 2 November 1704, *The Letters of Daniel Defoe*, ed. G. H. Healey (Oxford: Clarendon Press, 1955), p. 67.
15. J. A. Downie demonstrates Harley's awareness of the increasing importance of public opinion, and the ways in which it might be manipulated, during a period of intense electoral activity (Downie, *Robert Harley and the Press*, pp. 162–83). For a broader account of the development of the concept of public opinion during the later Stuart period, see Knights, *Representation and Misrepresentation*, pp. 67–205.
16. Addison to Charles Montagu, Earl of Manchester, Friday February 24 1707/8, *The Letters of Joseph Addison*, ed. W. J. Graham (Oxford: Clarendon Press, 1941), p. 91.
17. Cowper, *The Private Diary*, p. 56.
18. Loveman, *Reading Fictions*, p. 124, highlights the importance of ridicule in partisan debate during the first age of party politics.

19. R. Steele, *Spectator* 286 (28 January 1712), vol. 3, p. 17. Compare Astrea's speech to Intelligence in Manley's *New Atalantis*, in which Astrea asserts that 'to fit the Person for a Judge, he must be inform'd of the most minute particular, neither can we be polluted but by our own, not the Crimes of others. They stain nor reflect back upon us, but in our approbation of them' (Manley, *New Atalantis*, p. 116).
20. Steele, *Spectator*, 4 (5 March 1711), vol. 1, p. 19.
21. Steele, *Spectator*, 20 (23 March 1711), vol. 1, p. 86.
22. Steele, *Spectator*, 20 (23 March 1711), vol. 1, p. 86.
23. E. Ward, *The London-Spy Compleat*, 2 vols (1703), vol. 1, pp. 240–1.
24. Steele, *Spectator*, 4 (5 March 1711), vol. 1, p. 18.
25. Steele, *Spectator*, 4 (5 March 1711), vol. 1, p. 22.
26. Addison, *Spectator*, 1 (1 March 1711), vol. 1, pp. 4–5.
27. *OED*, 'speculation' (i) 2.a (*obs.*). When Macbeth sees Banquo's ghost, Shakespeare has him cry out in horror, 'Thou hast no speculation in those eyes / Which thou dost glare with!' (W. Shakespeare, *Macbeth*, III.iv.93–5, *The Riverside Shakespeare*, ed. G. B. Evans, 2nd edn (Boston, MA and New York: Houghton Mifflin Company: 1997), p. 1375). Achilles uses 'speculation' in the same sense when he addresses Ulysses in *Troilus and Cressida* III.iii.109, *Riverside Shakespeare*, p. 506.
28. By the time Samuel Johnson was compiling his *Dictionary of the English Language*, 2 vols (1755–6) the association between 'speculation' and visual, as opposed to cognitive, activity was obsolete. Johnson does provide, as the sixth meaning of 'speculation', 'power of sight', and cites the above example from *Macbeth* in support of this definition, but he adds that this meaning is 'not in use' (Johnson, *Dictionary*, 'speculation' (6)). Furthermore, the three quotations from the nineteenth century provided by the *Oxford English Dictionary* to illustrate 'speculation' as 'the faculty or power of seeing' are all found in heightened literary contexts, and constitute a deliberately archaic register. This means that the last non-archaic example in the *OED* of 'speculation' in its older, non-transferred sense comes from the *Spectator*, 3 (3 March 1711): 'In one of my late Rambles, or rather Speculations, I looked into the great Hall where the Bank is kept, and was not a little pleased to see the Directors, Secretaries, and Clerks, with all the other Members of that wealthy Corporation, ranged in their several Stations, according to the Parts they act in that just and regular Oeconomy' (Addison, *Spectator*, 3 (3 March 1711), vol. 1, p. 14). Although the *OED* uses this excerpt from *The Spectator* to illustrate 'speculation' in the sense of 'the exercise of the faculty of sight', the word 'speculation' in this context does not appear to refer exclusively to either visual or contemplative activity.
29. *Oxford Latin Dictionary*, 'speculator', 1a, b, and c.
30. *OED*, 'speculator', 2a. In support of this definition, the *OED* cites a sentence in Alexander Broome's *Observations in Pope's Odysseus* (1725): 'All the boats had one speculator in common, to give notice when the fish approach'd'.
31. Johnson, *Dictionary*, 'speculation' (2). Johnson may have added 'spy' as a synonym for 'speculator' because of this word's Latin derivation, but in his *Dictionary* he refers his readers to Shakespeare's *King Lear*. In act three, scene one of this play, Kent describes servants as, 'to France the spies and speculations / Intelligent of our state'. W. Shakespeare, *King Lear*, III.i.24–5, *Riverside Shakespeare*, p. 1322.
32. Referring to the aforementioned lines from *King Lear*, Johnson defines 'speculation' as 'examiner; spy', but adds that 'this word is found no where else, and probably is here misprinted for *speculator*' (Johnson, *Dictionary*, 'speculation' (2)).

33. Addison, *Guardian*, 71 (2 June 1713), in *The Guardian* ed. J. C. Stephens (Lexington, KY: University Press of Kentucky, 1982), p. 265. All subsequent references are to this edition.
34. It would add an interesting dimension to this word play if, in the early eighteenth century, the term 'speculator' was used in its modern sense, that is, to refer to a financial investor. According to the *OED*, however, the first use of 'speculation' to refer to a financial or commercial investment dates from 1774, and 'speculator' is first used in this sense in 1778. I have not found any earlier examples.
35. T. Smollett, *The Adventures of Peregrine Pickle* (1751), ed. J. L. Clifford (London: Oxford University Press, 1964), p. 387.
36. Addison, *Spectator*, 9, (10 March 1711), vol. 1, p. 39; Steele, *Spectator*, 4 (5 March 1711), vol. 1, p. 19.
37. We might compare Eliza Haywood's allusion to the opening sentence of the first number of the *Spectator* ('I have observed, that a Reader seldom peruses a Book with Pleasure 'till he knows whether the Writer of it be a black or a fair man, of a mild or cholerick Disposition, Married or a Batchelor, with other Particulars of the like nature, that conduce very much to the right Understanding of an Author', Addison, *Spectator*, 1 (1 March 1711), vol. 1, p. 1) at the opening of her novel, *The Invisible Spy* (1755): 'I have observed that when a new book begins to make any noise in the world, as I am pretty certain this will do, every one is desirous of becoming acquainted with the author; and this impatience increases the more, the more he endeavours to conceal himself' (E. Haywood, *The Invisible Spy*, 4 vols (1755), vol. 1, pp. 1–2). The title of Haywood's work suggests that it was not uncommon to perceive connections between Mr Spectator's activities and those of a spy.
38. Addison, *Spectator*, 12 (12 March 1711), vol. 1, p. 53.
39. Steele, *Spectator*, 390 (28 May 1712), vol. 3, pp. 465–6.
40. Steele, *Spectator*, 4 (5 March 1711), vol. 1, p. 22.
41. T. Tickell, *Spectator*, 619 (12 November 1714), vol. 5, p. 115. Donald Bond notes that John Nichols speculated that this bookseller turned alderman was the Tory mayor of London, John Barber, who was living with secret historian Delarivier Manley in 1714. John Barber never put his name to a published secret history, but Rachel Carnell has recently suggested that Barber was involved in printing *The New Atalantis*, in which case Tickell may be alluding to Barber's relationship with Manley (see Carnell, *Political Biography*, pp. 162–8).
42. The *Spectator* was published in two series. The first consists of 555 papers, published daily (except Sundays) between 1 March 1711 and 6 December 1712. The *Guardian* was launched by Richard Steele on 12 March 1713. At this time, Addison was preoccupied by his play, *Cato*, which opened in April 1713, although he did contribute several papers. Addison took over the editorship of the paper on 1 July 1713 to allow Steele to fight an election at Stockbridge (which he won). The *Guardian* is explicitly presented as a successor to the *Spectator*; like its predecessor, it addresses questions of social morals, manners, and polite society. It is, however, more overtly partisan than the *Spectator*, claiming in its first issue that neutrality was impossible under the grip of a Tory government. It ran until 1 October 1713, after which Steele launched the *Englishman*, which consists almost entirely of political commentary, and which lasted until 15 February 1714. On 18 June 1714, Addison began publishing the *Spectator* once more, which ran for a further eighty numbers until 20 December 1714.
43. Addison, *Guardian*, 134 (14 August 1713), p. 448.

44. Steele, *Spectator*, 252 (19 December 1711), vol. 2, pp. 479–80.
45. E. Budgell, *Spectator* 379 (15 May 1712), vol. 3, p. 423.
46. Addison, Spectator, 221 (13 November 1711), vol. 2, p. 360.
47. Steele, *Spectator*, 555 (6 December 1712), vol. 4, p. 492.
48. Addison, *Guardian*, 71 (2 June 1713), p. 266.
49. Ibid., p. 265.
50. Ibid., pp. 264–5.
51. Ibid., p. 266.
52. Addison, *Guardian*, 98 (3 July 1713), p. 350. The lion's head was erected at Button's and survived rather longer than Addison's short-lived periodical (see C. Richardson, *Notices and Extracts Relating to the Lion's Head, Which Was Erected at Button's Coffee-House in the Year 1713* (1828)).
53. S. P. Gordon, *The Power of the Passive Self in English Literature, 1640–1770* (Cambridge: Cambridge University Press, 2002), p. 88.
54. Addison, *Guardian*, 118 (27 July 1713), p. 397.
55. On the Societies for the Reformation of Manners, see S. Burtt, *Virtue Transformed: Political Argument in England, 1688–1740* (Cambridge: Cambridge University Press, 1992), pp. 39–63 and the earliest history of the Society: J. Woodward, *An Account of the Rise and Progress of the Religious Societies in the City of London &c and of the Endeavours for Reformation of Manners Which Have Been Made Therein* (1698).
56. F. Grant, *A Brief Account of the Nature, Rise and Progress of the Societies for Reformation of Manners* (Edinburgh, 1700), p. 11.
57. D. Defoe, *Defoe's Review*, ed. A. W. Secord, 22 vols (New York: Columbia University Press, 1938), vol. 2, p. 299; Ward, *London-Spy Compleat*, vol. 1 p. 361.
58. Addison, *Spectator*, 8 (9 March 1711), vol. 1, pp. 35–8.
59. Addison, *Spectator*, 10 (12 March 1711), vol. 1, p. 44.
60. Addison, *Spectator*, 225 (17 November 1711), vol. 2, p. 376. Mr Spectator's phrasing that echoes St Paul's disquisition on the Christian virtue of charity in 1 Corinthians 13.
61. Addison, *Spectator*, 225 (17 November 1711), vol. 2, p. 375.
62. Addison, *Spectator*, 228 (21 November 1711), vol. 2, p. 388.
63. Addison [and Pope], *Spectator*, 452 (8 August 1712), vol. 4, p. 92.
64. *Oxford Latin Dictionary*, 'discerno', 1 and 2.
65. *Oxford Latin Dictionary*, 'secerno', 'secretus'.
66. Addison, *Spectator*, 68 (18 May 1711), vol. 1, p. 289.
67. Addison, *Spectator*, 225 (17 November 1711), vol. 2, p. 375.
68. Ecclesiasticus 27:16–21.
69. Addison observes that the book of Ecclesiasticus 'would be regarded by our Modern Wits as one of the most shining Tracts of Morality that is extant, if it appeared under the Name of a *Confucius*, or of any celebrated *Grecian* Philosopher' (Addison, *Spectator*, 68 (18 May 1711), vol. 1, p. 289).
70. The Earl of Halifax and Lord Somers were particular friends and patrons of Addison. In 1708, Addison served as undersecretary of state to the elder Earl of Sunderland, whose son was a member of the Junto. In 1710, Addison was elected Member of Parliament for Malmesbury, a seat in which Wharton had a significant interest. Halifax and Somers were founders of the Whig Kit-Cat Club, of which Addison, Steele and the Junto peer, Lord Wharton, were also members. (*ODNB*, 'Joseph Addison').
71. E. Burke, *Thoughts on the Cause of the Present Discontents* (1770) in *The Writings and Speeches of Edmund Burke*, ed. P. Langford, 9 vols (Oxford: Clarendon Press, 1981–),

vol. 2, pp. 316–17; J. Addison, *The Campaign, A Poem, To his Grace the Duke of Marlborough* (1705), p. 3. I am grateful to Paddy Bullard for these references.
72. A. A. Cooper, *Letters from the Right Honourable the Late Earl of Shaftesbury, to Robert Molesworth, Esq; Now the Lord Viscount of that Name* (1721), p. 15.
73. Holmes, *British Politics*, p. 241.
74. Swift, *Examiner*, 31 (1 March 1710/11) in *Swift vs. Mainwaring* p. 272. If Addison read this paper, it is likely to have infuriated him, not only because it attacks the Junto but also because of the state of Addison's relationship with Swift by early 1711. Although they had been good friends and mutual admirers while Swift supported the Whigs, Swift's growing friendship with and service of Robert Harley created a rift with Addison that never fully healed.
75. As Geoffrey Holmes puts it, 'their sense of personal loyalty to each other, and their concept of the exacting nature of party ties, were alike remarkable' (Holmes, *British Politics*, pp. 237–8).
76. On the importance of the Kit-Cat Club to Whig politics, see P. Clark, *British Clubs and Societies, 1580–1800: the Origins of an Associational World* (Oxford: Clarendon Press, 2000), pp. 61–2; Holmes, *British Politics*, p. 21; and Williams, *Poetry and the Creation of a Whig Literary Culture*, pp. 220–39.
77. B. R., *Remarks on Mr Steele's Crisis &c., by One of the Clergy* (1714), p. 11.
78. J. Swift, *An Enquiry into the Behaviour of the Queen's Last Ministry*, in *Political Tracts 1713–1719*, pp. 129–80, pp. 137–8. Harley was linked to St John's Brothers' Club (1711–13) while in office and was a member the Scriblerus Club (including Jonathan Swift, Alexander Pope, John Arbuthnot, John Gay, and Thomas Parnell) from its inception in 1714. Harley's biographer, Brian Hill, notes that after his fall from office in 1714 his many friends rallied to his support (Hill, *Robert Harley*, p. 223). See also S. Biddle, *Bolingbroke and Harley* (New York: Knopf, 1974; London: George Allen and Unwin, 1975), p. 44.
79. Cowper, *The Private Diary*, p. 33.
80. A. Boyer, *Quadriennium Annæ Postremum; or The Political State of Great Britain. During the Four Last Years of the Late Queen's Reign*, 8 vols (1718–19), vol. 8, p. 614. In spite of having worked for Harley while he was in office, Boyer increasingly worked hard to position himself as a supporter of the Hanoverian succession during the final years of Anne's reign and immediately after the accession of George I.
81. T. Wentworth, *The Wentworth Papers, 1705–1739: Selected from the Private and Family Correspondence of Thomas Wentworth, Lord Raby, Created in 1711 Earl of Strafford, of Stainborough, C. York* ed. J. J. Cartwright (London: Wyman & Sons, 1883), pp. 132–3.
82. Steele, *Tatler*, 191 (29 June 1710), vol. 3, p. 33.
83. Swift, *Some Free Thoughts*, in *Political Tracts*, pp. 80–1.
84. Swift, *The History of the Four Last Years*, p. 74.
85. Addison, *Spectator*, 225 (17 November 1711), vol. 2, pp. 376–7.
86. In fact, Harley would have preferred to keep some Junto Whigs – particularly Halifax – in office in order to have formed a moderate ministry that drew on supporters of both parties. As many of the Whigs refused to enter into negotiations with him, however, Harley was increasingly forced to rely on the support of High Tories of Bolingbroke's faction (see Speck, *Birth of Britain*, pp. 184–5). Regardless of Harley's intentions, Addison's mistrust of this minister is unlikely to have been alleviated by the coincidence of Harley's return to office with the downfall of his friends and patrons.

87. If this analysis of Addison's efforts to distinguish discretion from cunning is correct, it corresponds with Lawrence Klein's analysis of Addison's attempt to distinguish Harley's notion of 'moderation' from that of the Whigs (see L. Klein, 'Joseph Addison's Whiggism' in D. Womersley (ed.), *"Cultures of Whiggism": New Essays on English Literature and Culture in the Long Eighteenth Century* (Newark, DE: University of Delaware Press, 2005), pp. 108–26). Klein focuses on the broad intellectual tradition of Whiggism within which Addison is operating, rather than the practical partisan quarrels between Whigs and Tories during the rage of party. While this is perhaps a safer route than the one that I have taken in this chapter, it does ignore the fact that, in 1711, the Whigs were a recently ousted political party determined to bring down the government – a political context which is, I believe, important to understanding the *Spectator*'s rhetorical strategies.
88. Addison, *Spectator*, 68 (18 May 1711), vol. 1, p. 289.
89. Addison, *Spectator*, 10 (12 March 1711), vol. 1, p. 44.
90. Addison, *Spectator*, 45 (21 April 1711), vol. 1, pp. 191–2.
91. S. Johnson, *The Lives of the Most Eminent English Poets; With Critical Observations on their Works*, ed. R. Lonsdale, 4 vols (Oxford: Clarendon Press, 2006), vol. 3, p. 8. For a more recent analysis of *The Spectator* as an attempt to restore public trust during the reign of Queen Anne, see Phillipson, 'Politics and Politeness', pp. 225–7.

6 Daniel Defoe: Harleyite Secret History and the Early Novel

1. McKeon, *Secret History*, p. 621.
2. J. H. Plumb, *The Growth of Political Stability in England, 1675–1725* (London: Macmillan, 1967).
3. The relationship between *Roxana* and secret history is discussed in L. B. Faller, *Crime and Defoe: A New Kind of Writing* (Cambridge: Cambridge University Press, 1993), p. 49; Warner, *Licensing Entertainment*, pp. 151–4; P. R. Backscheider, 'The Genesis of *Roxana*', *The Eighteenth Century: Theory and Interpretation*, 27:3 (1986), pp. 211–29.
4. Defoe to Harley, [July–August *c.* 1704], *Letters*, pp. 36, 38, 39.
5. Ibid.
6. Jonathan Swift to Alexander Pope, 10 January 1720/1, *The Correspondence of Jonathan Swift, D.D.* ed. D. Woolley, 4 vols (Frankfurt am Main and Oxford: Peter Lang, 1999), vol. 2, p. 124.
7. D. Defoe, *An Appeal to Honour and Justice, Tho' It Be of His Worst Enemies* (1715), p. 17.
8. Hill, *Robert Harley*, p. 159.
9. On Harley's impeachment, see Hill, *Robert Harley*, pp. 227–8.
10. Hill, *Robert Harley*, p. 227.
11. Swift, *History of the Four Last Years*, p. 74. Swift had written his character of Harley by January 3 1713/14, when he gave it to Harley to read (see Swift, *Journal to Stella*, vol. 2, pp. 613–4). The parallels between Harley's behaviour after his impeachment and this section of Swift's character of Harley are so striking, however, that it is tempting to believe that Swift revised it after 1714. For an overview of Swift's revisions to the manuscript of his *History*, see H. Williams, 'Jonathan Swift and the *Four Last Years of the Queen*', *The Library*, 4th series, 16 (1935–6), pp. 61–90 (pp. 66–73).
12. Hill, *Robert Harley*, p. 236.

13. Although Swift and Defoe were both propagandists for Harley, they had no direct contact with one another. For a detailed account of the relationship of each with Robert Harley, see Downie, *Robert Harley and the Press*.
14. Defoe had used such ironic titles on several previous occasions, most notably in *The Shortest Way with the Dissenters* (1702).
15. Downie, *Robert Harley and the Press*, p. 188.
16. *Considerations upon the Secret History of the White-Staff* (1714), p. 6; J. Oldmixon, *A Detection of the Sophistry and Falsities of the Pamphlet, Entitul'd the Secret History of the White-Staff*, 2 parts (1714), part 1, pp. 7–8.
17. Recent scholarship on *The Secret History of the White-Staff* has concurred with those contemporary polemicists who assert that Harley colluded with Defoe on these pamphlets (see Novak, *Daniel Defoe, Master of Fictions*, p. 462).
18. Defoe, *Secret History of the White-Staff*, part 1, p. 22.
19. Ibid., p. 24.
20. Ibid., p. 24.
21. See above, p. 66.
22. D. Defoe, *The Secret History of the White-Staff, Being an Account of Affairs under the Conduct of Some Later Ministers, and of What Might Probably Have Happened If Her Majesty Had Not Died*, 3 parts (1714–15), part 2, pp. 20–1.
23. For 'secret Springs', see Somers, *The True Secret History*, p. 1; for 'wheels within wheels' see Jones, *The Secret History of White-hall*, p. 318.
24. Defoe, *The Secret History of the White-Staff*, part 3, p. 20.
25. Daniel Defoe, *The Secret History of the October Club; from its Original to this Time*, 2 parts (1711), part 1, p. 56. C.f. Swift, *History of the Four Last Years*, p. 74: 'I have known him often suspected by his nearest Friends for some Months in Points of the highest Importance, to a degree that they were ready to break with him, and only undeceived by Time or Accident'.
26. An expository account of this text can be found in P. N. Furbank, 'Defoe's *Minutes of Mesnager*: The Art of Mendacity', *Eighteenth-Century Fiction*, 16:1 (2003), pp. 1–12.
27. D. Defoe, *Minutes of the Negotiations of Monsr Mesnager at the Court of England, Towards the Close of the Last Reign* (1717), p. 71. All italics are original.
28. Defoe, *Minutes of the Negotiations*, p. 185.
29. Ezekiel 1: 16.
30. R. Allestree, *The Vanity of the Creature* (1684), p. 34 (cf. J. Wilkins, *A Discourse Concerning the Beauty of Providence in All the Rugged Passages of it* (1649), p. 48). It seems that the mechanistic connotations of the wheel within a wheel appealed more to eighteenth-century writers than its mystical properties. The idea of God as a watchmaker and divine providence as the mechanism which turns the visible hands of earthly events was common during the late seventeenth and early eighteenth centuries (see, for instance, K. Philips, 'Submission', in *Poems. By the Incomparable, Mrs. K. P.* (1664), p. 210; J. Spalding, *A Sermon Preached Before His Grace George Earl of Melvil, Their Majesties High Commissioner, and the Nobility, Barons, and Burrows, Members of the High Court of Parliament* (Edinburgh, 1690), p. 5).
31. R. Saunders, *A View of the Soul, in Several Tracts*, 3 books (1682), book 3, p. 187.
32. Not all of Harley's supporters agreed. Jonathan Swift uses the same mechanistic metaphor as Defoe to condemn Harley's secretive style of management because it breeds unnecessary fear in those who feel excluded from Harley's secrets: 'Although the main Spring in a Watch be out of Sight, there is an intermediate Communication between

it and the smallest Wheel, or else no true Motion could be performed. This reserved mysterious way of acting, upon Points where there appeared not the least Occasion for it, and towards Persons who in right of their Posts expected a more open Treatment, was imputed to some hidden Design, which every Man conjectured to be the very Evil he was most afraid of' (Swift, *Some Free Thoughts*, p. 86). Swift suggests that Harley failed to act the part of the first moving cause because of his unwillingness to communicate directly with his agents. Perhaps the fact that Swift was engaged in writing his *History of the Four Last Years* at this time – a project which met with increasing obstruction from Harley – led him to make these remarks, which appear to have been written several months before the publication of the first part of Defoe's *Secret History of the White Staff* and to be independent of them.
33. On the analogy between God and the monarch in divine right theory, see Sommerville, 'Absolutism and royalism', p. 352.
34. McKeon, *Secret History*, pp. xix, 5–6.
35. This is something of a contemporary axiom. Even Addison, who strongly disapproved of political secrecy, acknowledged that spies are a necessary evil in *Spectator*, 439 (see above, pp. 112–15).
36. Defoe, *Minutes of the Negotiations*, p. 49.
37. Alluding to Harley's habit of refusing to disclose complete information to those – including Swift – who work as his agents, Swift observes that 'I suppose, when a Building is to be erected, the Model may be the Contrivance only of one Head; and it is sufficient that the under-workmen be ordered to cut Stones into certain Shapes, and place them in certain Positions; but the several Master Builders must have some general Knowledge of the Design, without which they can give no Orders at all' (Swift, *Some Free Thoughts,* p. 81).
38. Daniel Defoe to Robert Harley, [July–August *c.* 1704], *Letters*, p. 37.
39. Daniel Defoe to Robert Harley, 14 August 1705, *Letters*, p. 100.
40. Defoe, *Secret History of the White-Staff*, part 1, p. 22. By 'within Doors' Defoe means inside Parliament. Defoe articulates similar ideas in *The Secret History of the White-Staff* part 2, pp. 13–14.
41. Defoe, *Secret History of the White-Staff*, part 1, p. 4.
42. *OED*, 'counsel' *n.*, 2a.
43. *OED*, 'counsel' *n.*, 5b. Vestiges of this sense are still evident in the phrase 'to keep counsel' (see *OED*, 'counsel' *n.*, 5d).
44. Defoe, *Secret History of the White-Staff*, part 3, p. 13.
45. Defoe, *Secret History of the White-Staff*, part 1, p. 13. See also *OED*, 'clue' *n.*, 2a, 2b. Moll Flanders uses the same metaphor (mixed with another) when she describes her account of the methods taken by pickpockets to ply their trade as 'a Key to the Clue of *a Pick-Pockets* Motions, and whoever can follow it, will as certainly catch the Thief as he will be sure to miss if he does not' (D. Defoe, *The Fortunes and Misfortunes of the Famous Moll Flanders* (1722), ed. G. A. Starr as *Moll Flanders* (Oxford: Oxford University Press, 1971, repr. 1998), p. 213.
46. Oldmixon, *Detection*, part 1, p. 28.
47. Defoe, *The Secret History of the White-Staff*, part 3, p. 58.
48. Novak, *Daniel Defoe, Master of Fictions*, p. 460.
49. Defoe, *The Secret History of the White-Staff*, part 2, p. 4.
50. Ibid., part 3, pp. 27, 80

51. While all three parts of Defoe's original secret history were published by John Baker, this *Secret History of the Secret History* was published by Samuel Keimer. On the relationship between Defoe and Keimer, see Backscheider, *Daniel Defoe*, pp. 376–7.
52. D. Defoe, *The Secret History of the Secret History of the White-Staff, Purse and Mitre* (1715), p. 8.
53. Defoe, *The Secret History of the Secret History*, pp. 18–19 (italics in original).
54. On Edmund Curll, see P. Baines and P. Rogers, *Edmund Curll, Bookseller* (Oxford: Oxford University Press, 2007).
55. Defoe, *The Secret History of the White-Staff*, part 3, pp. 20–1.
56. S. Clement, *Faults on Both Sides: Or, An Essay upon the Original Cause, Progress, and Mischievous Consequences of the Factions in this Nation* (1710). Widely attributed to Harley, *Faults on Both Sides* is, according to Downie, 'the nearest thing we have, in print, to a full-scale exposition of Harleian ideology' (Downie, *Robert Harley and the Press*, p. 119).
57. *Considerations on the Secret History of the White-Staff* and *A History of the Mitre and Purse* are anonymous publications which have been variously attributed to Francis Atterbury, Bolingbroke, William Pittis and even John Oldmixon.
58. Defoe, *The Secret History of the Secret History*, p. 4.
59. *Considerations upon the Secret History of the White-Staff*, pp. 20–1; Oldmixon, *Detection*, part 1, pp. 16–17 and part 2, pp. 18–19;
60. Backscheider, *Daniel Defoe*, p. 354.
61. G. M. Sill, *Defoe and the Idea of Fiction, 1713–1719* (Newark, DE: University of Delaware Press, 1983), p. 88.
62. Sill, *Defoe and the Idea of Fiction*, pp. 87–93.
63. D. Defoe, *The Life, and Strange Surprizing Adventures of Robinson Crusoe of York, Mariner* (1719), ed. J. D. Crowley as *Robinson Crusoe* (Oxford: Oxford University Press, 1972), p. 156.
64. Defoe, *Robinson Crusoe*, p. 188.
65. The use of the 'secret springs' trope to refer to psychological rather than political phenomena is not unprecedented, but it is uncommon. The only other example that I have found occurs at the beginning of book 5 of Dryden's *Aeneis* (1697), which refers to the 'secret springs' that move the passions of 'Woman-kind' (J. Dryden, *The Works of John Dryden*, ed. V. A. Dearing, 20 vols (Berkeley and Los Angeles, CA: University of California Press, 1956–2000), vol. 5 (ed. W. Frost, 1987), p. 487).
66. Of course, both Moll and Roxana reveal that they do keep secrets from their readers. Moll's name remains hidden, as does Roxana's until she informs her readers that her daughter Susan is named after her. At one point in her narrative, Roxana comments 'There is a Scene which came in here, which I must cover from humane Eyes or Ears; for three Years and about a Month, *Roxana* liv'd retir'd, having been oblig'd to make an Excursion, in a Manner, and with a Person, which Duty, and private Vows, obliges her not to reveal, at least, not yet' (D. Defoe, *The Fortunate Mistress; or, a History of the Life and Vast Variety of Fortunes of Mademoiselle de Beleau, afterwards called the Countess of Wintelsheim in Germany, Being the Person known by the Name of the Lady Roxana in the time of Charles II* (1724), ed. J. Mullan as *Roxana* (Oxford: Oxford University Press, 1996), p. 181). The strange movement from first-person to third-person narration makes this intervention doubly unnerving, since it appears to be an editorial voice rather than Roxana's own that warns the reader about the gaps in this narrative. Nonetheless, both

Moll and Roxana are considerably more open with their readers than with the characters in their stories and they do confess many secrets in the course of their narratives.

67. N. Gallagher, 'Point of View and Narrative Form in *Moll Flanders* and the Eighteenth-Century Secret History', *Lumen: Selected Proceedings from the Canadian Society for Eighteenth-Century Studies*, 25 (2006), pp. 145–61, argues that *The Secret History of the White-Staff* are both first-person narratives which encourage their readers to feel privileged at receiving first-hand, inside information. This analysis ignores the important fact that the narrator of *The Secret History of the White-Staff* exposes the secrets of a third person (Robert Harley), while Moll Flanders confesses her own secrets – a difference which profoundly alters the relationship between the narrator and implied reader of these texts.
68. Defoe, *Moll Flanders*, p. 325.
69. Defoe, *Robinson Crusoe*, p. 188.
70. On friendship in the *Spectator*, see above, p. 81.
71. Defoe, *Moll Flanders*, p. 325. The motif of unwitting confession through sleep-talking was common in this period. In an episode in Manley's *New Atalantis*, a husband discovers his wife's lover when the lover, concealed in an upper room, begins loudly to recount his day's activities in his sleep (vol. 1, pp. 194–7). Moll's concern over the relationship between self-control and secrecy is made manifest early in her narrative, when she relates her fear that, while suffering a fever, she would reveal her affair with the older brother of the merchant's house in Colchester where she was living: 'I was reduc'd very low indeed, and was often Delirious and light Headed; but nothing lay so near me, as the fear, that when I was light Headed, I should say something or other to [the elder brother's] Prejudice' (p. 42).
72. See above, pp. 125–8.
73. Defoe, *Moll Flanders*, p. 128.
74. Ibid.
75. Ibid.
76. Ibid., p. 172.
77. Ibid., p. 290.
78. Ibid., p. 172.
79. Defoe, *Minutes of the Negotiations*, p. 49 (see above, p. 142).
80. Defoe, *Roxana*, p. 317.
81. See, for instance, H. O. Brown, 'The Displaced Self in the Novels of Daniel Defoe', *ELH* 38:4 (1971), pp. 562–90, p. 581–3; T. Castle, '*Amy*, who knew my Disease': A Psychosexual Pattern in Defoe's *Roxana*', *ELH*, 46:1 (1979), pp. 81–96; Faller, *Crime and Defoe*, p. 241; P. New, 'Why Roxana Can Never Find Herself', *Modern Language Review*, 91:2 (1996), pp. 317–29.
82. Defoe, *Roxana*, p. 318.
83. Ibid., pp. 188, 215.
84. There are, in this respect, interesting structural similarities between the discussion of secrecy and friendship in *Moll Flanders* and *Roxana*, since Moll's outburst about women's capacity to keep secrets occurs at a similar point in the narrative to Roxana's reflections upon Amy's knowledge of her secrets. In spite of the loose narrative structure of these novels, Defoe creates an impression that the burden of secrecy that has been building through each narrative breaks out towards the narrative's conclusion.
85. Defoe, *Roxana*, p. 317.
86. Ibid., p. 326.

87. This maxim represents an example of what Kate Loveman identifies as the tendency of Defoe's characters towards self-deception (see Loveman, *Reading Fictions*, p. 149).
88. In her reflections upon Amy, for instance, Roxana describes her as 'so faithful a Creature ... and a faithful Friend too' (p. 317).
89. See pp. 16, 25, 26, 36, 38, 45, 271, 326.
90. Defoe, *Roxana*, p. 269.
91. Ibid.
92. Ibid., p. 330.
93. On the textual history of *Roxana* see the Appendix to John Mullan's Oxford University Press edition, pp. 331–40.
94. G. A. Starr, *Defoe and Spiritual Autobiography* (Princeton, NJ: Princeton University Press, 1965), p. 164.
95. Ibid., pp. 165, 164.
96. Faller, *Crime and Defoe*, p. 232.
97. Defoe, *Moll Flanders*, p. 187.
98. Defoe, *Roxana*, p. 94.
99. Ibid., p. 215.
100. Defoe, *Moll Flanders*, p. 185.
101. Ibid., p. 186.
102. Ibid., p. 326.
103. Defoe, *Roxana*, pp. 5–6.
104. Ibid., p. 181.
105. P. K. Alkon, *Defoe and Fictional Time* (Athens, GA: University of Georgia Press, 1979), p. 54. See also D. Blewett, '*Roxana* and the Masquerades', *Modern Language Review*, 65:3 (1970), pp. 499–502, and 'The Double Time-Scheme of *Roxana*: Further Evidence', *Studies in Eighteenth-Century Culture*, 13 (1984), pp. 19–28.
106. For an account of the relationship between Defoe's fiction and early eighteenth century political thought, see M. Schonhorn, *Defoe's Politics: Parliament, Power, Kingship and Robinson Crusoe* (Cambridge: Cambridge University Press, 1991) and R. Carnell, *Partisan Politics, Narrative Realism, and the Rise of the British Novel* (Basingstoke: Palgrave Macmillan, 2006), pp. 75–102.
107. Novak, *Daniel Defoe, Master of Fictions*, p. 599, suggests that, in 1722, 'though he still retained some of his Revolution Principles ... Defoe was ready to plead for a stable government that continued to exemplify the principles of the Protestant succession and freedom within the limits of established laws. The agitation for repeal of the Test Act [which discriminated against both Roman Catholics and Protestant Nonconformists by refusing to allow them to take public office] had failed, but even so Defoe thought that the Dissenters should count their blessings under a government that supported religious toleration. By the end of the year, a new Jacobite plot was to make such a position even more desirable'. This analysis of Defoe's political views during the early 1720s supports my interpretation of his use of secret history in *Roxana*.
108. On these two different approaches towards the relationship between secret history and the novel, see above, pp. 23–4.

7 Eliza Haywood: Secret History, Curiosity and Disappointment

1. P. Spedding, *A Bibliography of Eliza Haywood* (London: Pickering and Chatto, 2004), p. 84–7.

2. G. F. Whicher, *The Life and Romances of Mrs. Eliza Haywood* (New York: Columbia University Press, 1915), p. 92.
3. Spedding suggests that Haywood's secret history of Mary Queen of Scots was probably a commission from the bookseller James Woodman, who had also published Jebb's *De Vita* (Spedding, *Bibliography*, pp. 233–4).
4. Paula Backscheider interprets *The Secret History of the Court of Caramania* in very broad political terms when she suggests that, in this narrative, Haywood 'gives us a George II character (Theodore) who is a promiscuous libertine whose wife *and* mistress are wiser and more admirable than he' (P. R. Backscheider, 'The Shadow of an Author: Eliza Haywood', *Eighteenth-Century Fiction*, 11:1 (1998), pp. 79–102 (p. 95)).
5. It is possible that Defoe was reacting against Haywood's slipshod use of the phrase 'secret history' in *Roxana*. Hammond, *Professional Imaginative Writing*, p. 223, suggests that 'when Haywood published *Idalia; or, The Unfortunate Mistress: A Novel* in 1723[,] ... Defoe felt compelled to respond with *The Fortunate Mistress* (the novel popularly known as *Roxana*) in the following year'. Hammond argues that the psychological depth of Defoe's characters is a response to the plot-driven narratives produced by Haywood. Perhaps *Roxana* is also a response to Haywood's apparent lack of political commitment in her self-styled secret histories such as *The British Recluse: or, Secret History of Cleomira*.
6. A. Hill, *The Plain Dealer*, 63 (26 October 1724); A. Pope, *The Dunciad Variorum* (1729), ed. J. Sutherland, 3rd (London: Methuen, 1963), p. 119.
7. *The Neuter: or, A Modest Satire on the Poets of the Age* (1733), p. 4.
8. Johnson, *Dictionary*, 'to conjure' (3).
9. Haywood herself gave the Hillarians their title (C. Gerrard, *Aaron Hill: The Muses' Projector* (Oxford: Oxford University Press, 2003), p. 62). On the relationship between Martha Fowke Sansom, Eliza Haywood, and the Hillarian Circle, see Gerrard, *Aaron Hill* pp. 66–101.
10. Haywood attacks Sansom through the figure of the lascivious Baroness de Tortillée whose servant, DuLache, represents Richard Savage in *The Injur'd Husband; or, The Mistaken Resentment* (1722); in *A Spy upon the Conjurer*, the narrator, Justicia, ridicules Mrs. F— (that is, Mrs Fowke or Martha Fowke Sansom) as a woman who shamelessly invents and circulates stories about her supposed affair with the nobleman to whom this narrative is ostensibly addressed (E. Haywood, *A Spy upon the Conjurer; or, A Collection of Surprising Stories, with Names, Places, and Particular Circumstances Relating to Mr Duncan Campbell* (1724), pp. 51–3). For Martha Fowke Sansom's attack on Haywood, see M. F. Sansom, *Clio: The Autobiography of Martha Fowke Sansom, 1689–1736*, ed. P. Guskin (Newark, DE: University of Delaware Press, 1997), p. 82.
11. In a recent article, Kathryn King undermines twentieth-century biographical accounts of Haywood which claim that she had an affair with Richard Savage during the early 1720s (see K. R. King, 'Eliza Haywood, Savage Love, and Biographical Uncertainty', *RES* Advance Access published 25 October 2007).
12. Gloatitia, a 'big-bon'd, buxom, brown Woman' who indulges in incestuous relations with her father, is represented in E. Haywood, *Memoirs of a Certain Island Adjacent to the Kingdom of Utopia*, 2 vols (1725–6), vol. 1, pp. 43–9.
13. On the prominent position of women in the Hillarian circle, see Gerrard, *Aaron Hill*, pp. 76–80.
14. Paula Backscheider observes that Haywood's involvement with literary coteries is 'among the unexplored aspects of Haywood's life' and suggests that 'in a time when connections and friendships were crucial for access to publication and production, Haywood could

not have been the solitary, bedraggled hack peddling her words bookseller to bookseller that she is so frequently described to be' (E. Haywood, *Selected Fiction and Drama of Eliza Haywood*, ed. P. R. Backscheider (Oxford: Oxford University Press, 1999), p. xvi). I demonstrate the role that Haywood's departure from her first coterie and the commencement of her career as a more commercial writer played in the development of her sophisticated, self-conscious approach towards secret history. On Haywood and professional authorship as well as gender and authorship more generally, see C. Ingrassia, *Authorship, Commerce, and Gender in Early Eighteenth-Century England: A Culture of Paper Credit* (Cambridge: Cambridge University Press, 1998), pp. 77–137.

15. K. R. King, 'New Contexts for Early Novels by Women: The Case of Eliza Haywood, Aaron Hill, and the Hillarians, 1719–1725' in P. R. Backscheider and C. Ingrassia (eds), *A Companion to the Eighteenth-Century Novel and Culture*, (Oxford: Blackwell, 2005), pp. 261–75, p. 266.
16. Spedding, *Bibliography*, pp. 819–20.
17. She remarks, 'one has to wonder what the usually shrewd and heretofore respected Haywood was thinking when she composed the lively, teeming, boundlessly ill-natured and still largely unstudied *Memoirs of a Certain Island*. If any single early work by Haywood calls out for close attention, it would surely be this scandal chronicle' (King, 'New Contexts', p. 267).
18. Although the date on the title page of the first volume of *Memoirs of a Certain Island* is 1725, Spedding, *Bibliography*, p. 211, shows that it was actually published in September 1724. *Secret Histories, Novels and Poems* was first advertised in December 1724 although the first edition appears not to have been published until August 1725 (Spedding, *Bibliography*, pp. 67, 74).
19. 1724–5 marks a peculiarly self-conscious moment in Haywood's career that sets *A Spy upon the Conjurer* and *Memoirs of a Certain Island* apart from all of Haywood's other publications. Even *The Secret History of the Present Intrigues of the Court of Caramania* (1727), which is often cited alongside *Memoirs of a Certain Island*, differs from Haywood's earlier work in this respect. Although it is a *roman à clef*, *The Secret History of... the Court of Caramania* lacks both the polemical force and the kind of self-referential exploration of the process of revealing secrets that characterizes *Memoirs of a Certain Island* and, indeed, most secret history from the late seventeenth to the early eighteenth century. Curiosity is an important motif in Haywood's later, anti-Walpole *roman à clef*, *The Adventures of Eovaai, Princess of Ijaveo: An Adamitical History* (1736). Princess Eovaai's curiosity leads her to lose the jewel that guarantees political stability in the kingdom of Ijaveo. Her quest to recover it involves avoiding the snares of Ochihatou (or Robert Walpole) – a corrupt minister who has usurped and enslaved the rightful King of Hypotofa – as well as receiving an education in the pitfalls of various modes of government, from arbitrary monarchy to republicanism. Eovaai's curiosity may be a cause of political conflict, but it is also the key to her successful political education; indeed, she and her nation are at greatest risk when she fails to use her curiosity to scrutinize the motives of Ochihatou. But although curiosity figures large in *The Adventures of Eovaai*, it is nowhere connected with the discovery of secrets, and instead is simply presented as a characteristically feminine trait. Moreover, Haywood does not appear to use curiosity here as a self-conscious point of connection between the action of the narrative and the act of reading the narrative. Haywood's very late work, *The Invisible Spy* (1755), returns to the idea of curiosity as a means of creating narrative movement, as the eponymous spy, Explorabilis, escorts readers of this work on a long satirical 'ramble' through mid-

eighteenth century society. In *The Invisible Spy*, however, the political connotations of the discourse of secrecy that are prominent in titles such as *A Spy upon the Conjurer* and *Memoirs of a Certain Island* have all but disappeared.

20. Sansom, *Clio*, p. 29.
21. J. Carswell, *The South Sea Bubble* (London: The Cresset Press, 1960; Stroud: Sutton Press, 2001), pp. 207–8; Plumb, *Sir Robert Walpole: The Making of A Statesman*, pp. 329–58.
22. J. H. Plumb, *Sir Robert Walpole: The King's Minister* (London: The Cresset Press, 1960), pp. 78–115.
23. The precise shades of Tory opinion that Haywood represents through her work are sometimes difficulty to gauge. Toni Bowers has convincingly read *Love in Excess* (1719) as Williamite Tory polemic (T. Bowers, 'Collusive Resistance: Sexual Agency and Partisan Politics in *Love in Excess*' in K. T. Saxton and R. P. Bocchicchio (eds), *The Passionate Fictions of Eliza Haywood: Essays on Her Life and Work* eds. (Lexington, KY: University Press of Kentucky, 2000), pp. 48–68). *The Adventures of Eovaai* seems to celebrate the careers of both James II and William III. Both monarchs are depicted as busts in the house of Alhahuza, a virtuous patriot who probably represents Henry St John, Viscount Bolingbroke (see E. Haywood, *The Adventures of Eovaai* (1736), ed. E. Wilputte (Peterborough, ON: Broadview Press, 1999) pp. 98–100). During the 1740s, Haywood was arrested and questioned by the government over her pamphlet, *A Letter from H—G—, Esq.* (1749), which appears to express Jacobite sentiments (see Spedding, *Bibliography*, pp. 520–5, 749–58). Kathryn King's forthcoming *Political Biography of Eliza Haywood* (London: Pickering and Chatto, 2012) will provide an invaluable account of Haywood's political thought.
24. E. Haywood, *Memoirs of a Certain Island Adjacent to the Kingdom of Utopia*, 2nd edn 2 vols (1726), vol. 1, p. 291. Abbreviated to *Memoirs 2* henceforth.
25. Carswell, *The South Sea Bubble*, pp. 206, 222.
26. Haywood, *Memoirs*, 2nd edn, vol. 1, p. 293.
27. Haywood, *Memoirs*, vol. 1, p. 277.
28. Haywood, *Memoirs*, vol. 1, p. 278. On literary Patriotism, see C. Gerrard, *The Patriot Opposition to Walpole: Politics, Poetry, and National Myth, 1725–1742* (Oxford: Clarendon Press, 1994).
29. Plumb, *Sir Robert Walpole: The King's Minister*, pp. 79, 113.
30. Haywood, *Memoirs*, 2nd edn, vol. 2, p. 4.
31. Plumb, *Sir Robert Walpole: The King's Minister*, pp. 100–2.
32. The key to this edition was obviously printed separately from the main text (the paper is different, with chain lines running in the opposite direction from those of the paper in the main text), although it has no separate title page.
33. Walpole's extant papers and correspondence are in the Cholmondley (Houghton) collection at the Cambridge University Library.
34. Haywood, *Memoirs*, vol. 1, p. 5.
35. Budgell is not accused elsewhere of debauching women but he was a soft target: he had lost a fortune in the South Sea bubble and was suffering from paranoid delusions. Convinced that Walpole had set spies on him and was attempting to have him murdered, Budgell eventually committed suicide in 1737 (*ODNB*, 'Eustace Budgell').
36. Haywood, *Memoirs*, vol. 1, p. 149.
37. Ibid., p. 109.

38. In *Memoirs of a Certain Island* Haywood explores the sexual misdemeanours of Flirtillaria [Aaron Hill's sister-in-law] and Gloatitia [Martha Sansom] at extraordinary length, although she seems to betray her awareness that the amount of time she spends on them is disproportionate to the level of readerly interest in they are likely to sustain. She has Cupid observe, 'I should wear out day [*sic*], to recount the thousandth part of her various Amours, or the unnumber'd changes of her roving Inclinations; — nor does a History, such as hers, become me to relate. – I wou'd have pass'd both hers and *Flirtillaria*'s in silence, if the signaliz'd Airs of these Coquets had not oblig'd you to remark them' (Haywood, *Memoirs*, vol. 1, p. 48).

39. As Michael McKeon puts it in his discussion of *Memoirs of a Certain Island*, 'it is as though the most basic priorities of the *roman à clef* have been not just muddled but inverted, so that the interpretative mystery we are asked to solve pertains not to the actual but to the virtual identity of the names, and the process of signification more often than not seems mysteriously to correlate one 'private' figure with another' (McKeon, *Secret History*, p. 631).

40. No character is identified between p. 60 and p. 110 (the story of Windusius and Wyaria) in the key to volume 1 of *Memoirs of a Certain Island* (Haywood, *Memoirs*, 2nd edn vol. 1, p. 294).

41. See, for instance, vol. 1, pp. 555–6.

42. Manley, *Adventures of Rivella*, p. 113.

43. W. Bond, *The History of the Life and Adventures of Mr. Duncan Campbell* (1720), p. 130.

44. Campbell's coterie included William Bond, Anthony Hammond, Philip Horneck, Ambrose Philips, Susanna Centlivre, Martha Fowke Sansom, and Haywood (D. Campbell, *Secret Memoirs of the Late Mr. Duncan Campbell, The Famous Deaf and Dumb Gentleman* (1732), pp. 131–2).

45. Cited in Spedding, *Bibliography*, p. 141.

46. Spedding, *Bibliography*, p. 145.

47. Haywood may have had personal as well as aesthetic reasons for using William Bond's text as a foil for her own exploration of the relationship between secrecy, curiosity and narrative. Bond was closely associated with Martha Fowke Sansom. In 1720, Bond had published not only his biography of Campbell but also, with Sansom, *The Epistles of Clio and Strephon* (1720), a series of letters in prose and verse celebrating Platonic love. Writing in opposition to Bond's text, perhaps Haywood also imagined that she was indirectly attacking her literary rival, Sansom. On the relationship between Sansom and Bond, see Gerrard, *Aaron Hill*, p. 73–4.

48. Bond, *History*, p. 7.

49. Ibid., p. 148.

50. *Oxford Latin Dictionary*, 'cura'. On the gendering of curiosity during the early modern period, and on the relationship between 'masculine' empirical or antiquarian enquiry and 'feminine' prurience, see N. Kenny, *The Uses of Curiosity in Early Modern France and Germany* (New York and Oxford: Oxford University Press, 2004), pp. 309–424, and B. M. Benedict, *Curiosity: a Cultural History of Early Modern Inquiry* (Chicago, IL and London: University of Chicago Press, 2001), pp. 118–244.

51. For a more recent perspective on Joseph Woodward, see J. M. Levine, *Dr. Woodward's Shield: History, Science and Satire in Augustan England* (Berkeley, CA: University of California Press, 1977).

52. Bond, *History*, p. 8.

53. Kenny, *Uses of Curiosity*, pp. 169–82.
54. Bond, *History*, p. 61.
55. Ibid., pp. 255–6.
56. Bond, *History*, pp. 38–55. In particular, Bond focuses on the work of the Oxford Professor of Geometry, John Wallis, in this area. On the education of deaf people during the early modern period, see J. Rée, *I See a Voice: A Philosophical History of Language, Deafness and the Senses* (London: Harper Collins, 1999), pp. 89–128.
57. For other examples of the way in which Haywood and her publishers manipulate her name on the title pages of her imprints, see Backscheider, 'Introduction' to Haywood, *Selected Works*, p. xxviii
58. *The Daily Post*, 19 March 1724 (cited in Spedding, *Bibliography*, p. 145).
59. *The Daily Post*, 23 March 1724 (cited in Spedding, *Bibliography*, p. 145).
60. Spedding, *Bibliography*, p. 145.
61. Bond, *History*, pp. iv–v.
62. One exception is, perhaps, Haywood's allusion to Mrs. F—, that is, Martha Fowke Sansom, who excites 'a mixture of Disdain and Wonder' in the narrator (Haywood, *The Spy upon the Conjurer*, p. 51).
63. Bond, *History*, p. 168.
64. Haywood, *The Spy upon the Conjurer*, p. 73.
65. Ibid., p. 73.
66. Kathryn King makes a similar point in her analysis of *A Spy upon the Conjurer* as a self-reflexive narrative that is 'obsessed with the guilty pleasures delivered up by (among other things) Haywood's own hugely popular fictions' (K. R. King, 'Spying upon the Conjurer: Haywood, Curiosity, and 'The Novel' in the 1720s', *Studies in the Novel*, 30:2 (1998), pp. 178–93 (p. 179)).
67. Haywood, *The Spy upon the Conjurer*, p. 70.
68. Ibid., p. 71.
69. Ingrassia, *Authorship, Commerce, and Gender*, p. 88.
70. E. Haywood, *Secret Histories, Novels and Poems*, 4 vols (1725), vol. 4, p. 74.
71. Haywood, *Memoirs*, vol. 1, pp. 224–5.
72. For instance, J. J. Richetti, *The English Novel in History, 1700–1780* (London: Routledge, 1999) p. 22, asserts that Haywood offers her reader 'intense and uncritical involvement in passion's white-hot excitements and deliciously unbearable tragedies'. Ballaster, *Seductive Forms*, p. 170, also claims that 'the business of Haywood's amatory plots is to engage the female reader's sympathy and erotic pleasure, rather than stimulate intellectual judgement', and she observe that Haywood's texts 'explicitly call upon the female readers to identify with the troubled heroine'. Although Warner, *Licensing Entertainment*, p. 151, argues that Haywood's narratives situate their reader in the position of a libertine, rather than a seduced victim, he suggests, like Ballaster and Richetti, that Haywood's narratives allow their readers to 'reach an extreme of sympathetic identification [with the characters in the narrative] in the big scenes of sex, in which purple-prose passages encourage absorption in the erotic rhythms of the action'.
73. Haywood, *Secret Histories, Novels and Poems*, vol. 3, p. 52.
74. Ibid., vol. 4, p. 10.
75. In a perceptive article on *Love in Excess* (1719), Scott Black also argues that Haywood uses the concept of curiosity as a way of indulging 'readerly play' and scrutinizing the factors that underpin the contemporary marketplace for fiction (S. Black, 'Trading Sex for Secrets in Haywood's *Love in Excess*', *Eighteenth-Century Fiction*, 15:2 (2003), pp. 207–

26). Haywood's fascination with curiosity is, however, more sophisticated than Black suggests. While Black argues that Haywood's readers are motivated not only by sexual desire, but also by the desire to know things that are hidden from them, I argue that Haywood is more interested in curiosity as a rootless emotion, not necessarily grounded in the hope of acquiring knowledge, but rather in the pleasure that the experience of curiosity yields in and of itself. A different reason for the repetitious quality of Haywood's narratives is provided by Barbara Benedict, who argues that Haywood's multivolume collected works allow 'addicted readers [to] linger over minor differences in the arrangement of their repetitive format of awakened desire, frustration, betrayal, and regret'. She goes on to argue that 'these cabinets and collections solicit and tout an unregulated, individualistic method of reading associated with the intellectual restlessness of curiosity' (Benedict, *Curiosity*, p. 136). I suggest that Haywood solicits both 'addicts' and 'sceptics' as her readers, cashing in on the curiosity 'addicts', while also creating space for more sceptical approaches towards her repetitious narratives.

76. Haywood, *Selected Fiction*, p. xxxv.

Conclusion

1. *A Cabinet Council; or Secret History of Lewis XIV* (1757), title page.
2. D. Hume, *The Letters of David Hume*, ed. J. Y. T. Greig, 2 vols (Oxford: Clarendon Press, 1932), p. 228.
3. Anon., *The Life, Amours, and Secret History of Francelia, Late D—ss of P—h, Favourite Mistress to Charles II* (1734), p. 4.
4. Sophia Lee's *The Recess* tells the story of the conflict between Elizabeth I and Mary Queen of Scots from the perspective of Mary's fictional daughters (who are held in captivity in the 'recess' of the title) in a manner that recalls *The Secret History of the Duke of Alançon and Q. Elizabeth* (1691), which recounts Elizbeth's efforts to exclude Mary's younger sister, a fictional character named Marianna, from the throne. On *The Recess* as a form of alternative, explicitly feminine historiography, see A. Stevens, 'Sophia Lee's Illegitimate History', *The Eighteenth-Century Novel* 3 (2003), pp. 263–91. Ann Yearsley's *The Royal Captives* is a version of the 'man in the iron mask' myth – the story of a mysterious masked prisoner during Louis XIV's reign who was held to be Louis' slightly older twin brother. On *The Royal Captives* as a form of political historiography, see J. Dorn, 'The Royal Captives, A Fragment of Secret History: Ann Yearsley's "Unnecessary Curiosity"', *1650–1850 Ideas, Aesthetics, and Inquiries in the Early Modern Era*, 5 (2000), pp. 163–89.
5. See above, p. 181.

WORKS CITED

Manuscripts

Bod. MS Rawl. 72.

Primary texts

Addison, J., *The Campaign, A Poem, To his Grace the Duke of Marlborough* (1705).

—, *The Letters of Joseph Addison*, ed. W. J. Graham (Oxford: Clarendon Press, 1941).

—, R. Steele and others, *The Tatler* (1709–11), ed. D. F. Bond, 3 vols (Oxford: Clarendon Press, 1987).

—, *The Spectator* (1711–14), ed. D. F. Bond, 5 vols (Oxford: Oxford University Press, 1965).

—, *The Guardian* (1713), ed. J. C. Stephens (Lexington, KY: University Press of Kentucky, 1982).

Allestree, R., *The Vanity of the Creature* (1684).

Anon., *The Kings Cabinet Opened; or, Certain Packets of Secret Letters & Papers, Written with the Kings Own Hand, and Taken in His Cabinet at Nasby-Field, June 14. 1645* (1645).

—, *Histoire Secrette de la Duchesse de Portsmouth* (1690).

—, *The Secret History of the Duchess of Portsmouth* (1690).

—, *The Secret History of the Reigns of K. Charles II and K. James II* (1690).

—, *The English Spy: or, The Intrigues, Pollicies, and Stratagems of the French KING with His Secret Contrivances, for Undermining the PRINCES OF CHRISTENDOM, DISCOVERED* (1695).

—, *Poems on Affairs of State: from the Time of Oliver Cromwell to the Abdication of K. James the Second* (1697).

—, *A Secret History of the Amours and Marriage of an English Nobleman with a Famous Italian Lady* (1712).

—, *Considerations upon the Secret History of the White-Staff* (1714).

—, *A Secret History of One Year* (1714).

—, *The Secret History of the Chevalier de St George* (1714).

The Neuter: or, A Modest Satire on the Poets of the Age (1733).

—, *The Life, Amours, and Secret History of Francelia, Late D—ss of P—h, Favourite Mistress to Charles II* (1734).

—, *An Examen of the New Comedy, Call'd the Suspicious Husband ...To Which Is Added ... A Piece of Secret History* (1747).

—, *A Cabinet Council; or Secret History of Lewis XIV* (1757).

Arbuthnot, J., *The History of John Bull*, ed. A. W. Bower and R. A. Erickson (Oxford: Clarendon Press, 1976).

Bacon, F., *The Essayes or Counsels, Civill and Morall*, ed. M. Kiernan (Oxford: Clarendon Press, 1985).

Barksdale, C., *Memorials of Worthy Persons. (Lights and Ornaments of the Church of England.) The Fourth Decade* (Oxford, 1663).

Besogne, N., *Galliae Notitia: or, The Present State of France*, trans. R. Wolley (1691).

Bond, W., *The History of the Life and Adventures of Mr. Duncan Campbell* (1720).

— and M. F. Sansom, *The Epistles of Clio and Strephon* (1720).

Boyer, A., *Quadriennium Annæ Postremum; or The Political State of Great Britain. During the Four Last Years of the Late Queen's Reign*, 8 vols (1718–19).

B. R., *Remarks on Mr Steele's* Crisis *&c., by One of the Clergy* (1714).

Broughton, T., *The Mottoes of the Spectators, Tatlers, and Guardians Translated into English* (1735).

Burke, E., *The Writings and Speeches of Edmund Burke*, ed. P. Langford, 9 vols (Oxford: Clarendon Press, 1981).

Campbell, D., *Secret Memoirs of the Late Mr. Duncan Campbell, The Famous Deaf and Dumb Gentleman* (1732).

Clement, S., *Faults on Both Sides: Or, An Essay upon the Original Cause, Progress, and Mischievous Consequences of the Factions in this Nation* (1710).

Coke, R., *A Detection of the Court and State of England During the Four Last Reigns and the Interregnum* (1694).

Cooper, A. A., *Letters from the Right Honourable the Late Earl of Shaftesbury, to Robert Molesworth, Esq; Now the Lord Viscount of that Name* (1721).

Corneille, T., *Le Comte d'Essex* (1678), ed. W. Gibson (Exeter: University of Exeter Press, 2000).

Courtilz de Sandras, G. de, *The French Spy: or, The Memoirs of John Baptist de la Fontaine*, trans. J. C. M. D. (1700).

Cowper, William, *The Private Diary of William, First Earl Cowper, Lord Chancellor of England, 1705–14*, ed. E. C. Hawtrey (Eton: Roxburghe Club, 1833).

Curll, E., *A Complete Key to the Tale of a Tub* (1710).

Defoe, D., *The Secret History of the October Club; from its Original to this Time*, 2 parts (1711).

—, *And What if the Pretender Should Come? Or, Some Considerations of the Advantages and Real Consequences of the Pretender's Possessing the Crown of Great Britain* (1713).

—, *Reasons Against the Succession of the House of Hanover* (1713).

—, *An Answer to a Question That No Body Thinks of, viz. But What If the Queen Should Die?* (1713).

—, *The Secret History of the White-Staff, Being an Account of Affairs under the Conduct of Some Later Ministers, and of What Might Probably Have Happened If Her Majesty Had Not Died*, 3 parts (1714–15).

—, *An Appeal to Honour and Justice, Tho' It Be of His Worst Enemies* (1715).

—, *The Secret History of the Secret History of the White-Staff, Purse and Mitre* (1715).

—, *Minutes of the Negotiations of Monsr Mesnager at the Court of England, Towards the Close of the Last Reign* (1717).

—, *The Life, and Strange Surprizing Adventures of Robinson Crusoe of York, Mariner* (1719), ed. J. D. Crowley as *Robinson Crusoe* (Oxford: Oxford University Press, 1972).

—, *The Fortunes and Misfortunes of the Famous Moll Flanders* (1722), ed. G. A. Starr as *Moll Flanders* (Oxford: Oxford University Press, 1971, repr. 1998).

—, *The Fortunate Mistress; or, a History of the Life and Vast Variety of Fortunes of Mademoiselle de Beleau, Afterwards Called the Countess of Wintelsheim in Germany, Being the Person Known by the Name of the Lady Roxana in the Time of Charles II* (1724), ed. J. Mullan as *Roxana* (Oxford: Oxford University Press, 1996).

—, *Defoe's Review*, ed. A. W. Secord, 22 vols (New York: Columbia University Press, 1938).

—, *The Letters of Daniel Defoe*, ed. G. H. Healey (Oxford: Clarendon Press, 1955).

Dryden, J., *The Works of John Dryden*, ed. V. A. Dearing, 20 vols (Berkeley and Los Angeles, CA: University of California Press, 1956–2000).

Dunton, J., *The Art of Living Incognito, Being a Thousand Letters on As Many Uncommon Subjects* (1700).

—, *The Case of John Dunton, Citizen of London* (1700).

—, *A Satyr upon King William; Being the Secret History of His Life and Reign* (1703).

—, *Athenae Redivivae: or, the New Athenian Oracle* (1704)

—, *The Life and Errors of John Dunton, Late Citizen of London* (1705).

—, *The Athenian Spy*, 2nd edn (1706).

—, *Dunton's Whipping Post; or, a Satyr upon Every Body* (1706).

—, *The Christians Gazette: or, Nice and Curious Speculations Chiefly Respecting the Invisible World* (1713).

—, *The Court-Spy* (1713)

—, *Neck or Nothing: in a Letter to the Right Honourable the Lord —* (1713).

—, *Queen Robin: or The Second Part of Neck or Nothing, Detecting the Secret Reign of the Four Last Years* (1714).

—, *The Shortest Way with the King: or, Plain English Spoke to His Majesty* (1715).

—, *The Hanover-Spy; or, Secret History of St. James's* (1718).

—, *The State-Weathercocks: or, a New Secret History of the Most Distinguished Favourites of the Late and Present Reigns* (1711)

Echard, L., *The Roman History*, 5 vols (the last three by an anonymous 'continuator') (1695–1704).

Evelyn, J., *The Diary of John Evelyn*, ed. E. S. de Beer, 6 vols (Oxford: Clarendon Press, 1955).

Gibbon, E., *The Decline and Fall of the Roman Empire* (1776–88), ed. D. Womersley, 3 vols (Harmondsworth: Penguin, 1994).

Gildon, C., *The Golden Spy: or, A Political Journal of the British Nights Entertainments of War and Peace, and Love and Politics* (1709).

Grant, F., *A Brief Account of the Nature, Rise and Progress of the Societies for Reformation of Manners* (Edinburgh, 1700).

Haywood, E., *A Spy upon the Conjurer; or, A Collection of Surprising Stories, with Names, Places, and Particular Circumstances Relating to Mr Duncan Campbell* (1724).

—, *Secret Histories, Novels and Poems*, 4 vols (1725).

—, *Memoirs of a Certain Island Adjacent to the Kingdom of Utopia*, 2 vols (1725–6; 2nd edn 1726).

—, *The Secret History of the Present Intrigues of the Court of Caramania* (1727).

—, *The Adventures of Eovaai, Princess of Ijaveo: A Pre-Adamitical History* (1736), ed. E. Wilputte (Peterborough, ON: Broadview Press, 1999).

—, *A Letter from H—G—, Esq.* (1749).

—, *The Invisible Spy*, 4 vols (1755).

—, *Selected Fiction and Drama of Eliza Haywood*, ed. P. R. Backscheider (Oxford: Oxford University Press, 1999).

Hearne, T., *Ductor Historicus or, a Short System of Universal History and an Introduction to the Study of that Science* (1698).

Hill, A., *The Plain Dealer* (1724).

Hoffman, F., *Secret Transactions During the Hundred Days Mr William Gregg Lay in Newgate Under Sentence of Death for High Treason* (1711).

Hotoman, F., *Franco-Gallia: or, An Account of the Ancient Free State of France*, trans. R. Molesworth (2nd edn, 1721).

Hume, D., *The Letters of David Hume*, ed. J. Y. T. Greig, 2 vols (Oxford: Clarendon Press, 1932).

Johnson, S., *The Works of the Late Reverend Mr. Samuel Johnson, Sometime Chaplain to the Right Honourable William Lord Russel* (1710).

—, *A Dictionary of the English Language*, 2 vols (1755–6).

—, *The Lives of the Most Eminent English Poets; With Critical Observations on their Works*, ed. R. Lonsdale, 4 vols (Oxford: Clarendon Press, 2006).

Jones, D., *The Secret History of White-hall, from the Restoration of Charles II down to the Abdication of the Late K. James* (1697; 2nd edn 1717).

Jortin, J., *Remarks on Ecclesiastical History*, 5 vols (1751–73).

Journals of the House of Commons, 55 vols (1803).

Lenglet Dufresnoy, N., *A New Method of Studying History, Geography, and Chronology*, trans. R. Rawlinson, 2 vols (1728).

Luttrell, N., *A Brief Historical Relation of State Affairs from September 1678 to April 1714*, 6 vols (Oxford: Oxford University Press, 1857).

Manley, D., *Secret Memoirs and Manners of Several Persons of Quality, of Both Sexes. From the New Atalantis, an Island in the Mediterranean*, 2 vols (1709).

—, *Memoirs of Europe, Towards the Close of the Eighth Century*, 2 vols (1710).

—, *The Adventures of Rivella; or, the History of the Author of the Atalantis* (1714).

—, *The New Atalantis*, ed. R. Ballaster (London: Pickering and Chatto, 1991).

—, *The Selected Works of Delarivier Manley*, ed. R. Carnell and R. Herman, 5 vols (London: Pickering and Chatto, 2005).

Marana, G. P., *Letters Writ by a Turkish Spy*, 8 vols (1687–94).

Marvell, A., *The Prose Works of Andrew Marvell*, ed. A. Patterson, M. Dzelzainis, N. H. Keeble, and N. von Maltzahn, 2 vols (New Haven, CT and London: Yale University Press, 2003).

Ménage, G., *Menagiana, ou Les bons mots et remarques critiques, historiques, morales et d'érudition de Monsieur Ménage*, 3rd edn, 2 vols (1715).

Mothe le Vayer, F. de la, *Oeuvres*, 2 vols (3rd edn, Paris, 1662).

Nani, B., *A History of the Affairs of Europe in this Present Age, But More Particularly of the Republick of Venice*, trans. R. Honywood (1673).

Nedham, M., *The Germane Spie: Truly Discovering the Deplorable Condition of the Kingdom and Subjects of the French King* (1691).

N. N., *The Blatant Beast Muzzl'd: or, Reflexions on a Late Libel, Entituled The Secret History of the Reigns of K. Charles II and K. James II* (1691).

North, R., *Examen: or, an Enquiry into the Credit and Veracity of a Pretended Complete History* (1740).

Oldmixon, J., *A Letter to the Seven Lords of the Committee, Appointed to Examine Gregg* (1711).

—, *The Secret History of Europe*, 4 vols (1712–14).

—, *Arcana Gallica: or, the Secret History of France, for the Last Century* (1714).

—, *A Detection of the Sophistry and Falsities of the Pamphlet, Entitul'd the Secret History of the White-Staff*, 2 parts (1714).

Philips, K., *Poems. By the Incomparable, Mrs. K. P.* (1664).

Pope, A., *The Temple of Fame: A Vision*, 2nd edn (1715).

—, *The Dunciad Variorum* (1729), 3rd edn, ed. J. Sutherland (London: Methuen, 1963).

Procopius of Caesarea, *The History of the Warres of the Emperour Justinian in Eight Books*, trans. H. Holcroft (1653).

—, *The Secret History of the Court of the Emperor Justinian* (1674).

—, *The Debaucht Court; or, The Lives of the Emperor Justinian, and His Empress Theodora the Comedian* (1682).

Rapin, R., *Instructions pour l'histoire* (Paris, 1677).

—, *Instructions for History, with a Character of the Most Considerable Historians Ancient and Modern*, trans. J. Davies (1680).

Richardson, C., *Notices and Extracts Relating to the Lion's Head, Which Was Erected at Button's Coffee-House in the Year 1713* (1828).

Ryves, T., *Imperatoris Iustiniani defensio aduersus Alemannum* (1626).

Saint-Evremond, C. de Marguetel de Saint-Denis, seigneur de, *Miscellaneous Essays by Monsieur St. Euremont* (1692).

Saunders, R., *A View of the Soul, in Several Tracts*, 3 books (1682).

St John, H., *A Letter to the Examiner* (1710).

Sansom, M. F., *Clio: The Autobiography of Martha Fowke Sansom, 1689–1736*, ed. P. J. Guskin (Newark, DE: University of Delaware Press, 1997).

Shakespeare, W., *The Riverside Shakespeare*, ed. G. B. Evans, 2nd edn (Boston, MA and New York: Houghton Mifflin Company, 1997).

Sidney, A., *Colonel Sidney's Speech, Delivered to the Sheriff on the Scaffold, December 7th 1683* (1683).

Smith, M., *Memoirs of Secret Service* (1699).

Smollett, T., *The Adventures of Peregrine Pickle* (1751), ed. J. L. Clifford (London: Oxford University Press, 1964).

Somers, J., *The True Secret History of the Lives and Reigns of all the Kings and Queens of England, from King William the First, Called, the Conqueror* (1702).

Spalding, J., *A Sermon Preached Before His Grace George Earl of Melvil, Their Majesties High Commissioner, and the Nobility, Barons, and Burrows, Members of the High Court of Parliament* (Edinburgh, 1690).

Speke, H., *The Secret History of the Happy Revolution in 1688* (1715).

Stoughton, W., *The Secret History of the late Ministry; from their Admission, to the Death of the Queen* (1715).

Swift, J., *A Discourse of the Contests and Dissensions between the Nobles and the Commons in Athens and Rome* (1701)

—, *The Conduct of the Allies, and of the Late Ministry, in Beginning and Carrying on the Present War* (1711).

—, *The Importance of the Guardian Considered, in a Second Letter to the Bailiff of Stockbridge* (1713).

—, *Political Tracts 1713–1719*, ed. H. Davis and I. Ehrenpreis (Oxford: Basil Blackwell, 1953).

—, *Travels into Several Remote Nations of the World* (1726), ed. R. DeMaria Jr. as *Gulliver's Travels* (London: Penguin Books, 2001).

—, *Journal to Stella*, ed. H. Williams, 2 vols (Oxford: Clarendon Press, 1948; Oxford: Basil Blackwell & Mott, 1974)

—, *The History of the Four Last Years of the Queen* (1758), ed. H. Williams (Oxford: Basil Blackwell, 1951).

—, *The Correspondence of Jonathan Swift, D.D.* ed. D. Woolley, 4 vols (Frankfurt am Main and Oxford: Peter Lang, 1999).

— and A. Mainwaring, *Swift vs. Mainwaring:* The Examiner *and* The Medley, ed. F. H. Ellis (Oxford: Clarendon Press, 1985).

Vanel, C., *The Royal Mistresses of France, or, The Secret History of the Amours of all the French Kings, from Pharamond the First Monarch, Anno 418. to this Present Time* (1695).

Varillas, A., *Anekdota Heterouiaka. Or, The Secret History of the House of Medicis*, trans. F. Spence (London, 1686).

Ward, E., *The London-Spy Compleat*, 2 vols (1703).

Wentworth, T., *The Wentworth Papers, 1705–1739: Selected from the Private and Family Correspondence of Thomas Wentworth, Lord Raby, Created in 1711 Earl of Strafford*, ed. J. J. Cartwright (London: Wyman, 1883).

Wilkins, J., *A Discourse Concerning the Beauty of Providence in All the Rugged Passages of it* (1649).

Wood, A., *Athenae Oxonienses*, 2nd edn, 2 vols (1721).

Woodward, J., *An Account of the Rise and Progress of the Religious Societies in the City of London &c and of the Endeavours for Reformation of Manners Which Have Been Made Therein* (1698).

Secondary texts

Alkon, P. K., *Defoe and Fictional Time* (Athens, GA: University of Georgia Press, 1979).

Ascoli, G., *La Grande-Bretagne devant l'opinion française au XVII siècle*, 2 vols (Paris: Libraire Universitaire J. Gamber, 1930).

Ashcraft, R., 'The Language of Political Conflict in Restoration Literature', in *Politics as Reflected in Literature: Papers Presented at a Clark Library Seminar, 24 January 1987* (Los Angeles, CA: The William Andrews Clark Memorial Library, University of California, 1989), pp. 1–28.

Backscheider, P. R., 'The Genesis of *Roxana*', *The Eighteenth Century: Theory and Interpretation*, 27:3 (1986), pp. 211–29.

—, *Daniel Defoe: His Life* (Baltimore, MD and London: Johns Hopkins University Press, 1989).

—, 'The Shadow of an Author: Eliza Haywood', *Eighteenth-Century Fiction*, 11:1 (1998), pp. 79–102.

— and C. Ingrassia (eds), *A Companion to the Eighteenth-Century Novel and Culture*, (Malden, MA and Oxford: Blackwell, 2005).

Baines, P. and P. Rogers, *Edmund Curll, Bookseller* (Oxford: Clarendon Press, 2007).

Bakhtin, M. M., *The Dialogic Imagination: Four Essays by M. M. Bakhtin*, ed. M. Holquist, trans. C. Emerson and M. Holquist (Austin, TX: University of Texas Press, 1981).

Ballaster, R., *Seductive Forms: Women's Amatory Fiction from 1684–1740* (Oxford: Clarendon Press, 1992).

—, *Fabulous Orients: Fictions of the East in England, 1662–1785* (Oxford: Oxford University Press, 2005).

Bannet, E. T., '"Secret History": Or, Talebaring Inside and Outside the Secretorie' in P. Kewes (ed.), *The Uses of History in Early Modern England* (San Marino, CA: Huntington Library, 2006), pp. 367–88.

Beasley, F. E., *Revising Memory: Women's Fiction and Memoirs in Seventeenth-Century France* (New Brunswick, NJ: Rutgers University Press, 1990).

Benedict, B. M., *Curiosity: a Cultural History of Early Modern Inquiry* (Chicago, IL and London: University of Chicago Press, 2001).

Berry, H., *Gender, Society and Print Culture in Late-Stuart England: The Cultural World of the Athenian Mercury* (Aldershot: Ashgate, 2003).

Biddle, S., *Bolingbroke and Harley* (London: George Allen and Unwin, 1975 (first published, New York: Knopf, 1974)).

Black, S., 'Trading Sex for Secrets in Haywood's *Love in Excess*', *Eighteenth-Century Fiction*, 15:2 (2003), pp. 207–26.

Blewett, D., '*Roxana* and the Masquerades', *Modern Language Review*, 65:3 (1970), pp. 499–502.

—, 'The Double Time-Scheme of *Roxana*: Further Evidence', *Studies in Eighteenth-Century Culture*, 13 (1984), pp. 19–28.

Bok, S., *Secrets: on the Ethics of Concealment and Revelation* (Oxford: Oxford University Press, 1984).

Bowers, T., 'Collusive Resistance: Sexual Agency and Partisan Politics in *Love in Excess*' in K. T. Saxton and R. P. Bocchicchio (eds), *The Passionate Fictions of Eliza Haywood: Essays on Her Life and Work* (Lexington, KY: University Press of Kentucky, 2000), pp. 48–68.

Brown, H. O., 'The Displaced Self in the Novels of Daniel Defoe', *ELH* 38:4 (1971), pp. 562–90.

Browning, A. (ed.), *English Historical Documents, 1660–1714* (London: Eyre and Spottiswoode, 1953; London: Routledge, 1996).

Burke, P., 'Tacitism' in T. A. Dorey (ed.), *Tacitus* (London: Routledge and Kegan Paul, 1969), pp. 149–71.

—, 'Tacitism, Scepticism and Reason of State' in J. H. Burns (ed.), *The Cambridge History of Political Thought, 1450–1700* (Cambridge: Cambridge University Press, 1991), pp. 479–98.

Burns, J. H. (ed.), *The Cambridge History of Political Thought, 1450–1700* (Cambridge: Cambridge University Press, 1991).

Burtt, S., *Virtue Transformed: Political Argument in England, 1688–1740* (Cambridge: Cambridge University Press, 1992).

Butterfield, H., *The Whig Interpretation of History* (London: G. Bell and Sons, 1931).

Cameron, A., *Procopius and the Sixth Century* (London: Gerald Duckworth & Co., 1985; reissued, London and New York: Routledge, 1996).

Carnell, R., *Partisan Politics, Narrative Realism, and the Rise of the British Novel* (Basingstoke: Palgrave Macmillan, 2006).

—, *A Political Biography of Delarivier Manley* (London: Pickering and Chatto, 2008).

Carswell, J., *The South Sea Bubble* (London: The Cresset Press, 1960; Stroud: Sutton Press, 2001).

Castle, T., ''Amy, who knew my Disease': A Psychosexual Pattern in Defoe's *Roxana*', *ELH*, 46:1 (1979), pp. 81–96.

Chernaik, W. and M. Dzelzainis (eds.), *Marvell and Liberty* (Basingstoke: Macmillan, 1999).

Clark, P., *British Clubs and Societies, 1580–1800: the Origins of an Associational World* (Oxford: Clarendon Press, 2000).

Claydon, T., *William III and the Godly Revolution* (Cambridge: Cambridge University Press, 1996).

Condren, C., *Satire, Lies and Politics: The Case of Dr Arbuthnot* (Basingstoke: Macmillan, 1997).

Coward B. and J. Swann (eds), *Conspiracies and Conspiracy Theory in Early Modern Europe: from the Waldesians to the French Revolution* (Aldershot: Ashgate, 2004).

Cruickshanks, E., *Ideology and Conspiracy: Aspects of Jacobitism, 1689–1759* (Edinburgh: John Donald, 1982).

Darnton, R., *The Forbidden Best-Sellers of Pre-Revolutionary France* (New York: W.W. Norton, 1995).

Davis, L., *Factual Fictions: the Origins of the English Novel* (New York: Columbia University Press, 1983)

deJean, J., *Tender Geographies: Women and the Origins of the Novel in France* (New York: Columbia University Press, 1991).

DePorte, M., 'Riddles, Mysteries, and Lies: Swift and Secrecy' in *Reading Swift: Papers from the Fourth Münster Symposium on Jonathan Swift*, ed. H. J. Real and H. Stöver-Leidig (München: Wilhelm Fink Herlag, 2003), pp. 115–31.

Donaldson, P. S., *Machiavelli and Mystery of State* (Cambridge: Cambridge University Press, 1988).

Dorey, T. A. (ed.), *Tacitus* (London: Routledge and Kegan Paul, 1969).

Dorn, J., 'The Royal Captives, A Fragment of Secret History: Ann Yearsley's "Unnecessary Curiosity"', *1650–1850 Ideas, Aesthetics, and Inquiries in the Early Modern Era*, 5 (2000), pp. 163–89.

Downie, J. A., *Robert Harley and the Press: Propaganda and Public Opinion in the Age of Swift and Defoe* (Cambridge: Cambridge University Press, 1979).

—, 'What if Delarivier Manley Did *Not* Write *The Secret History of Queen Zarah*?' *The Library*, 5:3 (2004), pp. 247–64.

Eamon, W., *Science and the Secrets of Nature: Books of Secrets in Medieval and Early Modern Culture* (Princeton, NJ: Princeton University Press, 1994).

Ehrenpreis, I., *Swift: The Man, His Works, and the Age*, 3 vols (London: Methuen, 1962–83).

Elkin, P. K., *The Augustan Defence of Satire* (Oxford: Clarendon Press, 1973).

Faller, L. B., *Crime and Defoe: A New Kind of Writing* (Cambridge: Cambridge University Press, 1993).

Furbank, P. N., 'Defoe's *Minutes of Mesnager*: The Art of Mendacity', *Eighteenth-Century Fiction*, 16:1 (2003), pp. 1–12.

— and W. R. Owens, *Defoe De-Attributions: A Critique of J.R. Moore's Checklist*, (London and Rio Grande, OH: The Hambledon Press, 1990).

Gallagher, C., *Nobody's Story: The Vanishing Acts of Women Writers in the Marketplace, 1670–1820* (Berkley and Los Angeles, CA: University of California Press, 1994).

Gallagher, N., 'Point of View and Narrative Form in *Moll Flanders* and the Eighteenth-Century Secret History', *Lumen: Selected Proceedings from the Canadian Society for Eighteenth-Century Studies*, 25 (2006), pp. 145–61.

Gerrard, C., *The Patriot Opposition to Walpole: Politics, Poetry, and National Myth, 1725–1742* (Oxford: Clarendon Press, 1994).

—, *Aaron Hill: The Muses' Projector* (Oxford: Oxford University Press, 2003).

Gordon, S. P., *The Power of the Passive Self in English Literature, 1640–1770* (Cambridge: Cambridge University Press, 2002).

Gossman, L., 'Anecdote and History', *History and Theory*, 42:2 (2003), pp. 143–68.

Greaves, R., *Deliver Us From Evil: the Radical Underground in Britain, 1660–1663* (Oxford: Oxford University Press, 1986).

—, *Enemies Under His Feet: Radicals and Nonconformists in Britain, 1664–1677* (Stanford, CA: Stanford University Press, 1990).

—, *Secrets of the Kingdom: British Radicals from the Popish Plot to the Revolution of 1688–9* (Stanford, CA: Stanford University Press, 1992).

Gregg, E., 'Was Queen Anne a Jacobite?', *History*, 57 (1972), pp. 358–75.

Habermas, J., *The Structural Transformation of the Public Sphere: An Inquiry into a Category of Bourgeois Society*, trans. T. Burger (Boston, MA: MIT Press, 1989).

Hammond, B., *Professional Imaginative Writing in England, 1670–1740: 'Hackney for Bread'* (Oxford: Clarendon Press, 1997)

Harth, E., *Ideology and Culture in Seventeenth-Century France* (Ithaca, NY and London: Cornell University Press, 1983).

Herman, R., 'Similarities between Delarivier Manley's *Secret History of Queen Zarah* and the English Translation of *Hattigé*', *Notes and Queries*, 47:2 (2000), pp. 193–6.

—, *The Business of a Woman: The Political Writings of Delarivier Manley* (Newark, DE: University of Delaware Press, 2003).

Hicks, P., *Neoclassical History and English Culture from Clarendon to Hume* (Basingstoke: Macmillan, 1996).

Hill, B. W., *Robert Harley: Speaker, Secretary of State, and Premier Minister* (New Haven, CT and London: Yale University Press, 1988).

Holmes, G., *British Politics in the Age of Anne* (London: Macmillan, 1967).

Hopkins, P., 'Sham Plots and Real Plots in the 1690s' in E. Cruickshanks, *Ideology and Conspiracy: Aspects of Jacobitism, 1689–1759* (Edinburgh: John Donald, 1982), pp. 89–109.

Hunter, J. P., *Before Novels: the Cultural Contexts of Eighteenth-Century English Fiction* (New York and London: Norton, 1990).

Ingrassia, C., *Authorship, Commerce, and Gender in Early Eighteenth-Century England: A Culture of Paper Credit* (Cambridge: Cambridge University Press, 1998).

Jones, J. R., *Country and Court: England, 1658–1714* (London: Edward Arnold, 1978).

Kaldellis, A., *Procopius of Caesarea: Tyranny, History, and Philosophy at the End of Antiquity* (Philadelphia, PA: University of Pennsylvania Press, 2004).

Kenny, N., *The Uses of Curiosity in Early Modern France and Germany* (New York and Oxford: Oxford University Press, 2004).

Kenyon, J. P., *Revolution Principles: The Politics of Party, 1689–1720* (Cambridge: Cambridge University Press, 1977).

Kewes P., (ed.), *The Uses of History in Early Modern England* (San Marino, CA: Huntington Library, 2006).

King, K. R., 'Spying upon the Conjurer: Haywood, Curiosity, and 'The Novel' in the 1720s', *Studies in the Novel*, 30:2 (1998), pp. 178–93.

—, 'New Contexts for Early Novels by Women: The Case of Eliza Haywood, Aaron Hill, and the Hillarians, 1719–1725' in P. R. Backscheider and C. Ingrassia (eds), *A Companion to the Eighteenth-Century Novel and Culture*, (Malden, MA and Oxford: Blackwell, 2005), pp. 261–75.

—, 'Eliza Haywood, Savage Love, and Biographical Uncertainty', *RES* Advance Access published 25 October 2007.

Klein, L. E., *Shaftesbury and the Culture of Politness: Moral Discourses and Cultural Politics in Early Eighteenth-Century England* (Cambridge: Cambirdge University Press, 1994).

—, 'Joseph Addison's Whiggism' in D. Womersley (ed.), *"Cultures of Whiggism": New Essays on English Literature and Culture in the Long Eighteenth Century* (Newark, DE: University of Delaware Press, 2005), pp. 108–26.

Knights, M., *Politics and Opinion in Crisis, 1678–81* (Cambridge: Cambridge University Press, 1994).

—, 'Faults on Both Sides: The Conspiracies of Party Politics under the Later Stuarts' in Coward, B. and J. Swann (eds), *Conspiracies and Conspiracy Theory in Early Modern Europe: from the Waldesians to the French Revolution* (Aldershot: Ashgate, 2004), pp. 153–72.

—, *Representation and Misrepresentation in Later Stuart Britain: Partisanship and Political Culture* (Oxford: Oxford University Press, 2005).

—, 'The Tory Interpretation of History in the Rage of Parties' in P. Kewes (ed.), *The Uses of History in Early Modern England* (San Marino, CA: Huntington Library, 2006), pp. 347–66.

Cruickshanks, E., S. Handley and D. W. Hayton (eds), *The History of Parliament: The House of Commons, 1690–1715*, 5 vols (Cambridge: Cambridge University Press for the History of Parliament Trust, 2002).

Kropf, C. R., 'Libel and Satire in the Eighteenth Century', *Eighteenth-Century Studies*, 8:2 (1974–5), pp. 153–68.

Levine, J. M., *Dr. Woodward's Shield: History, Science and Satire in Augustan England* (Berkeley, CA: University of California Press, 1977).

Lochrie, K., *Covert Operations: The Medieval Uses of Secrecy* (Philadelphia, PA: University of Pennsylvania Press, 1999).

Love, H., *English Clandestine Satire, 1660–1702* (Oxford: Oxford University Press, 2004).

Loveman, K., *Reading Fictions, 1660–1740: Deception in English Literary and Political Culture* (Aldershot: Ashgate, 2008).

Mascuch, M., *Origins of the Individualist Self: Autobiography and Self-Identity in England, 1591–1791* (Cambridge: Polity Press, 1997).

Mayer, R., *History and the Early English Novel: Matters of Fact from Bacon to Defoe* (Cambridge: Cambridge University Press, 1997).

McInnes, A., *Robert Harley: Puritan Politician* (London: Victor Gollancz, 1970).

McKeon, M., *The Origins of the English Novel, 1600–1740* (Baltimore, MD and London: Johns Hopkins University Press, 1987).

—, *The Secret History of Domesticity: Public, Private and the Division of Knowledge* (Baltimore, MD: Johns Hopkins University Press, 2005)

New, P., 'Why Roxana Can Never Find Herself', *Modern Language Review*, 91:2 (1996), pp. 317–29.

Novak, M. E., *Daniel Defoe, Master of Fictions: His Life and Ideas* (Oxford: Oxford University Press, 2001).

O'Brien, K., 'History and the Novel in Eighteenth-Century Britain', in P. Kewes (ed.), *The Uses of History in Early Modern England* (San Marino, CA: Huntington Library, 2006), pp. 389–405.

Patey, D. L., *Probability and Literary Form: Philosophic Theory and Literary Practice in the Augustan Age* (Cambridge: Cambridge University Press, 1984).

Patterson, A., *Early Modern Liberalism* (Cambridge: Cambridge University Press, 1997).

—, 'Marvell and Secret History' in W. Chernaik and M. Dzelzainis (eds), *Marvell and Liberty* (Basingstoke: Macmillan, 1999), pp. 23–49.

Plumb, J. H., *Sir Robert Walpole: The Making of a Statesman* (London: The Cresset Press, 1956).

—, *Sir Robert Walpole: The King's Minister* (London: The Cresset Press, 1960).

—, *The Growth of Political Stability in England, 1675–1725* (London: Macmillan, 1967).

Phillipson, N., 'Politics and Politeness in the Reigns of Anne and the Early Hanoverians' in J. G. A. Pocock (ed.), *The Varieties of British Political Thought, 1500–1800*, (Cambridge: Cambridge University Press, 1993), pp. 211–45.

—, and Q. Skinner (eds), *Political Discourse in Early Modern Britain* (Cambridge: Cambridge University Press, 1993), pp. 232–52.

Pocock, J. G. A., *Virtue, Commerce, and History: Essays on Political Thought and History, Chiefly in the Eighteenth Century* (Cambridge: Cambridge University Press, 1985).

—, (ed.), *The Varities of British Political Thought, 1500–1800*, (Cambridge: Cambridge University Press, 1993).

Popkin J. and B. Fort (eds), *The Mémoires secrets and the Culture of Publicity in Eighteenth-Century France* (Oxford: Voltaire Foundation, 1998).

Potter, L., *Secret Rites and Secret Writing: Royalist Literature, 1641–1660* (Cambridge: Cambridge University Press, 1989).

Rabb, M. A., *Satire and Secrecy in English Literature from 1650–1750* (New York: Palgrave Macmillan, 2007).

Real, H. J. and H. Stöver-Leidig (eds), *Reading Swift: Papers from the Fourth Münster Symposium on Jonathan Swift* (München: Wilhelm Fink Herlag, 2003).

Rée, J., *I See a Voice: A Philosophical History of Language, Deafness and the Senses* (London: Harper Collins, 1999).

Richetti, J. J., *The English Novel in History, 1700–1780* (London: Routledge, 1999).

Ridley, R. T., 'The Forgotten Historian: Laurence Echard and the First History of the Roman Republic', *Ancient Society*, 27 (1996), pp. 277–315.

Roper, A., 'Drawing Parallels and Making Applications in Restoration Literature' in *Politics as Reflected in Literature: Papers Presented at a Clark Library Seminar, 24 January 1987* (Los Angeles, CA: The William Andrews Clark Memorial Library, University of California, 1989), pp. 29–65.

Rose, C., *England in the 1690s: Revolution, Religion, and War* (Oxford: Blackwell, 1999).

Rostenberg, L., *Literary, Political, Scientific, Religious & Legal Publishing, Printing & Bookselling in England, 1551–1700: Twelve Studies*, 2 vols (New York: Burt Franklin, 1965).

Sachse, W. L., *Lord Somers: A Political Portrait* (Manchester: Manchester University Press, 1975).

St Clair, W., *The Reading Nation in the Romantic Period* (Cambridge: Cambridge University Press, 2004).

Saxton, K. T. and R. P. Bocchicchio (eds), *The Passionate Fictions of Eliza Haywood: Essays on Her Life and Work* eds. (Lexington: University Press of Kentucky, 2000).

Schonhorn, M., *Defoe's Politics: Parliament, Power, Kingship and Robinson Crusoe* (Cambridge: Cambridge University Press, 1991).

Schwoerer, L., 'The Right to Resist : Whig Resistance Theory, 1688 to 1694' in *Political Discourse in Early Modern Britain*, ed. N. Phillipson and Q. Skinner (Cambridge: Cambridge University Press, 1993), pp. 232–52.

Shapin S., and S. Schaffer, *Leviathan and the Air-Pump: Hobbes, Boyle and the Experimental Life* (Princeton, NJ: Princeton University Press, 1985).

Shapiro, B., *Probability and Certainty in Seventeenth-Century England: a Study of the Relationships Between Natural Science, Religion, Law, and Literature* (Princeton, NJ: Princeton University Press, 1983).

—, *A Culture of Fact: England, 1550–1720* (Ithaca, NY and London: Cornell University Press, 2000).

Sill, G. M., *Defoe and the Idea of Fiction, 1713–1719* (Newark, DE: University of Delaware Press, 1983).

Somerville, D. H., *The King of Hearts: Charles Talbot, Duke of Shrewsbury* (London: Allen and Unwin, 1961).

Sommerville, J. P., 'Absolutism and Royalism' in J. H. Burns (ed.), *The Cambridge History of Political Thought, 1450–1700* (Cambridge: Cambridge University Press, 1991), pp. 347–73.

Speck, W. A., *The Birth of Britain: A New Nation* (Oxford: Blackwell, 1994).

Spedding, P., *A Bibliography of Eliza Haywood* (London: Pickering and Chatto, 2004).

Spurr, J., *England in the 1670s: 'This Masquerading Age'* (Oxford: Blackwell, 2000).

—, *The Post-Reformation: Religion, Politics and Society in Britain, 1603–1714* (Harlow: Longman, 2006).

Starr, G. A., *Defoe and Spiritual Autobiography* (Princeton, NJ: Princeton University Press, 1965).

Stevens, A., 'Sophia Lee's Illegitimate History', *The Eighteenth-Century Novel* 3 (2003), pp. 263–91.

Toffanin, G., *Machiavelli e il 'Tacitismo', la 'politica storia' al tempo della Controriforma* (Padova: A Draghi, 1921).

Treadwell, M., 'London Trade Publishers 1675–1750', *Library*, 6th series, 4 (1982), pp. 99–134.

Tully, J. (ed.), *Meaning and Context: Quentin Skinner and his Critics* (Cambridge: Polity Press, 1988).

Warner, W. B., *Licensing Entertainment: The Elevation of Novel Reading in Britain, 1684–1750* (Berkeley and Los Angeles, CA: University of California Press, 1998).

Weber, H., *Paper Bullets: Print and Kingship under Charles II* (Lexington, KY: University Press of Kentucky, 1996).

Weil, R., *Political Passions: Gender, the Family and Political Argument in England, 1680–1714* (Manchester: Manchester University Press, 1999).

Welsh, A., *Strong Representations: Narrative and Circumstantial Evidence in England* (Baltimore, MD and London: Johns Hopkins University Press, 1992).

Whicher, G. F., *The Life and Romances of Mrs. Eliza Haywood* (New York: Columbia University Press, 1915).

Williams, A., *Poetry and the Creation of a Whig Literary Culture, 1681–1714* (Oxford: Oxford University Press, 2005).

Williams, H., 'Jonathan Swift and the *Four Last Years of the Queen*', *The Library*, 4th series, 16 (1935–6), pp. 61–90.

Wilson, P. H., *Absolutism in Central Europe* (London: Routledge, 2000).

Womersley, D. (ed.), *"Cultures of Whiggism": New Essays on English Literature and Culture in the Long Eighteenth Century* (Newark, DE: University of Delaware Press, 2005).

Wood, G. S., 'Conspiracy and the Paranoid Style: Causality and Deceit in the Eighteenth Century', *William and Mary Quarterly*, 3rd series, 39:3 (1982), pp. 401–44.

Zook, M. S., *Radical Whigs and Conspiratorial Politics in Late Stuart England* (University Park, PA: Pennsylvania State University Press, 1999).

—, 'The Restoration Remembered: The First Whigs and the Making of their History', *The Seventeenth Century*, 17:2 (2002), pp. 213–34.

Zwicker, S., *Lines of Authority: Politics and English Literary Culture, 1649–1689* (Ithaca, NY and London: Cornell University Press, 1993).

INDEX

Act of Settlement (1701), 100–1
Addison, Joseph, *see also Guardian, The; Spectator, The; and Tatler, The*, 76, 127, 136, 169, 187
Albemarle, Duke of, *see* Monck, Christopher
Alemannus, Nicolaus, *see* Procopius of Caesarea, *Arcana Historia*
Alkon, Paul K., 156
Allestree, Richard, 140
Anne (Queen), 4, 65, 86, 92, 98–109, 133
Arbuthnot, John, 89
Argyll, Duke of, *see* Campbell, Archibald
Assassination Plot, 3, 185
Atterbury, Francis, 138

Backscheider, Paula, 146–7, 181
Bacon, Francis, 111
Bakhtin, Mikhail, 23
Baldwin / Baldwyn, Richard, 36, 49
Ballaster, Ros, 88, 96, 100
Bannet, Eve Tavor, 52, 89
Barclay, John, 94
Barkesdale, Clement, 35–6
Barksdale / Barkesdale, John, 35–6
Behn, Aphra, 22, 88
Belisarius (General), 29, 35, 39, 40, 42
Bentinck, William (Earl of Portland), 67, 92, 93
Blatant Beast Muzzl'd, The, 13–14, 20–1, 41, 46, 51, 53, 59, 94
Bolingbroke, Viscount, *see* St John, Henry, 67
Bond, Donald, 128
Bond, William, 171–5
Boyer, Abel, 128
Broughton, Thomas, 113

Browne, Joseph, 63, 86, 92
Buckingham, Duke of, *see* John Sheffield
Budgell, Eustace, 169
Burke, Edmund, 127–8
Burnet, Gilbert, 22, 104–6
Butterfield, Herbert, 48, 50
Button's coffeehouse, 120, 122–3

Cabinet Council; or, Secret History of Lewis XIV, A, 185
Cabinet Open'd: or, The Secret History of the Amours of Madam de Maintenon with the French King, The, 2, 45, 49, 157
Campbell, Archibald (Duke of Argyll), 167
Campbell, Duncan, 171–7
Catherine of Braganza, 105
censorship, *see* press regulation
Charlemagne, 108–9
Charles II, 1, 2, 4, 9, 10, 11, 16, 20, 29, 36, 37, 38, 45, 46, 50, 53, 58, 59, 64, 70, 91, 94, 95, 105, 156–7, 185, 186, 187
Chilmead, Edmund, 34–5
Churchill, John (Duke of Marlborough), 9, 89, 91–2, 100, 102, 107, 109, 128
Churchill, Sarah (Duchess of Marlborough), 9, 63, 86, 89, 91–2, 95, 99, 102–4, 106, 107–8
Cibber, Colley, 63
Clarendon, Earl of, *see* Hyde, Edward
Clement, Simon, *see Faults on Both Sides*
Cleveland, Duchess of, *see* Palmer (*née* Villiers), Barbara
Coke, Roger, 7, 14, 59–60
Considerations on the Secret History of the White-Staff, 146

– 245 –

Cooper, Anthony Ashley (Earl of Shaftesbury), 127
Courtilz de Sandras, Gatien de, *see French Spy, The*
Court of St Germains: or, The Secret History of James II, The, 16, 45
Cowper, William, 65, 92, 115, 128, 136
Cowper, Spencer, 92
Craggs, James, 76, 166, 167
curiosity, 33, 73–4, 76, 117, 168–81
Curll, Edmund, 145

Defoe, Daniel, 22, 65, 114–5, 124, 134–59, 162, 184, 187
  Appeal to Honour and Justice, 136
  Minutes of the Neogtiations of Monsr Mesnager, 140, 141–2
  Moll Flanders, 23, 82, 134, 147–51, 153–6, 158, 159, 161
  Review, 116
  Robinson Crusoe, 147, 148, 149
  Roxana, 3, 23, 82, 134, 147–8, 150–8, 159, 161
  Secret History of the October Club, The, 66, 139–40
  Secret History of the Secret History of the White-Staff, The, 144–6, 159
  Secret History of the White-Staff, The, 19, 66, 82, 134, 137–47, 148, 152–3, 157–9
  Shortest Way with the Dissenters, 73
Dionysius of Syracuse, 114
discretion, 125–32
Dryden, John, 113
Dunton, John, 11, 28, 54–5, 68–80, 131, 133, 135, 136, 138, 159, 180, 183–4, 185
  Athenian texts (including *The Athenian Mercury*), 73–6
  Court-Spy, The, 69, 71
  Hanover-Spy, The, 10, 69–73, 76–8
  K—ng G—rge Prov'd a Usurper, 73
  Neck or Nothing, 71
  Queen Robin, 137
  Satyr upon King William, A, 72–3
  Shortest Way with the King, 71, 73
  State-Weathercocks, The, 77, 135

Ecclesiasticus, 126–7
Echard, Laurence, 103–8
epistemic questions, 4–5, 8, 13–15, 18, 19, 23, 55–8, 62, 159
eroticism, 7, 31, 33, 52–4, 162, 179, 186–7
Exclusion crisis, 3, 36, 58, 110
Ezekiel, 140

Fair Concubine, The, 186
Faller, Lincoln, 153
Faults on Both Sides, 145
fiction, *see* epistemic questions
French Spy, The, 56
friendship, 126–32, 148–51, 156, 163, 185

Gallagher, Catherine, 95, 97
George I, 67–8, 73, 133, 136, 156–7, 158, 167, 187–8
George II, 162
George of Denmark, 99, 105
Gerrard, Anne (Countess of Macclesfield), 92
Gibbon, Edward, 33–4, 42
Glorious Revolution, *see* Revolution of 1688–9
Godolphin, Sidney (Earl of Godolphin), 9, 63–4, 89, 91, 94, 99–100, 107, 109, 128, 138
Gordon, Scott Paul, 123–4
Gothic fiction, 187
Grainger, Lydia, 186
Gregg, William, 65
Guardian, The, 118, 120–5
Gwyn, Nell, 37

Harcourt, Simon, 138
Harley, Robert (Earl of Oxford), viii, 2, 3, 9, 28, 63–7, 69, 71, 77–8, 79, 81, 83, 86–7, 94, 96, hearn 99, 100, 109, 112, 114–5, 116, 128–9, 131, 134–47, 152, 153, 155, 158–9, 183
Haywood, Eliza, 22, 82, 83, 161–81, 185, 187
  Adventures of Eovaai, The, 166
  Arragonian Queen, The, 161
  British Recluse, The, 161, 165
  Fantomina, 177
  Fatal Secret, 161

Frederick, Prince of Brunswick-Lunenburgh, 166
Idalia, 178
Love in Excess, 164
Mary Stuart, Queen of Scots, 161, 162
Masqueraders, The, 161, 165
Memoirs of a Certain Island, 82, 162–70, 174, 178, 179–81
Rash Resolve, The, 164, 177
Secret Histories, Novels & Poems, 161, 165
Secret History of the Present Intrigues of the Court of Caramania, 161, 162
Spy upon the Conjurer, A, 162–3, 170–1, 173–7, 179
Surprize, The, 161
Wife to be Lett, 164
Works of Mrs Eliza Haywood, The, 165
Hearne, Thomas, 21, 45
Henrietta Maria (Queen), 114
Henriette-Anne (Duchess of Orléans), 2, 64
Hill, Aaron, 162, 163–4, 170
Hillarian circle (*see also* Hill, Aaron; Sansom, Matha Fowke; and Savage, Richard), 163–5, 168
histoire galante (*see also histoire secrète*), 15–16, 18
histoire secrète, 49–52
historicity, *see* epistemic questions
historiography (whig), *see* whig interpretation of history
History of the Mitre and Purse, A, 145–6
Holcroft, Henry, 34–5
Holmes, Geoffrey, 87, 127
Howard, Henrietta (Countess of Suffolk), 162
Hume, David, 186
Hyde, Edward (Earl of Clarendon), 17, 22

Incestuous Mother, The, 186
Ingrassia, Catherine, 177

Jacobites / Jacobitism (*see also* James, Duke of York / James II; Pretender, the), 2, 3, 4, 21, 45–6, 51, 56, 57, 59, 66, 69, 71, 73, 77, 78, 79, 86, 87, 88, 89, 101, 105, 106, 108, 109, 110, 128, 138–40, 142, 184, 185
James, Duke of York / James II (*see also* Jacobites, Jacobitism), 2, 3, 4, 10, 11, 28, 45, 46, 49, 50, 57, 58, 59, 64, 66, 68, 69, 70, 89, 91, 98–9, 101, 102–3, 105
Johnson, Samuel, 131
Jones, David, 2, 7, 9, 10, 14–15, 19, 20, 27, 54–62, 68, 70–1, 78, 146, 184
Jortin, John, 33
Junto, The, 81, 86, 87, 109, 112, 127–9, 138
Justinian (Emperor), 1, 29–31, 34, 36–42

Kéroualle, Louise de, Duchess of Portsmouth, 2, 37, 94
King, Kathryn, 164
Kings Cabinet Open'd, 49, 55
Kit-Cat Club, 127–8
Knights of the Bath, *see* Order of the Bath
Knights, Mark, 4, 24–5, 89, 100

Lee, Sophia, 187
Lenglet Dufresnoy, Nicolas, 13, 21
L'Estrange, Roger, 116
Letters Writ by a Turkish Spy, 55, 56–7, 136
Licensing Acts, *see* press regulation
Life, Amours, and Secret History of Francelia, Late D—ss of P—h, 186
linguistic turn, the, 24–5
Louis XIV, 2, 37, 45, 49, 50, 57, 58, 64, 185
Loveman, Kate, 4, 75

Macclesfield, Countess of, *see* Gerrard, Anne
MacPherson, James, 186
Manley, Delarivier, 22, 63, 85–110, 131, 135, 166, 187
Adventures of Rivella, The, 87
Memoirs of Europe, 81, 82, 87, 102–110, 121, 184–5
New Atalantis, The, 3, 81, 85–6, 89, 90–102, 109–110, 121, 168–70, 180, 184–5
Marana, Giovanni Paolo, *see Letters Writ by a Turkish Spy*
Marlborough, Duchess and Duke, *see* Churchill, Sarah and John
Marvell, Andrew, 3–4, 8–9, 9–10
Mascuch, Michael, 74

Masham, Abigail, 99, 100, 102–3, 106
Mary II, 47, 50, 52, 98–9, 101
Mary of Modena, 4, 68, 98–9
McKeon, Michael, 23, 24, 133, 135, 141, 147, 156, 157–8
Mauger, Leonor de, *see* Procopius of Caesarea, Ἀνέκδοτα, *ou Histoire secrète de Justinien*
Mayer, Robert, 23
Memoirs of the Nobility, Gentry &c. of Thule, 186
metaphors (mechanistic), 17, 19, 21, 28, 59, 71, 139–41, 147
Monck, Christopher (Duke of Albemarle), 92
Montagu, Mary Wortley, 162
Molesworth, Robert, 127
Mothe le Vayer, François de la, 32–3, 34, 42

narrative (*see also* revisionism), 134, 143–4, 152–4, 159
Natural Secret History of Both Sexes, 186–7
neoclassical historiography (*see also* Tacitism), 8, 15–18, 37, 39, 40, 47, 62
Neuter, The, 162
North, Roger, 21, 45–6
N. N., *see Blatant Beast Muzzl'd, The*
novel, the (and secret history), 23–4, 38, 147–59

Oldmixon, John, 133, 135, 138, 159
  Arcana Gallica, 67, 78–9
  Detection of the Sophistry and Falsities, 143, 145–6
  The Secret History of Europe, 10, 63–4, 67, 79
Order of the Bath, 167–8
Orléans, Duchess of, *see* Henriette-Anne
Ovid, 112–13

Palmer (*née* Villiers), Barbara (Duchess of Cleveland), 91–2
partisan language, 24–5, 105, 110
patronage, 76–7, 79, 82, 87, 115, 137, 147, 164, 167, 8, 180–1
Patterson, Annabel, 24, 46, 59, 88, 110, 184
Pittis, William, 145–6
Plumb, J. H., 133

poems on affairs of state, 22, 133
Pope, Alexander, 162
Popish Plot, 3, 55, 58
Portland, Earl of, *see* Bentinck, William, or Weston, Richard
Portsmouth, Duchess of, *see* Kéroualle, Louise de
Pretender, the (*see also* Jacobites / Jacobitism) 2, 4, 10, 64–9, 78, 79, 88, 98, 101, 109, 110, 135, 138, 185
print, 6–7, 34–5, 41–3
Procopius of Caesarea
  Anekdota, 1, 7, 15, 27, 29–43, 49, 62
  Ἀνέκδοτα, *ou Histoire secrète de Justinien*, 29, 31, 49
  Arcana Historia, 15, 29, 30, 32, 41
  Debaucht Court, The, 36
  History of the Wars, 7, 31, 34, 35, 38–40, 45
  On Buildings, 31
  Secret History of the Court of the Emperor Justinian, 1, 29–30, 35–8, 45, 46, 47, 48, 135, 183, 187
press regulation, 4, 31, 35, 49, 51–2, 74
public sphere, 4

Rabb, Melinda Alliker, 23
Raby, Baron (later Earl of Strafford), *see* Wentworth, Thomas
raison d'état, 6
Rapin, René, 15, 17, 18, 21
Reformation of Manners, *see* Societies for the Reformation of Manners
revisionism, 5, 7, 15, 18, 19–20, 38–40, 58–61, 64, 66–798–101, 146, 183
Revolution of 1688–9, 1, 4, 27, 45–52, 56, 57, 66–8, 71, 77, 92, 103–6, 138
Revolution principles, 3, 22, 28, 70–1, 77–8, 89, 180
roman à clef, 3, 63, 81, 82, 88, 94–8, 101, 102, 103, 105–6, 109, 110, 163–4, 166, 167, 170, 174, 184
Royal Mistresses of France, or, The Secret History of the Amours of all the French Kings, The 2, 16, 45, 52
Rye-House Plot, 3, 4, 185
Ryves, Thomas, 15, 18, 31, 34, 41

St Evremond, Charles Sieur de, 17
St John, Henry (Viscount Bolingbroke), 2, 67, 86, 89, 136–7
Sansom, Martha Fowke, 163, 170
satire, 8, 15, 18, 23, 73, 82, 88–90, 93, 102, 105–6, 109, 111, 120–1, 123, 124, 129, 133, 156–7, 166, 168, 179–80
Sault, Richard, 73
Savage, Richard, 163–4, 170
secret (definitions of), 8–12, 32, 40–3, 62, 69–76, 78–9, 90–3, 170, 176–7, 183–4
Secret History of Colonel Hooke's Negotiations in Scotland, The, 185–6
Secret History of Miss Blandy, The, 186
Secret History of One Year, A, 66, 133
Secret History of Pandora's Box, 187
Secret History of Queen Zarah and the Zarazians, see Browne, Joseph
Secret History of the Chevalier de St George, The, 10, 68, 133
Secret History of the Duchess of Portsmouth, The, 2, 16, 49, 52–3, 94, 95, 157, 186
Secret History of the Duke of Alançon and Q. Elizabeth, The, 51
Secret History of the Four Last Monarchs of Great Britain, The, 45
Secret History of the Last Two S-ss-ns of Parliament, The, 185
Secret History of the Reigns of K. Charles II and K. James II, The, 2, 13, 15, 20–1, 27, 41, 45, 46, 47, 48, 49, 50, 53, 59, 61, 71–2, 94
Secret History of the Reigns of King James I and King Charles I, The, 45
Secret History of the Renown'd Queen Elizabeth with the Earl of Essex, 51
Secret History of the Rye-House Plot, The, 185
secret springs, *see* metaphors (mechanistic)
secret treaty of Dover, 2, 9–10, 64
sexual intrigue, *see* eroticism
Shaftesbury, Earl of, *see* Cooper, Anthony Ashley
Sheffield, John (Duke of Buckingham), 89
Shrewsbury, Duke of, *see* Talbot, Charles
Sidney, Algernon, 48, 61
Sidney, Philip, 94
Sill, Geoffrey, 147
Smith, Matthew, 56

Smollett, Tobias, 118–9
Societies for the Reformation of Manners, 123–4
Somers, John Baron, 7, 14–15, 17, 19, 20, 21, 27, 47–51, 61–2, 64, 72, 78, 127, 184
South Sea Bubble, 166, 167, 177, 179
Spencer, Charles (Earl of Sunderland), 77, 115, 127, 170
Spectator, The, 3, 22, 81, 82, 83, 111–32, 136, 149, 169, 185, 187
Speke, Hugh, 67–8, 133
Spence, Ferrand, 12
spies / spying, 14, 25, 37, 54–7, 59, 61–2, 70–2, 78, 85, 112–6, 118–9, 120, 121–3, 127, 131, 134, 135–6, 151, 154, 162–3, 173, 174–5, 184, 185
Stanhope, James, 76–7
Starr, G. A., 153
Steele, Richard, *see also Guardian, The; Spectator, The;* and *Tatler, The*, 87, 95, 128
Stoughton, William, 67, 137–8, 158
Stout, Sarah, 92
Suetonius, 40, 47–8, 72
Suffolk, Countess of, *see* Henrietta Howard, 162
Sunderland, Earl of, *see* Spencer, Charles
Swift, Jonathan, 128–9, 136, 138, 142
  Conduct of the Allies, The, 9
  Examiner, The, 116, 127
  Gulliver's Travels, 13, 22
  History of the Four Last Years of the Queen, The, 66, 129, 137
  Importance of The Guardian Considered, The, 94
  Journal to Stella, The, 96–8
  Tale of a Tub, A, 89

Tacitism (*see also* neoclassical historiography), 15, 17–18
Talbot, Charles (Duke of Shrewsbury), 91
Tatler, The, 128–9, 131
Temple, William, 7, 14, 59
Terrae-Filius; or, Secret History of the University of Oxford, 185
Theodora (Empress), 29, 31, 32, 36–7, 39, 42
Third Dutch War, 2, 10, 29, 37, 58

Three Hours After Marriage, 172
Tickell, Thomas, 120
Tonson, Jacob, 127
Triple League, The, 2, 64
Turkish Spy, The, see Letters Writ by a Turkish Spy
Tutchin, John, 116

Vanel, Claude, *see Royal Mistresses of France, or, The Secret History of the Amours of all the French Kings, The*
Varillas, Antoine, 12, 16, 18–20, 31–2, 49

Walpole, Robert, 3, 77–8, 82, 158, 163, 166–8, 179–81, 185
War (Third Dutch), *see* Third Dutch War
War of Spanish Succession, 9, 64–5, 92, 130–1, 133, 136
Ward, Edward (Ned), 63, 89, 116, 117, 124

warming pan scandal, 68
'wheels within wheels', *see* metaphors (mechanistic)
Warner, William B., 23
Wentworth, Thomas (Baron Raby, later Earl of Strafford), 128
Wesley, Samuel, 73
Weston, Richard (Earl of Portland), 114
Whicher, George Frisbie, 161–2
whig interpretation of history, 48–50, 52–4, 57–8, 62, 67
William III, 3, 22, 27, 43, 47, 50, 52, 54, 56, 57–8, 66, 67, 68, 71, 72–3, 91, 92, 98–101, 102–3, 104, 185
Williams, Harold, 96
Wolley, Richard, 54–6, 58, 60, 61
Wood, Anthony, 46

Yearsley, Ann, 187